OVEN TEMPERATURES

To convert temperature from Fahrenheit to Celsius: subtract 32, multiply by 5, and divide by 9.
To convert from Celsius to Fahrenheit: multiply by 9, divide by 5, and add 32.

Fahrenheit	Celsius	Gas Mark	Description
250	120	$1/2$	very low
275	140	1	very low
300	150	2	low
325	160	3	low/moderate
350	175	4	moderate
375	190	5	moderately hot
400	200	6	hot
425	220	7	very hot
450	230	8	very hot

SOME USEFUL DRY VOLUME MEASURE EQUIVALENTS

Ingredient	American Standard	Imperial Weight	Metric
Coarse salt	1 teaspoon	$1/5$ oz	5 g
	$1^{1}/_{2}$ teaspoons	$1/4$ oz	8 g
	1 tablespoon	$1/2$ oz	15 g
Grated cheese	1 tablespoon	$1/6$ oz	5 g
	$1/4$ cup	1 scant oz	20–25 g
Breadcrumbs	1 tablespoon	$1/8$ oz	4 g
	$1/4$ cup	$1/2$ oz	16 g
All-purpose flour	1 tablespoon	$1/4$ oz	8 g
	$1/4$ cup	1 oz	30g
	$1/2$ cup	$2^{1}/_{2}$ oz	70 g
Granulated sugar	1 tablespoon	$1/2$ oz	15 g

USEFUL EQUIVALENTS

All-purpose flour = plain flour
Kosher salt = coarse salt
Cornstarch = corn flour
Cheesecloth = muslin
Parchment paper = greaseproof paper

Mrs. Wheelbarrow's Practical Pantry

Mrs. Wheelbarrow's Practical Pantry

RECIPES AND TECHNIQUES FOR YEAR-ROUND PRESERVING

Cathy Barrow

PHOTOGRAPHY BY
Christopher Hirsheimer and Melissa Hamilton

W. W. NORTON & COMPANY
NEW YORK • LONDON

For information about permission to reproduce selections from this book, write to
Permissions, W. W. Norton & Company, Inc., 500 Fifth Avenue, New York, NY 10110

For information about special discounts for bulk purchases, please contact
W. W. Norton Special Sales at specialsales@wwnorton.com or 800-233-4830

Manufacturing by Toppan Leefung Pte. Ltd.

Book design by BTDnyc

Production manager: Devon Zahn

Library of Congress Cataloging-in-Publication Data

Barrow, Cathy.

Mrs. Wheelbarrow's practical pantry : recipes and techniques for year-round preserving / Cathy Barrow ;
photographs by Christopher Hirsheimer and Melissa Hamilton. — First edition.

pages cm

Includes bibliographical references and index.

ISBN 978-0-393-24073-3 (hardcover)

1. Canning and preserving. I. Title.

TX601.B325 2014

641.4'2—dc23

2014017291

W. W. Norton & Company, Inc., 500 Fifth Avenue, New York, N.Y. 10110
www.wwnorton.com

W. W. Norton & Company Ltd., Castle House, 75/76 Wells Street, London W1T 3QT

1 2 3 4 5 6 7 8 9 0

FOR DENNIS,

without whom there would be no Mrs. Wheelbarrow

Fresh beets

Contents

Fresh okra

Mrs. Wheelbarrow's Practical Pantry

Introduction

To make the most of a preserving habit, have a plan for what is preserved.

It's 8:30 in the morning and I am reluctantly heading to the basement to get on the treadmill. Because I live in Washington, DC, I tune the television to a wonky news show hoping it will distract me long enough to get through this exercise routine. Instead, my eye is drawn to the shelves along two of the basement walls. Sharing space with large cooking vessels are hundreds of jars filled with edible treasures. A grocery store of my own making, evidence of weekends spent in the kitchen. This is my practical pantry.

I've canned since I could stand on a stool next to the stove, first with my great-grandmother, and later with my mother. We made just a few things, fruit jams, pickled peaches, and pepper jelly. My mother's mango chutney was my first food obsession, and I can still recall the year I started my own home preserving habit with that treat, putting a few jars away for myself.

So, the idea of canning wasn't foreign when I read *Animal, Vegetable, Miracle*, Barbara Kingsolver's book chronicling her family's efforts to "live locally." We bandy that word around, "local," and I know many people who make every effort to shop at farmers' markets all summer, picking up fresh tomatoes and corn straight from the growers. They stop for peaches at an orchard and buy apples and cider on fall weekend road trips. But in the winter, when the choices at the grocery store are from Chile and Mexico, they put all good intentions aside in favor of convenience. Until Kingsolver's

book, I hadn't drawn the connection between home canning and local eating. The idea that I could "put up" food for the winter was different from the idea of canning for fun, as a kitchen hobby. This was planned, organized, thoughtful.

I began to shop for fresh produce at the farmers' markets popping up around DC. My husband, Dennis, and I would have a Sunday morning date, walk the dog around the market, and enjoy coffee outside. I purchased what I could, learned the seasonal flow, took note of what to expect in different months: the early onions of April and the wine grapes of October. I became aware of which farmers grew which foods, who had eggs, who had tastier turkey, better greens, foraged mushrooms. I became acquainted with the farmers who displayed their products with love. The flavor of those market-fresh foods was a revelation, and not the only one I had.

Plastic. Waste. We had been overtaken by packaging. It was humbling to see the pile of recycling that left the house every week. We were surprised at the number of cans (beans and tomatoes), jars (jams, mustards, and sauces), and plastic quart and pint containers (cottage cheese, yogurt, soup, salads) we used. Slowly we began to turn away from the giant plastic clamshells filled with produce at the grocery store. We began to make buying decisions based on packaging.

Then another revelation. I began to read labels and notice salt content, high fructose corn syrup and palm oil. I will admit that for the longest time, I was quite unaware not only of what I was putting in my body, but also of how those decisions factored in to all that concerned me environmentally. Michael Pollan, Temple Grandin, Barry Estabrook. Manufactured food, GMOs, feedlots, changing weather patterns, animal waste poisoning streams, pesticides on berries, carbon footprints, pink slime, E. coli. There were many eloquent writers telling terrible stories, and now I was paying attention.

And then there were the stories chronicling the demise of the American small farmer. I grew up in the Midwest, surrounded by waving fields of grain, and the thought of families unable to continue their life's work—well, it all hit home. I woke up. After reading Kingsolver's book, I remembered my childhood of canning again, and somehow an idea for a new way of living fell into place.

I could start canning, supplementing what I remembered with classic and new cookbooks, asking people who canned to tell me what they knew. On Saturdays, at my farmers' market, I chatted up Susanne Behling, the energetic and razor-sharp orchardist at West Virginia's Nob Hill Farm. She and I talked about fruit varieties, her bee population, how rain would thin the taste of berries. We waited patiently for alternate Augusts, for the Mirabelle plums that bear fruit only every other year. We shared information about pectins and how to recognize a properly set jam.

Because Suzanne is a jam maker, she grows varieties of fruit particularly good for preserving, with sensational flavors, all harvested with great care. I felt compelled to experiment with each new variety, making jams, sauces, and chutneys; with some, because their flavors were so spectacular, I simply canned the fruit in syrup. Preserving books became my nightstand reading, and I cooked through each one as I learned my way.

That first year of preserving was reasonable, but the second and third years were out of control. I loved the act of canning, the rhythm, the quiet time, the slow stirring, the satisfying "pings" indicating the jars were safe for storage, but Dennis and I couldn't possibly consume all that food. Holiday giving got a lot easier, sure, but even gifting jars to neighbors, the UPS driver, and every farmer at the market didn't put a dent in my inventory.

Another revelation was about to smack me upside the head. Why make anything we wouldn't eat? There were some jams that were ignored, pickles that languished. I gathered three dozen unopened jars at the beginning of year four and began experimenting, using the contents to make barbeque sauces and marinades, vinaigrettes, and brines. I glazed tarts and filled cookies. Suddenly the pantry meant more than having something to spread on toast or garnish a sandwich; it meant more variety in our meals.

Things changed again as soon as I added basic canned tomatoes to my pantry shelves. In September, when tomatoes were plentiful, I bought a twenty-five-pound box and peeled, seeded and crushed them into jars. Practical? Canned tomatoes have to be the most practical jar in the pantry. I make thirty quarts of tomatoes each fall, because that will take Dennis and me from October to July. Those jars start marinaras, moussakas, masalas, and more and are central to our diet.

Farmers' markets began to flourish in DC, and others opened in our region, on more days of the week. It was possible to go to a market every day, and I went to as many as I could. I met farmers from West Virginia, Maryland, Pennsylvania, and Virginia and suddenly I had a point of reference, noticing how produce came to the market first from the southern tip of Virginia and then, moving geographically, later from the cooler hills of central Pennsylvania. I learned how some areas got more rain and had different crops fail and thrive than those areas hampered by drought conditions.

I was working as a landscape designer, and I had received my Master Gardener certification, so I knew enough about gardening to start a conversation with the farmers. Certified organic or best practices? Heirloom or heritage seed? Grass fed and finished? Line caught? Hothouse grown? I asked a lot of questions and found that everyone was very happy to tell me more. (If they weren't willing, why would I buy what they were selling?)

In 2009, I started writing a blog (Mrs. Wheelbarrow's Kitchen). It was a place to record recipes, put up pictures of the garden, and tell stories. Soon after, with this new blog to fill up, I decided to start visiting my favorite farms. I had long conversations about each farmer's dreams and challenges, walked across pastures with warm turkey eggs in my pockets, gazed at apples turning red only on the sunny side of the orchard, saw tiny seedlings protected by light-as-air cloth. I broke bread at these farmers' tables, lavishing homemade butter on freshly dug potatoes, with a panfried recently slaughtered chicken on the plates.

My canning matured. It became goal-oriented, with recipes for dinner connected to what was in the jars. And the canning recipes were informed by my friends the farmers, by their crop successes and failures. When late blight wiped out the tomato crop, Dennis and I went through that winter without tomatoes.

I bought a pressure canner to ramp up production, using it to make more of the items I had previously bought at the grocery store. Jars of black and white beans, limas and butter beans, black-eyed peas and other Southern field peas, home canned and stacked on a shelf in October, made us one dinner a week for a full year. I canned stocks and soups, former denizens of the deep freeze. Chicken stock on the shelf: a lifesaver.

So began a rapid conversion from simple home canning to an expanded view of preserving. Charcuterie was the first technique to interest me, and a two-day workshop at Bethesda's L'Academie de Cuisine set my mind spinning. I developed a cured-meat obsession, using it to garnish my por-

tion of the mostly vegetarian meals I cooked for dinner, but I wondered where that meat came from and what the salt content was—not to mention all that packaging. It was time to start making my own. I educated myself by cooking my way through Michael Ruhlman and Brian Polcyn's *Charcuterie*. The book became more than a guide; it inspired me to think in new and different ways about the meat on my table.

Two years later, I cocreated (with Kim Foster) Charcutepalooza, a year-long blogger challenge to make charcuterie at home. Charcutepalooza gave me the chance to study briefly with the American-born charcuterie impresario Kate Hill in her adopted French home in Gascony. There I learned about raising animals, butchering, and using every bit.

From meat curing, I moved on to fresh-cheese making. Crème fraîche, one of my favorite spoonful-added-at-the-last-minute tricks, and ricotta were everyday items that were exceedingly helpful in creating meat-free dishes, yet, from the store, both came in those wasteful plastic containers, and crème fraîche was expensive. Soon making my own ricotta and crème fraîche, stored in glass jars, was a snap. In time, I added cream cheese and Camembert to my repertoire.

Now we just live this way, without thinking about it much. Food preservation is part of the household routine. A walk through the weekend farmers' market is a chance not only to shop for the week ahead, but also to plan for the winter months. I can't taste a raspberry without thinking of jam. I spy a pile of tiny Kirby cucumbers and my mouth waters—soon they will be cornichons. When October rolls around, there are plump ducks at the market—time for confit. In April, the sweet taste of new spring milk translates to buttery, grassy Camembert.

Summer is a busy time. Each weekend, at least one day is devoted to preserving. And I've become very efficient during the week. I might start jam while dinner is simmering, popping the fruit into the refrigerator to macerate overnight. The next night, I multitask again, ladling the jam into jars to process while eggplant sizzles on the grill. I make a jar of quick pickles in a flash, rub a salty cure into a piece of salmon, or add a culture to warmed milk. Over time, these tasks have become integrated into the rest of my cooking life, as background.

The time investment pays back all year long, whenever I gaze at those shelves wondering what's for dinner. And financially? Certainly and unfortunately, organic food is more expensive than commercially grown food, but I cannot be convinced to preserve anything but the best. Our summertime food costs are higher, but our winter food costs are considerably lower. On average, we spend about the same amount annually on groceries as we did before I started all this preserving, but now I know exactly where the food comes from, how it is grown, and who grows it. I feel good about contributing to the economic growth of my community. I call that winning.

After what can only be called a deliberate, extensive education, Dennis and I are living nearly locally. This is not to say that a craving for salad greens in January is ignored. I use imported olive oil, drink coffee and tea from around the world, eat imported French cheese and Italian cured meats. I embrace international spices. I eat enthusiastically from food trucks. I'm not a fanatic, but I do want my impact on our world to be thoughtful, less harmful. That intention colors every purchasing decision. For many years, when I asked myself, "What can I do?" I felt helpless, incapable of pushing back against the devolution of our environment. But this preservation habit, this practical, organized way to be principled, to care about farmers, the earth, and the food I feed my loved ones, connects me to the world around me.

Is preserving kitchen science? Or a culinary

Hot peppers in vinegar. *See Three Ways to Hot Sauce recipe, page 175.*

art? I'm not sure, but I enjoy the process and the rewards. For now, I will continue to stretch, to learn more about preserving. I'm experimenting with aged cheeses, fresh and cured sausages, fermentation, dehydrating, and freezing, and I'm developing new recipes for using what's preserved. There is no limit to the potential with all that good food in my pantry.

Your pantry is different from my pantry—and it should be.

The pages that follow offer an education in four types of preserving. This is where we will begin together, but where you end up is your decision. While I have an extensive preserving plan, what you do needs to fit your lifestyle, the foods you love, and the way you eat.

Would you like to learn to make cheese? Turn to page 357 and go. Are you an experienced water-bath canner but haven't tried pressure-canning? Go to page 219. Each section stands alone. All are organized seasonally, when appropriate, and they move from the easiest preparations to the more complex. Making ricotta informs the process when making cream cheese. Understanding the way a wet brine changes texture makes smoked brisket more comprehensible. And making a great raspberry jam teaches the principles of evaporation and building a gel, which paves the way for crystal-clear, wiggly grape jelly.

Not sure you're ready to take on preserving? There are 36 bonus recipes that require no preserving at all. This is the practical angle to my pantry. Linked to the preserving recipes are appetizer, salad, dinner, and dessert recipes that are part of our everyday diet. Bonus recipes use what's preserved, sure, but all those foods are also available on the grocery store shelves. No judgment, I just want to feed you. And inspire you.

I certainly don't want to cajole or imply that you must do it my way. You will find your own way to preservation and that doesn't necessarily assume a big, comprehensive program. Perhaps you love dill pickles, and that is what you want to make. I do hope to engage your curiosity, thinking that dill pickles might lead you to dilly beans. And dilly beans might encourage you to try roasted peppers, and from there, a salsa. It's a slippery slope, this preserving habit.

I have come to a comfortable place, and pace, of preserving projects, and there is always something happening in the kitchen. It might be strawberry jam, pie filling, sweet pickles, or a Camembert aging in the small wine refrigerator, even a *bresaola* hanging in the garage. Central to the concept is my own nature. Cooking projects, preserving, baking—that is how I relax. Managing the pantry, knowing what I have available when I plan a week's meals, this is my idea of convenience. Your pantry will be different for many reasons, but especially the time you have available, the size of your family, what they like to eat, the growing season in your part of the world, and what equipment you have at your disposal.

I wrote this book to make preserving accessible, both less frightening and more useful. To show how preserving fits into everyday life, how a well-stocked pantry contributes to easing the weeknight dinner challenge, and, first and foremost, to preach the local food message.

What is this, the State Fair?

The pursuit of perfection can get us in trouble. I am particularly hard on myself when things aren't exactly perfect. I want every jar that emerges from the canner to be State Fair ready to garner a blue ribbon. But that doesn't always happen.

Some jars may end up with floating fruit, two inches of liquid at the bottom of the jar and the fruit crowding the top. Some may have siphoned (liquid escaped from the jar during processing) leaving more headspace at the top of the jar than you want. I give you permission to relax. It's not perfect? So what? Eat the imperfect jars first.

I cover these issues and more in the Troubleshooting pages in each chapter. I'll tell you when to worry and when it's simply an aesthetic issue.

And if you do want to enter the State Fair, I wish you a wall full of blue ribbons.

Straight talk on safety

There is a story that plays in my head every single time I set out to preserve. When I was growing up in Ohio, we would drive nearly an hour to eat at a small Mexican restaurant near Detroit. There weren't many places to get authentic Mexican food, and this was especially delicious. I remember their salsa, the first I ever tasted. And that salsa killed thirteen diners one night. Improper preservation techniques. We could all use a little fear, and that is why I tell you this story.

I know you may be nervous. I can tell you, very seriously, that the likelihood of killing your family or making someone sick, or of something exploding in the kitchen or pantry, is slim. But follow the rules. Don't get "creative," don't riff on cooking times, processing times, or processing methods, and you will be just fine. Most errors will become evident. There will be mold; the contents of the jar will smell awful; the sealed lids will lift up from the force of gases created from an unhealthy environment, breaking the seal; or, in some cases, a jar will shatter.

Because it has no markers, *Clostridium botulinum* is the biggest anxiety producer, but *Staphylococcus aureus*, *Salmonella*, *Clostridium perfringens*, *Campylobacter*, *Listeria monocytogenes*, *Vibrio parahaemolyticus*, *Bacillus cereus*, and enteropathogenic *Escherichia coli* are just a few of the other bacteria that create food-borne illnesses. Fewer than one hundred people die from food-borne illnesses each year, and most people get sick not from home-canned foods, but from food from commercial producers.

I want you to be a confident home food preserver, but one who carries around a healthy dose of fear. It will make you careful. The minute you decide that there's too much sugar or too much vinegar in a recipe, or that adding a couple of garlic cloves would make it tastier, or to use orange instead of lemon juice, or to skip the pasteurizing step, you are making a risky move. Respect the recipes. They are the science ensuring that the food you make, and the people who eat it, will not suffer.

STAY SAFE

These low-acid foods may harbor pathogens and must be supplemented with a significant amount of balancing acid: figs, tomatoes, onions, shallots, garlic, garlic scapes, peppers and chiles, cantaloupe.

These foods must be pressure-canned: poultry, meat, fish, beans, some salsas, some tomato products, vegetables that are not pickled. See Chapter Two, page 219.

These foods should never be canned: dairy products, grains and flours (for instance, rice, noodles, kasha, or barley added to soups), bananas, watermelon (except the rind, pickled), summer squash, winter squash, pumpkin.

SOME RULES OF THE ROAD: STAYING SAFE

- Start with a clean kitchen. Wipe up any spills on the stove, wash down the counters and sink. Cooking pots should be clean and free of any residual oil.

- Follow recipes, keep to the processing times, and use recipes from trusted sources. Who are those trusted sources? See the Bibliography (page 403) for some links and the books I rely on. If your interest is in canning a favorite family recipe, your County Extension office may be willing to evaluate the safety of that recipe for a reasonable fee.

- Read through the instructions several times before starting. If you haven't canned before, talk a friend into preserving together; two heads are better than one. Or ask to help a veteran canner and learn by doing—it's the best way.

- If you start preserving frequently, you will develop a rhythm and have a body memory of the process. If you only can once a year, reread all the recipes and all the other instructions before you get going. There will be things you forget. Give yourself plenty of time.

- Keep your equipment in top shape. Scrub any hot spots from the bottom of your large pre-serving pot. If you pressure-can, check the gauge every year; most hardware stores and many auto mechanics can check it for you. The rubber gasket on a pressure canner will wear out. Check carefully for rips and tears, and replace it when needed.

- If you grab a jar from the pantry and it is no longer sealed, throw it away. Do not taste it, just toss it—jar and all. If it is sealed but there is mold growing inside the jar, throw it away. If it smells like something died in the jar, throw it away. Don't feed it to the dog. Don't taste a little, just to see. It's not worth it. If at any time you are suspicious of the food in front of you, don't eat it.

- Finally, be smart about all of this. I give away jars of food all the time with confidence, but I would never give home-canned meats and other pressure-canned and low-acid foods to someone with a compromised immune system. Never.

- If you are new to preserving, start with pickles or jam, move on to putting crushed tomatoes or tomato puree in jars, and then consider pres-sure-canning. Make ricotta before you leap into Camembert. Become familiar with brining before smoking. Just as with any new endeavor, warm up and stretch before going for the gold.

- After opening a jar, keep it covered and in the refrigerator. As a rule of thumb, most home-canned jams and pickles will keep for a month or more in the refrigerator, but tomatoes, meats, fish, soups, and all pressure-canned foods should be consumed within a week after opening the jar.

Fresh apricots,
rhubarb, and
raspberries

Chapter One

THE BASICS OF WATER-BATH CANNING: ANSWERING THE SIREN CALL OF SEASONAL ABUNDANCE

In the pages that follow, I introduce you to the basics of water-bath canning. This is the most commonly used form of preserving, and if you make a few of these recipes every year, you will have your own practical pantry. Before cooking anything, though, let's talk about safely sealing the jars. The purpose is to put away some food for later. Peaches for March, strawberries for December, jars of tomatoes to start stews in January. While that jam you just made tastes sensational, and it's tempting to eat it all up and skip the canning, winter is coming. There will be no berries and no jam then. So put aside at least one jar, maybe two, from each batch. One for you, one to give away. But in order to set some of these seasonal treasures aside, you must know how to safely seal the jars.

If I told you to submerge covered filled jars in a pot of boiling water for a specified number of minutes, then remove them, would you be afraid? I didn't think so. Of course, there are other skills and techniques that are valuable when filling the jars. Creating ethereal jams, remarkable fruits, astonishing pickles, and ketchup that makes you need a French fry: these come from the recipes. But the basics of putting foods on the shelf for the cold months is really that simple: put jars in water, boil, and take them out.

The process of water-bath canning makes foods shelf stable by heating the contents of the jar to 212°F, the same temperature as boiling water. I refer throughout the book to sea-level temperatures and times. If you live above sea level, follow the charts on page 30 to adjust the processing times and temperatures as necessary. Go ahead and write them in here so you don't forget. Yes, right on the recipe page. I believe in writing in books.

Sanitize the jars and keep them warm until you fill them with hot liquids to the appropriate headspace, the space between the food and the top of the jar, a measurement noted in each recipe. Then submerge the jars in boiling water in the canning kettle, where the temperature will equalize between the boiling water and the contents in the jars. Heat the jars for the processing time noted in the recipe; when the temperature of the contents of the jars reaches 212°F, the air in the headspace is expelled from the jar, escaping under the lid. When all the air is removed, a vacuum forms and the lid pulls down and makes a pinging sound—"plink," what I call the music of the jars. In a nutshell, that is the science of water-bath canning.

There is an interrelationship between the size of the jars, the processing time, and the headspace, all of which are noted in each recipe. If changes are made—if the jars are larger, the headspace smaller, or the processing time is adjusted—failure is likely. Follow the recipes exactly, or all bets are off.

While I could spend more time extolling the magic of canning, the rhythm, the charm of the pinging jars, I'd rather focus on the benefits. It is hard work, but the real joy comes months later, when you discover a lost jar of strawberry jam in the back of the cupboard, months before a local strawberry will be picked. Or imagine offering friends gathered to watch the game a big platter of nachos with salsa and pickled jalapeños, even candied chiles, from your own home-canned jars of good food. When dinner is "chicken-yet-again," make it special by glazing it with a pan sauce made from last summer's currant jelly. Your pantry is far more convenient than running off to the supermarket. Reach in and find inspiration.

Put the very best in the jar

Of course, only the very best foods should go in the jar. Really, why would I want to eat anything but the healthiest food available? Whether I grow it or purchase it at a market or farm stand, or harvest it at Pick Your Own farms, I look for food in season from the very best sources. Then I rush right home and preserve that flavor, the scent of the field, the warmth of the sun. All captured inside a beautiful jar.

When shopping for fruits and vegetables, I often start with a recipe in mind, but just as often I let the abundance at the market lead me to the recipe. It might be the first box of plump blueberries, a late-season plum or a tumble of ripe Roma tomatoes.

Some fruits and vegetables are better suited to certain applications. There is no better example than the peach, with two forms—cling and freestone. The first must be cut off the pit, while the second slips beautifully off the stone after cutting around it from north to south and gently twisting the two hemispheres. Clings are better suited to pie filling or preserves, freestones are exquisite suspended in scented syrup.

If at all possible, taste before making a big investment: looks can be deceiving. The quality of the fruit, the color, and the scent all collaborate in the experience, but knowledge of the fruit is how I determine what I will do. Is it totally ripe or still slightly underripe? Is the skin tough? Is the fruit mushy or grainy? Is it tart and acidic or velvety sweet? Should it be chutney or sauce? Is the color extraordinary? Then, make jelly. Be inspired by what you see, smell, taste, and touch.

Avoid purchasing fruit after a heavy rainstorm. Stone fruits (peaches, plums, cherries, apricots) and berries will have absorbed too much water, resulting in thin flavor and unappealing texture. Inspect the bottom of a berry box or box of tomatoes to check for mold or rotting fruit. Yes, one rotten apple really will spoil the whole batch.

When you get home, spread your bounty out in a single layer and look over each piece for signs of bugs, bruising, or other unappealing elements.

Rinse fruit and vegetables just before cooking, and only if absolutely necessary.

Don't bite off more than you can chew. Try to plan your purchases, preserving, and time. I can say this, but trust me, I don't do it all the time. You'll find me preserving until 10 p.m. one night because I overbought, seduced by a plum or taunted by the last of the strawberries. Find the circumstances that make you happy when canning. Do you want music? To listen to a book? To sing show tunes? Or to gather with a roomful of friends? Create the experiences that encourage preserving, and the two become intertwined, a part of life that is joyous, not onerous.

FREEZING

Too busy to can? **Jams and preserves made from frozen fruit work equally well and taste just as good.** If the fruit is picked at the height of the season and quickly frozen, it can be used to make marvelous preserves up to eight months later. Don't let time constraints deprive you of a favorite jam.

Freeze dry whole berries, carefully separated, on baking sheets. These IQF (individually quick frozen) fruits are delicate but will retain all the qualities of fresh berries. Once the berries are frozen, pack into zip-lock bags, remove the air, and store flat. Mark the weight and date on the bag. Use while still frozen. Make jam in January, stir into muffins, or cook into sauce.

Stone fruits like cherries, peaches, plums, and apricots should be pitted before freezing. The peels will fall away after defrosting, a bonus for peaches especially. Freeze solid on baking sheets, then put in large zip-lock bags, carefully expelling all the air, and mark with the weight and date.

Most of the recipes in this book call for 3 pounds of fruit or vegetables, which will fit in a one-gallon bag.

Equipment: the necessary pieces and those that are nice to have

I wish I could say no special equipment is needed to make any of the recipes in this chapter. I can't, but there are many preserving recipes requiring nothing more than some sturdy cookware and the basic utensils found in most cooks' kitchens. In fact, skip ahead to quick pickles (page 187) or refrigerator pickles (page 191) for preserving projects requiring no special equipment whatsoever. Other recipes call for specific pieces of equipment. Some of them cost just a few dollars; others are more of an investment. Rest assured, many of the recipes require only four items: a canning kettle with a rack, a preserving pot, a scale, and a thermometer.

For online sources for canning equipment, see Resources, page 401.

A **canning kettle,** a good-sized pot, is key. It needs to be deep, ideally with a 10- to 16-quart capacity, and to have a lid. This is a piece of equipment with broad usefulness in the preserving kitchen: for stock, for blanching tomatoes, for sanitizing cheese-making equipment, and for water-bath processing. If you are planning to use the pot for cooking stock, look for stainless steel, which is non-reactive. The pot takes up space, but I can promise that you will never regret having a big pot like this. Look at flea markets, yard sales, restaurant supply stores, and even big box stores for bargains.

There are also inexpensive graniteware and aluminum pots made and sold expressly for can-

Water-bath canning equipment

ning. Or use a lobster pot. Really, any pot that will hold the jars upright on a rack and is tall enough so the water can cover the jars by at least an inch or two will work. If you do not have a pot large enough to hold quart jars, consider canning only in the shorter pint jars.

The jars must rest on **a rack**. If glass jars are placed willy-nilly directly onto the bottom of the canning kettle, the boiling water will rattle them against one another and as they jiggle and jangle, all that action could very easily nick or crack the glass, bursting the jar. Canning kits and canning pots often come with a rack, but most are oddly constructed and the jars won't sit level, putting the seal in jeopardy every time they tip over. It can be so frustrating, trying to balance all the jars and keep them upright while preventing the rack from collapsing into the water. Many canners turn to a common DIY trick, a rack made from canning rings tied together in a honeycomb pattern. Even with this clever repurposing, it's still difficult to get the jars to sit level. Some canners fold a towel in the bottom of the pot, but that tends to rise like a specter. This whole rack business can make a first-time canner crazy.

Here's a better idea. Measure the inside diameter of your canning kettle and find a similarly sized round baking rack, one you might cool a cake on. It's perfect for the jars. Cake racks all have little feet, so they sit up above the bottom of the canning kettle, preventing the jars from rattling against it. Most round baking racks are stainless steel and so will not rust. I found mine at the hardware store.

Throughout the following pages, I refer often to a **preserving pot**. This will be your companion in the canning kitchen, a pot you reach for over and over, so find one you love. A 5-quart heavy pot will work like a charm. An 8-quart pot is even better, providing a wider surface area to evaporate water from

Copper preserving pots

jams and jellies more quickly. The best preserving pots are heavy bottomed and allow for a long vigorous boil at high heat without scorching. I have a beautiful all-copper French preserving pot in my arsenal, but it is a little too large for the small batches I prefer to make. (However, it is superb for candy making, pie fillings, fruit halves in syrup, and other large-batch projects.) Stainless steel cookware is another good option, the heavier the better. For my own cooking, I turn to my 8-quart Le Creuset enameled cast-iron Dutch oven: it maintains heat beautifully, keeps jams at a constant boil, and cleans up easily—it is a great investment.

Some recipes call for a nonreactive pot. Aluminum reacts with acids or vinegars, and the food will taste of metal and will turn black. This is not a color you want for your chutney. Avoid all-aluminum pots. By the same token, your beautiful all-copper pot should not be used with vinegar-based preparations like chutney or pickles and any tomato recipes, as they are acidic and could pit the metal.

During cleanup, scrub away any hot spots, those darkened areas on the bottom of the pot. The heat gravitates to these hot spots and your next batch of jam or jelly could scorch. Any burned jam or jelly will flavor the entire batch. Burned sugary jam is a cleanup problem too. If you do scorch or burn the jam, fill the pot with water and boil hard for a few minutes. The scorched food will lift off without having to scratch the surface to get it clean.

Mine is not the first cookbook to suggest using a **scale** for precision, nor will it be the last. Precision is important in baking, less vital in much of cooking, more critical in science. And preserving food is a science. Why take chances?

Just as vital to the science of preserving is a **candy thermometer**. I like the all-metal ones that clip on to the side of the pot (see Resources, page 401). I want you to be successful, and without a thermometer, you'll just be guessing; this is a smart, inexpensive investment.

And then there are items that ease the process. They aren't essential, but I like their functionality and wouldn't consider canning without them.

A **1- to 3-quart saucepan** to warm the lids and rings. This is nice to have, but if your stove is too small to hold another pan once the preserving pot and canning kettle have taken up residence, just warm the lids and rings in the canning kettle.

A **jar lifter** is enormously useful and a safety measure against boiling water splashing everywhere. This rubber-coated grabber is shaped to fit the jars. It's inexpensive and well worth the money.

A **metallic lid lifter** is a clever little tool. It's about the size and shape of a pencil, with a magnet on one end. No more fishing lids from boiling water with your fingers!

A **bubbler** can be a plastic knife or a chopstick, but the flat plastic bubbler that's sold expressly for canning works like a charm and even has a handy headspace measure on the end. Run this flat tool around the inside of the jar and through the preserves to dislodge and burst air bubbles. During processing, air bubbles make the preserves bubble up in a slow sputter, often lifting the entire lid with the force of the bubbles and allowing food to escape. That food may lodge on the rim of the jar, which ultimately leads to seal failure. Dislodge the bubbles before this happens. Do not use a metal knife. The hot metal could scratch the jar, add to glass fatigue, and even the very slightest chip can cause jars to crack under the intense heat of the canning kettle.

Jar funnels, available in plastic, glass, or stainless steel, fit inside the top of the jar and make filling so much easier. I use glass and stainless steel funnels, as plastic will absorb, for example, the garlic smell from chutney and pass it on to the raspberry jam.

A **sturdy food mill** uses elbow grease to seed and remove the skin of various fruits and vegetables. I couldn't live without mine. If a recipe calls for a food mill and you don't have one, use a strainer and press the food through the mesh using a wooden spoon. However, your yield may be lower than the recipe specifies; a food mill is much more efficient.

Some jams, jellies, and sauces need a little mashing to achieve the correct consistency. I use a **heavy-duty stainless steel potato masher**. Immersion blenders also work well, or use a classic blender, but pulse carefully to avoid pureeing the mixture. A masher is best when the preserves should have a chunky consistency.

My batterie de cuisine also includes plenty of long-handled wooden spoons and **silicone spatulas**. And to fill the jars, a **stainless steel ladle**. For removing foam, a perforated stainless steel skimmer. A rasp and a citrus zester. A citrus reamer. Small, medium, and large stainless steel sieves. A 3-quart **footed colander** from OXO. And Pyrex **measuring cups** in 1-, 2-, 4- and 8-cup sizes.

Because I do so much cooking, I couldn't manage without my frequently sharpened excellent **chef's knife** and a couple of sharp **paring knives**. A **food processor, sturdy blender** (a glass beaker is a sign of a strong motor), and **stand mixer** are also useful every day, whether or not you are canning.

Clean cotton kitchen towels, and plenty of them, are essential. Preserving is messy.

And, finally, **music for dancing.** It is going to be a long, hot day in the canning kitchen. Get yourself an upbeat playlist and have fun.

Jars and lids and rings

Think of the canning jar as the frame around your artful preserving project. Each jar suits certain foods not only aesthetically, but also in terms of processing. The processing time in a particular recipe is based on the size of the jar used, the density of the product preserved, and the time it will take to heat the food in the jar through to the very center. For this reason, canning jars come in many shapes but only a few sizes, and recipes are gauged to the jar sizes. New jars are widely available at hardware, grocery, and big box stores. Old jars are often found for pennies at flea markets, junk stores, and garage sales. The brilliant thing about preserving in jars is how very green it is: jars can be used over and over, requiring only new lids each time.

At the beginning of the twentieth century, there were many companies making jars, but now, after many an acquisition, and smaller companies coming and going, most jars sold in the United States are made by Jarden Home Products, makers of the Ball jar. The jars are often still called Mason jars, even though Ball purchased Mason and Atlas and many other small companies.

I have been acquiring vintage canning jars for years, first as a storage option for all the grains, flours, and sugars in my pantry. Later, fascinated by the variation in shapes and colors, I began to collect them, and then I started using these old jars. Throughout the book there are photographs of some of my favorites, in both traditional classic and rare shapes. But as unusual as some of the shapes may seem, the openings are exactly the same as in the jars sold today: regular or wide-mouth. Smart design endures.

While European jars, such as Weck and others are stunning, with their glass tops, rubber rings, and metal clips, they are too expensive for preserving on my scale. I do keep a few around for setting a breakfast table, for gifts, and for holding thumbtacks.

Process only in jars meant for canning. Not all glass is tempered to withstand the high temperatures required, and even those that are eventually suffer "fatigue" and may crack in the canner. When I process in my antique jars, I know that every bath could be their last. Think of using these jars instead to store everything from grains to buttons and shells to candy kisses. Fill jars with wildflowers. Pack leftovers in a jar and then reheat in the microwave at the office in the same container. Every time you reach for a jar, consider the plastic that isn't being used.

Every jar is sealed with a two-part lid, a flat metal piece and a ring. The rings can be used over and over but should not be left on the jars when they are stored. The rings have only one purpose— to hold the lid in place during processing, before the seal has formed.

Each lid has a rubber gasket that, as it warms, softens and spreads against the jar rim, allowing the air to ease out of the jar. Once the air is expressed, the button in the center is pulled down, making a pinging sound.

Lids should be used only once and be discarded after the contents of the jar are used. A multiuse lid is available from Tattler, but I have not been satisfied with the stability of the seal. Antique zinc lids are not recommended for processing.

Assorted canning jars, lids, and rings

CANNING JARS

Canning jars are made with either wide-mouth or regular openings. When tucking items such as Kirby cucumbers or plump peach halves into a jar, the wide-mouth openings are pretty handy. Because there are only two sizes for the openings, there are only two sizes of lids. Here are the common jar sizes.

Quarter pint (4-oz., 120-ml). This small jar works well for jams, jellies, and sauces. It is a perfect size for gifting, lovely in a basket packed with cheese or bread, a little butter spreader, and a pretty napkin.

Half pint (8-oz., 235-ml). This is the most useful jar for jam makers. The low wide-mouth versions make pretty containers for conserves and chunkier confitures like peach and apricot.

One-and-a-half cups (12-oz., 355-ml). This is a newer size that is perfect for juice and for pickling tall asparagus or onion stalks. It's also a good size for ketchup, for conserves with whole nuts such as macadamia or pistachios, and fruity sauces.

Pint (16-oz., 475-ml). These jars are good for pickles, tomatoes, soup for two, juices, and corn, beets, and beans. Most recipes for these are scaled to pint jars.

One-and-a-half pints (24-oz., 710-ml). This larger jar size works beautifully for pickle chunks, dilly beans, carrots, and other tall produce. I like this size for crushed tomatoes and tomato puree.

Quart (32-oz., 950-ml). The handiest size for pie fillings, stock, beans, soups, whole peaches, and pears.

Half-gallon. While not recommended for processing, these jars are great for brining pickles. And big **one-, three-, and five-gallon crocks or clamp-top jars** are also useful for brining, infusing liquor, and large-scale fermenting, but they cannot be used for processing.

Preparing jars for canning

Before using any jars, wash them with warm soapy water and rinse well. If you will be processing for 10 minutes or less, you must sanitize the jars. (This isn't an operating room; it's a kitchen. Sterile is not probable—sanitary is possible.) If you will be processing for more than 10 minutes, jars do not require sanitizing.

To sanitize jars, either boil the jars in the canning kettle for 10 minutes or run the jars through a hot dishwasher cycle. Leave the jars in the canning kettle or the dishwasher to keep warm. Always put the warm food into warm jars before processing them.

Fresh nonchlorinated water

Throughout the book, many recipes specify nonchlorinated water. For pickling, particularly, the quality of the water is critical. If your water is highly chlorinated (you smell chlorine in a glass of water fresh from the tap), that smell will carry through to your preserved foods. If that is the case, for any recipe that calls for nonchlorinated water, either purchase filtered water or measure out the water needed for the recipe and leave it on the counter, uncovered, overnight, or for at least 8 hours, before starting. Chlorine is a gas, and gases disperse over time.

Fluorides, base metals, and other elements naturally floating around in your tap water may play havoc with pickles so use filtered water. And when there is a good portion of water in a recipe, as in brining or making syrups, use filtered water.

Six steps to successful water-bath canning

1. Preserve. Process. Can. These are the basic steps to water-bath canning. Making the jam or the pickles or putting up peaches—we'll get to that. But first, here is all you need to know about putting jars in boiling water and taking them out. These are the dance steps. Let them become second nature through repetition. If the seal on your jar fails, either refrigerate the jar and use it up within a month, or empty the jar into the preserving pot, reheat the preserves, and reprocess. If an entire canner load failed, it's time to review your actions. They should not fail at that rate. See Troubleshooting Water-Bath canning, page 31.

2. Fill a canning kettle with enough water so that the jars will be submerged by 1 to 2 inches. If your water tends to leave spots, add 2 tablespoons white vinegar to the canning kettle to ensure sparkling jars. Add a rack—preferably a footed cake rack. Bring the water to a boil, then reduce to a simmer, cover, and keep warm until ready to process the jars. Sanitize the jars by boiling in the canning kettle for 10 minutes or in the dishwasher. Fill a small saucepan with water and add the rings. Have the lids close by.

3. Prepare the food to be preserved according to the recipe. When the food is ready, drop the lids into the saucepan holding the rings, bring the water to a simmer to warm and soften the rubber gaskets, then turn off the heat. Do not boil the lids, as prolonged high heat weakens the rubber. Warm them, don't cook them.

4. Remove the jars from the canner (or dishwasher) and place them on a clean towel. Ladle the hot preserves into the warm jars. Be aware of the headspace noted in every recipe, the amount of space to leave between the food and the top of the jar. Do not overfill the jars, put any excess into a little bowl for sampling; and do not underfill the jars, either. Run a bubbler around the inside of each jar and then make an X through the center to release any air bubbles.

5. Clean the rim of each jar carefully with a towel dipped in the hot water in the small saucepan. Place the lids on the jars, then add the rings and screw on "finger tight." The ring keeps the lid in place. As the contents of the jar heat, air is forced out of the jar under the lid. If the ring is too tight, air cannot get out, so the seal will fail or, worse, the jar will crack. Tighten the rings using your fingertips, no brute force necessary.

6. Lower the jars, upright, into the boiling water. Add more hot water as necessary to cover them by 1 or 2 inches. Bring the water back to a murmuring boil with big bubbles. Cover the pot and process for the entire time indicated in the recipe. Turn off the heat and let the jars rest in the canning kettle for a few minutes to reduce siphoning (hot liquid boiling up and out under the lids.) Remove the jars and place apart on a folded towel. When the jars are cool, remove the rings and check the seal on each one by lifting the jar by the lid. Wash the jars, label with the contents and date, and store in a cool, dark, dry spot.

The old ways

I am a big believer in a lot of the "old ways of doing things" when I cook, but when I'm processing, it's safety first. The USDA does not recommend any of these "old-fashioned" methods, and neither do I. Even if you have "always done it this way," please stop now.

- Flipping the jars upside down to seal
- Oven processing
- Open-kettle processing
- Steam-canner processing
- Paraffin caps

Labeling and storing

Every recipe in this book includes a note on shelf stability, how long the jars will keep on the shelf. But that isn't always a hard-and-fast rule. As long as the jar was processed within the last couple of years and is still sealed, it will be fine. However, the contents may not be as tasty after the time given: the flavors will fade, the color will change, the texture may alter. The purpose of preserving is to keep what is in season for the off season. So try to plan accordingly. By the time tomatoes are back at the market, they should be out of your pantry. Do your kids eat PB&J every day? You'll go through a hundred jars of jam. If you live alone, maybe ten jars will be enough. Keep records, if you are an organized person like that. I try, really I do.

Mark every jar with the contents and the date. You think you will remember what's in every one, but you won't. I write on the lid with a permanent marker. I've tried all sorts of labels, but they often leave a gummy residue that is difficult to remove. I'll put labels on jars I give as gifts, but there's no need to get fancy in my own pantry.

Your home-canned foods will last longer if kept in a cool, dark, dry place. If you are not living in a house with a root cellar (and, really, how many of us are?), put your jars in a cool garage, the closet in a spare room, or under the bed. Always store the jars without the rings: if there is a problem with the food in the jar, the lid will often lift up. If the ring is left on the jar, the lid cannot lift, and the jar may burst. If possible, don't stack the jars on top of one another, again so the lids can release if necessary. If you must stack, just check the seal carefully when opening the jar. To open any home-canned food, use a church-key-style bottle opener and listen for the sound of the seal releasing.

Altitude adjustments for water-bath canning

This book was written with processing times and temperatures for working at sea level. If you live at a higher elevation, see the charts below.

Altitude	Add to Processing Time
1,000–2,999 ft	5 minutes
3,000–5,999 ft	10 minutes
6,000–7,999 ft	15 minutes
8,000–10,000 ft	20 minutes

Water boils at a lower temperature than 212°F at higher altitudes. The temperature at which preserves set, 220°F, will adjust downward as well.

Altitude	Temperature at Which Water Boils	Adjustment for 220°F
2,000 ft	208°F	218°F
4,000 ft	204°F	216°F
6,000 ft	201°F	214°F
8,000 ft	197°F	212°F
10,000 ft	194°F	210°F

TROUBLESHOOTING WATER-BATH CANNING

Water-bath canning is straightforward and, for the most part, any failures are going to be straightforward too. Of course, this assumes you have followed the recipe, have not doubled or tripled it, have not reduced or increased any of the ingredients, have used jars of the correct size, and have processed them for the recommended time.

With that said, the most frequent and annoying problem is **seal failure**. After processing, let the jars cool, remove the rings and lift each jar by the flat lid; if it does not remain securely attached, the seal has failed. Or, if, when the ring is removed, the lid lifts up, or if the button in the center of the flat lid is not depressed but can be pushed in and out, that also is seal failure. The most common cause of seal failure is not cleaning the jar's rim completely before putting the lid on. Be sure to clean the top and the inner lip of the jar using a towel dipped in hot water. The warm water should cut through any sugars and fruits. To be extra certain, you can use white vinegar, particularly if processing with oil or with finely ground spices, both of which seem to adhere relentlessly to the lips of the jars.

The science of water-bath canning tells us that when the contents of the jar reach 212°F, the air at the top of the jar (the headspace you left) will be expelled, thus forming a vacuum. If there are air bubbles left in the jar and the liquid in the jar burbles up along with that air, some food can escape under the lid, and any food trapped between the rubber surface and the jar will interfere with seal formation. This burbling up, the escape of food and liquids from the filled jars, is called **siphoning**.

The first sign of siphoning is the food floating in the water of the canning kettle. This is unsettling, I know. Sometimes the food and liquid siphons out and the seals still form but the liquid in the jar is well below the food (as in, for example, canned peaches). This is not a problem per se. (It is a State Fair issue; see page 15.) But there may be some discoloration on the surface of any foods exposed to air inside the jar. My rule of thumb is to use those jars first, and soon.

One seal failing is annoying. An entire canner load failing is a big problem. Review the headspace you left, and measure it to be sure. Review the timing. Do not cut corners anywhere. And don't be too hard on yourself, you will get better at this. Reprocess and consider it a lesson learned.

Reprocessing is possible with any jar that has seal failure, but you must do it within 24 hours of the original processing. Empty the contents of the jar(s) into the preserving pot and bring the food back to a strong boil. Ladle into a warm, clean, sanitized jar (or jars), clean the rim of the jar, and cover with a brand-new, never-used flat lid. Add the ring, finger tighten, and reprocess. Reprocessing will change the texture of the preserved food (it's twice-cooked, after all), so if only one jar has failed, I put that one into the refrigerator, eat it up within a month, and move on.

Some seals fail in the pantry, most likely as a result of food being trapped under the lid during processing. The seal will form but then releases sometime down the road. This is the best reason for carefully removing the rings and testing the seals after processed jars have cooled, because coming upon a jar of homemade anything covered in fluffy white fuzz is awful.

Mold inside the sealed jar is an indication of underprocessing. Always give yourself plenty of time when starting any preserving project, follow the recipe, and process for the entire time indicated. If an emergency arises and you must stop processing, turn off the heat and remove the jars from the canning kettle. Then, within 24 hours empty the contents of the jars into the preserving pot and bring back to a strong boil. Ladle into clean sanitized jars and reprocess. This may affect the preserved food's color, texture, or taste, but it will be safe to eat.

If the **pantry is too cold or too warm,** seals may release and mold may grow inside the jars. Throw those out, jars and all. I keep a thermometer on a shelf in my pantry. The ideal temperature for storage is between 50° and 70°F.

If the lids of the **jars bulge** in any way, it is a sign of gases building up inside. When a jar has been properly canned, all the air has been expressed, leaving no room for gases. Something is wrong if the jar is bulging, and the next thing that will happen could be it exploding. Throw it out. If a jar **explodes** or if food and liquids **bubble out under the lid**, throw it all away.

In a nutshell, **if in doubt, throw it out**. And never sample questionable food to see if it's okay—never.

OPPOSITE (left to right): Jars of Roasted Tomato Puree (page 163), Crushed Tomatoes (page 156), and Tomato Puree (page 161)

JAM, CONFITURE, PRESERVES, CHUTNEY, SAUCE, AND CONSERVE

OPPOSITE: Fresh strawberries

What's in a name?

From the first tiny strawberries to the last pear, preserve through the seasons with these recipes. Once you learn to make one jam, you'll be enjoying a world of different flavors in no time. Jams and preserves, confitures, sauces and chutneys are all ways of preserving fruit. There are others in the next section, but let's start with these, the most straightforward of all fruit-preserving methods. First, a review of the taxonomy, keeping in mind that whatever it is called, it's all heavenly on toast.

In a classic **jam**, the fruit is diced small and partially mashed and the suspending syrup is thick and opaque. **Confitures and preserves** are kissing cousins: whole or elegantly sliced fruit suspended in syrup is a confiture from the French verb *confire*, meaning "to preserve." In confitures, the fruit is shown to great advantage, glistening in a clear gel. The set tends to be looser than for jam. Add confitures to yogurt or crepes and spoon over waffles. Preserves are made from roughly chopped fruit and are more rustic, less fussy. Neither as evenly textured as jam nor as refined as confiture, preserves are the middle child of the fruit spread family.

The fruit often determines the method. Beautiful first-of-the-season strawberries are small, the size of a thumbnail, and so I make confiture, cosseting the berries, turning them gently so they hold their shape. Because there is little pectin in the berries, the result is loose and even a little runny, which I expect. Come November, when tiny, sweet local strawberries are just a memory, consistency is the last thing I worry about. Those individual jewels look spectacular on a slice of grilled pound cake.

I use the words "jam," "confiture," and "preserves" fairly interchangeably in the book, and in recipes. Any of them makes a quick tart, served with a spoonful of crème fraîche. Bake a pan of shortbread and spread jam across the surface once cooled (see Jam Tarts, page 69). Layer preserves in granola bars or dab in thumbprint cookies. Some fruits make sensational sauces, ready for trifle or ice cream. There are myriad savory applications too. Mix with mustard, Chinese fermented black beans, or soy sauce to make quick marinades or barbeque sauces (see, for example, Chipotle Barbeque Sauce, page 263), suitable for tofu, chicken, fish, or meat.

Once you have gained experience with jam making, turn to **chutneys**, where savory dances with sweet. Chutney is a condiment, a shape shifter, made like a jam, with fruit suspended in a syrup of vinegar and sugar. These tangy combinations can be spicy or not, and they often include dried fruit as well as fresh.

Add a handful of pecans or pistachios, walnuts or almonds, any nut at all (toasted are tastier) to jam. That's what we call a **conserve**.

NO ANGST

All jams will develop a firmer set as they cool and some jams will firm up over the course of a week, or even a month, after processing. Be patient—and flexible. If your preserves are too loose to call jam, just rename them as syrup and spoon over ice cream or pancakes, stir into sparkling water, blend into a smoothie, or use as a base for a fruity cocktail. Next time, cook the jam a little longer and test, test, test the set.

And here's a tip. Don't label your jars "jam" or "preserves"—instead, just write the flavor (cherry, apricot, strawberry) on the label. If the set is loose, serve it as syrup without a second thought. Never apologize; rebrand instead.

Water, water everywhere

When food professionals talk about food safety and canning, there are two primary concerns: the food's pH (see High-Acid and Low-Acid Foods, page 38) and the water activity. In their natural form, most foods have moisture levels that keep them fresh and appealing. But that moisture also supports the growth of microorganisms, bacteria, yeasts, and mold. That's why fresh food spoils.

To preserve foods, we must consider their water content. Water makes up most of the cells of everything on this earth—remember science class? Osmosis moves molecules through the permeable "skin" of each cell. Water content, called water activity in preserving terms, is what determines the shelf stability of preserved foods.

Cooking down jams and sauces reduces the amount of water harbored in the cells. Through osmosis, the remaining water is exchanged with the sugary syrup, reducing water activity to a level considered safe and lasting. This is why we test the "set" (see page 44); why loose, undercooked jams may lose their bright color and fresh flavor more quickly; and why the balance of sugar, fruit, and lemon (added acid) is important to successful preserving.

This is a simplified explanation, but it's the way I've come to understand what is happening when I cook and can. Jams and other fruit preserves are boiled, and boiled hard (see The Boil That Will Not Stir Down, page 38), before canning. The foam that forms during that boil is the water activity reducing. If all the water were simply removed, the food would be dehydrated, tough, and rubbery. But surrounding the fruit with a sugary syrup instead means the fruit takes on the syrup, staying plump and retaining its bright color. This method of cooking leads to safe preserving.

If a jam is undercooked, resulting in a syrupy liquid with floating fruit, the water content is likely to be higher than recommended. High water activity is likely to result in mold, color loss, and textural problems. Moderate water activity (when a jam is more like a syrup) will not make you sick, but the product may lose flavor and color over time.

Sugar and lemon play nicely together

There is a certain alchemy that occurs when fruit, sugar, and lemon are stirred together. That action is what makes the preserves set, or gel, as the sugar and lemon juice activate the fruit's natural pectin. When the sugar in a recipe is reduced or the lemon juice replaced with another citrus juice or omitted, the gel will fail. Most of the recipes in this book use no added pectin, making the ratios of sugar, fruit, and lemon juice essential to their success and the foods' safety.

To ensure a good set, do not use fruit that is overripe. Fruits lose pectin strength as they age, so the best choice is a blend of perfectly ripe and slightly underripe fruit.

Whether white or brown, organic or unprocessed, all sugar works in the same way, assisting the gel formation in tandem with the fruit's natural pectin and the lemon juice. Sugar ensures that the fruit retains its shape, color, and flavor. Reducing the amount of sugar will change the texture of the finished product. If substituting one sugar for another, always use a scale, swapping by weight, not volume.

Lemon juice has a reliable pH level of 2.3. When combined with fruit and sugar, it activates the fruit's natural pectin and regulates the pH of the preserves. Lemon juice also helps preserve the color. Oranges, limes, and grapefruit have different pH levels and will not reliably form a gel. The only acceptable substitution is citric acid: ⅛ teaspoon is equivalent to the juice of 1 lemon in any recipe.

Neither lemon juice nor sugar is a preserving agent per se, but each is essential to successful preserving.

High-acid and low-acid foods: what is pH?

If it's been a few years since chemistry class, and the whole pH thing is a little fuzzy, that's all right. For canning purposes, you need only remember that low pH is good (high acidity=low pH) and high pH is bad. A pH value ranges from zero to 14; lemons, which are very acidic, have a pH of 2.3, and baking soda, which is alkaline, has a pH of 9. For preserving, I focus on a pH range of between 4 and 5. At a pH of 4.6, the food in the jar is safe.

The measure of a food's acidity determines the canning method that will kill off botulinum and other microorganisms that can carry food-borne illnesses. High-acid foods can be safely canned using water-bath processing. Most jams, jellies, and pickles are high-acid. Water-bath canning brings the temperature of the processed foods to 212°F, sufficient to kill bacteria or other dangerous microorganisms in foods with a pH under 4.6.

To safely can variably acidic foods, like tomatoes and figs, the recipe must include sufficient added acid (from lemon juice or citric acid). Most vegetables are low-acid, and unless pickled, must be pressure-canned. These foods may harbor *Clostridium botulinum* spores, and sealing those spores in the jar after insufficient processing temperatures or times just encourages them to grow willy nilly so these foods must be processed in a pressure canner, with the temperature brought to 240° to 250°F (See Chapter 2, page 219.)

The only way to be certain your canned goods will be safe to eat is to follow trusted recipes.

The boil that will not stir down (TBTWNSD)

Canning how-tos have included the phrase "the boil that will not stir down" for decades. Embrace the phrase and learn what it means, for this is where jams form.

Bring the fruit and syrup to a boil that will not stir down: you will see this direction repeated over and over in my recipes. What does TBTWNSD look like? It should be a little scary. It might spit (be careful, and stand back—hot sugar causes a nasty burn). It will be roiling and, as much as you stir, it will not stop boiling at its fast, foamy, rolling pace. You can't stop the boiling unless the pot is removed from the heat, and even then it will take a little while to settle down.

Continues on p. 44.

ACIDITY (PH) VALUES FOR COMMONLY PRESERVED FOODS

These fruits have suitable acidity (pH) to be safely processed in a water-bath canner:

Apple	3.30–4.00
Blackberries	3.85–4.50
Blueberries	3.12–3.33
Cherries	4.01–4.54
Gooseberries	2.80–3.10
Grapes	3.20–3.40
Nectarines	3.92–4.18
Oranges	3.69–4.34
Peaches	3.30–4.05
Pears	3.50–4.60
Pineapple	3.20–4.00
Plums, late-season	2.90–3.10
Plums, early season	3.60–4.30
Raspberries	3.22–3.95
Strawberries	3.00–3.90

These fruits and vegetables, with pH values near or above 4.6, require added acid (lemon juice or citric acid) to bring the pH to 4.6 or below:

Figs	4.92–5.00
Papaya	5.20–6.00
Tomatoes	4.30–4.90

These low-acid fruits must be pickled to lower the pH for safe processing in a water-bath canner:

Cantaloupe	6.13–6.58
Watermelon	5.18–5.60

These low-acid vegetables must be pickled to reduce the pH for safe water-bath processing (otherwise, process in a pressure canner):

Artichokes	5.60–6.00
Asparagus	6.00–6.70
Beans, dried or field peas	6.50
Beans, string	5.60
Beets	5.30–6.60
Brussels sprouts	6.00–6.30
Cabbage	5.20–6.80
Carrots	5.88–6.40
Cauliflower	5.60
Chickpeas (garbanzo beans)	6.48–6.80
Corn	5.90–7.30
Cucumbers	5.12–5.78
Eggplant	5.50–6.50
Garlic	5.80
Mushrooms	6.00–6.70
Okra	5.50–6.60
Onions, yellow	5.32–5.60
Peas (English)	6.22–6.88
Peppers, chile and bell	4.65–5.45
Potatoes	5.40–5.90
Turnips	5.29–5.90

These meats, poultry, and seafoods must be pressure-canned:

Beef	5.1–6.2
Chicken	6.2–6.4
Clams	6.0–7.1
Fish	5.3–6.1
Shellfish	6.5–7.0
Ham	5.9–6.1
Shrimp	6.5–7.0
Veal	6.0
Oysters	5.68–6.17

Source: USDA Complete Guide to Home Canning, 2009 revision, National Center for Home Food Preservation (nchfp.uga.edu/publications).

Eight steps to making fruit preserves

1. Prepare for water-bath canning. Fill a large stockpot with water and bring to a boil. Gather the necessary jars, lids, and rings. Sanitize the jars by boiling in the waterbath for 10 minutes or by running through the dishwasher. Keep the jars warm until the fruit preserves are ready to process.

   Have a small saucepan filled with water ready for warming the lids and rings. Have the jar lifter, lid lifter, and bubbler at hand, as well as a candy thermometer, ladle, funnel, and several clean kitchen towels. I always have a ramekin to hold any last bits of jam from the pot. The cook's treat.

   Put three small plates and metal teaspoons in the freezer. Dropping a spoonful of hot jam on a cold plate is the most accurate way to test the set. This is called the wrinkle test.

2. Place a 3-quart or larger glass or ceramic bowl on the scale. Zero (tare) the weight of the bowl, then add the fruit and the sugar by weight. Squeeze the juice of one lemon over the fruit, making sure to dispose of the seeds. Add any herbs, spices, or other flavorings (see pages 45 and 49). Let the mixture sit for 10 minutes while the sugar begins to dissolve.

   With a flexible spatula or a wide, shallow wooden spoon, stir gently but thoroughly until the sugar is fully distributed through the fruit. The trick is to combine well enough to avoid leaving a quantity of sugar languishing in the bottom of the bowl and yet not stir so aggressively as to break up the fruit.

3. To encourage a syrup to form, macerate the fruit. Letting the fruit rest for two hours begins the process, but a full overnight rest in the refrigerator will make a more deeply flavored confiture as well as speed the gel.

The sugar forms a syrup and, during maceration, the sugar syrup replaces the fruit's natural cellular water. When the mixture is heated to 220°F, the water activity slows and the fruit preserves. By beginning with less water to reduce, the jam cooks more quickly and the freshest flavors are retained.

Do not discount the role of the lemon juice. Not only does it keep the color bright, but it builds pectin with the fruit's naturally occurring pectins.

4. Place your preserving pot on the stove. I use a 5- or 8-quart Le Creuset enamel over cast iron Dutch oven for most of my preserving, but copper and heavy-duty stainless steel are also suitable. The pan needs to be heavy bottomed so the fruit will not scorch at high temperatures. The wider the pan, the more rapidly the jam will reduce, which is a good thing. If making only half a recipe, use a 3-quart pot.

Pour the macerated fruit into a colander suspended over the preserving pot. Collect the syrup in the pot, stir the fruit in the colander a few times, then set the colander aside in a bowl to catch any last bits of syrup.

Turn the heat to high and clip a candy thermometer to the side of the pot. Bring the syrup to a rollicking boil, stirring from time to time. It will take about 20 minutes to reach 220°F.

5. Add the fruit and use a potato masher to release the pulp, especially with plums, cherries, blueberries, and other fruits with a sturdy skin. Fruits like peaches, apricots, and raspberries and blackberries will change texture, thickening the mixture.

   If using a seedy berry, put half the fruit through a food mill to remove some of the seeds. If the fruit is being preserved whole, or in careful slices or a pretty dice, forego the masher and stir more gently. The texture will be looser, but the fruit will be extraordinary in every bite.

6. Finally, cook the heck out of it. Yes, boil those preserves until the water content is reduced and a lovely jammy consistency emerges. This stage is called The Boil That Will Not Stir Down (see page 38). The jam will foam and bubble, and as it cooks at a very high strong boil, the foam will move off to the edges. Stir constantly. When the foam is almost gone, the jam is done.

7. Test the set. Remove the pan from the heat. (Leaving the jam on the stove, cooking away, could turn your perfectly gelled preserves into rubber in the time it takes to cross the room to the refrigerator.) Retrieve a chilled plate and spoon from the freezer.

Drop a healthy two tablespoons of jam onto the cold plate. Let it chill for about a minute. Now push the jam with your fingertip. Does it form a wrinkle? Now pull your finger through the jam. Does it form a clean trail through the gel?

If the set is still very loose, place the pan back on the stove and heat again to that big boil for two or three minutes. Repeat until you are satisfied. Keep in mind that the recipes in this book are for a slumpy set, a gentle gel.

8. Clarify, or polish, the jam. This old jammer's trick was taught to me by my great grandmother and never fails to make the jam picture perfect. Just drop a pinch of butter into the jam and stir well to remove any trace of foam. This tiny bit of fat gathers up the last of the water (foam) and makes the preserves shiny and clear.

Ladle the jam into the warm, sanitized jars and follow the instructions for water-bath processing (see page 28).

The heat under the pot should be as high as possible. This is why a heavy-bottomed preserving pot is optimal. Lightweight cookware will scorch and burn. All fruit preserves must reach this boil, the point where the water is released and where the sugar and lemon juice act with the fruit to form a gel. Stand back a little, and stir with a long-handled spoon, but don't reduce the heat.

Yes, you must stir constantly through that terrifying boil. Even as the preserves threaten to rise up and out of the pot, stir like the dickens to avoid hot spots.

The setup

Achieving the perfect gel, or set, in fruit preserves can be frustrating. It takes time, nuance, and experience. Your first jams might not be perfect. Understanding the moment when the jam is ready for the jar is the most difficult part of jam making. Don't get frustrated, just take your time. This is an art form, and you are learning the techniques. Experience is the best teacher.

As the water activity is lowered, the foam disperses naturally. Cook the jam until the foam disappears, then remove from the heat and start testing the set. New jammers often fail to cook jam long enough. As a rule of thumb, cook jams for about 40 minutes from start to finish.

Please remember to remove the pot from the heat when testing the set: even a minute of overcooking can turn a perfectly set jam to rubber. It's impossible to uncook a jam.

There are two ways to measure the set. The first one is **the wrinkle test**, long employed as the most dependable of all tests, but it requires some planning ahead. Before starting to make the jam, put three small plates in the freezer. At the point in the recipe when the jam is set, or should be set, or you think it is set, remove from the burner.

Take one plate from the freezer, drop a bit of jam onto the plate, and let the cold take effect—a minute or two. The set you see on that plate is what you will get. Pull your finger through the preserves and see whether a clear path remains—or does it fill in again? You want to see a clear path. The jam should firm up and, when pressed lightly, wrinkle a bit.

The other test is **the sheeting test.** When you believe the jam is ready, remove from the heat and let the boil settle down. Lift up the spatula or spoon you have been using to stir the jam, turn it sideways, and let the jam sheet off it. It should gather along the edge of the spatula and drop slowly back into the pot. It should look like jam! Evaluating set with the sheeting method gets easier with experience. I do not recommend it as the only test when new to canning. Rely on the wrinkle test, but always do the sheeting test too to learn.

You can stop and start the jam-making process as many times as necessary until you are satisfied with the set. When you are new to making preserves, stop and start often. To further evaluate the set, ask yourself if the fruit is suspended throughout the jam. When the water activity is reduced (see page 37), the fruit will be distributed throughout the syrup, not floating on the surface.

In addition to the wrinkle and/or sheeting test, after the preserving pot has cooled for 3 or 4 minutes, before ladling the preserves into the jars, push against the surface of the jam with the spatula or spoon. Look for slight wrinkling, like the rings on a pond after skipping a stone. It should be starting to set already.

Be patient: give yourself time to understand gel—it will take a few batches of jam. Rely not just on the cold plates but on all your senses. Learning to judge set is one of the artistic aspects of this science. And be kind to yourself. If the jam is loose after processing, just find another use for it.

Flavoring with herbs, spices, extracts, and liquor

Some fruits need nothing more than sugar and lemon to become ethereal jam. Others benefit from imaginative uses of flavoring agents. Be bold and creative, but use a light hand, or you risk burying the fruit flavor.

For fresh herbs, use 6 to 8 sprigs tied together with kitchen string. Green herbs turn dull and dark over time; remove the bundle from the jam before processing.

Spices should be used sparingly, as their flavor grows while the jam sits on the shelf. Some spices, like star anise and cinnamon sticks, are pretty, and small pieces can be left in the jam as decoration, or removed—your choice.

Split a vanilla bean, scrape out the seeds, and add the pod and seeds to the macerating fruit. Pluck the pod out before cooking the jam.

If using an extract, liqueur, or liquor, add it at the end of cooking. Cooked longer, these flavors leave less of an impression in the final product.

Experiment and use your imagination to make delicious bespoke preserves.

SET TRICKS

If the proper set is eluding you, there are a few possible reasons:

- **The fruit was overripe.** As fruit ripens, it loses pectin. Older fruit doesn't have the same get-up-and-go as young, slightly immature fruit. Select a mix of ripe and underripe fruit for the best results, but make sure the fruit has an appealing scent, because some fruit picked green never develops flavor.

- **The jam was not cooked long enough.** Always test the set, using the wrinkle test or sheeting test (see The Setup, page 44), before ladling the preserves into the jars.

- **The jam was overcooked.** Yes, it's a conundrum. The preserves can achieve the correct set and then move beyond it, so test frequently, with the pan off the heat.

- **The jam was cooked too slowly.** Slow cooking will break down the pectin and the preserves will never set.

- **You used the wrong amount of sugar and/or lemon.** Changes in the proportions will result in failure to gel and shorter shelf life (see Water, Water Everywhere, page 37).

- **You doubled (or tripled) the recipe.** There is no way to reduce water activity and retain texture and flavor in a big batch. It requires too much cooking, at lower temperatures to avoid burning, and it's a disaster waiting to happen. If you want a bigger yield, make batches consecutively. Recipes can be halved, because they cook down quickly. Why bother canning one or two jars of jam? I might make a tiny batch of jam with precious fruit in short supply. I might even process it, because I'm like that. But it's not a practical thing to do.

Pitted fresh apricots

TROUBLESHOOTING FRUIT PRESERVES

Even veteran canners are not immune to problems. While canning or preserving is a science, making the food that goes in the jars is an art. Each season brings differences. If the weather is cooler, the fruit may ripen differently than over a hot summer. Rain is a factor. There are very few hard-and-fast rules for jam making, and timing for jam varies depending on the fruit's water activity (see page 37). Fruits are fickle. I overcook a jam from time to time, either because I am doing too many things at once or because I don't trust my instincts.

The most common frustration is improperly gelled preserves: **the jam is either too runny or rubbery**. Most of the recipes in this book make a "slumpy" jam. It's a relaxed, not sit-up-and-take-notice-of-me jam. But if it is syrupy, the Set Tricks (page 45) will help.

The jam loses the bright, appealing color of the fresh fruit, especially at the top of the jar. Color loss is usually caused by storing preserves in a place that is too warm or too bright. Cool, dark spots are best for long-term storage. But, these less-colorful preserves are certainly edible, as long as there is no mold present and the seal is intact.

The fruit floats at the top of the preserves. Always chop the fruit into uniform pieces; fruit floats because the pieces are too large for the syrup to fully penetrate it in the time it takes to firm the gel. The most common reason for "fruit float" is undercooked jam. When the preserves are properly set, after removing them from the heat and letting them cool for 3 or 4 minutes, stir slowly a few times, then check to see if the fruit is suspended in the gel or floating. If the fruit is still floating but the gel has properly set, cook at a brisk boil for 1 or 2 additional minutes—no longer, or you risk rubbery, tight jam. Even if the fruit is floating, it is still edible jam.

Air bubbles appear in the preserves. It takes a while to remove all the air bubbles from thicker preparations, so go slowly, be precise, and take the time to run the bubbler around and around and through the jar.

Tough or rubbery jams either are overcooked or underacidified. Overcooking happens when there is too little sugar. Fruit that is underripe will also make a tough jam.

Jam that is **too seedy** is annoying. Start by putting half the fruit through a food mill to remove most of the seeds.

Some jams and especially jellies may **weep**: when the jar is opened, a small bit of moisture is evident. **Weeping** happens when storage temperatures are too high or fluxuate.

If the jam has **a fermented flavor**, almost vinegary, the fruit was overripe or was macerated too long in too warm a spot. There is no fix for fermented jam.

Mold grows when air is present inside the jar. Although this is usually the result of seal failure, mold can also grow in a jar that is under- or overfilled, or one that is underprocessed. Throw away moldy jams.

Double Strawberry Preserves (page 53)

Straight-Up Preserves with Any Fruit

MAKES: 4 half-pint jars

ACTIVE TIME: 90 minutes

MACERATING TIME: 2 to 48 hours

Once the light changes and spring arrives, weekends include trips to the farmers' markets. Everywhere I look, I see fruit that wants to be jam. The recipe below is my starting point. All I need to know is: 3 pounds of fruit, any fruit, 3 cups of sugar, and a lemon.

This jam is fruity and tart, not sweet. It slumps on the spoon. It is not a firm set. I might add homemade pectin or kiwi or green apple to stiffen the set with those fruits devoid of natural pectin (see page 57) or add herbs, spices, or other flavorings (see pages 45 and 49), but this recipe, this ratio, is always the starting point.

The jam is all about the fruit: keep small fruits whole and halve larger fruits or cut into beautiful slices or equal-sized chunks.

The ratio of sugar to fruit ensures sufficient syrup to enrobe the fruit. The recipe uses less sugar than many classic American jam recipes and because there is less sugar, there is also a lower yield, about four half-pint jars from 3 pounds of most fruits. Should you choose to reduce the sugar, the preserves will not set as well, nor will they have the same long shelf life.

Halve the recipe if you wish, and in that case, use a 3-quart pot, as a larger pot may lead to burning or overcooking the jam. But don't double the recipe. That would require too much time to cook and could result in a burned undertone or overcooked, rubbery fruit.

3 **pounds (1350 g) fruit, a mixture of slightly underripe and ripe (not overripe)**

3 **cups (21 oz., 600 g) granulated sugar**

• **Juice of 1 lemon**

• **Fresh herbs, spices, or citrus zest (see page 45; optional)**

One **4-ounce jar homemade Pectin (page 60), 1 green apple, grated, or 1 kiwi, peeled and diced, if needed**

½ **teaspoon unsalted butter optional**

¼ **cup (2 oz., 60 ml) liquor or liqueur (see page 45; optional)**

1. Clean, hull, peel, pit, seed, or otherwise prepare the fruit. Leave whole if small, or cut into bite-sized pieces or slices. Transfer to a large bowl. If the whole fruit has a firm outer skin (like blueberries), use a potato masher to get the juices flowing.

2. Stir in the sugar and lemon juice. Add any herbs, spices, or citrus zest. Cover and macerate for anywhere from 2 hours to 2 days. (Longer maceration is not better, but the timing is elastic to work with your schedule). Leave it on the counter for up to 12 hours, but refrigerate after that, or it may ferment.

3. Discard any herbs or whole spices and pour the mixture into a colander suspended over your preserving pot. Allow the syrup to drip for 20 minutes or so, then, working over the pot, stir the fruit to release more syrup. Place the colander of fruit in a bowl to capture any additional syrup.

4. Turn the heat to high, clip on a candy thermometer, and bring the syrup to a sturdy boil. When the foam clears, at 220°F (about 10 minutes), add the fruit and any syrup in the catch bowl and bring the jam to a foamy boil. Depending on the fruit, this will take anywhere from 20 to 40 minutes. Stir well and often.

5. Continue to boil vigorously, and, if using it, add the pectin boost. Stir constantly until the jam has set, anywhere from 5 to 12 minutes. At first the boil will be vigorous, hardy, and at a boil that will not stir down (see page 38), then it will become lazy and languid as the jam thickens, and the bubbles will take longer to burst. This is when all your senses must be employed: Listen for the crackle along the bottom of the pot as you stir. Watch for evidence of the fruit sinking—it will float when first added, but as it absorbs the syrup, it will become suspended throughout the gel. Lean over the pot and inhale the full, rich scent of sweet, ripe fruit. When the foam has almost totally cleared, remove from the heat and let the jam cool for 2 minutes.

6. Test the set, using the wrinkle test or sheeting test. If the jam has not yet gelled to your satisfaction, turn the heat back on to high for 2 or 3 minutes, then turn it off and test again. Repeat as necessary. When the jam is ready, stir in the butter, if using, to disperse any remaining foam; the butter will add a slight sheen and clarity to the jam, not flavor, so you need only a pinch. Add the liquor, if using.

7. Stir well, then ladle the jam into the jars, leaving ½-inch headspace. Clean the rims of the jars well with a damp paper towel. Place the warmed lids and rings on the jars and finger-tighten the rings.

8. Lower the jars upright into the water bath. Process for 10 minutes, starting the timing at the moment the water comes back to a vigorous boil.

9. Remove from the canner and listen for the pings telling you the jars have sealed. Cool the jars for at least 12 hours, then test the seals, wash the jars, label them, and store.

The preserves are shelf stable for 1 year.

FRUITS AND THEIR BEST FRIENDS
AND COMPATRIOTS

- **Strawberries:** peppermint, lemon verbena, balsamic vinegar, black pepper, thyme, vanilla, dark rum
- **Blueberries:** allspice, almonds, vanilla, lemon peel, Frangelico
- **Raspberries:** Cognac, cloves, mint, rum, vanilla, star anise, orange
- **Blackberries:** ginger, orange liqueur, vanilla, cinnamon, gin
- **Rhubarb:** cinnamon, cardamom, ginger, lime, vanilla, kirsch
- **Cherries:** almond extract, bourbon, vanilla, fennel, ginger, orange peel, pepper, sage, amaretto
- **Peaches:** basil, anise, bourbon, chiles, ginger, lemon verbena, lavender, thyme, mint, saffron
- **Nectarines:** allspice, maple, wine, ginger, violet, anise
- **Plums:** anise, bay, ginger, juniper, lavender, lemon, rum, thyme
- **Apples:** Calvados, cinnamon, garam masala, anise, ginger, nutmeg, pepper, rosemary, tarragon, star anise
- **Pears:** basil, Scotch, pink peppercorn, cassis, mint, rosemary
- **Figs:** Vanilla, rosemary, almond extract, ginger, thyme, lemon peel

Bonus Recipe: Rugelach

MAKES: 16 cookies

ACTIVE TIME: 2 hours

CHILLING TIME: 4 hours, then at least 2 hours

If I could only eat one cookie for the rest of my life, it would be rugelach. There is so much to love about these rolled-up nuggets. If you're anything like me and might have a hard time stopping at one, two, or three, store the unbaked cookies in an airtight container in the freezer, then remove just what you want to eat and bake (a toaster oven works fine).

Make the cream cheese dough ahead; it needs to chill well, or it will be challenging under the rolling pin. Work quickly when rolling, slicing, and forming the cookies to keep the dough cold. Then freeze the unbaked rugelach for another few hours. They must be chilled before baking, or the very rich dough will lose its shape in the oven.

The filling recipe uses only preserves, nuts, and bread crumbs, so the flavor possibilities are endless. Omit the nuts if you wish, but I like them for the texture they bring to this sweet, silky, crunchy treat. Any preserves will work, but the best results come from smooth-textured jam. If you want to use a jam that is loose and runny or has large chunks of fruit, blend, chop, or crush the fruit and warm the jam to create a thicker, smoother texture, then cool completely before using.

FOR THE DOUGH

- 4 ounces (110 g) cream cheese, homemade (page 389) or store-bought
- 8 tablespoons (4 oz., 110 g) unsalted butter
- 1 cup (4.25 oz., 125 g) all-purpose flour
- ¼ teaspoon kosher salt

1. To make the dough, cut the butter and cream cheese into 1-inch cubes. Place the butter, cream cheese, flour, and salt in a metal bowl and freeze for 30 minutes.

2. Transfer the chilled ingredients to a food processor and pulse until the dough forms a shaggy ball, about 20 pulses. Alternatively, cut the butter and cream cheese into the flour with a pastry cutter or two table knives to combine. Scrape the moist, sticky dough onto a floured countertop and form into a 6-inch disk. Wrap in wax paper and refrigerate for at least 4 hours, or overnight.

Recipe continues

OPPOSITE: Rugelach

¼ cup (1.5 oz., 40 g) toasted nuts (see suggestions below), finely chopped

1 tablespoon granulated sugar

2 tablespoons soft fresh bread crumbs

½ cup (4 oz., 120 ml) any preserves

1 egg yolk, beaten

3. Line a baking sheet with parchment. In a small bowl, mix together the nuts, sugar, and bread crumbs.

4. On a lightly floured surface, roll out the dough into a 9-inch circle. Spread the jam across the surface of the dough, leaving a ½-inch border. Sprinkle the nut mixture over the jam.

5. Using a sharp knife or pizza cutter, cut the disk into 16 wedges. Starting from the wide end of the long triangle, roll each segment up and press on the pointy end to seal. Place seam side down on the baking sheet and place the pan in the freezer for at least 2 hours. (*Once frozen hard, the rugelach can be transferred to zip-lock bags and kept frozen for up to 6 months.*)

6. Preheat the oven to 375°F. Brush the egg yolk gently on the tops of the cookies. Place another baking sheet under the cookie-filled sheet. (Stacking will keep the rugelach from burning on the bottom.) Bake for 22 to 25 minutes. The nuts and jam will have squished out a little and be a little messy; that's okay. The bottoms of the rugelach should be caramelized, not burned. Transfer to a rack to cool completely, about 1 hour.

7. Stored between layers of wax paper in a tightly covered container, rugelach keep well for up to 3 weeks.

OTHER FAVORITE FILLING COMBINATIONS
- Raspberry jam and macadamia nuts
- Apricot jam and almonds
- Plum jam and hazelnuts
- Pear jam and walnuts
- Bacon-Onion Jam (page 295) and salted roasted peanuts

Double Strawberry Preserves

MAKES: 6 or 7 half-pint jars
ACTIVE TIME: 90 minutes
MACERATING TIME: 1 to 2 days

This recipe reduces the sugar and doubles the fruity flavor of a basic strawberry jam. It is a rich and satisfying spread. For anyone who prefers a more spreadable, stick-to-the-spoon jam. Adding dried fruit deepens the flavor. The jam is sweet and sultry, intense and fruity, with a complex flavor reminiscent of good hard candy. It's also tart, with touches of peppermint and black pepper elevating the berry flavor so subtly you're not even sure they are really there.

Chop all the fruit well before maceration. For even more spreadable preserves, use a food processor to chop the dried fruit with some of the sugar for small pieces that will be evenly distributed throughout the preserves, giving them more body. Be careful cooking this jam: stop before you think it's thick enough—it will thicken further as it cools, and overcooking it is unfortunate.

2 cups (11 oz., 300 g) dried strawberries

3 pounds (1350 g) strawberries hulled and quartered or cut into ½-inch dice (about 6 cups)

3 cups (21 oz., 600 g) granulated sugar

• Juice of 2 lemons (about ¼ cup, 60 ml)

4 fresh peppermint sprigs or ¼ teaspoon peppermint extract

6 black peppercorns, crushed

½ teaspoon unsalted butter (optional)

1. If the pieces of dried fruit are larger than one bite, cut into smaller pieces with a sharp knife or scissors (see Note).

2. Stir the fresh and dried berries together with the sugar and lemon juice in a large bowl. Add the fresh peppermint if using, and peppercorns (do not add the extract now, if using). Stir well to dissolve the sugar. Cover and refrigerate for at least 12 hours, or up to 2 days. (This allows the fresh fruit to soak up the sugar and the dried fruit to soften.)

3. Remove and discard the peppermint, if you used it, and pour the berry mixture into the preserving pot. Turn the heat to medium-high and then gradually increase the temperature to bring the syrup to a sturdy boil that will not stir down; this will take 30 to 40 minutes. Stir well and often.

4. Continue to boil vigorously. The foam will disperse and the mixture will start to clear. Stir constantly and until the jam has set, anywhere from 5 to 12 minutes. When the foam has nearly cleared, remove the pot from the heat and let cool for 2 minutes.

Recipe continues

5. Check the set using the wrinkle test or sheeting test. If the preserves have not yet gelled to your satisfaction, turn the heat back on for 2 or 3 minutes, then turn it off and test again. Repeat as necessary. To polish the jam, stir in the optional butter, dispersing any remaining foam. Add the extract, if using, and stir well.

6. Ladle into the warm jars, leaving ½-inch headspace. Clean the rims of the jars with a damp towel. Place the lids and rings on the jars and finger-tighten the rings.

7. Process in a boiling-water bath for 10 minutes.

The jam is shelf stable for 1 year.

Note: To finely chop the dried fruit in a food processor, combine 1 cup of the sugar and the dried fruit in the processor bowl. Pulse a few times to reduce the pieces of fruit to a very small mince. Then proceed with the recipe, stirring the fruity sugar together with the fruit, the remaining 2 cups sugar, and the lemon juice.

DOUBLE THE FLAVOR

This is a very versatile technique that not only boosts the yield from fresh fruit, but also reduces the overall sugar. Select and match any fresh and dried fruit for these thick, rich preserves. Try plums and prunes, peaches and dried peaches, or mango and dried mango. Or mix and match: strawberries with cranberries, or peaches with dried cherries. It's all delicious. Sadly, this preparation is very unreliable when made with fresh cherries. If using thicker-skinned fruits like blueberries, currants, plums, and the fusion fruits like pluots or apriums, mash them well to encourage a syrup to develop before cooking.

OPPOSITE: Fresh and dried strawberries

Fresh gooseberries

To pectin or not to pectin

Woe to the first-time jam maker seduced by the new fruits of summer, most of which are without the secret ingredient that helps a jam gel. Pectin, a naturally occurring agent, is low or nonexistent in most berries and cherries, so the early days of summer, when jammers are at the stove, taunt and toy with us. Any jam made with low-pectin fruit is difficult to set without added pectin. And that is where the rubber hits the road. Literally. Cooked too long, jam becomes rubbery and the fruit is glacéed, not preserved. Too little cooking results in fruit floating at the top of the jam, a syrupy consistency, and, sometimes, a shorter shelf life.

Pectin is what makes jellies and jams gain structure and gel. There are several commercial options available: powdered, liquid, low-sugar, and no-sugar, as well as pectin activated with calcium chloride. Look for these in the grocery store, lurking on the shelf above the cornstarch in the baking aisle. Commercial pectin is derived from citrus rinds and seeds as well as apple peelings and cores.

Traditional pectin packets require copious amounts of sugar to bolster their gelling properties. All that sugar makes a very sweet jam and also guarantees a big batch. It is traditional pectin that perpetuates the assumption that all canning must involve dozens of jars.

When health concerns about vast quantities of sugar in our diet first surfaced, we learned it has been added to every imaginable processed food. The pectin companies responded by developing low- and no-sugar versions, many requiring sugar-free fruit juices (apple or grape) to activate them. In the early 2000s, Pomona-brand pectin reinvigorated a method calling for very little or no sugar but requiring calcium chloride to boost the gelling action. I understand the value of commercial pectin and use it in a couple of instances—making preserves out of foods that have no pectin (see herb jellies) or foods that have very low pectin (like pepper jelly), but for the most part, I prefer the flexibility that comes from making jam with my own pectin, or easy substitutes like grated apple and kiwi—even at the risk of inconsistent gelling. The benefit of commercial pectin is consistency.

The single greatest benefit of making preserves without commercial pectin is the ability to macerate fruits and develop flavors. Commercial pectins call for the fruit to be mixed and heated to boiling with the pectin, after which the sugar is added.

Many fruits make a suitable gel without any pectin at all. In her 2002 book *Mes Confitures*, Christine Ferber was the first to reconnect with Escoffier's method for confiture, macerating the fruit with sugar and flavorings, then straining the mixture and cooking the syrup to what, in candy-making terms, is called the soft-ball stage (220°F). Then fruit is returned to the hot syrup and, when suitably suffused, is ready to be put in jars. From this process, a modern jam—fruit-forward, less sweet, and more tart—emerges.

The more jam I made, the more I wondered about making it without any commercial products. Certainly preserves had been made for centuries before boxes of pectin were on the shelf. After some research and experimentation, I began making my own pectin.

I don't mean to disparage traditional pectins. They are effective and useful. But for the preserves I put in jars, I am happier keeping to a balance of fruit, sugar, and lemon. Should you prefer to work with traditional pectins, the recipes in this book will serve as guidelines. Follow the pectin's package directions, and use my recipes for new flavor combinations. But I hope you will try my methods. Choose among my variations on Escoffier's theme, or simply employ kiwi fruit or grated green apple to offer a little body to a jam made with a low-pectin fruit. The flavors are tart, fruit forward, and not too sugary.

Ways to build gel with low pectin fruits

- **Ripeness.** Select the fruit carefully. At least one-third of the fruit should be slightly underripe; none of the fruit should be overripe.
- **Add kiwi.** Peel and finely dice 1 kiwi for every 3 pounds of fruit. Add at the maceration stage, and do not increase the sugar or lemon juice. The kiwi pulp melts away, but the little black seeds will remain.
- **Add green apple.** Grate 1 unpeeled green apple right down to the core (unripe is best, Granny Smith will stand in) for every 3 pounds of fruit. Add at the maceration stage, and do not increase the sugar or lemon juice. The apple will change the texture of the finished preserves very slightly.
- **Add citrus seeds.** Tie up the seeds from 2 lemons in a cheesecloth bundle. Cook the preserves with this bundle, removing it before ladling the jam into the jars. This is less precise, as all lemons do not have the same number of seeds.
- **Give it time.** Many jams continue to set up as they rest on the shelf. This is especially true of cherry jam, many jellies, and some marmalades. If the wrinkle test works on a cold plate, in time the jam will gel in the jar. Be patient. It might take a week or even as long as a month.

How to use homemade pectin

Use one 4-ounce jar of Homemade Pectin (page 60) for every 3 pounds of fruit. Occasionally a fruit will require 8 ounces for a firmer set. Add more if the set is in question; it will not change the flavor in any way. If your pectin doesn't deliver a good set, it's possible the fruits were too ripe. The greener the fruit, the more underripe, the stronger the pectin.

PECTIN PRIMER

Homemade pectin will add structure to preserves made with the fruits and vegetables listed below, but they will never be stiff. This book is filled with recipes for preserves that slump.

- Raspberry, boysenberry, tayberry, wine berry, black raspberry, blackberry, rhubarb, gooseberry, currant, apple, pear, quince, cranberry, and citrus fruits set up without added pectin.

- Apricots, apriums, peaches, nectarines, pluots, plums, grapes, mango, pineapple, and papaya may or may not need pectin. Use half a kiwi, half a grated apple, or 4 ounces of homemade pectin for every 3 pounds of fruit.

- Strawberries, cherries, and blueberries always require something extra to strengthen the gel. Use 1 kiwi, 1 green apple, grated, or 4 to 8 ounces homemade pectin for every 3 pounds of fruit.

- Beets, corn, beans, figs, melon, tomatoes, onions, chiles, and peppers fall into a special category, as they are not only low in pectin, but also very low in acid (pH). This is why every jar of tomatoes has added citric acid, and why the Figgy Marmalade (page 99) has whole lemons cooked into the jam. Pressure-canning is one option here, as is pickling in vinegar. When in doubt, don't can it—some foods are meant to be enjoyed in season only.

- The USDA has declared the following produce unsafe for any type of processing due to water-activity and density issues: summer squash, winter squash, pumpkins, and bananas.

OPPOSITE: Draining gooseberries in a jelly bag for Homemade Pectin (page 60)

Homemade Pectin

MAKES: eight 4-ounce jars
ACTIVE TIME: 3 hours
DRAINING TIME: 6 hours

This homemade pectin is one way to firm up preserves. It's shelf stable and ready when you are.

Most apple growers will happily part with a few pounds of underripe apples. Early season windfall apples (on the ground after a storm) are the classic pectin source, but plan on additional pounds to account for removing the bruised or buggy parts.

4 pounds (about 12 cups, 1.8 kg) gooseberries, mostly underripe and green, OR 4 pounds (1.8 kg) underripe apples (see headnote), chopped, including core and peel (about 12 cups), OR 4 pounds (1.8 kg) underripe crabapples (see headnote), including core and peel (about 12 cups)

6 cups (1.5 l) water

1. Put the gooseberries and water into your preserving pot and bring to a boil. Mash the fruit well with a potato masher. Reduce the heat and cook at a slow, consistent simmer for 45 minutes.

2. Suspend a jelly bag over a catch bowl, or use a colander lined with three layers of cheesecloth. Spoon and carefully pour the mixture into the bag. Drain for 4 to 6 hours, until the fruit seems almost dry. Do not squeeze; just let the liquid drip into the bowl.

3. Pour the pectin into the preserving pot and clip on a candy thermometer. Bring to a boil you can't stir down (210°F); this will take about 30 minutes. Skim any foam or floating bits that come to the surface, then continue to cook to 220°F to a thick, syrupy consistency.

4. Ladle the pectin into the warm jars, leaving ¼-inch headspace. Attach the flat lids and rings and finger-tighten the rings.

5. Process in a boiling-water bath for 10 minutes.

The pectin is shelf stable for 1 year, but it loses some oomph after about 8 months—so make just enough to use up during one canning season.

TOP LEFT: Fresh gooseberries in a preserving pot. TOP RIGHT: Mashing the gooseberries with a potato masher. BOTTOM LEFT: Suspending a jelly bag over a bowl to drain the gooseberry mixture. BOTTOM RIGHT: Jars of homemade pectin.

Strawberry Mango Jam

MAKES: 4 half-pint jars

ACTIVE TIME: 90 minutes

MACERATING TIME: 2 to 48 hours

Tantalizing flavors are created when you combine the last of one season's fruit and the first of the next one. This jam teeters on tropical, with a slightly floral, bright, sassy flavor that brings out the candy sweetness of strawberries. Because the berries are mashed, the texture is thick and studded with pearls of berry and mango.

- 3 **pints (40 oz., 1125 g) ripe strawberries, hulled and diced (5 cups)**
- 3 **large (24 oz., 680 g) ripe, juicy mangoes, diced (about 1½ cups)**
- 3 **cups (21 oz., 600 g) sugar**
- **Juice of 1 lemon**
- ½ **teaspoon unsalted butter (optional)**

1. Combine the strawberries and mango in a large bowl and add the sugar and lemon juice and stir well until dissolved. Cover and set aside on the counter for 2 hours, or refrigerate for up to 48 hours.

2. Mash the mixture with a potato masher or use an immersion blender, leaving a slightly lumpy texture. Pour into your preserving pot, clip on a candy thermometer, and turn the heat to high. It will take about 15 minutes for the berry mixture to come to a boil that will not stir down, with foam covering the surface of the jam. Continue to stir frequently to avoid scorching.

3. Over the next 20 minutes, the jam will foam thickly and then the foam will disperse to the edges of the pot. Remove from the heat and confirm the set with the wrinkle test or sheeting test. When the set is satisfactory, if you like, stir in the butter to make the preserves shiny.

4. Ladle into the warm jars, leaving ½-inch headspace. Clean the rims of the jars with a damp towel. Place the flat lids and rings on the jars and finger-tighten the rings.

5. Process in a boiling-water bath for 10 minutes.

The jam is shelf stable for 1 year.

OPPOSITE: Fresh strawberries

Strawberry Rhubarb Sauce

MAKES: 4 pint jars or five 12-ounce jars, plus some extra to enjoy right now
ACTIVE TIME: 90 minutes
MACERATING TIME: 4 hours to 2 days

The large leaves of rhubarb unfurling and the stalks turning carmine red are harbingers of summer. When rhubarb comes into season, I go a little crazy. I make pies and infuse simple syrup. I roast the stalks and serve warm with a big spoonful of crème fraîche (page 385). It is one of those special seasonal foods, the ones that come and go and leave you wanting more.

The happy marriage of strawberries and rhubarb here makes a sauce to pour over everything, all year round. Its bright, tangy taste will bring back summer even in February. Try it warm, spooned over yogurt or granola, oatmeal, angel food cake, semifreddo, or ice cream. It's thick for a sauce, but it's not quite a jam; the texture resembles applesauce (and it's fantastic with pork). It's also an essential ingredient in the barbeque sauce on page 263.

- 4 pints (48 oz., 1380 g) ripe strawberries, hulled and quartered (about 8 cups)
- 3 pounds (1350 g) rosy-red rhubarb, cut into ½-inch dice (5 cups)
- 5 cups (35 oz., 1 kg) granulated sugar
- Juice of 3 lemons
- 1 star anise

1. Put the berries in a large glass or ceramic bowl and, using a potato masher or wooden spoon, gently crush them. Add the rhubarb, sugar, lemon juice, and star anise and stir well and completely until the sugar has dissolved. Cover and macerate for at least 4 hours, or, refrigerated, for as long as 2 days.

2. Scrape the mixture into the preserving pot and clip on a candy thermometer. Slowly bring to a simmer over medium-high heat, stirring frequently to prevent scorching. Then bring to a vigorous boil and stir constantly until the sauce thickens to the consistency of ketchup, about 25 minutes.

3. Turn off the heat and discard the star anise. Ladle the sauce into the warm jars, leaving ½-inch headspace. Clean the rims of the jars well with a damp paper towel. Place the lids and rings on the jars and finger-tighten the rings.

4. Process in a boiling-water bath for 15 minutes.

This sauce is shelf stable for 1 year.

Spiced Rhubarb Chutney

MAKES: 4 half-pint jars
ACTIVE TIME: 90 minutes

The tang of rhubarb is the predominant flavor in this springtime chutney. It contributes to the sweet, sour, spicy profile of the chutney and provides luxurious body. Buy only bright-pink or red rhubarb stalks; while green rhubarb offers the same taste and texture, the color is not as appealing in the final product. I'd been making this chutney with dried cranberries for years, but when I added dried strawberries instead, I fell in love with this savory take on the classic combination. (Really, any dried fruit will do.) Serve with grilled chicken or pork, or use as a glaze for broiled tofu. For instant party finger food, top baguette toasts with thinly sliced sharp cheddar cheese and a dab of chutney.

3 pounds (1350 g) rosy-red rhubarb, diced (5 cups)

1 medium red onion, (4.5 oz., 130 g) diced (1 cup)

2 garlic cloves, slivered (about 1 tablespoon)

¾ cup (2.5 oz., 70 g) crystallized ginger, chopped

2 cups (12 oz., 340 g) dried strawberries or dried cranberries

1 teaspoon mustard seeds

½ teaspoon coriander seeds

½ teaspoon kosher salt

1 cup (8 oz., 235 ml) cider vinegar

1 cup (6 ½ oz., 185 g) firmly packed light brown sugar

4 small Thai bird chiles

1. Combine the rhubarb, onion, garlic, ginger, strawberries, mustard seeds, coriander seeds, salt, vinegar, brown sugar, and chiles in the preserving pot and set over medium-low heat. Stir well and constantly to dissolve the sugar, while increasing the heat to medium-high. Bring the mixture to a slow simmer, and continue stirring the chutney as it thickens and the rhubarb breaks down. When a spoon leaves a trail along the bottom of the pot and the mixture is as thick as ketchup, about 45 minutes, the chutney is ready to process.

2. Ladle into the warm jars, leaving ½-inch headspace. Clean the rims of the jars with a damp paper towel. Attach the flat lids and rings and finger-tighten the rings.

3. Process in a boiling-water bath for 10 minutes. Turn off the heat and let the jars rest in the water about 5 minutes, then remove to a towel on the counter.

The chutney is shelf stable for 1 year.

Raspberry Violette Jam

MAKES: 4 half-pint jars, plus a little extra

ACTIVE TIME: 2 hours

MACERATING TIME: 3 to 4 hours

If I had my way, every first-time canner would start with raspberry jam. It's practically foolproof; require nothing more than berries, sugar, and lemon juice; and sets up beautifully with a little time and a lot of stirring. Because there are so few ingredients, it's critical to use the very best. Buy (or pick your own) organic berries from a farmer you trust, and always select berries picked in dry weather, not in rain (those picked in the rain will be more delicate and the preserves will have a thinner flavor.) Taste, smell, and carefully look over the berries before bringing them home. Are they full of flavor? Do they smell incredible? Skip them if there is any sign of mold at the bottom of the container.

For this jam, I like to add a whisper of the floral liqueur crème de violette. Its flavor is exquisite and delicate, not unlike the raspberries' sweet and tart combination, so each flatters the other, but you can omit it. Seediness in raspberry jam is a topic of much discussion in canning circles. Without seeds, the yield is lower, the texture smooth and satiny. With all the seeds, the texture can be annoying and crunchy—not a quality I like in preserves. Putting half the mixture through a food mill results in preserves full of flavor with just enough seeds to remember what it is you're enjoying. If your preference runs to seedless jam, the food mill is your friend.

8 cups (3 pounds, 1350 g) ripe raspberries

3 cups (21 oz., 600 g) granulated sugar

• Juice of 1 lemon

½ teaspoon unsalted butter (optional)

2 tablespoons (1 oz.) crème de violette, elderflower, or other floral liqueur (see headnote)

OPPOSITE: Fresh raspberries

1. Gently but thoroughly, stir the berries together with the sugar and lemon juice in a large glass or ceramic bowl. Cover and allow to macerate for 3 to 4 hours.

2. Transfer the berry mixture to a colander set over the preserving pot and allow the syrup to drip into the pot. Set the raspberries aside (put the colander in a bowl to capture any additional syrup). Clip a candy thermometer onto the pot, set over high heat, and bring the syrup to 220°F, about 10 minutes. Remove the pot from the heat.

3. Place a food mill over the pot and mill half the berries into the syrup. Stir in the remaining berries (see the headnote). From the moment the jam begins to boil, it must be stirred relentlessly. It's the simplest of all preserves, elegant and richly raspberryish, but it's also very easy to burn. When the foam has cleared, remove from the heat and cool for 3 minutes.

Recipe continues

4. Check the set, using the wrinkle test or sheeting test. If the preserves aren't yet gelled to your satisfaction, turn the heat on again for no more than 3 minutes, then turn it off and test again. When the jam is ready, stir in the butter if you like, to disperse any remaining foam and clarify the gel. Stir in the crème de violette.

5. Ladle into the warm jars, leaving ½-inch headspace. Clean the rims of the jars well with a damp paper towel. Place the lids and rings on the jars and finger-tighten the rings.

6. Process in a boiling-water bath for 10 minutes.

The jam is shelf stable for 1 year.

TIP

Raspberries, blackberries, and certain other berries are called drupelet fruits, referring to the little individual orbs that make up the whole berry. Because of their structure, washing will thin the flavor and destroy their texture. Buy from organic or IPM (Integrated Pest Management) berry farms, and you can eat the berries without washing without concern.

For longer shelf life, spread dry raspberries or other drupelet berries on a paper-towel-lined plate or baking sheet, well separated from one another. Leave uncovered, and refrigerate.

Bonus Recipe: Jam Tarts

MAKES: 12 tiny tarts (1 by 2 inches), six 3-inch tarts, or one 9-inch tart
ACTIVE TIME: 30 minutes
CHILLING TIME: 30 minutes

This combination of shortbread and jam is both a perfect ending to a dinner party and a lovely treat for teatime. I've made them tiny, in financier molds, medium sized in classic small tart molds, and in a 9-inch tart pan. The shortbread crust is pantry-friendly, it's ready in an instant, and it marries perfectly with whatever leftover jam is lurking in your refrigerator. The crust can be made by hand or with a mixer; I use a mixer.

See photograph on page 70.

- 1 stick (4 oz., 110 g) unsalted butter, softened
- ½ cup (3.5 oz., 100 g) granulated sugar
- 1 large egg yolk
- 2 cups (8.5 oz., 250 g) all-purpose flour
- • Big pinch of kosher or sea salt
- 1 half-pint jar any jam, preserves, or conserves

1. In the bowl of a stand mixer fitted with the paddle attachment, or in a large bowl, using a hand mixer, beat the butter and sugar until light and creamy. Add the egg yolk and blend until combined. Add the flour and salt and blend until combined. Turn out the dough, gather it together, and form into a disk. Keep covered with a slightly dampened towel as you work.

2. If making tiny tarts, set out twelve 1-by-2-inch molds. Pinch off pieces of dough the size of a walnut and press one into each mold. Place the mold(s) on a baking sheet. Alternatively, press the dough over the bottom and up the sides of a 9-inch tart pan with a removable bottom. Chill the crust for 30 minutes.

3. Preheat the oven to 350°F.

4. Prick the crust all over with a fork. This will keep the crust from ballooning up in the oven, although it still may rise a bit; don't worry, it will go back down. Bake tartlets for 8 to 12 minutes, 15 to 20 minutes if using a tart pan, until the crust is very lightly browned, about the color of sand. Watch carefully and do not overbake. Remove to a rack and cool completely.

5. Using a toothpick, carefully release the tiny tart shells from the pans; or, remove the large tart shell from its pan. Warm the jam in a small saucepan and spoon it into the baked shells. Let the tarts cool before serving.

Jam tarts are best when enjoyed within 3 days.

Blackberry Hazelnut Conserve

MAKES: 6 half-pint jars

ACTIVE TIME: 90 minutes

MACERATING TIME: 1 to 24 hours

The charms of blackberries eluded me for years. They seemed seedy and were often too tart in the center and too mushy on the outside. But it turns out that cooked blackberries are everything I want in a berry. The tartness remains, and underneath is sweet, deeply flavored fruit. Some blackberries ripen on the outside but have a green, hard center. Avoid using these berries by tasting a few before you commit.

When I discovered the ethereal combination of blackberry and hazelnut, I was completely won over. This conserve, a jam with added nuts, is especially welcome on a cheese board, where it adds textural complexity. Try it with sharp Cheddar, Camembert (page 395), or aged Manchego.

3   pounds (1350 g) ripe blackberries, picked over to remove any leaves, debris, or unripe berries

3   cups (21 oz., 600 g) granulated sugar

•   Juice of 1 lemon

1   orange

1   cup (4.5 oz., 125 g) toasted, skinned hazelnuts (see box, page 72), roughly chopped

2   tablespoons (1 oz.) orange liqueur (optional)

1. Combine the berries, sugar, and lemon juice in a large glass or ceramic bowl and stir well to dissolve the sugar and break up the berries.

2. Remove the zest from the orange, leaving the white pith behind. I use a zester; this charming little implement spiral-cuts the entire orange in impossibly narrow, long strips of zest. As the mixture cooks, these strips break down and give the conserve a marmalade undertone. (If you don't have a zester, use a vegetable peeler to remove the zest, then cut it into a fine julienne.) Juice the orange and add the zest and juice to the berry mixture. Set the mixture aside to macerate for at least 1 hour; optionally, cover and refrigerate for up to 24 hours.

3. Pour the mixture into the preserving pot and set over medium-low heat. Smash the berries with a potato masher or the back of a large spoon; leave some texture, but give them a good smooshing. As the mixture cooks, gradually increase the heat to high until it reaches a strong boil, stirring all the while. Then, stirring, bring the mixture to a boil that will not stir down, about 40 minutes total.

OPPOSITE: Jam Tarts (page 69)

4. Remove from the heat and test the set with the wrinkle test or sheeting test. If the jam has not yet gelled to your satisfaction, turn the heat on again for 2 or 3 minutes, then turn it off and test again. Continue to cook for 3 minute increments, checking the set, until satisfied. When the conserve is set, stir in the hazelnuts and orange liqueur if using, and bring back to a boil. Remove from the heat.

5. Ladle into the warm jars, leaving ½-inch headspace. Wipe the rims of the jars and clean with a damp paper towel. Place the lids and rings on the jars and finger-tighten the rings.

6. Process in a boiling-water bath for 15 minutes. Let the jars rest in the canning kettle for a few minutes after processing to prevent siphoning.

The conserve is shelf stable for 1 year.

TOASTING AND SKINNING HAZELNUTS

To toast and skin hazelnuts (an odius kitchen task), preheat the oven to 350°F. Spread the hazelnuts on a rimmed baking sheet and toast for 12 to 15 minutes, until fragrant. Pour the warm nuts onto a clean tea towel and rub them against one another until the brown skin releases (it's messy). Pluck out the pale skinned hazelnuts and transfer them to a bowl as they are skinned, then continue to rub the remaining hazelnuts together until they look pale and only a bit of the skin remains. This takes a lot of effort and they will never really be perfect. You can freeze skinned and toasted hazelnuts for up to 6 months, so work on a couple of pounds at a time; they can turn rancid quickly if not frozen. You won't want to do this again for awhile.

OPPOSITE: Double Strawberry Preserves (page 53)

Instead of Pie: Apricot, Rhubarb, and Raspberry Preserves

MAKES: 4 half-pint jars

ACTIVE TIME: 1 hour

MACERATING TIME: 3 to 8 hours

Early summer is a dangerous time for me. My preserving passion ramps up in a big way with the first sight of glorious fresh fruit: blueberries and cherries and apricots, rhubarb and currants and gooseberries. Inevitably, after a weekend at the farmers' markets, the refrigerator is bursting. I make jams and jellies, conserves, and chutney, filling jar after jar.

And then there comes a point when there are bits and pieces of all those glorious fruits littering the counters and fatigue sets in. There are two options. One is pie. The other is preserves made with a medley of flavors that will rarely be the same from one year to the next but will always be delicious.

In this version, early summer fruits play nicely together to make a tart, sweet, and velvety spread. If you can find them, the rose petals add an undercurrent not of perfume, like rosewater, but a fresh and floral note. They melt away, leaving behind a faint bit of their color.

The only obligatory element here is some form of gel strengthener, whether grated apple, kiwi, or the humble gooseberry, either topped and tailed and used whole or in the form of pectin. Without a little boost, these early summer fruits simply will not set. This is a very tart jam, lovely spread across buttery shortbread and equally appealing slathered on a turkey sandwich.

2 pounds (900 g) ripe apricots, pitted and sliced into 8 pieces each (about 6 cups)

1 pound (450 g) rosy-red rhubarb, cut into 1-inch dice (about 3 cups)

4 cups (28 oz., 800 g) granulated sugar

• Juice of 1 lemon

1 pint (8 oz., 225 g) ripe gooseberries or 4 ounces Homemade Pectin (page 60), ½ green apple, grated, or ½ kiwi, peeled and diced

1. Add the apricots and rhubarb to a large glass or ceramic bowl and stir together, then sprinkle the sugar over the fruit and stir well and thoroughly. Drizzle the lemon juice over the fruit and stir again. Cover the bowl and macerate for 3 hours at room temperature, or refrigerate for up to 8 hours.

2. If using fresh gooseberries, top and tail them, snipping off the blossom and stem ends (or risk a mouthful of tough unpleasantness later). I use tiny kitchen scissors. Set aside.

3. Pour the fruit and sugar mixture into the preserving pot and clip on a candy thermometer. Bring to a sturdy boil, then gently stir in the raspberries and the rose petals and gooseberries, if using. Bring back to a boil and stir constantly while it foams and burbles, about 25 minutes.

OPPOSITE: Apricots and rhubarb macerating

Recipe continues

2 **half-pints (about 2 cups, 8 oz.,**
  225 g) red, purple, or black
  raspberries
½ **ounce (14 g) organic fresh**
  rose petals (optional)
½ **teaspoon unsalted butter**
  (optional)

4. The mixture will be saucy and then will begin to thicken. When it reaches 205°F, stir in the pectin, apple, or kiwi, if using. Continue to cook at a boil that will not stir down for about 15 more minutes for a total of about 40 minutes. Remove from the heat and let cool for 5 minutes.

5. Check the set: The jam should very clearly wrinkle on the surface, like ripples on a pond. If it does not, turn the heat back on and continue to cook and test the jam as necessary. To make the jam shiny and prettier, swirl in the optional butter, then stir the jam thoroughly.

6. Ladle the preserves into the warm jars, leaving ½-inch headspace. Clean the rims of the jars well with a damp towel. Place the flat lids and rings on the jars and finger-tighten the rings.

7. Process in a boiling-water bath for 10 minutes.

The preserves are shelf stable for 1 year.

Tart-and-Sweet Cherry Preserves

MAKES: 4 half-pint jars

ACTIVE TIME: 1 hour

MACERATING TIME: 12 hours to 2 days

Summer cherries sing a siren song to me. I cannot walk by a table of these beauties without putting some in my basket. I eat them greedily from the moment they arrive in late June for just a few short weeks, then disappear for another year. There are dozens of varieties of cherries, and the local cherries available will depend on where you live.

Bing is a bright red, sweet cherry with bright red juice. Rainier cherries, yellow with a red blush, are also sweet, but the juice is clear and any preserves made only from these cherries will have a disappointing color. The late-season, deep maroon cherries called coeur de boeuf or Dark Hudson have wine-tinted juice and very sweet flesh.

And then there are the elusive tart, or sour, cherries, including Morellos and Montmorency, sometimes called pie cherries. Their juice is clear and the fruit is tart and not for eating out of hand. These cherries make the very best pies (see Sour Cherry Pie Filling, page 137). Because they are easily bruised and have an extremely short shelf life, tart cherries are rarely sold in the grocery store. Look for them at farmers' markets, usually around the last week of June and the first week of July. I have spent many Fourth of July weekends pitting sour cherries.

While most varieties independently make a lovely classic preserve on their own, blending the different cherries can create a complex interplay of sweet and tart, with the juicy fruit floating in a delicious syrup. This is a tricky jam to make. Overcook it, and it will be rubbery and sticky. But at its best, the set is loose and the fruit is plump and suspended. In any form whatsoever, it's delightful ribboned through vanilla ice cream.

1½ pounds (680 g) ripe tart sweet cherries, preferably varied colors

1½ pounds (680 g) ripe, plump tart cherries

3 cups (21 oz., 600 g) granulated sugar

• Juice of 1 lemon

1. Stem the cherries, then pit them over a bowl to catch the juices. Combine the cherries, sugar, and lemon juice in a large glass or ceramic bowl. Stir well, cover, and refrigerate for at least 12 hours, but no more than 48 hours.

2. Pour the mixture into a colander set over the preserving pot and allow the syrup to drip for a few minutes. Stir the fruit, gently pressing on it to extract more syrup, then transfer the colander of fruit to a bowl, to capture any last bits of syrup.

Recipe continues

One 4-ounce jar Homemade Pectin (page 60), 1 green apple, grated, or 1 kiwi, peeled and diced

2 tablespoons (1 oz.) St-Germaine liqueur (optional)

½ teaspoon unsalted butter (optional)

3. Clip a candy thermometer onto the pot. Turn the heat to high and bring the syrup to a sturdy boil. When the foam clears, at 220°F (about 10 minutes), add the fruit and any collected syrup and bring to a foamy boil. Devoid of pectin, cherries are fickle fruits, tending more to becoming candied or *glacéed* than preserved; watch them carefully and stir well and often. Once the mixture has come back to a boil, add the pectin (or apple or kiwi). Bring to a boil that will not stir down and stir constantly until the jam has set, about 5 minutes. Listen for the crackle along the bottom of the pot as you stir, and watch as the fruit begins to sink—it will float initially, then, as it absorbs the syrup, become suspended in the gel. When the foam has nearly cleared again, remove from the heat and let cool for 3 minutes.

4. Check the preserves, using the sheeting test and wrinkle test. There will not be a strong set, but it will sheet off the spoon and it will slightly wrinkle. If you boil until a firm set is achieved, the cherries will overcook. The best indication that the jam is ready is that the cherries no longer float on the surface of the syrup; stop cooking at that moment, and stir in the St-Germaine and butter, if using.

5. Ladle into the warm jars, leaving ½-inch headspace. Clean the rims of the jars with a damp towel. Place the lids and rings on the jars and finger-tighten the rings.

6. Process in a boiling-water bath for 10 minutes.

The preserves are shelf stable for 1 year.

OPPOSITE: Bundles of Joy (page 80)

Bonus Recipe: Bundles of Joy

MAKES: 24 bundles

ACTIVE TIME: 45 minutes

PREP TIME: about 6 hours to defrost the phyllo, if frozen

FREEZING TIME: at least 30 minutes

For an almost-instant snack, bundle your beautiful preserves into flaky phyllo pastry. Add a nugget of cheese for a special kind of deliciousness. These two-bite charmers are welcome snacks at any time of day. Whenever the refrigerator is being overrun with jars of tiny amounts of preserves, I settle in to make some bundles of joy. This recipe makes a lot—freeze the extras, to be popped into the oven and ready in minutes.

Phyllo is available in boxes of full-size or half-size sheets. The half sheets make 6 bundles per every 4 sheets; the full size will make 12 bundles from 4 sheets.

See photograph on page 79.

8 tablespoons (4 oz., 110 g) unsalted butter, melted

One 1-pound (454 g) box of phyllo sheets, defrosted in the refrigerator if frozen (plan on at least 6 hours)

1 half-pint jar Tart-and-Sweet Cherry Preserves (page 77)

8 ounces (225 g) fresh goat cheese

1. Line two baking sheets with parchment.

2. Unfurl the phyllo onto another baking sheet. Cover with a barely damp kitchen towel. Pluck one sheet from the pile of phyllo and place it on a clean, dry countertop; keep the remaining phyllo covered to prevent it from drying out. Using a pastry brush, brush the phyllo sheet with melted butter. The phyllo may stick to the brush and tear, but just go with it. Place another sheet of phyllo over the first, hiding any issues, and brush with more butter. Be generous—the phyllo has no fat in it and needs the butter. Do this two more times, so 4 sheets are stacked. Lightly butter the final sheet.

3. Using a sharp knife or a pizza or pastry cutter, cut the phyllo stack into 3-inch squares. Place 1 teaspoon of preserves and 1 nugget of cheese onto each stack. Gather the edges of each square and carefully form into a hobo bundle. The butter will hold it together—just lift the bundle and squeeze shut around the equator, holding it from the bottom to avoid smooshing the gathered top. Set the bundles on one of the parchment-lined pans. Repeat with the remaining phyllo and filling. Freeze the bundles for 30 minutes.

4. Preheat the oven to 400°F.

5. Place the pans in the oven and bake the bundles for 4 to 8 minutes, depending on size, until browned. Watch carefully. Burned bundles are not joyful. Cool slightly and serve warm or at room temperature.

Apricot Jam with Ginger and Rosemary

MAKES: 5 to 6 half-pint jars
ACTIVE TIME: 3 hours
MACERATING TIME: 12 to 24 hours

I was nineteen before I ever tasted a fresh apricot. And that first taste of the real thing remains one of the most vivid food memories of my life. It was summertime in Paris. Tender fruit melting in my mouth. Of course I was hooked. And as soon as I took up canning, I envisioned apricots year-round.

Truly perfect ripe apricots are difficult to get in much of the United States. The season is short, around the end of June or beginning of July. Because it is so short, often the fruit is picked all at once and so may benefit from a few days ripening before eating or making preserves (or making tarts, pies, grilling apricots with mascarpone and every other magical way to enjoy these spectacular fruits). Wait for the scent of apricots to fill your kitchen.

Every apricot cooks up beautifully, even mealy ones. If you have a choice (you lucky Californians), opt for Blenheim apricots. Some apricots break down to a saucy texture, others stay intact. If the apricot pieces remain whole, you will need to add homemade pectin or a substitute (see page 57) for a sturdier set. Do not skip the long maceration for these preserves; it's essential to the final product's silken texture.

3 pounds (1350 g) ripe apricots, washed
3 cups (21 oz., 600 g) granulated sugar
3 tablespoons grated fresh ginger
Juice of 1 lemon
Four 4-inch fresh rosemary sprigs
One 4-ounce jar Homemade Pectin (page 60), 1 green apple, grated, or kiwi, diced and peeled (optional; see headnote)
½ teaspoon unsalted butter optional

1. Cut the apricots in half, pit, slice each half lengthwise into 3 or 4 wedges, and place in a large bowl. Stir in the sugar and ginger and drizzle the lemon juice over the apricots. Stir well for several minutes, until the sugar begins to dissolve; be gentle, so the apricot pieces stay as intact as possible.

2. Crush the rosemary sprigs in your hand, add to the bowl, and stir again. Cover and refrigerate for at least 12 hours, or overnight. Some of the fruit on top may darken a bit; don't worry.

3. Remove and discard the rosemary, pour the apricots into a colander set over the preserving pot, and let drain for a few minutes. Transfer the colander to a bowl to capture any additional syrup.

4. Set the preserving pot over medium-high heat, clip on a candy thermometer, and bring the syrup to 220°F. Add the apricots and any syrup in the bowl and stir well. Continue to stir as the

Recipe continues

mixture reaches a boil that will not stir down. Be hyperaware: this is when the fruit may scorch. Cook the preserves at this vigorous boil until the fruit is no longer floating and the foam has dispersed to the edges of the pot. Remove from the heat and let cool for 2 minutes.

5. Check the set, using the sheeting test or wrinkle test. Or, if the preserves are still very saucy and not at all set, add the homemade pectin or substitute, then return the jam to a boil that will not stir down and cook for about 5 minutes. Test the set again. Stir in the butter, if using.

6. Ladle the preserves into the warm jars, leaving ½-inch headspace. Clean the rims of the jars well with a damp towel. Place the lids and rings on the jars and finger-tighten the rings.

7. Process in a boiling-water bath for 10 minutes.

The jam is shelf stable for 1 year.

VARIATIONS
- Substitute sweet cherries for the apricots.
- Swap 1 star anise for the ginger and 2 stalks of smashed lemongrass for the rosemary; remove both before cooking the preserves.
- Instead of rosemary opt for culinary lavender or minced spruce tips, but beware: these flavors are bold and too much will overpower the fruit. Use no more than ¼ teaspoon of either one.

Fresh apricots

Bonus Recipe: Focaccia with Apricot Jam, Caramelized Onion, and Fennel

MAKES: one 14-by-10-inch focaccia
ACTIVE TIME: 1 hour
RISING TIME: 1 hour

A first course, a cheese course, a teatime snack, or a brunch food. In other words, this focaccia is pretty fabulous at any time. Herbal preserves dancing with savory: one of my favorite performances.

This dough is my go-to for pizza and almost any flatbread-type recipe. It's quite wet, and it is soft and full of bubbles when baked. The bubbles get larger and the tangy sour flavor deepens with a longer, cool rise. (For pizza dough, let it rise for 3 days in the refrigerator.)

See photograph on page 85.

FOR THE DOUGH

- 1½ teaspoons active dry yeast
- 1 cup (8 oz., 235 ml) warm water
- About 2½ cups (10 oz., 310 g) all-purpose flour
- 3 tablespoons olive oil, plus extra for the bowl
- 1 teaspoon chopped rosemary
- 2 teaspoons kosher salt

1. In a large bowl, sprinkle the yeast over the warm water and stir well. When small bubbles start to form on the surface, after 5 minutes or so, add 1 cup of the flour and stir well. Let rest for 10 minutes.

2. Add another cup of the flour, the oil, rosemary, and salt and stir until you have a shaggy mass. Turn out onto a well-floured work surface and sprinkle the dough with about a tablespoon of flour. Allow the dough to rest and absorb the flour for about 10 minutes. Wash the bowl, dry well, and lightly oil it.

3. Using a spatula or a bench scraper, gently lift, fold, and press down the dough, then give it a quarter turn. Continue this gentle kneading until the dough is smooth and elastic, about twelve turns, adding as little additional flour as possible. This is a wet, sticky, dough.

4. Place the dough in the bowl and turn to coat in the oil, then cover with a tea towel and let rise for an hour. (Or, for a tangier focaccia, place the covered bowl in the refrigerator for up to 2 days for a slow rise. Bring to room temperature before proceeding.)

Recipe continues

- 2 tablespoons olive oil, plus extra for brushing and drizzling
- 2 medium onions (9 oz., 260 g), halved lengthwise and sliced into thin half-moons
- 2 cups (16 oz., 450 g) sliced fennel
- Kosher salt and freshly ground black pepper
- 1 half-pint jar Apricot Jam with Ginger and Rosemary (page 81) (or ½ cup store-bought apricot preserves)
- 4 ounces (110 g) goat cheese (I like a tangy, crumbly aged cheese, but fresh goat cheese also works well)
- Crunchy sea salt

5. Heat the 2 tablespoons olive oil in a large sauté pan over low heat. Add the onions and fennel, season with plenty of salt and pepper, and cook slowly until well browned and caramelized, 14 to 20 minutes. Remove from the heat.

6. Preheat the oven to 450°F. Line a baking sheet with a piece of parchment. Brush the parchment with oil.

7. Place the dough on the parchment-lined baking sheet and press out into a 14-by-10-inch rectangle. If the dough shrinks back and fights you, let it relax for 10 minutes, then press it out gently. It does not need to be perfect by any means. Dimple the focaccia all over with your fingertips (as though you were lightly playing the piano). Let rest for 20 minutes.

8. Brush the focaccia lightly with olive oil. Using an offset spatula, spread the preserves to within ½ inch of the edges. Cover the preserves with the onions and fennel. Break up the cheese and dot it over the onions. Drizzle with olive oil and sprinkle with crunchy salt and pepper.

9. Bake the focacccia until it is golden brown and the cheese is bubbly and toasty, 20 to 25 minutes; the internal temperature will register 190°F.

10. Serve warm or at room temperature.

OPPOSITE: Focaccia with Apricot Jam, Caramelized Onion, and Fennel (page 83)

The Best of Both Worlds:
Apricot and Tart Cherry Preserves

MAKES: 6 half-pint jars
ACTIVE TIME: 1 hour
MACERATING TIME: 8 to 24 hours

People have often asked me to name my favorite jam—what an unfair question! If pressed, I waffle endlessly, because, quite simply, any fruit at the height of its season makes an exceptional jam, and every year brings different fruits to the forefront. I'll admit to a soft spot for apricots and sour cherries. One day, it occurred to me these two tastes might be good together. Now, if you ask me to name my favorite jam, I still hate to call out just one because they all give me so much pleasure, but I point to this one, "The Best of Both Worlds," as evidence that, really, you can't have too much of a good thing.

If you have two favorite fruits, experiment with blending them into a jam. Try different ratios and different sugars, and enhance the flavors with spices or liqueurs. Create a signature flavor that's all yours.

1½	**pounds (680 g) apricots, pitted and quartered**
1½	**pounds (680 g) tart cherries**
3½	**cups (24.5 oz., 650 g) granulated sugar**
•	**Juice of 1 lemon**
4	**drops orange blossom water (optional)**
2	**tablespoons (1 oz.) apricot or orange liqueur**
½	**teaspoon unsalted butter (optional)**

1. Put the apricots in the preserving pot. Halve and pit the cherries, working over the pot to capture the juices. Add the sugar, lemon juice, and orange blossom water, if using, and bring just to a simmer. Pour into a glass or ceramic bowl, cover, and macerate in the refrigerator for at least 8 hours, or overnight.

2. The next day, scrape the apricot and cherry mixture into a colander set over the preserving pot and let the syrup drip for 15 minutes. Stir the fruit well in the colander to release more syrup, then transfer the colander to a bowl to capture any syrup that remains.

3. Turn the heat to high under the preserving pot, clip on a candy thermometer, and stir frequently as the syrup comes up to 220°F. Add the apricots, cherries, and any syrup in the bowl and bring to a boil that will not stir down.

4. After about 25 minutes, the apricots will break down and form a silky backdrop for the cherries and the preserves will begin to gel. Watch for the foam to disperse to the edges of the pot, then remove from the heat.

5. Test the set, using the wrinkle test or sheeting test. Once the jam has set to your satisfaction, add the liqueur and butter, if using. Stir well and return to a boil, then remove from the heat.

6. Ladle into the warm jars, leaving ½-inch headspace. Clean the rims of the jars well with a damp paper towel. Place the lids and rings on the jars and finger-tighten the rings.

7. Process in a boiling-water bath for 10 minutes.

The jam is shelf stable for 1 year.

VARIATIONS

- Substitute rose water and 1 ounce organic fresh rose petals for the orange blossom water and liqueur.
- If you are not a fan of floral tones, add spices like 1 teaspoon of ground cardamom, 1 teaspoon of crushed pink peppercorns, or ½ teaspoon of nutmeg.
- Or make a jam with no added herbs, spices, or waters and let the fruit flavors shine.

Early Plum and Pecan Conserve

MAKES: 6 half-pint jars

ACTIVE TIME: 90 minutes

MACERATING TIME: 8 hours to overnight

In the middle of summer, plums, the last of the stone fruits, begin to arrive in the market. After the bright orange of apricots and peaches, their pretty yellow, red, pale rose, and deep purple colors are alluring. Although those jewel tones beg to be put behind glass, most early plums are very juicy, making them great for eating out of hand but difficult to reduce to a jam without caramelizing. There are varieties that will work for jam, such as the small firm-fleshed Methany, the honey-flavored Mirabelle, and the gorgeous, though hard to find, greengage.

In this conserve, I've added dried fruit for texture, weight, and flavor. I prefer dried pluots, the apricot/plum hybrid, which are more tart than prunes, but they can be difficult to find. A combination of prunes and dried cherries achieves a similar balance.

This is a beautiful conserve, smooth textured, with nuggets of toasted pecan. It pairs with any cheese, but don't stop there. Slather some on a roast pork sandwich or in a panini layered with thin slices of salty country ham and Swiss cheese.

3 pounds (48 oz., 1350 g) ripe, plump early Methany, Mirabelle, greengage, or other firm plums, pitted and chopped into ½-inch dice (about 4 cups)

• Juice of 1 lemon

½ cup (6 oz., 160 g) wildflower honey

2 cups (14 oz., 400 g) granulated sugar

1 cup (5 oz., 150 g) dried pluots or ½ cup pitted prunes plus ½ cup dried cherries

⅔ cup (3 oz., 86 g) toasted pecans, coarsely chopped

2 tablespoons (1 oz.) Sauerkirsch, kirsch, or Grand Marnier

1. Combine the plums, lemon juice, honey, and half the sugar in a large glass or ceramic bowl and stir well.

2. Combine the remaining sugar and the dried pluots in a food processor and process together to a damp paste. Add to the plum mixture, cover, and refrigerate for 8 hours, or overnight.

3. Pour the fruit mixture into the preserving pot. Start the heat at medium-low and increase to high as the mixture comes to a boil. The plums will break down and thicken the mixture; they can easily scorch, so keep stirring well. Boil for 30 to 35 minutes. Remove the pan from the heat.

4. Use the wrinkle test or sheeting test to evaluate the set. If satisfied, stir in the pecans and brandy, return to a boil, and remove from the heat.

5. Ladle into the warm jars, leaving ½-inch headspace. Clean the rims of the jars well with a damp paper towel. Place the lids and rings on the jars and finger-tighten the rings.

6. Process in a boiling-water bath for 15 minutes.

The conserve is shelf stable for 1 year.

Methany plums

Chai-Spiced Plum Preserves with Balsamic

MAKES: 6 half-pint jars

ACTIVE TIME: 90 minutes

MACERATING TIME: 8 to 24 hours

One day I was reading a description of a Cabernet—plumy, peppery, and full-bodied— and it inspired me to include similar flavors in this late-season jam. Once I got started with the black pepper, it was *chai*, the Indian spiced tea, that further inspired me, and cardamom, anise, and black tea were added to the mix.

The balsamic vinegar provides the tang that makes this jam simply irresistible. I have tried an inexpensive grocery store balsamic, reduced to a syrup (and I substituted pomegranate molasses once), but the best incarnation was with a heavenly fig balsamic I found on the back shelf of a little shop in New York City. Even a thin red or sherry wine vinegar helps to build the complex layered flavors in these preserves, dancing with the pepper and bay to create a savory jam on the verge of becoming a chutney.

Late-season plums have many names. Alternatively called prune plums or Italian plums, Damsons or Quetsches, all make a deeply flavored fruit spread. A freestone variety saves work, but every late plum makes divine jam. Plum lovers rejoice.

½ **teaspoon cardamom seeds (from green cardamom pods)**

½ **teaspoon anise seeds**

½ **teaspoon black peppercorns**

1 **dried bay leaf, crumbled**

1 **teaspoon loose black tea**

3 **pounds (1350 g) slightly underripe Quetsch, Damson, or Italian prune plums, pitted and quartered**

3½ **cups (24.5 oz., 700 g) granulated sugar**

• **Juice of 1 lemon**

2 **tablespoons aged balsamic vinegar (don't hold back, use the good stuff—see headnote)**

1. Toast the cardamom, anise, peppercorns, bay, and tea in a small dry skillet over medium heat until fragrant, just a minute or two. Transfer to a spice grinder or clean coffee grinder or to a mortar and grind the mixture to a powder (or use two bowls that fit one inside the other).

2. Stir together the plums, sugar, lemon juice, and ground spices in your preserving pot and bring just to a boil over medium-high heat. Pour into a glass or ceramic bowl, cover, and refrigerate for at least 8 hours, or overnight. (This releases the plum flavor, softens the skins, and makes quick work the following day.)

3. Pour the preserves into the preserving pot and set over medium heat. Cook, increasing the temperature to high, until the mixture comes to a boil that will not stir down. Remove the pot from the heat and mash the fruit with a potato masher for rustic preserves, or puree with an immersion blender for a smooth spread.

Recipe continues

OPPOSITE: Italian prune plums

4. Return the pot to medium-high to high heat and cook the preserves until jammy and thick, about 25 minutes, stirring all the while to avoid scorching. Turn off the heat.

5. Check the set, using the sheeting test or wrinkle test and cook again for 2 to 3 minutes if necessary. When the preserves have set to your satisfaction, stir in the balsamic vinegar. Ladle into the warm jars leaving ½-inch headspace. Clean the rims of the jars well with a damp paper towel. Place the lids and rings on the jars and finger-tighten the rings.

6. Process in a boiling-water bath for 10 minutes.

The preserves are shelf stable for 1 year.

VARIATIONS

- Turn this intense jam into a conserve by adding ½ cup of toasted slivered almonds, chopped walnuts, or pine nuts. Whole and roughly broken macadamia nuts sends it over the top, in only the very best way. Serve with creamy mild cheeses.
- Try this jam in rugelach (page 51) to create a cookie that pairs with wine, port, and sherry. Use any of the nuts listed above.

Asian-Style Plum Sauce

MAKES: 4 half-pint jars
ACTIVE TIME: 90 minutes

Late-season plums, arriving at the end of summer, are dusky and deep, dark violet, with golden, sweet flesh. When cooked, they turn a deeper purple with reddish undertones, like garnets. This is a very versatile sauce. Bright and fruity, acidic, and eye-opening with the surprise of heat from the chile, it's wonderful with Spiced Pork Chops (page 307), mixed with hot mustard for dipping spring rolls or dumplings, or stirred together with fermented black beans and brushed on grilled tofu. Just one jar has the potential to bring many new flavors to the table.

1½ cups (12 oz., 340 g) firmly packed light brown sugar

¾ cup (5 oz., 138 g) granulated sugar

¾ cup (6 oz., 180 ml) cider vinegar

1 cup (4 oz., 110 g) finely minced onion

1 medium jalapeño pepper, seeds removed and finely chopped

3 garlic cloves, minced

1½ tablespoons grated peeled fresh ginger

1 tablespoon mustard seeds

1½ teaspoons salt

½ teaspoon Szechuan peppercorns

3 pounds (1350 g) late-season or Damson plums, pitted and chopped into ½-inch dice

1. Combine the two sugars, vinegar, onion, chile, garlic, and ginger in your preserving pot and bring to a boil that will not stir down.

2. Add the plums and bring back to a boil. Mash the mixture with a potato masher, or use an immersion blender, pureeing for as long as you wish, depending on whether you want a smooth or chunky sauce. I like mine a little chunky.

3. Lower the heat and simmer until the sauce is reduced by half, thick, and syrupy, about 30 minutes. Stir well in the last 10 minutes to avoid scorching.

4. Ladle into the warm jars, leaving ½-inch headspace. Clean the rims of the jars well with a damp paper towel. Place the lids and rings on the jars and finger-tighten the rings.

5. Process in a boiling-water bath for 20 minutes.

The sauce is shelf stable for 1 year.

Peach Melba in a Jar:
White Peach, Raspberry, and Thai Basil Sauce

MAKES: four 12-ounce jars
ACTIVE TIME: 90 minutes
MACERATING TIME: 8 hours to overnight

Perhaps I have loved peach Melba all my life because of the romantic story. Escoffier, that rogue, was known to name his desserts for his amour of the moment. Imagine how flattered Nellie Melba, the Australian opera singer, was when she learned she was the inspiration for the glorious combination of peach and raspberry. Or perhaps I love it for the floral combination of peach and raspberry. The basil adds a whisper of anise tones to keep the sauce from turning the corner toward cloying. Buy a mixture of slightly underripe and barely ripe white peaches; if you use overripe fruit, the flavor may taste fermented. Not in a good way.

Serve over crumbled meringues, stir into yogurt, ribbon through a *semifreddo* or use for a trifle with pound cake.

3 pounds (1350 g) white peaches (a mixture of slightly underripe and ripe)
• Juice of 1 lemon
1 pound (450 g) raspberries
3 cups (21 oz., 600 g) granulated sugar
1 ounce (28 g) fresh Thai basil sprigs (about 8), tied together with kitchen string (optional)

1. Fill a large pot with water and bring to a boil. Make an X in the base of each peach, slicing just through the skin, not into the fruit. Blanch the peaches in the boiling water for about 30 seconds (the time depends on the size of the peach); when the peaches rise to the surface, pluck them out and drop into a bowl of ice water.

2. Peel, pit, and halve the peaches. Slice each half into 4 long crescents and place in a large glass or ceramic bowl. Drizzle the lemon juice over the peaches and stir. Run the raspberries through a food mill right into the bowl. (Alternatively, press the berries through a fine sieve to remove the seeds and add to the bowl.) Add the sugar and basil, if using, and stir well. Cover and refrigerate for 8 to 12 hours.

Recipe continues

OPPOSITE: Fresh peach

3. Pour the fruit into a colander set over the preserving pot. Let the syrup drain into the pot for about 20 minutes. Transfer the colander to a bowl to catch any additional syrup.

4. Place the preserving pot over medium-high heat, clip a candy thermometer to the pot, and bring the syrup to 215°F, gradually increasing the heat to high. Add the peaches and cook until the sauce has thickened, the peaches no longer float on the surface of the syrup, and the foam has cleared, about 25 minutes.

5. Ladle into the warm jars, leaving ½-inch head-space. Clean the rims of the jars well with a damp paper towel. Place the lids and rings on the jars and finger-tighten the rings.

6. Process in a boiling-water bath for 15 minutes.

The sauce is shelf stable for 1 year.

Nectarine, Rosemary, and Honey Preserves

MAKES: 4 or 5 half-pint jars

ACTIVE TIME: 90 minutes

MACERATING TIME: 1 to 12 hours

For years, I made this jam with lavender, its piney tones tempering the sweetness of the honey and intensifying the fruit flavor. Then it occurred to me to explore the blend with rosemary. This was a natural evolution, as garden and kitchen collaborated in my brain. The two plants, lavender (Lavendula) and rosemary (Rosmarinus), are often interchangeable in the garden for both form and flower, so why shouldn't they be exchanged in the kitchen? Each is delicious, heady, and unusual—with the potential for a medicinal overtone if overused.

1 lemon

3 pounds (1350 g) slightly underripe, firm nectarines, peeled, pitted, and diced (about 6 cups)

2½ cups (17 oz., 500 g) granulated sugar

¾ cup (9 oz., 255 g) light honey, preferably acacia or Tupelo

1 tablespoon dried rosemary

½ teaspoon pink peppercorns, crushed

½ teaspoon unsalted butter (optional)

1. Remove 5 wide strips of zest from the lemon with a sharp vegetable peeler, then juice the lemon. Combine the nectarines, sugar, honey, lemon strips, lemon juice, rosemary, and peppercorns in a large glass or ceramic bowl. Cover and macerate for at least an hour at room temperature or refrigerate for as long as overnight.

2. Pour the nectarine mixture into a colander set over your preserving pot. Transfer the colander to a bowl to capture any additional syrup.

3. Put the preserving pot over high heat, clip on a candy thermometer, and bring the syrup to 220°F, about 10 minutes. Remove the lemon zest and set aside to decorate the jars, if desired.

4. Add the nectarines and any accumulated syrup to the preserving pot and bring to a boil that will not stir down, about 15 minutes. Stir gently and boil until the foam mostly clears, about 5 additional minutes. Remove from the heat.

5. Test the set, using the wrinkle test or sheeting test. Continue to cook if necessary until you are satisfied. Stir in the butter, if using, to clear and clarify the jam.

6. Ladle into the warm jars, leaving ½-inch headspace. Clean the rims of the jars well with a damp paper towel. Place the lids and rings on the jars and finger-tighten the rings.

7. Process in a boiling-water bath for 10 minutes.

The preserves are shelf stable for 1 year.

Figgy Marmalade with Macadamia Nuts

MAKES: 6 half-pint jars

ACTIVE TIME: 90 minutes

MACERATING TIME: 12 to 18 hours

Look for fresh figs in late summer for this rich, exotic conserve. Figs are a very low-acid fruit and not safe for canning without a substantial amount of balancing acid. When I originally tried simply increasing the lemon juice, it made an overly tart jam, but as with a marmalade, including lemon rind for texture (and to increase the pH), it is just right.

This is a slumping conserve; sweet and sultry, with the buttery accent of the nuts. It's luscious in grilled cheese sandwiches (page 100), stirred into yogurt, or dolloped on crackers.

3 pounds (1350 g) fresh figs (Black Mission or other purple figs are preferable to green), stemmed

1 vanilla bean, split

8 ounces (225 g) organic lemons, sliced into very thin rounds, seeds removed

½ cup (5 oz., 140 g) wildflower, acacia, or clover honey

1½ cups (10.5 oz., 300 g) granulated sugar

¾ cup (4 oz., 110 g) salted roasted macadamia nuts, roughly broken or chopped (optional)

1. Put the figs into a medium heatproof bowl and pour boiling water over them to cover. This thoroughly cleans the figs, loosening any environmental dirts that get stuck in the wrinkly parts; it will also dislodge any bugs that might be slumbering inside them. Let stand for 10 minutes, then drain.

2. Quarter the figs and transfer to a nonreactive preserving pot. Scrape the seeds from the vanilla bean and add the bean, seeds, lemons, honey, and sugar to the pot. Bring the mixture to a simmer, stirring just until the sugar has dissolved. Pour into a glass or ceramic bowl, cover and refrigerate for 12 to 18 hours.

3. The next day, pour the fig mixture back into the preserving pot. Remove the vanilla bean, cut into 6 equal pieces, and set aside.

4. Bring the mixture up to a rolling boil, about 30 minutes. It will become thick and jammy; you're looking for softened figs surrounded by velvety syrup. In the last few minutes, the marmalade tends to scorch, so stir constantly. Stir in the macadamia nuts, if using.

5. Press a piece of vanilla bean against the side of each jar. Ladle the marmalade into the jars, leaving ½-inch headspace. Clean the rims of the jars well with a damp paper towel. Place the lids and rings on the jars and finger-tighten the rings.

6. Process in a boiling-water bath for 15 minutes.

OPPOSITE: Fresh figs on fig leaves

The jars are shelf stable for 1 year.

Bonus Recipe: Grilled Cheese with Figgy Marmalade

MAKES: 2 sandwiches
ACTIVE TIME: 30 minutes

Some nights, particularly when it is cold and snowy, a bowl of soup (see pages 238–42 for four of my favorites) and a grilled cheese sandwich make a perfect supper. For a great grilled cheese sandwich, the bread must have some density and not too many big holes. I opt for whole-grain breads, *pain ordinaire*, artisanal boules, dense sourdough, brioche, or challah. Match the bread to the cheese and fruit. Also try oat bread with Caramel Pear Preserves (page 101) and sharp Cheddar. Challah with cream cheese (page 389) and Blackberry Hazelnut Conserve (page 71). Rye bread with Swiss cheese, mustard, and Sweet Pickle Relish (page 205). And so on. You can't go wrong.

4	**thick slices dense, hearty bread**
One	**4-ounce jar Figgy Marmalade with Macadamia Nuts (page 99)**
2	**ounces (55 g) Manchego cheese, sliced**
1	**ounces (30 g) Fontina cheese, sliced**
2	**tablespoons (1 oz., 20 g) Cultured butter (page 369), softened (use store-bought butter only if you must)**

1. Line up the bread slices side by side, like the Rockettes. Spread the marmalade from edge to edge on each piece of bread. Divide the sliced cheeses among 2 of the slices. Cover with the other slices of bread, jammy side down, to make 2 oozy sandwiches.

2. Heat a griddle or a heavy cast-iron skillet over low heat. Generously butter the tops of the sandwiches. Place butter side down on the griddle and press gently. Slowly griddle the sandwiches until nice and brown on the bottom, about 6 minutes; if they are pressed, the sandwiches take on a brown butter flavor; so place a piece of parchment over the sandwiches (push them close together in the pan), then place a small baking sheet or skillet or whatever heatproof object you have that best covers both sandwiches and weight it down with a couple of (filled) quart jars. (Admittedly, my Rube Goldberg setup usually falls at some point, so I never stray far from the stove.)

3. Undo your weighted construction, butter the tops of the sandwiches, and turn them over. Griddle the other side until toasty (no need to weight them down again). When the smell drives you batty, they're ready. Cool slightly so you don't burn the roof of your mouth, like you know you will.

Caramel Pear Preserves

MAKES: 5 or 6 half-pint jars
ACTIVE TIME: 1 hour

When October comes and caramel apples are on display at local farm stands, my mind, of course, turns to jams and flavors. And that is how this recipe came to be. I can't explain the spice, except to call it divine intervention.

There are many types of pears. Some are velvety, soft, and juicy; others are a little firmer, grainier, and drier. That's the kind you want for this jam, one that stands up to cooking, leaving distinct pieces of pear surrounded by the smooth, silky caramel.

3   **pounds (1350 g) firm slightly underripe Bosc or Seckel pears, peeled, cored, and cut into fine julienne**

3½   **cups (24.5 oz., 700 g) granulated sugar**

½   **teaspoon Quatre Épices (recipe follows)**

¾   **cup (180 ml) orange juice**

•   **Juice of 1 lemon**

1. Mix the pears, 2 cups of the sugar, the quatre épices, and orange and lemon juices in a bowl. Cover and let macerate while you make the caramel.

2. Slowly melt the remaining 1½ cups sugar in your preserving pot over low heat, without stirring (you can shake the pan for even cooking), and cook until it becomes a caramel. Let it turn from golden to a deep amber color. Don't rush the process, and watch it carefully. Do not walk away. Do not read your e-mail or fold laundry. Stand there and watch.

3. Here's the really scary part, the part that will make you think you've wrecked it all. Pour in the pears and all their liquids. The caramel will seize and break. It will make you want to cry. It will look wrong. Don't worry. Just heat the whole mixture up again very slowly, stirring carefully and frequently to work the pieces of caramel off the bottom of the pot and incorporate them into the preserves. It's a hellish moment. Then bring the preserves up to 220°F, which will take at least 30 minutes, by which time all the caramel will have melted again and it will be heavenly. You'll smell those spices. You'll be happy again.

4. Keep the preserves at a boil that will not stir down for about 5 minutes, then remove from the heat and test the set, using the wrinkle test or sheeting test to determine if the jam has set to a

Recipe continues

gentle slump. If not, heat it again and boil for 2 to 3 minutes, then test again.

5. Ladle the hot preserves into the warm jars, leaving a ½-inch headspace. Clean the rims of the jars well with a damp paper towel. Place the lids and rings on the jars and finger-tighten the rings.

6. Process in a boiling-water bath for 10 minutes.

The preserves are shelf stable for 1 year.

Quatre Épices

MAKES: about ⅓ cup

Quatre épices is a French four-spice mix used in many sausages and pâtés. I like the floral bite of white pepper blended with cloves, ginger, and nutmeg. It's a great mix to have in the cupboard. This recipe makes much more than is needed for the preserves, so there will be plenty left for experimentation. Sprinkle it on pork, chicken, and fish; summer and winter squash; panna cotta; and grilled nectarines.

2 tablespoons freshly ground white pepper
1 tablespoon ground ginger
1 tablespoon ground nutmeg
1 tablespoon ground cloves

Combine all the spices. Store in a tightly closed jar.

Whole-Cranberry Raspberry Sauce

MAKES: 5 half-pint jars

ACTIVE TIME: 1 hour

Over the years, I've heard many people complain about the horrid canned cranberry sauce they were served as a child. I have no such memories. These same people initially shun my glistening, ruby-red cranberry sauce, but quickly revise their thinking after just one taste. Tangy, sweet, fruity in November, when many fruits are only a memory, this is a welcome addition to any holiday meal.

If you feel the need to serve this as a mold, as though it had slipped from a can, just run a palette knife around the inside of the jar and slide the cylinder onto a relish dish. Slice and serve shamelessly.

4 cups (28 oz., 800 g) granulated sugar
4 cups (32 oz., 950 ml) nonchlorinated water
• Grated zest of 1 orange
• Juice of 1 lemon
4 cups (14 oz., 390 g) cranberries
1 cup (8 oz., 225 g) fresh raspberries
½ teaspoon unsalted butter (optional)

1. Combine the sugar, water, zest, and juice in your preserving pot and bring to a boil over high heat, stirring to dissolve the sugar. When the mixture is briskly boiling, carefully add the cranberries. The berries will burst when heated and may splatter. Cook until most of the berries have burst and the sauce is thickening, about 12 minutes.

2. Add the raspberries and bring back to a boil that will not stir down. Boil hard for about 10 more minutes. Test the set using the wrinkle test or the sheeting test. Add the butter, if using, to clarify and clear the sauce.

3. Ladle into the warm jars, leaving ½-inch headspace. Clean the rims of the jars well with a damp paper towel. Place the lids and rings on the jars and finger-tighten the rings.

4. Process in a boiling-water bath for 10 minutes.

The sauce is shelf stable for 1 year.

Mango Chutney

MAKES: 3 pint jars

ACTIVE TIME: 2 hours

MACERATING TIME: 8 hours to overnight

My mother made curry regularly. This was long ago, before Indian food was really popular in the United States. She discovered curry for what it is, an inexpensive way to stretch a little bit of meat, fish, or a handful of vegetables into dinner for four. For me, the pleasure of curry resided in the toppings: Chopped tomato and scallion, cucumber in yogurt, chopped hard-boiled eggs, salted peanuts, golden raisins, and mango chutney. At the time, the only chutney we knew was Major Grey's, but it was surely my gateway to the world of condiments. A decade later, my mother and I started to make mango chutney together.

It's sweet, yes, but it's also hot. It's bright with vinegar and tangy from onions and garlic. The complex texture, combining the chew of dried fruit and tenderness of fresh mango, is why it holds a special place in my heart, and I hope you'll add it to your pantry.

7½ pounds (3.5 kg) firm but ripe mangoes, peeled, seeded, and diced (about 5 cups)

1 cup (8 oz., 225 g) diced onion

2 garlic cloves, slivered

½ cup (4 oz., 110 g) crystallized ginger

½ cup (4 oz., 110 g) golden raisins

½ cup (4 oz., 110 g) dried sour cherries

1 teaspoon mustard seeds

½ teaspoon kosher salt

1 cup (8 oz., 235 ml) cider vinegar

1 cup (7 oz., 200 g) firmly packed light brown sugar

3 superhot Thai bird chiles, pierced 2 times with the tip of a paring knife

1. Combine all the ingredients in a large glass or ceramic bowl, stir, and cover. Refrigerate for at least 8 hours, or overnight.

2. Pour the mixture into the preserving pot and bring to a boil, stirring constantly. Turn the heat down to a low, slow simmer and cook, uncovered, until the chutney is thick and jammy, about 40 minutes. Stir regularly but gently to keep the mango pieces intact, being careful not to let it burn or stick.

3. Ladle into the warm jars, leaving a ½-inch headspace. Clean the rims of the jars well with a damp paper towel. Place the lids and rings on the jars and finger-tighten the rings.

4. Process in a boiling-water bath for 15 minutes.

The chutney is shelf stable for 1 year.

WHAT TO DO WITH CHUTNEY

If you have never made chutney, or are wondering what to do with chutney, please do try this version of mango chutney. It's delicious enough to eat from the jar with a spoon, but here are some other ways to enjoy this sensational condiment.

- **Serve it on the side** as a condiment with any poultry, particularly leftover Thanksgiving turkey.

- **Take a trip back to the 1960s** and pour some chutney over a wheel of Brie. Wrap it in puff pastry, and bake in a 325°F oven for 10 to 15 minutes.

- **Serve with Ritz crackers**.

- **Top Inside-Out Samosas** (page 107) with the chutney.

- **Stir some into a chicken salad** and add grapes and almonds.

- **Use it as a barbeque sauce** for halibut and other firm fish.

- **For a dip or sandwich spread**, mix it with sour cream or Greek yogurt.

- **Enjoy chutney with softly scrambled eggs**.

- **Top deviled eggs** with a dollop of chutney.

- **Spread on a roast pork sandwich**.

Bonus Recipe: Inside-Out Samosas

SERVES: 4 as an appetizer or 2 for dinner

ACTIVE TIME: 45 minutes

When we eat at our local Indian restaurant, we automatically order samosas. These little pastries are crackly and flaky and the dough is so thin and rich. I decided to find a way to enjoy everything about the samosa without the dough, instead holding the mixture together with the soft, fluffy potatoes enhanced with toasted spices and seeds. Dice the vegetables about the same size as the peas so every bite includes each element and ensures that everything cooks in the same amount of time.

This is a tasty appetizer for an Indian-inspired dinner party or a simple supper, full of flavor, for two. The mango chutney brings it all together for a Bollywood-worthy mouthful.

- 4   medium Yukon Gold potatoes (24 oz., 680 g), rinsed
- •   Kosher salt
- ¼   cup (4 oz., 110 g) diced carrot
- 2   tablespoons (1 oz., 28 g) unsalted butter
- 1½ teaspoons coriander seeds
- ½   teaspoon cumin seeds
- ½   cup (4 oz., 110 g) diced onion
- 2   teaspoons minced ginger
- 1   garlic clove, minced
- ½   cup (3 oz., 90 g) frozen peas
- ¾   teaspoon garam masala
- ¼   teaspoon cayenne pepper
- ¼   teaspoon freshly ground black pepper
- ¼   cup (1 oz., 28 g) all-purpose flour
- •   About 3 tablespoons grapeseed or canola oil
- •   Mango Chutney (page 104)

OPPOSITE: Inside-Out Samosas served with Mango Chutney (page 104)

1. Put the potatoes in a 3-quart saucepan, cover with cold water, and add a big pinch of salt. Bring to a boil and boil until a fork easily pierces the fresh, about 20 minutes. Remove the potatoes from the boiling water with a slotted spoon and cool slightly.

2. In the meantime, drop the diced carrots into the boiling water and blanch for 2 minutes, then drain.

3. Slip off the potato skins, transfer the potatoes to a medium bowl, and smash with a fork or a potato masher, leaving some lumps for texture.

4. Melt the butter in a small sauté pan. Add the coriander and cumin seeds and toast in the butter for 2 minutes. Add the onion, ginger, and garlic and cook until just starting to brown on the edges. Remove from the heat.

5. Add the onion mixture, carrots, peas, garam masala, cayenne, 1 teaspoon salt, and the pepper to the potatoes and mix gently with your hands. Use a ¼-cup measure for easy portioning, and pat the potatoes into a fat little cake. Form the remaining cakes in the same way.

6. Spread the flour out on a plate or tray. Dredge each cake lightly in flour; use a light touch—don't smush the cakes.

7. Add a slick of oil to a large nonstick skillet (trust me, you want nonstick) and get it nice and hot. Working in batches, carefully place the cakes in the pan and get them good and brown, about 3 minutes on each side. Keep the finished cakes covered and warm, and add more oil to the pan as necessary.

8. Serve with mango chutney.

Drunken Pineapple Sauce

MAKES: four 12-ounce jars

ACTIVE TIME: 90 minutes

MACERATING TIME: 1 hour

From time to time, I get a hankering for tropical fruit. It usually starts sometime in February, when the apples seem tired. That is when tastes of the islands (and thoughts of the beach) are never far from my mind. Breakfast features fruit salad with bananas, mango, and pineapple. I've been known to make my way through the snow to the patio grill with wedges of pineapple. Such foods are the best antidote to winter I know.

In the depths of winter, I yearn for a little canning too. I miss the rhythms and the meditative nature, the quiet of being in the kitchen. And that is when I make this sauce, to feed my canning needs, fill the kitchen with the sounds and smells of preserves, and (ultimately) indulge in a Tropical Tart (see photograph on opposite page). This sauce will taste familiar yet even better: like the sauce from a banana split but it's all grown up, with plenty of spicy dark rum and a hint of bay.

10 cups (53 oz., 1.5 kg) finely diced ripe pineapple (from 3 pineapples; see page 109)

1½ cups (10 oz., 300 g) granulated sugar

1½ cups (10 oz., 300 g) firmly packed light brown sugar

1 dried bay leaf

• Juice of 2 lemons

½ cup (4 oz., 120 ml) Myers's or Gosling's dark rum

1. Combine the diced pineapple, both sugars, the bay, and lemon juice in a glass or ceramic bowl and let macerate for 1 hour.

2. Remove and discard the bay leaf. Add the pineapple mixture to the preserving pot, scraping the bowl to get every drop. Clip a candy thermometer to the pot. Slowly bring to a simmer and cook, stirring regularly, for about 1 hour, until the sauce is very thick, the foam has cleared, and it registers 220°F.

3. Add the rum and stir constantly until the sauce is thick and clear again, about 3 minutes.

4. Ladle into the warm jars, leaving ½-inch headspace. Clean the rims of the jars well with a damp paper towel. Place the warmed lids and rings on the jar and finger-tighten the rings.

5. Process in a boiling-water bath for 15 minutes.

The sauce is shelf stable for 1 year.

HOW TO SELECT A RIPE PINEAPPLE

• Most pineapples are harvested when still a little green; some are picked entirely green. Like many other fruits that travel long distances, pineapples are gassed to encourage ripening. This is an unfortunate practice. Look for pineapple during early winter, when it is abundant and in season in Hawaii, the Philippines, Brazil, and Mexico and properly ripened fruit is more likely to be in the store.

- The fruit will ripen further on your counter, so purchase a slightly underripe pineapple and wait for the moment to arrive: you'll smell pineapple when you walk into the kitchen. One sure test? When a leaf pulls away easily, the pineapple is ripe.

HOW TO DICE A PINEAPPLE

- First slice off the top and bottom of the pineapple. Sit the pineapple upright on the cutting board and slice away the fruit, removing the tough outer skin. With a small paring knife, cut away any brown "eyes." Slice the pineapple vertically into 4 equal pieces, then cut away the tough core. Dice the pineapple into small pieces, no bigger than a pea.

Tropical Tart (recipe page 383)

Carmen Miranda Tropical Fruit Preserves

MAKES: 4 to 5 half-pint jars
ACTIVE TIME: 90 minutes
MACERATING TIME: 8 to 24 hours

Most of us think of Carmen Miranda as a kitschy cultural icon, the lady in a slinky dress with a turban made up of every tropical fruit imaginable. I named this complex preserve after that hat, but also after her sassy nature. It is strong flavored, aggressive, and spiced. The sweet mango, the bright ginger, and the tart papaya work as well with scones as with poultry or red meat. Use these jammy preserves as a marinade for a breezy skirt steak in a snap (page 113). You'll be hearing Don Ho's ukulele in no time.

When working with tropical fruits, choose the ripe and juicy ones, not those that are sold completely green and underripe. Often picked green and traveling long distances to the grocery store produce department, these fruits can be disappointing. Make sure to taste before you preserve. Papaya is deliciously astringent and mango adds a glorious silky texture. For the best results, both should be fully ripe before being preserved.

- 4 pounds (1.8 kg) ripe mangoes, peeled, seeded, and diced (about 2½ cups)
- 2 pounds (90 g) ripe papayas, peeled, seeded, and diced (about 4 cups)
- • Juice of 2 lemons
- 2 limes
- 4 cups (28 oz., 800 g) granulated sugar
- ½ cup (4 oz., 110 g) finely minced crystallized ginger
- ¼ cup (2 oz., 60 ml) dark rum
- 1 teaspoon coriander seeds
- 1 teaspoon black pepper
- ½ teaspoon unsalted butter (optional)

1. Put the mangoes and papaya in a large glass or ceramic bowl, add the lemon juice, and stir together.

2. Using a vegetable peeler, remove the zest, not the white pith, from the limes. Add the zest and 1 cup of the sugar to a food processor or blender and blitz the bejeezus out of it until the lime is distributed throughout the sugar. Take a whiff: it will smell amazing. Add it and the remaining 3 cups sugar to the fruit.

3. Juice the limes and add the juice, ginger, and rum to the fruit mixture. Crush the coriander seeds under the side of a heavy knife and add the seeds and pepper to the fruit. (I originally tried toasting the spices, but they turned bitter in the jar, so don't be tempted to do that.) Cover and refrigerate for at least 8 hours, or overnight.

4. Pour the fruit mixture into a colander set over the preserving pot. Then set the colander of fruit in a bowl to catch any additional syrup. Clip a candy thermometer to the pot and bring the syrup to a strong, rolling boil. Continue boiling until it reaches 220°F, about 10 minutes. Add the fruit and any accumulated

syrup, stir well, and continue to stir as the mixture comes back to a boil that will not stir down, about 30 minutes longer.

5. Continue to stir, stir, stir until the foam has nearly cleared, about 10 minutes. Remove from the heat and let cool for 2 minutes.

6. Test the set using the sheeting test or wrinkle test. If necessary, continue to cook until the set is achieved. Then stir in the butter, if using, to disperse any remaining foam and clarify the gel.

7. Ladle into the warm jars, leaving ½-inch headspace. Clean the rims of the jars well with a damp paper towel. Place the lids and rings on the jars and finger-tighten the rings.

8. Process in a boiling-water bath for 10 minutes.

The preserves are shelf stable for 1 year.

Bonus Recipe: Hula Skirt Steak

SERVES: 2, with leftovers

ACTIVE TIME: 15 minutes

MARINATING TIME: 20 to 40 minutes

A conversation with a butcher taught me that pineapple and papaya are enzymatic agents and great for tenderizing tougher cuts of meat. It was that and a jar of Carmen Miranda Preserves that inspired this weeknight dinner. Serve the steak with garlic-laced sautéed Swiss chard, crispy plantains, and basmati rice made green and gloriously herbal with copious amounts of chopped fresh cilantro or flat-leaf parsley.

A grill is preferable, but a grill pan or searingly hot cast-iron pan will work too. (If using a grill pan or cast-iron pan, you may need to cut the skirt steak into smaller pieces to fit it in the pan.) Hanger steak also works well in this recipe.

1½ **to 2 pounds (680 to 900 g) skirt steak**

½ **cup (4 oz., 120 ml) Carmen Miranda Tropical Fruit Preserves (page 110)**

• **Kosher salt and freshly ground black pepper**

1. Place the steak in a single layer in a shallow nonreactive dish, such as a baking dish. Pour the preserves over the steak and turn to coat both sides of the meat. Cover and set aside for 20 to 40 minutes; no longer, or the meat will get mushy. (Those enzymes don't fool around.)

2. Prepare a hot fire in a grill.

3. Brush the grill with oil. Wipe away the jam from the meat, using a paper towel. Set the steak on the grill. Leave it alone for 5 minutes, then lift the meat with tongs (not a fork—that lets all the juices flow out). If it sticks to the grill, it is not ready to be turned; wait another minute or two and try again. When it's ready, the steak will release easily. Cook on the other side for 4 minutes, or until it easily releases again. Remove from the grill and place on a cutting board. Loosely cover the steak with aluminum foil and let rest for 10 minutes.

4. Unwrap the meat and slice across the grain into pieces about ½-inch thick. The meat should be rosy pink and juicy, with a nice crusty edge all around.

OPPOSITE: Hula Skirt Steak with Carmen Miranda Tropical Fruit Preserves (page 110)

JUICE, JELLY, PIE FILLING, AND FRUIT IN SYRUP

OPPOSITE: Currants juicing in a jelly bag

Once you've developed some expertise with jams and preserves, it's time to dive into the trickier preparations. These are my pantry treasures, the jars I will admit to hoarding. Some fruits just call out for elegant treatment.

Jellies are a little fussy, but even a loose jelly makes a delicious ice cream syrup, so don't despair. The pie fillings and whole fruit preparations are delicate; some require fancy knife work, others demand keen attention. All are sensational additions to the larder.

Consider the currant: so rare, special, and jewel-like, and the flavor so substantial for such a little thing. I just have to preserve them. A garden full of fresh green herbs—bottle that scent. Baskets of wine grapes in late summer, bees buzzing around them, call out to me.

Every jelly starts with juice, and the method of juicing is critical to the final product. The fruit is chopped if necessary. Seeds and skins are pectin builders, as are cores, so nothing is thrown away. The fruit is heated with just enough water and mashed, then the fruit mash is suspended in a bag over a catch bowl for several hours. For crystal-clear jelly, the juice must be extracted without rushing; no squeezing, or the jelly will be cloudy. Plan plenty of time for proper juicing.

While most fruits can be cooked into jam, only certain ones deserve to be jelly. I want brilliant color, intense flavor, and, most important of all, freshly harvested fruit, mostly perfectly ripe, but with some underripe fruit. The natural pectin is most evident in underripe fruit, and it dissipates the longer the fruit is off the vine, bush, or tree. And that pectin is essential to jelly's jelly-ness. Jelly should sit up on the spoon. There is more precision to jelly making. Building the structure requires a critical balance of lemon, sugar, and pectin-rich fruit juice.

As if the gel specifics aren't tricky enough, cooking to the precise moment of perfect gel is a skill, and here experience is the best teacher. The gel occurs when the water activity is low and the temperature of the jelly is around 220°F. I say "around," because the two elements, water activity and temperature, work hand in hand—and because of the way weather and seasonal differences can change the water activity of the fruit, time and temperature are just estimates. You need to use all the skills developed making jams and preserves to make jelly, and then some. So, give in to it. You will probably make some rubbery jelly. I certainly have. Don't despair, just warm it and add some liquid, and that bouncy jelly will contribute substantial flavor to a smoothie, a pan sauce, or a (well-shaken) cocktail.

Some fruits lead me in a completely different direction. Peaches are big, juicy, sunshine-filled fruits. In season, when boxes are a bargain, I settle in to put up peaches in syrup. This is a technique that truly preserves all of the best qualities of a peach, and its simplicity belies the pile of dishes at the end of the day. It's worth it. Some February snow day, I'll open that jar, spoon on some cottage cheese (page 391), and plan a beach vacation. A peach in the winter is a wonderful thing.

Jars of fruit pie fillings are also practical in the winter months. Beyond pie, they work as a base for crisps, cobblers, Bettys, or buckles. Having fresh-tasting fruity desserts all winter long makes the short, dark days tolerable. I love pie, whether deep-dish or free-form, hand pie, or pop tart, and I've included my family's piecrust recipe so you can make blue-ribbon pies too.

These recipes take some finesse, time, and (usually) more pots and pans than jams and preserves, but I think you will agree that they are worth it.

Making jelly

There are times when jelly is the perfect preservation technique. Because jelly is made from juice, which is extracted from whole fruit that is cooked until softened and strained, there is very little prep work. Currant jelly, for instance, is made without the tedium of plucking the tiny little seed from each and every fruit, necessary for a truly lovely currant jam. Jelly can be stirred into a pan sauce, adding complexity to even ordinary fare. Jelly can be diced and scattered over salads or sliced into disks and served alongside almost any savory dish.

Jelly making is based on a simple equation: juice the fruit, measure the juice, and add an equal amount of sugar and the juice of 1 lemon. Stir well. Boil to 220°F, until set. Yes, that's it.

Any fruit will make a jelly following these steps, but overcooking the fruit while extracting the juice will destroy the pectin and the jelly will never set. Cook it only until softened.

Underripe fruit has the most pectin, but less flavor. For jelly, use mostly ripe fruit with about one-quarter underripe fruit. Do not use overripe fruit for jelly as it will impart a fermented flavor to the finished product. Bruised fruit can be salvaged as a jelly as long as it is not also overripe.

Equipment

If you have the equipment needed to make jams, sauces, and chutneys (see Equipment, page 22), you're nearly there. Add to that a **jelly bag and stand** (see photograph, page 114), which is a great contraption for hands-free juicing. If you don't want to acquire any more equipment, though, you can just use a smooth, threadbare cotton tea towel. Rename it jelly-making equipment and use it over and over for these and other projects (see Cream Cheese,

page 389). Fashion the towel into a tidy packet—a hobo bundle—using one of the four corners to snugly tie the other three together. Then figure out a way to suspend the packet over a catch bowl so gravity does your work. I have suspended bundles from the handles of my upper cabinets, from a faucet handle, and from the handle of a wooden spoon balanced on a deep pitcher. Find a setup that lets the juice flow freely.

Power-tool juicers are not appropriate for jelly making. The fruit is battered and beaten, the juice is cloudy, and the pectin is too dispersed to be useful. By the same token, a steam juice extractor is fantastic for large-batch juicing (see page 147), but the steam overheats the fruit and destroys the jelly-making pectin.

Altitude adjustments

At sea level, cook jellies to 220°F. If needed, make altitude adjustments as shown in the chart below.

Altitude	Jelly-Making Temperature
1,000 ft	218°F
2,000 ft	216°F
3,000 ft	214°F
4,000 ft	212°F
5,000 ft	211°F
6,000 ft	209°F
7,000 ft	207°F
8,000 ft	205°F

Four steps to jelly making

1. Underripe fruit has the most pectin. For jelly, use mostly ripe fruit with about one-quarter underripe fruit. Chop the fruit and place in the preserving pot along with any peel, seeds, pits, or cores to help build pectin. Barely cover the fruit with cool water. Heat the water to boiling and cook the fruit just until soft, mashing it with a potato masher to get the juices flowing. Any fruit will make a jelly following these steps, but overcooking the fruit at this stage, while extracting the juice, will destroy the pectin and the jelly will never set.

2. Set a colander lined with cheesecloth or a soft threadbare cotton kitchen towel over a large bowl. Ladle the fruit and accumulated juices into the colander, capturing the juice below, tie the cheesecloth or towel into a bundle, suspend this bundle over the bowl, and extract the juice. Or use a jelly bag and stand—it's much easier. Let the fruit juice drip for up to four hours. Refrigerate after four hours to avoid fermentation or fruit flies. It's perfectly fine to break this task into two days, but do use the juice within a day or the pectin loses its oomph.

3. The jelly-making premise is based on a simple equation. Juice the fruit, measure the juice, add an equal amount of sugar and lemon juice, and stir well. The lemon activates the pectin when combined with the sugar. This is a delicate balance and will fail with insufficient sugar.

Prepare for water-bath canning (see page 28). Sanitize the jars, fill the canning kettle with water, and bring to a boil. Fill a small saucepan with water and bring to a boil to warm the lids and rings. Gather the lid lifter, jar lifter, bubbler, funnel, and ladle, as well as a stack of clean cotton towels.

4. Add the fruit juice, sugar, and lemon juice to the preserving pot and bring to a boil over high heat, stirring all the while. Boil until the temperature of the jelly reaches 220°F, when the jelly should be set. Yes, that's all it takes. Jellies continue to firm up, so do not judge the gel when it is still warm. If the jelly sheets off the spoon and passes the wrinkle test (see page 44), it will gel. Give it time.

I usually pack jelly into 4-ounce jars.

Red Currant Jelly

MAKES: six 4-ounce jars
ACTIVE TIME: 1½ hours
JUICING TIME: 4 hours

Making currant jelly is thoroughly satisfying. It's beautiful, it has sufficient pectin to gel on its own, and it is endlessly useful in the kitchen. It is my secret weapon for a pan sauce (page 123) that enlivens everything from chicken to tofu to veal.

Currants appear in the market in early summer in colors ranging from pale pink to deep purple, almost black. Black currants are the most common, but they make a dark, murky jelly. Instead, look for the tiny carmine-red currants still attached to their fragile stems. Pale pink or violet currents are a charming addition, making the red even more jewel-like, but alone, these pale berries result in a wan jelly.

2 **pounds (900 g) red currants (about 6 half pints)**

½ **cup (4 oz., 120 ml) water**

2½ **to 3 cups (17 to 21 oz., 475 to 600 g) granulated sugar**

• **Juice of 1 lemon**

1. Gently rinse the berries and pluck from the stems directly into a 3-quart saucepan. Add the water and bring to a boil, then mash the currants well with a potato masher. Remove from the heat and cool for 30 minutes.

2. Ladle the fruit into a jelly bag or cheesecloth-lined colander and set it over a catch bowl. Let drip for at least 4 hours. Do not squeeze or press the fruit, or the jelly will be cloudy. Just let gravity and time do the work for you.

3. Measure the juice and measure out an equal amount of sugar. Pour the juice into the preserving pot and bring to a strong boil.

4. Clip a candy thermometer onto the pot. Add the sugar and lemon juice, start stirring, and keep stirring. Bring the mixture to a boil that will not stir down and boil hard for 5 minutes. Then turn down the heat and continue to stir so no hot spots develop—a burned jelly is a terrible thing. Soon the jelly will begin to gel slightly. When the foam recedes, the temperature should be 220°F, after about 15 minutes. Confirm the gel using the wrinkle test or sheeting test.

5. Ladle the jelly into the warm jars leaving ½-inch headspace. Wipe the rims of the jars well with a damp paper towel. Place the lids and rings on the jars, and finger-tighten the rings.

6. Process in a boiling-water bath for 5 minutes.

The jelly is shelf stable for 1 year.

OPPOSITE: Fresh currants

Bonus Recipe: Chicken Breasts with Currant Jelly Sauce

SERVES: 4
ACTIVE TIME: 40 minutes

A good pan sauce elevates any simple meal and takes nothing more than a well-stocked pantry. That and the skill to build a *fond*, a crusty, flavorful base on the bottom of the skillet that will release with liquid and flavor the sauce.

This sauce is made with currant jelly, but almost any jelly will work. My mother made this whenever "chicken-whatever" was for dinner. The next time the thought of dinner seems just too difficult, make this chicken dish. It's easy to put together and a little bit fancy. While it's cooking away, pour a glass of wine, light a candle, and get out the cloth napkins.

Grilled broccoli rabe, radicchio, or another bitter green would be the perfect accompaniment. And some bread to sop up the delicious sauce.

½ cup (2 oz., 57 g) all-purpose flour

• Kosher salt and freshly ground black pepper

4 plump boneless chicken breasts (about 3 pounds, 1350 g total), tenderloins removed and reserved for another use

2 tablespoons olive oil

3 tablespoons (1.5 oz., 42 g) unsalted butter

1 shallot, finely minced

½ cup (4 oz., 120 ml) dry white wine or water

One 4-ounce jar Red Currant Jelly (page 121)

2 teaspoons thyme leaves

1 tablespoon Dijon mustard

1. Preheat the oven to 250°F.

2. Season the flour aggressively with salt and pepper. Dry the chicken breasts well with paper towels and dredge in the flour. Heat the olive oil and 2 tablespoons of the butter in a wide heavy sauté pan over medium-high heat. When the oil and butter shimmer, slip in the chicken breasts, skin side down, and brown well on the first side, 8 to 10 minutes. Don't fuss and keep moving them in the pan; just let them cook. Turn and brown the other side, about 6 more minutes. Remove the chicken breasts to an ovenproof plate and keep warm in the oven while you whisk together the sauce.

3. Return the pan to the stove, turn up the heat, and add the shallot. Cook until translucent. Add the wine, scrape up all the good browned bits, and bring to a boil to release all the flavor. Add the jelly, thyme, and mustard and whisk everything together, then heat until simmering and slightly thickened, 3 or 4 more minutes. Taste and add salt and pepper as needed. Whisk in the remaining 1 tablespoon butter.

4. Place one chicken breast on each plate. Pour the sauce over the chicken breasts and serve.

OPPOSITE: Chicken Breasts with Currant Jelly Sauce

Blueberry Jelly

MAKES: 4 half-pint jars
ACTIVE TIME: 1½ hours
JUICING TIME: 4 to 12 hours

I love the flavor of blueberries but find the skins and blossom-end bit of toughness bothersome in a jam. Blueberry jelly, on the other hand, is pristine and purple and just plain perfect. Spread this jelly across a warm crepe or spoon an obscene amount on a scone. Whir a spoonful into a smoothie with a banana and some plain yogurt. Or stir into a gin cocktail and add lime. This is a multitalented spread.

4   pounds (8 cups, 1800 g) fresh blueberries
½   cup (235 ml) water
•   About 4 cups (28 oz., 800 g) granulated sugar
•   Juice of 1 lemon

1. Rinse the blueberries well, then pick through and remove any leaves or stems. Place the blueberries in a preserving pot, add the water, and crush about half the berries with a potato masher or the back of a spoon. Turn the heat to low and bring to a simmer.

2. Pour the fruit mash into a jelly bag or a colander lined with cheesecloth and set it over a catch bowl. Let drain, without squeezing, pressing, or otherwise fiddling with the fruit, for at least 4 and up to 12 hours.

3. Measure the juice and measure out an equal amount of sugar. Add the juice, sugar, and lemon juice to the clean preserving pot. Bring to a rapid boil and boil hard until the jelly gels, about 10 minutes longer. When most of the foam clears, check the set with the sheeting test or wrinkle test.

4. Ladle into the warm jars, leaving ½-inch headspace. Wipe the rims of the jars well with a damp paper towel. Place the lids and rings on the jars and finger-tighten the rings.

5. Process in a boiling-water bath for 10 minutes.

The jelly is shelf stable for 1 year.

VARIATION
•   Make any fruit jelly using the same method and ratios.

OPPOSITE: Fresh blueberries

Mint Jelly

MAKES: 4 half-pint jars
ACTIVE TIME: 1 hour
STEEPING TIME: 15 minutes to 1 hour

When I was growing up, Friday night dinners at my grandparents' always meant a substantial main course. My Grandmother Mary, even decades after immigrating from Lithuania, still found the abundance at the butcher counter a little startling. She would look at the display case, count the number of guests in her head, and ask the butcher for "a nice piece of meat." This might mean brisket, chuck roast, steamship round, or, my favorite, leg of lamb. As a nod to her Bostonian-born daughter-in-law, there was always a cut-glass bowl of shocking-green mint jelly served with it. Making my own minty jelly elevated my expectations well beyond that Crayola-colored condiment.

Because herbs have no pectin, added pectin is a must. In this case, I opt for commercial pectin over homemade, for a crystal-clear appearance. I prefer a slightly loose jelly, so I use 2 tablespoons of pectin, but if you want a firm jelly (one that can be sliced or cut into forms, for instance) use a full 3 tablespoons. If clarity is not important to you, you can substitute any of the pectin options on page 60 for commercial pectin.

Any herb makes a lovely jelly. An acidic note is necessary not only for taste, but also for pectin activation. Many older recipes use white vinegar, but wine vinegar adds complexity and depth to the jelly's subtle herbal flavor. Get creative with herbs, spices, and more, making small batches to serve with meat, cheese, or fruit. And if you miss that electric tint, feel free to drop in a tiny bit of green food coloring.

2 cups (16 oz., 475 ml) Riesling or other fruity white wine

2 cups (2.5 oz., 70 g) lightly packed fresh peppermint or spearmint leaves

1 tablespoon fresh lemon juice

1 tablespoon white wine vinegar

2 to 3 tablespoons powdered pectin

2½ cups (17 oz., 500 g) granulated sugar

• Green food coloring (if you must)

½ teaspoon unsalted butter

1. Combine the wine and mint in a 3-quart heavy saucepan, crushing the mint leaves with the back of a spoon. Bring to a simmer, then turn off the heat. Cover and steep for 15 minutes to 1 hour, tasting until the herb flavor is pleasing to you.

2. Strain the wine through a fine-mesh sieve into a 2-cup measure. Add water if necessary to achieve 2 cups. Pour the wine into a 3-quart heavy nonreactive saucepan, add the lemon juice, vinegar, and pectin, and stir together. Bring to a boil over medium-high heat, stirring well and often. Add the sugar, stirring constantly, and bring to a boil. When the jelly reaches an active boil that will not stir down, set the timer for exactly 1 minute and continue to boil hard. Remove from the heat and test the set using the sheeting test or wrinkle test.

3. Add food coloring, if you are doing that. To disperse any foam still visible in the jelly and to further clarify the gel, add the butter and stir well.

4. Ladle into the warm jars, leaving ½-inch headspace. Wipe the rims well with a damp paper towel. Place the lids and rings on the jars and finger-tighten the rings.

5. Process in a boiling-water bath for 5 minutes.

The jelly is shelf stable for 1 year.

VARIATIONS

- Try fresh bay leaves for an intense emerald-green jelly, appealingly medicinal.
- Rosemary or lavender imparts a strong woodsy tone.
- For a more subtle jelly, turn to thyme and any basil variety (especially lemon basil, Thai basil or chocolate basil).
- Gentle herbs like chervil and parsley are too subtle to effectively flavor a jelly.
- Or use 2 or 3 juniper berries, boldly aromatic peppercorns, or a couple of star anise.
- Substitute almost any wine, including Chablis, rosé, or Zinfandel (essentially, whatever might be languishing in the refrigerator or pantry), or sake. Or use cider vinegar. Try a Sauternes with rosemary, rosé with herbes de Provence: Chardonnay is elevated by the piney flavor of bay leaves; ice wine comes alive with a few allspice berries; Pinot Noir is enhanced by star anise; and Zinfandel and Tellicherry peppercorns go hand in hand. Are you getting the idea?

Cocktail Cherries with Maraschino Liqueur

MAKES: 3 pint jars
ACTIVE TIME: 2 hours
BRINING TIME: overnight
CURING TIME: 1 month

Plumped with a salty brine, then cured, these are sensational cocktail cherries. If the chipotle is included, they are smoky, sweet, and spicy, ready to make an appearance with bourbon. Without the chile, they are sweet but bring on a pucker, settling into a Negroni.

Although almost any cherry will work here, from sweet Bing to sour Montmorency, Rainier and other yellow cherries do not retain their color and end up muddy and unappealing. I prefer to make these with tart cherries. I like the firm flesh and piquant flavor, which balances somewhere between candied and pickled. Even mixing sweet and tart cherries will make a terrific jar of cocktail cherries. I'll admit—I usually make this recipe after working my way through many pounds of cherries, pitting and stirring and canning jams and pie fillings. These cocktail cherries are the last recipe after a long weekend of cherry preservation, so they get short shrift, and there are years when I end up with only one or two jars. I hoard them, and I'll bet you will, too.

Add a few cherries to a pan sauce (see page 278) for duck or pork. Skewer with fresh peaches and grill for dessert. Stir a few into softened ice cream, ribbon with bittersweet chocolate, and refreeze. Gloat in January when others are buying those horrid things from the grocery store to cheer up their Manhattans or Negronis. These make great gifts, if you are willing to part with a jar. Start planning now to make more next year.

2 pounds (900 g) tart (sour) cherries

1 tablespoon kosher salt

3 cups (24 oz., 700 ml) boiling water

1½ cups (10 oz., 300 g) granulated sugar

1 cup (8 oz., 240 ml) water

1 star anise

3 dried chipotle peppers (optional)

1. Pit the cherries over a bowl, capturing all the juice. Strain and refrigerate the juice.

2. Stir the cherries together with the salt in a glass or ceramic bowl. Add the boiling water, cover, and brine overnight on the counter.

3. Rinse the cherries well, drain, and pack tightly into sanitized jars.

4. Bring the reserved juice to a boil in a medium saucepan over high heat and reduce to ½ cup, about 20 minutes. Add the sugar, water, star anise, chiles, if using, and lemon juice and cook, stirring, until the sugar is dissolved. Remove from the heat, cover, and steep for 1 hour.

5. Remove star anise and chipotles, if you used them, from the juice. Stir in the liqueur and bring the syrup to a simmer, then

1 tablespoon fresh lemon juice
1 cup (8 oz., 235 ml)
   maraschino liqueur (substitute
   bourbon for a boozier, less
   sweet flavor)

pour over the cherries, leaving ½-inch headspace. Remove the air bubbles using a bubbler or plastic knife, running it around the inside of the jars and through the fruit; add more syrup, if needed, to achieve the ½-inch headspace. Wipe the rims well with a damp paper towel. Place the lids and rings on the jars and finger-tighten the rings.

6. Process in a boiling-water bath for 25 minutes.

7. Cure the cherries out of direct sunlight for 1 month; this rest removes the saltiness and balances the flavors.

The cherries are shelf stable for 1 year.

Tart cherries, also called pie, or sour, cherries

Many-Berry Pie Filling

MAKES: four 1-quart jars
ACTIVE TIME: 2 hours

Berries are so abundant in the early part of summer that I make tarts and pies and crisps almost daily. I become complacent, thinking they will be around forever, and then suddenly it's all over and the only available berries are sad imposters in the grocery store. Don't let that happen to you. Make this pie filling for the berry-free cold months.

I like the mix of tart, sweet, and tangy that comes from combining different types of berries. Feel free to mix and match berries with abandon, or even make a Single-Berry Pie Filling, if you want, but do not use more than 12 total cups of berries.

Berries range in sweetness, as do our personal preferences. Mix the berries and taste them together. Are they very tart or very sweet? I'm happy with a tart pie and usually opt for just 2 cups of sugar in this recipe, but if you prefer a sweeter pie, use more, up to the whole 3 cups.

The ClearJel or cornstarch will begin to thicken the filling, but don't expect it to be as gelled as it will be once it is cooked in a pie. Instead, pay close attention to the timing, cooking the filling for just 1 minute before filling and processing the jars.

4½ cups (27 oz., 775 g) blackberries

4½ cups (25 oz., 725 g) blueberries

3 cups (18 oz., 750 g) raspberries

1 cup (8 oz., 240ml) water

2 to 3 cups (14 to 21 oz., 400 to 600 g) granulated sugar

⅓ cup (2½ oz., 80 ml) fresh lemon juice

¾ cup (3 oz., 85 g) ClearJel (not instant) or cornstarch

6 tablespoons (3 oz., 90 ml) St-Germain, plum, or orange liqueur (optional)

1. Pick through the berries carefully to remove any stems or leaves. Stir together all the berries in a large bowl.

2. Combine the water, sugar, ClearJel, and lemon juice, in your preserving pot and whisk until smooth. Bring to a boil and add the berries. Stir gently and thoroughly and return the mixture to a rolling boil for precisely 1 minute. Remove from the heat. Add the St-Germaine, if using, and stir well.

3. Ladle into the warm jars, leaving 1-inch headspace. Wipe the rims well with a damp paper towel. Place the lids and rings on the jars and finger-tighten the rings.

4. Process in a boiling-water bath for 30 minutes. Turn off the heat and leave the jars in the canner for 10 minutes to prevent siphoning.

The filling is shelf stable for 1 year.

Thickeners for pie filling

Many thickeners work wonders in a fresh pie but are not appropriate, or safe, for preserving. The best and most effective pie thickener for home-canned pie filling is ClearJel, a modified cornstarch made for industrial use, but it is difficult, to find ClearJel in quantities appropriate for the home cook. It was introduced to the industrial food community about fifty years ago, and there were hopes it would eventually be made available for the home cook, but those hopes have dwindled. Instant ClearJel can be found online at many baking sites, and although it works perfectly for fresh pies, it is not meant for canning.

ClearJel improves the aesthetics of a pie filling—the gel. Cornstarch is a suitable substitute but will not result in the same see-through gel. If you can let go of the need for this transparency and accept that, over time (after 9 to 12 months), the color may fade a bit, the results from cornstarch will be perfectly adequate.

For safety's sake, do not use flour, tapioca, tapioca flour, or anything other than ClearJel or cornstarch to thicken canned pie filling.

Fresh raspberries

Bonus Recipe: Mrs. Wheelbarrow's Perfect Piecrust

MAKES: enough dough for one 9-inch pie or 10-inch tart, or four 3-inch hand pies, or 12 tiny single-crust pies
ACTIVE TIME: 10 minutes
CHILLING TIME: 4½ hours

My mother was a pie maker, though later in life, she preferred to make tarts, carefully arranged fruit decorating the tops, her own jelly glazing the surface. Her crust was always ethereal. Buttery and flaky, but sturdy enough to set an upright piece of pie on the plate and to hold a crimped edge.

I've tried many piecrusts. I've substituted lard or duck fat for some or all of the butter. I've even tried shortening. But my mother's piecrust recipe is the one that I turn to over and over. It suits any filling, sweet or savory, because there is no added salt or sugar. It's easy to roll out, and it freezes beautifully.

No food processor? No problem. Using your fingertips, blend the butter and flour in a wide deep bowl. When the mixture feels sandy and the butter is in pea-sized lumps, add the ice water and blend, using your fingers and the heel of your hand against the side of the bowl, until it all comes together. Turn the dough out onto a countertop and press the mass out with the heel of your hand, pushing away from you. Gather the dough and push away again, then gather the dough together and stop fussing. Form into a disk, even if you think it's not very homogenous, and continue with the recipe.

8 tablespoons (4 oz., 113 g) unsalted butter, cut into ½-inch cubes

1⅓ cups (5.25 oz., 150 g) all-purpose flour

¼ cup (2 oz., 60 ml) ice water

1. Put the butter and flour in the freezer for 30 minutes. Fill a tall glass with ice and then water and put that in the freezer too. You want the water to be very cold.

2. Add the butter and flour to a food processor and pulse about 15 times, until the mixture is sandy and the butter is in pea-sized lumps. Measure out ¼ cup of the very cold water (no ice), add to the processor all at once, and process until the crust comes together in a shaggy mass, about 1 minute.

3. Dump the dough out of the work bowl onto a sheet of plastic wrap or wax paper. Quickly form it into a disk about 6 inches across. Wrap in the plastic or wax paper and refrigerate for at least 4 hours. The dough can be frozen for up to 1 month; defrost overnight in the refrigerator.

OPPOSITE: A Pie Straight from the Pantry (page 134) with Sour Cherry Pie Filling (page 137)

Bonus Recipe: A Pie Straight from the Pantry

MAKES: 1 double-crusted 9-inch pie

ACTIVE TIME: 90 minutes

FREEZING TIME: 1 hour

For years, I left the pies and tarts to my mother. It took most of my thirties to get the hang of making a good crust, and another few years before I would dare to make a pie for her.

At first, I just pressed the crusts together with the tines of a fork. Each pie gave me a chance to practice crimping techniques, learning to make that wave-like edge that holds the filling in the pan. Now, years later, it is entirely second nature.

Making a pretty piecrust can be a little daunting, but a pie always tastes good, even if it is a little, um, rustic. The special pie skills—crimping or fluting, venting, and decorating—come with practice. Keep making pies, and soon you, too, will be known as the pie baker in your family. I say this with confidence. I was fifty-two years old when I won my first blue ribbon (for a sour cherry pie).

- **Double recipe Mrs. Wheelbarrow's Perfect Piecrust (page 133), chilled**
- 1 **quart jar home-canned pie filling (page 130, 137, or 138)**
- 1 **tablespoon (½ oz., 14 g) unsalted butter**
- 2 **tablespoon heavy cream**

1. Place one disk of cold dough on a lightly floured counter. (If it is very hot in your kitchen, chill the counter first with a bag of ice. Dry the counter well before flouring.) Smack the dough with the rolling pin, whacking it three times. Turn one quarter turn and smack it again three times. Roll from the center of the dough out. Flip the disk over, turn it a quarter turn, and roll from the center again. Continue to flip, roll, and turn, lightly dusting with flour as needed, about four times. Then continue without flipping the dough over, just rolling it out from the center to the edges, leaving the edges a little thicker than the center.

2. When the crust is about 13 inches across, roll the crust up around the pin, then unroll it over the pie pan. Gently press the crust into the bottom and up the sides of the pan, letting the overhang drape over the edges of the pan.

3. Pour in the filling and dot the top with the butter. Roll out the remaining crust in the same way. Drape the crust over the filling, trim the edges, and crimp or flute the two crusts together. With a sharp knife, make three 3-inch slits in the top of the pie to vent and allow steam to escape.

4. Brush the top crust, but not the edges, with the cream. Freeze the pie for 1 hour. (This helps keep the bottom crust from getting soggy and makes the crust extra flaky.)

5. Position a rack in the lower third of the oven, slide in a baking sheet on a lower rack to catch drips, and preheat the oven to 425°F.

6. Bake the pie for 20 minutes, then reduce the heat to 350°F and bake for an additional 45 minutes, or until the filling is bubbling. If the crust begins to brown too quickly, cover loosely with foil. Cool the pie on a rack for at least 1 hour before serving.

STEAM VENTS

There are many ways to vent decoratively: Stamp out a 1-inch circle or star or heart shape from the center of the top crust. Or make a lattice top or stamp out stars or hearts or fluted circles from the rolled-out dough with a cookie cutter and arrange them on top of the filling to form a top crust with plenty of room for steam to escape.

Sour Cherry Pie Filling

MAKES: 4 quart jars
ACTIVE TIME: 2 hours

Tart cherries are a weakness of mine. They remind me of my step-father, Bill, whose July 10th birthday falls in the midst of the brief tart cherry season. Every year, instead of birthday cake, Bill would ask for a sour cherry pie. For years, we only enjoyed this pie in season, meaning three or four pies in a two-week period. But now that I preserve this sour cherry pie filling, there is a pie on the Thanksgiving table every year, and another served up for my February birthday, deep in the cold winter months.

In the mood for a crisp, a crumble, a slump, or a Betty? This pie filling works in any of these incarnations.

8 pounds (3.6 kg) tart (sour) cherries weighed before pitting
1 cup (8 oz., 240 ml) water
3 cups (21 oz., 600 g) granulated sugar
⅓ cup (scant 3 oz., 80 ml) fresh lemon juice
¾ cup (3 oz., 85 g) ClearJel (not instant) or cornstarch
2 teaspoons almond extract (optional)

1. Pit the cherries over a bowl to capture all the juices.

2. Whisk together the water, sugar, lemon juice, and ClearJel in an 8-quart heavy preserving pot and bring to a boil, stirring constantly. Add the fruit and juices, bring to a rolling boil, and let boil for exactly 1 minute. Remove from the heat.

3. Funnel the filling into the warm jars leaving 1-inch headspace. Add ½ teaspoon almond extract to each jar, if using. Using a bubbler or plastic knife, remove any air bubbles (which also helps incorporate the extract). Wipe the rims of the jars well with a damp paper towel. Place the lids and rings on the jars and finger-tighten the rings.

4. Process in a boiling-water bath for 30 minutes. Turn off the heat but leave the jars in the canner for 10 minutes to prevent siphoning.

The pie filling is shelf stable for a year.

OPPOSITE: Fresh tart (sour) cherries

Cardamom Peach Pie Filling

MAKES: 4 quart jars

ACTIVE TIME: 2 hours

Eaten out of hand, just picked, while I'm standing in soft, green grass with the sweet, sticky juices running down my arms: that's how I like peaches. The rest of the time, I make pies or crisps. Peaches need to be warm, either from the sun or from the oven.

For this filling, a highly spiced gel is studded with plump pieces of peach. A step away from the usual cinnamon-based peach pie, it is exotic and heady. No time to make a crust? Use the filling for a crisp, or cover it with buttermilk biscuits and bake up a cobbler.

3 tablespoons ascorbic acid, Fruit Fresh, or fresh lemon juice

12 pounds (5.4 kg) freestone peaches

2 teaspoons ground ginger

2 teaspoons ground cinnamon

1 teaspoon ground nutmeg

1 teaspoon cardamom seeds (from 12 to 15 green cardamom pods)

¾ teaspoon ground allspice

¼ teaspoon ground cloves

⅛ teaspoon cracked black pepper

1 cup (8 oz., 240 ml) water

2 cups (14 oz., 400 g) granulated sugar

1 cup (7 oz., 200 g) firmly packed light brown sugar

½ cup (4 oz., 120 ml) fresh lemon juice

¾ cup (3 oz., 85 g) ClearJel (not instant) or cornstarch

2 tablespoons (1 oz.) light rum or bourbon (optional)

1. Bring a 5-quart pot of water to a boil. Fill a large bowl with 8 cups of water and dissolve the ascorbic acid (or Fruit Fresh) in the water, or add the lemon juice (this acidulated water will prevent the peaches from turning brown). Fill another large bowl with ice water.

2. Working in batches, blanch the peaches in the boiling water for 30 to 60 seconds. Scoop the peaches out of the boiling water and transfer to the bowl of ice water. Make an X in the bottom of each cooled peach and peel the skin off in large swaths; if it does not peel easily, leave the next batch in the boiling water a little longer. Cut each peach into 8 slices. Hold the slices in the acidulated water.

3. In your preserving pot, combine all the spices, water, sugars, ClearJel, and lemon juice, and whisk until smooth. Bring to a boil and add the drained peach slices. The mixture will look gloppy—just keep stirring. Bring the mixture to a rolling boil for exactly 1 minute. Add the liquor, if using, stir, and remove from the heat.

4. Funnel into the warm jars, leaving 1-inch headspace. Wipe the rims clean with a damp paper towel. Place the lids and rings on the jars and finger-tighten the rings.

5. Process in a boiling-water bath for 30 minutes. Leave the jars in the canner for 10 minutes after processing to prevent siphoning.

The pie filling is shelf stable for 1 year.

Peaches in Ginger Syrup

MAKES: 5 quart or 10 pint jars

ACTIVE TIME: 2 hours

STEEPING TIME: 1 hour

When I was growing up, my great-grandmother had jars of canned peaches lining the shelves of her basement. The peaches were pickled or brandied.

Now I've come to understand the sense of loss when peach season ends, the realization there will be no more truly wonderful peaches for another year, and I, too, wish for jars of peaches on the shelf. But while pickled or brandied peaches were all the rage in the 1960s, I want fresh-tasting peach halves or slices for my morning yogurt (page 376) or to pair with cottage cheese (page 391).

To keep the peaches firm and flavorful, this raw-pack method is best. Raw-packing may result in "fruit float": all the peaches gathered at the top of the jar. Fruit float will not affect the flavor in any way, but it can be somewhat reduced if you pack the jars extra tight and get all the air bubbles out.

2½ cups (17.5 oz., 625 g) granulated sugar

6 cups (48 oz., 1.5 l) water

• 3-inch knob (about 3 oz., 85 g) fresh ginger, peeled and sliced into coins

3 tablespoons ascorbic acid, Fruit Fresh, or fresh lemon juice

10 pounds (4.5 kg) perfect freestone peaches

1. Combine the sugar, water, and ginger in a saucepan and bring to a boil, then reduce to a simmer and stir until the sugar has dissolved. Remove the syrup from the heat and let steep for 1 hour.

2. Bring a large pot of water to a boil. Prepare a large bowl of ice water. Fill another bowl with 8 cups water and dissolve the ascorbic acid in the water. Blanch and peel the peaches (as described on page 138, Step 2). Halve and pit the peaches; cut into slices, if desired.

3. Remove the ginger coins and reheat the syrup to a simmer.

4. Pack the peaches into the warm jars—pack tightly, without bruising; you can nestle the peaches together like spoons. The packing is the hardest part of this recipe. After processing, the fruit will probably float to the surface, so get as many peaches as possible into your jars. (While it will be tempting to use wide-mouth jars, the shoulders of a regular jar help hold the peaches down in the syrup.)

Recipe continues

5. Pour the hot syrup over the fruit, leaving ½-inch headspace. Using a bubbler or plastic knife, remove the air bubbles, then check the headspace again and add more syrup if necessary. Wipe the rims of the jars clean with a damp paper towel. Place the lids and rings on the jars and finger-tighten the rings.

6. Process in a boiling-water bath for 25 minutes. Leave the jars in the canner for 10 minutes after processing to prevent siphoning.

The peaches are shelf stable for 1 year.

WASTE NOT, WANT NOT

Combine the peach pits in a quart jar and cover with cider vinegar or white vinegar. Let sit, covered, in a dark place, for about a month. Strain through cheesecloth and enjoy peach-flavored vinegar in light salad dressings or as a splash on roasted vegetables. This works with plum, apricot, cherry, and other stone fruit pits too.

VARIATIONS

Any fruit is lovely preserved in sweet syrup, but some are just prettier—and more useful.

- Although plums have a short (six-month) shelf life, they are simply marvelous warmed and served over ice cream.
- Apricots sing in a vanilla syrup (substitute 1 vanilla bean, split and scraped, for the ginger) and can be plucked from the jar and arranged in a baked tart shell slathered with pastry cream.
- Pears in syrup (made with 2 star anise instead of the ginger), especially tiny Seckle pears, are fantastic in a twist on *tarte Tatin*.

Bonus Recipe: Gingery Peach Daiquiri

SERVES: 2

ACTIVE TIME: 5 minutes

The daiquiri falls into the category of cocktails consumed in the warmer months, with ocean breezes and sand between the toes. The gingery syrup from home-canned peaches is a superb start to this classic cocktail.

Serve this cocktail over ice in an appropriately festive glass, or frozen (instead of combining the ingredients in a cocktail shaker, puree in a blender with 1 cup of ice), and abandon tradition. Bring summer memories flooding back in January.

6 tablespoons (3 oz., 90 ml) light rum

3 tablespoons fresh lime juice

¼ cup (2 oz., 60 ml) syrup from Peaches in Ginger Syrup (page 139)

1. Pour all the ingredients over ice in a cocktail shaker and shake until the shaker is thoroughly frosted.

2. Strain into stemmed glasses. Yes, that's all there is to it.

Heat-and-Sweet Habanero Jelly

MAKES: six 4-ounce jars
ACTIVE TIME: 1 hour

Pepper jelly is a beautiful gift and a quick-to-the-table cracker topper with cream cheese or chèvre. This is no ordinary pepper jelly, this is crowd-pleaser jelly. It has a little of everything: sweet, tart, and, hello, spicy!

Most pepper jellies are made with jalapeños, but I like to go for incendiary habaneros, tempered with sweet, tart dried apricots. Pick the prettiest, brightest peppers for the most attractive final product. Avoid green at all costs as they turn mud colored.

I hope you have a food processor. This jelly can be made without one, but the fine mincing necessary takes a sharp knife, intense focus, protective gloves, and time.

Check the set well before putting this jelly in the jars. It can be tricky (chile peppers have almost no pectin), but success is certain if you wait until the pepper pieces stop floating on the surface and disperse throughout the amber gel.

2½ cups (17.5 oz., 500 g) granulated sugar

¼ cup (3 oz., 85 g) wildflower honey

¾ cup (6 oz., 175 ml) cider vinegar

• Juice of 1 lemon

¼ cup (1.5 oz., 40 g) finely minced habanero or Scotch Bonnet peppers

½ cup (3 oz., 85 g) finely minced sweet red pepper

½ cup (3 oz., 85 g) finely minced red onion

½ cup (4 oz., 110 g) finely minced dried apricots (about 12)

½ teaspoon unsalted butter (optional)

1. Combine the sugar, honey, vinegar, and lemon juice in your preserving pot, clip a candy thermometer to it, and bring to a strong boil, stirring to dissolve the sugar. Add the hot and sweet peppers, onions, and apricots and bring to a boil that will not stir down, 220°F, and hold at that heat. When the foam has nearly cleared, after about 10 minutes, remove from the heat and let the jelly cool for 2 minutes.

2. Check the set, using the wrinkle test or sheeting test. If the jelly has not yet set to your satisfaction, turn the heat on again for 2 or 3 minutes, then turn it off and test again. Repeat as necessary. Stir in the butter, if using, to disperse any last bits of foam and polish the jelly.

3. Ladle into the warm jars, leaving ½-inch headspace. Wipe the rims clean with a damp paper towel. Place the lids and rings on the jars and finger-tighten the rings.

4. Process in a boiling-water bath for 10 minutes.

The jelly is shelf stable for 1 year. Turn the jars over from time to time during the first week to distribute the pieces of pepper as the jelly firms up.

Grape Jelly

MAKES: 4 or 5 half-pint jars
ACTIVE TIME: 1½ hours
JUICING TIME: 2 hours

Grape jelly is one of the lost pleasures of childhood—it was satisfying like no other jelly. And then we expanded our palates and left grape jelly in the dust. Embrace it again.

Late-season wine grapes, like Concord, Ontario, and muscadet, have thicker skins and seedy interiors that plop out of the skin. Do not make this with Thompson or other seedless grapes, as the seeds are essential for their pectin. If you come across very fresh Champagne grapes, make this jelly immediately.

Grape jelly is a versatile pantry item. Pair it with pâté or duck liver mousse. Substitute for the currant jelly in the Chicken Breasts with Currant Jelly Sauce (page 123). Or make a peanut butter and grape jelly sandwich on white bread, slice the crusts off, cut into triangles, and remember kindergarten.

3 pounds (1350 g) wine grapes, plucked from the stems (see page 148, Step 1)

4 cups (28 oz., 800 g) granulated sugar

• Juice of 1 lemon

1. Put the grapes in an 8-quart nonreactive pot and lightly crush with a potato masher. Barely cover with cold water, bring to a brisk boil, and boil hard for 5 minutes.

2. Ladle the boiled grapes into a jelly bag or cheesecloth-lined colander set over a catch bowl. Let drip for 2 hours. Do not press or squeeze, or the jelly will be cloudy. You need 4 cups juice for the recipe. Put any extra juice in the refrigerator, then enjoy, just as it is, or top off with sparkling water or Champagne. It's divine.

3. Combine the 4 cups of juice, the sugar, and the lemon juice in a nonreactive preserving pot, clip on a candy thermometer, and bring to a boil that will not stir down. The jelly will threaten to rise up and out of the pot. Stir and be brave, and keep the heat on high until the foam clears, about 10 minutes; the temperature will reach 220°F. Remove from the heat and evaluate the set, using the wrinkle test or sheeting test.

4. Ladle into the warm jars, leaving ½-inch headspace. Wipe the rims clean with a damp paper towel. Place the lids and rings on the jars and finger-tighten the rings.

5. Process in a boiling-water bath for 10 minutes.

The jelly is shelf stable for 1 year.

Bonus Recipe: Crispy Buttermilk-Brined Chicken Livers on Toast

SERVES: 1

ACTIVE TIME: 30 minutes

BRINING TIME: 1 to 3 hours

This is a favorite dinner when I'm all alone. It's indulgent and rich, so I keep the portion small and savor every bite.

3 **plump chicken livers, rinsed and trimmed of fatty bits**

½ **cup (4 oz., 125 ml) buttermilk, homemade (page 369) or store-bought**

1 **teaspoon to 1 tablespoon Hot Sauce (page 175), Tabasco, or Sriracha (optional)**

¼ **cup (1 oz., 28 g) all-purpose flour**

½ **teaspoon cornstarch**

• **Kosher salt and freshly ground black pepper**

• **Grapeseed or canola oil for deep-frying**

1 **thick slice brioche, toasted**

2 **tablespoons Grape Jelly (page 143)**

½ **teaspoon fresh chives, minced**

• **Maldon or other large-crystal sea salt**

1. In a small bowl, combine the livers and buttermilk, then add hot sauce according to your preference for heat. I like them spicy so go for the full tablespoon. Cover and brine in the refrigerator for at least 1 hour, or as long as 3 hours.

2. Combine the flour and cornstarch on a plate. Generously salt and pepper the flour and stir together. Pluck the livers from the buttermilk brine and coat well in the flour mixture. Shake to remove excess flour and place the dredged livers on a clean plate.

3. Heat 1 inch of oil to 375°F in a small straight-sided sauté pan or cast-iron skillet. Fry the livers in the hot oil, turning to brown well on all sides, about 6 to 8 minutes. They should still be pale pink when cut open. Drain on paper towels.

4. Pick your prettiest small plate and place the toasted brioche on it. Spread the jelly over the bread. Top with the livers, garnish with the chives, and sprinkle with coarse salt. Serve piping hot.

OPPOSITE: Crispy Buttermilk-Brined Chicken Livers on Toast

Home-canned juice

Any fruit will make juice, but for my pantry, and speaking practically, grape, apple, and cranberry, and combinations of the three, are all the fruit juices I need. Juicing is a great way to deal with imperfect, slightly overripe, bruised, or windfall fruit. It may seem like a lot of fruit, but work in 10-pound batches so you'll get at least one gallon of juice. Otherwise, you'll be wondering if all that mess was worth it. If you have children, this is the juice you want to feed them. No sugar, nothing but fruit and water.

Steam juice extractors

A steam juice extractor is a clever, albeit pricey, piece of preserving equipment. After splattering the kitchen with grape juice for a few years, I invested in one and couldn't be happier. (Dennis loves grape juice more than anything else I can, so I had to do it.) This three-tiered wonder holds about ten pounds of fruit in the perforated top basket. The second tier, shaped like a donut with a funnel in the center, captures the juice that drips through the perforations. The lower tier holds water, which is held at a simmer, so steam is forced up through the funnel to heat the fruit.

It is efficient, tidy, and makes delicious, crystal-clear juice. While I had hoped the steam juice extractor would provide juice that could then be transformed to jelly, the process removes the pectin.

TOP: Boiled grapes
BOTTOM: Grape juice dripping through a jelly bag

OPPOSITE: Smashing grapes for jelly or juice

Grape Juice

MAKES: twelve 12-ounce jars or 4 quart jars, or any combination of sizes to total 1 gallon
ACTIVE TIME: 2 hours over 2 days
JUICING TIME: 3 periods of 1 to 6 hours, 2 hours, and overnight

Wine grapes, the ones with seedy centers that pop right out of the thick skin when squeezed, make delicious juice. This is the flavor we think of when we think of grape soda or grape-flavored hard candy. Make grape juice if only for the opportunity to smell it cooking. Make jelly from the juice (see page 143), if you wish, or just preserve the juice.

- 10 **pounds, 4.5 kg wine grapes**
- • **About 10 cups (2.37 l) filtered water**

1. Stem the grapes: Either do this by hand while watching the U.S. Open, and get your husband or kids or friends to help, or pop them, stems and all, into the bowl of a stand mixer fitted with the paddle attachment. Turn the mixer on low and watch the grapes release from the stems.

2. As each batch of grapes is stemmed, transfer the fruit to a deep 8-quart or larger nonreactive pot. Once a quart of grapes is in the pot, crush with a potato masher or the back of a broad spoon. Continue to add the grapes by the quart and crush them well.

3. Add enough filtered water to cover the grapes by 1 inch. Bring to a rolling boil and boil for 5 minutes. Turn off the heat and let the boiled grapes sit for 1 hour to develop a rich color and flavor. If using green wine grapes, let sit even longer, up to 6 hours, to develop a deeper color; some wine grapes make pale juice, but color does not determine flavor.

4. Ladle the boiled grapes into a jelly bag or a cheesecloth-lined colander set over a catch bowl. Let the juice drip for 2 hours. Resist the urge to squeeze the bag—it will make the juice cloudy. Cover the strained juice and place in the refrigerator overnight to settle the sediment.

5. The next day, carefully pour the juice into a deep 5-quart or larger pot, leaving as much of the sediment as possible behind. Or "polish" the juice by straining it through a coffee filter. Polishing reduces the yield, but if you do not polish, the jars may have a little sediment at the bottom. This is one of those State Fair questions—aesthetics are the only thing at risk. Bring the juice up to a full rolling boil and boil for 5 minutes.

6. Ladle into the warm jars, leaving ¼-inch headspace. Place the lids and rings on the jars and finger-tighten the rings.

7. Process in a boiling-water bath for 10 minutes.

The juice is shelf stable for 1 year.

VARIATION
- Apple juice, cranberry juice, apple-cranberry, apple-grape, and every other combination are made using the same method. Use a total of 10 pounds of fruit and proceed.

Fresh wine grapes

TOMATOES, SALSA, KETCHUP, PEPPERS, AND HOT SAUCE

These are my workhorse recipes, the very epitome of practicality, the foods I use almost every day. Foods that inspire a menu or save the day when everyone's hungry and there's nothing to eat but a few eggs (see Eggs and Tomatoes Make Friends, page 160). They are the jars that fancy up a simple salad (Marinated Roasted Red Peppers, page 171), and make the most of a sandwich (Tomato Chutney, page 167). These recipes represent the essence of self-sufficiency.

And they all start with tomatoes.

Deciding to can tomatoes is a no-brainer for most canners: this is the food that feeds a family for months to come. No jam or pickle has the same versatility. Before starting, understand that the recipes are bound by rules that must not be ignored.

Select ripe or slightly underripe tomatoes and cut away any bruised or black spots. Do not can overripe or bruised tomatoes. While any tomato can be canned, some work better than others. The Rutgers varieties were developed specifically for canning, and all their genetic offspring are terrific. Look for Brandywines, Beefsteaks, and all the Reds—Jersey Reds and Ramapos, sometimes called Big Reds or field tomatoes.

All paste, plum, and Roma tomatoes work especially well for canning. Romas hold up to the rigors of canning, the heat and long processing, retaining a very rich flavor. Avoid yellow, green, or maroon tomatoes; their colors do not translate well to sauce. Do look, always, for the seconds or not-quite-perfect tomatoes on sale at many farmers' markets and spend a little extra time cutting away the bad parts while patting yourself on the back for saving some money.

Tomato skins and seeds can bring bitterness and an unpleasant aftertaste to canned tomatoes. But the seeds are slippery and small and entirely-seed-free jars are nearly impossible without a Squeezo (see Equipment, page 155), so give yourself a break. There will be some seeds.

There are really only two options when faced with a mountain of red tomatoes: Blanch them (see page 158) to remove the skins. Or force slightly cooked tomatoes through a food mill. The former requires vats of boiling water. The latter requires elbow grease. A lot of elbow grease. The former gives you crushed tomatoes, infinitely useful, and, if I were to can only one tomato product, crushed tomatoes would be my choice. But, yet another example of the practical pantry, the puree can stand in for vegetable stock in soup and cooks down to ethereal pasta sauces, and it brings the taste of summer even in winter, when hope-filled gardeners are just selecting tomato varieties from seed catalogs.

A third canned tomato option, a roasted puree, requires no blanching and uses a blender instead of a food mill, but it requires a hot oven on what is likely to be a blistering summer day. For this lovely sauce, cooking the skins and reducing the liquid avoids any bitterness. It is a very useful sauce, smoky, rich, and sweet. It's impossible to resist when smeared on toasts for quick crostini.

While it may be tempting to jazz up these recipes and put your family's famous pasta sauce in the jar, please don't. The addition of peppers, onions, garlic, mushrooms, meat, carrots, celery, and/or oil will affect the acidity and balance, potentially filling that jar with a sauce teeming with botulinum spores. Process crushed or pureed tomatoes and make the pasta sauce later, just as you would with canned tomato products from the store.

When choosing a tomato canning recipe, I make them all, rotating through the recipes each weekend for as long as the fruits are on the vine. And then I rotate through the jars, allowing their remarkable contents to inspire a meal.

OPPOSITE: Roasted plum tomatoes

Tomatoes and acidity

Tomatoes vary widely in acidity—which refers not to the flavor, but to the pH (the measure of alkaline or acid in a substance; see page 38). Some heirloom tomato varieties, especially, have very low acidity and very high water content, making them better for salad or sandwiches than canning. Ensuring that each jar has a consistent pH level is critical to safe tomato canning. You can manage pH levels by adding lemon juice or citric acid. Choose juice from the classic Eureka lemon (found in any supermarket), and do not substitute Meyer lemons or any other citrus, as they will not have the same acidifying effect. But my choice is citric acid, as it adds a milder flavor to the final product, is less expensive than fresh lemons, and is very reliable. Citric acid is found in the canning section of the grocery store or hardware store, or online (see Resources, page 401).

Pureeing tomatoes in a food mill (see page 161)

Equipment

Tomato canning requires no special equipment, but is easier with a few key pieces, because putting tomatoes in jars is one of a handful of canning projects worth doing in very large batches. Not just a little larger, but really large. Think of it in terms of 25 or 50 pounds at a time, dividing the tomatoes among a few recipes. It will be a long day, but it will be worth it. Or gather friends and family and get 100 pounds. Share the labor and split the proceeds—about 25 quarts of lovely farm-fresh tomatoes. Once you've committed to the process, and with many people helping, the volume just doesn't matter that much.

It's very handy to have a **10-quart or larger stainless steel pot with lid**. I found mine at a discount kitchen store. It is a multitalented pot—it serves as my canner for smaller batches of jams and jellies (with a cake rack accommodating up to seven half-pint jars). It's also a convenient size for making large batches of stock (page 229) and soup (page 237). I use it to sanitize cheese-making tools and, really, for about a hundred other tasks in the kitchen. If you do not have a 10-quart or larger pot, divide the large recipe among several pots. Both stainless steel and enameled cast-iron are nonreactive. Aluminum is reactive, meaning it will turn the tomatoes a dark color and will leach a metallic taste into your tomatoes. Never use aluminum cookware for tomatoes or other highly acidic mixtures (like chutneys and pickles).

A **food mill** is a versatile and especially useful kitchen tool. It may be bulky and inconvenient to store, but it is essential for pureeing tomatoes, as well as seeding berries for jams and jellies. The best food mills come with an assortment of disks for fine, medium, and coarse purees. If you don't have a food mill, use a sturdy sieve or colander and press against the solids to achieve a smooth consistency in the resulting puree. A China cap, or *chinois*, will also suffice, but using one is a lot of work. The goal is to remove skin and seeds, so if you have none of these tools, make crushed tomatoes instead of a puree. Crushed tomatoes require only two hands, a sharp knife, and a vat of boiling water.

The roasted tomato puree calls for a **blender**, and I recommend one with a strong motor and sharp blade. I have an ancient Oster with only two speeds—fast and faster—and it works like a charm.

If you have a stand mixer, KitchenAid makes a **grinding attachment** with an assortment of milling disks. The attachment functions like a hand-cranked food mill, using the power of the mixer to drive the effort. I have used this attachment with great success, and when I'm facing down one hundred pounds of fresh tomatoes, it works like a charm, fast and efficient. Most of the time, though, I just think of the hand-cranked food mill as a good workout, and I try to remember to use both arms equally.

Veteran canners extoll the virtues of the magical **Squeezo**, a sturdy metal mill that's been around for nearly a century. The Squeezo clamps onto a countertop or table with a large C-clamp (it's clear that this is machinery). Tomatoes are fed into the hopper and pour out of one spout as a smooth puree, while the seeds and skins are spit out a second spout into a waiting bowl. Although pricey, it is superfast, and if you plan to process more than two hundred pounds of tomatoes a summer, well worth the investment.

Crushed Tomatoes

MAKES: 6 to 7 quart jars or 12 to 14 pint jars, or a combination of sizes
ACTIVE TIME: 2 hours

This is the beginner's canned tomato recipe, requiring no special equipment to make. I process more crushed tomatoes than any other product in this section of the book. It's the most useful and the most versatile, and it's relatively quick to make. One quart of home-canned tomatoes substitutes for a can of grocery store tomatoes in any recipe. If you are wondering how many quarts of crushed tomatoes you will need, keep track of how many cans of tomatoes you lug home in a month and multiply by twelve. We go through at least 40 quarts a year.

See photograph on page 33.

25 **pounds (11.3 kg) ripe but firm red tomatoes (about 30 to 45, depending on size)**
- **About 4 teaspoons citric acid or 1 cup (8 oz., 240 ml) fresh lemon juice**
- **Kosher, pickling, or fine sea salt (optional)**

1. Blanch, core, and peel the tomatoes (see page 158). Halve them and scoop out the seeds and gel with your fingers, then crush and tear the tomatoes using your hands, letting the crushed fruit fall into a 4-cup measure. (You can capture the seeds and gel in another bowl for tomato water; see box, page 157.)

2. When you have 1 quart of tomatoes in the measuring cup, add them to an 8-quart or larger nonreactive pot, bring to a boil, and crush with a potato masher to generate some juices. Continue to add the crushed tomatoes 1 quart at a time, mashing and heating to a boil. When they are all added, bring the entire batch to a brisk boil and boil for 5 minutes.

3. All this mashing and scooping is useful for two reasons: First, the tomatoes will be less likely to separate from the liquid in the jar (only an aesthetic concern) and second, keeping count of the quarts that go into the pot helps plan for the number of jars needed.

4. Ladle the hot tomatoes into the warm jars, leaving about an inch headspace. Add ½ teaspoon citric acid (or 2 tablespoons lemon juice) to each quart jar, or ¼ teaspoon (or 1 tablespoon lemon juice) to each pint jar. If using salt, add it now: 1 teaspoon per quart jar, ½ teaspoon per pint jar. Check the headspace, you want ½ inch, so add more tomatoes if necessary. Clean the rims with a damp paper towel. Place the lids and rings on the jars, and finger-tighten the rings.

5. Process in a boiling-water bath for 45 minutes if using quart jars, 35 minutes if using pint jars. A mixed batch should be processed for the full 45 minutes.

6. Let the jars rest in the canning kettle for 10 minutes after processing to prevent siphoning.

Crushed tomatoes are shelf stable for 1 year.

WASTE NOT, WANT NOT

There's another treasure lurking in the scooped-out tomato gel and seeds: Press the seeds and solids through a not-too-fine mesh strainer to discover the fresh flavor of tomato water. Use it to make a tomato martini. Or a vegetable broth for a summer soup. Cook rice in it. Substitute tomato water for the liquid in bread baking. Chill it and sip it over ice with a basil leaf garnish. Make a savory smoothie with plain yogurt (page 376), spinach, and a pinch of curry powder. Reduce it to a syrup and add an equal measure of honey, then brush on fish or chicken or in sandwiches. Whatever you do, don't waste it.

The tomato peels have plenty of flavor, too. Place them in a single layer on a parchment-lined baking sheet and slowly dry in a very low oven (175° to 200°F) for 2 hours. Blitz the dry peels in a spice grinder or blender and store the powder in a sealed glass jar. Sprinkle liberally on salads or on eggs. Put a generous pinch in any pan sauce, or add to labneh for a savory complement to hummus and pita. You'll find plenty of reasons to add a touch of tomato.

Peeling tomatoes

1. To blanch and peel tomatoes, bring a large pot of water to a boil. Slice an X through just the skin at the bottom of each tomato. Drop a few tomatoes at a time into the boiling water for 30 to 60 seconds (depending on the size of the tomato).

   Let the water return to a steady simmer between batches. Do not overfill the pot, just blanch a few tomatoes at a time.

2. The tomatoes will float to the surface at about the same time the peel has loosened. When the tomato bobs to the surface, lift it out with a perforated skimmer and drop it into a bowl of ice water to stop the cooking and cool. When working with a very large batch, hold the blanched tomatoes in an ice-filled cooler.

3. Core and then peel the tomatoes from the cut X, removing the skin in large pieces. If it does not remove easily, blanch the next batches for slightly longer. Dunk a few tomatoes, then peel a few, then dunk a few, and so on.

By the way, use the same method to peel peaches for Cardamom Peach Pie Filling (page 138) and Peaches in Ginger Syrup (page 139).

4. Halve the tomatoes and scoop out the seeds and gel for a denser, more robust jar of tomatoes. There is no need to be obsessive about the seeds, but do try to get most of them out. Too many and your tomatoes may be bitter. Only a few? No problem. Just remove as many as you can.

Put the tomato flesh in a large bowl as you go. Then go ahead and crush the tomatoes. Get in there and smush them with your hands and tear the flesh apart, mixing the flesh with the juices. The more work you do here to combine the textures, the less likely your tomatoes will separate in the jar, with the liquid rising to the top.

Bonus Recipe: Eggs and Tomatoes Make Friends

SERVES: 4 as a light supper or brunch
ACTIVE TIME: 30 minutes

Eggs and tomatoes are best friends, and that will become apparent as soon as you taste eggs poached in tomato sauce. The idea shows up in several cuisines. The Italian-American favorite eggs in purgatory is one example, and the classic Middle Eastern dish shakshuka is another.

This is a dinner that appears when I am plumb out of ideas, have no energy, or have an excellent loaf of bread that demands a sauce for sopping. With a jar of tomatoes, a jar of peppers, and a carton of eggs, dinner is on the table in a flash, and those gathered at the table quiet into that special silence that comes from a particularly satisfying meal.

2	tablespoons mild olive oil
1	medium onion (4 oz., 110 g), diced
2	garlic cloves, slivered
1	quart jar Crushed Tomatoes (page 156)
1	teaspoon kosher salt
½	teaspoon dried oregano
½	teaspoon red pepper flakes
3	Marinated Roasted Red Peppers (page 171), drained and cut into slivers
8	large fresh eggs
¼	cup (0.75 oz., 20 g) fresh flat-leaf parsley, chopped
•	Freshly grated Pecorino cheese for serving

1. In a 12-inch cast-iron or other heavy skillet, heat the olive oil over medium heat. Add the onion and cook for 6 or 7 minutes until translucent. Add the garlic and cook for 1 minute, then add the tomatoes, salt, oregano, and red pepper flakes and bring to a simmer. Lower the heat and cook until the sauce is slightly thickened, about 10 minutes.

2. Stir the roasted peppers into the tomato sauce. Make a small well in the sauce and carefully crack in an egg. Keeping the eggs apart, continue making wells and adding the remaining eggs and cook for about 5 minutes for a runny yolk. Cook longer if you like a firmer egg, spooning the sauce over the eggs.

3. Scatter with the parsley and shower with a substantial amount of grated cheese. Spoon out the eggs and sauce into warm shallow bowls. Serve with a salad, a loaf of crusty bread, and a gutsy red wine.

Tomato Puree

MAKES: 6 quart jars or 11 to 12 pint jars, or a combination of sizes
ACTIVE TIME: 2 hours

When canning tomatoes as a puree, I prefer a thinner one, as I frequently use it for braises, sauces, and stews. If I want a thicker texture, I reduce the puree after I open the jar. I use this puree for pasta and pizza sauce, in chana masala and cioppino, and as a fresh-tasting base for vegetarian minestrone.

See photograph on page 33.

25 **pounds (11.3 kg) ripe but firm red tomatoes (about 30 to 45)**
• **About 4 teaspoons citric acid or 1 cup (240 ml) fresh lemon juice**
• **Kosher, pickling, or fine sea salt (optional)**

1. Core and chop the tomatoes. Once you have 4 cups of tomatoes, add them to an 8-quart or larger nonreactive pot, crush with a potato masher, and bring to a sturdy boil. Continue to add the tomatoes by the quart, mashing each addition and bringing to a boil before adding more. When all tomatoes have been added to the pot, reduce the heat, cover, and simmer for 10 minutes.

2. Set a food mill fitted with a medium disk over another pot (or empty the tomatoes into a large bowl and use the same pot) and force the tomatoes through the mill to remove the skin and as many seeds as possible. Bring the puree to a sturdy simmer and cook, uncovered, stirring frequently, to reduce by one-third, about 30 minutes. Look for the consistency of heavy cream. If you'd like a thicker puree, simmer for as much as 1 hour longer.

3. Ladle the hot tomato puree into the warm jars, leaving room for the lemon juice or citric acid. Add ½ teaspoon citric acid (or 2 tablespoons lemon juice) to each quart jar, or ¼ teaspoon citric acid (or 1 tablespoon lemon juice to each pint jar. If using salt, add 1 teaspoon to each quart jar, or ½ teaspoon to each pint jar. Review the headspace, you want ½ inch, so add more puree if necessary. Clean the rims with a damp paper towel. Place the lids and rings on the jars and finger-tighten the rings.

4. Process in a boiling-water bath for 45 minutes if using quart jars, 35 minutes if using pint jars. A mixed batch should be processed for 45 minutes. Let the jars rest in the canner for 10 minutes after processing to prevent siphoning.

The tomato puree is shelf stable for 1 year.

Roasted Tomato Puree

MAKES: 9 pint jars
ACTIVE TIME: 3 hours

A *passata* is a tomato puree, "passed" through a food mill or sieve—not unlike the previous recipe, but in this version, the tomatoes are roasted first to concentrate and deepen the flavor. Use this passata to make sauces, spread it on bruschetta, or toss it with pasta.

See additional photographs on page 33.

25 pounds (11.3 kg) ripe but firm red paste or Roma tomatoes
• Kosher salt
• About 2½ teaspoons citric acid or ½ cup (120 ml) fresh lemon juice

1. Position the racks in the top, middle, and bottom of the oven and preheat the oven to 325°F. Line three baking sheets with foil. (Work in batches if your oven will not accommodate three baking sheets.)

2. Cut away the cores and any bruised or discolored spots from the tomatoes, then cut lengthwise in half. Arrange the tomatoes on the baking sheets, cut side up, in one layer, and salt liberally. Slide the pans into the oven and bake for 2 hours, rotating the pans from back to front and from top to bottom every 30 minutes to ensure even cooking. Look for the tomatoes to soften, but do not let them blacken. Cool the tomatoes briefly.

3. In batches, transfer the tomatoes to a blender and puree until smooth. Alternatively, use a food mill to puree the tomatoes.

4. In a 5-quart or larger nonreactive pot, bring the tomato puree to a boil and cook for 5 minutes. The passata will be thick and the flavor will be rich.

5. Ladle into the hot jars, leaving about 1-inch headspace. Add ¼ teaspoon citric acid (or 1 tablespoon lemon juice) to each jar, and check the headspace; you want ½ inch, so add more puree if necessary. Clean the rims of the jars with a damp paper towel. Place the lids and rings on the jars and finger-tighten the rings.

6. Process in a boiling-water bath for 35 minutes. Leave the jars in the canner for 10 minutes after processing to prevent siphoning.

The sauce is shelf stable for 1 year.

OPPOSITE: Pureeing tomatoes in a blender

Garden in a Glass: Spicy Tomato-Vegetable Juice

MAKES: 6 pint jars
ACTIVE TIME: 2 hours

A few years ago, I kept a horse way out in Virginia, about an hour from DC, and made the long drive at every opportunity for the chance to ride. Each weekend in August, on the road to the barn, a charming elderly Virginian set up a small stand by the road. He sat there happily under an umbrella, waiting for people to stop. There was a hand-lettered sign declaring "Real Good Tomato Juice." The juice became an obsession of mine, and every week I would buy a couple of jars. As I handed over a few dollars, he'd say, "When you open this jar, you will hear a little voice telling you it wants to be a Bloody Mary." And we would laugh a little. But we both knew he was right.

It was a sprightly, bright tomato juice. Nothing like the juice in cans that often carries a faint metallic tang. It was full of vegetable flavors, with chiles and green flecks of spinach. I would drink it right from the jar as I drove home.

As I should have anticipated, one year there was a House for Sale sign. I thought about that lovely man and his juice and how very proud he was of this delicious concoction, and I decided there was nothing to do but try to re-create it. Be forewarned, this juice is eye-opening: I add two jalapeños, with all the seeds. Start with a less chile heat, and bump it up according to your own taste. Serve icy cold, with or without vodka.

7 pounds (3.2 kg) ripe red tomatoes
12 ounces (325 g) sweet red peppers, cored, seeded, and roughly chopped
¼ cup (1.25 oz., 33 g) roughly chopped onion
½ cup (4 oz., 110 g) roughly chopped carrot
5 stalks Swiss chard or kale (4 oz., 110 g) or 2 cups (4 oz., 110 g) spinach leaves, rinsed very well and roughly chopped
1 to 2 jalapeños, seeded, seeds reserved (optional)

1. Core and roughly chop the tomatoes. Once you have 4 cups of tomatoes, add to an 8-quart or larger nonreactive pot, crush with a potato masher, and bring to a brisk boil. Continue to add the tomatoes to the pot 1 quart at a time, mashing each addition and bringing to a boil. This step keeps the juice from separating in the jar, but if the juice separates anyway, just shake before serving. There's nothing wrong with it. When all the tomatoes have been added, reduce to a simmer.

2. Add the chopped red pepper, onion, carrot, chard, and jalapeños (not the seeds) to a food processor (or a sturdy blender) and puree thoroughly to ensure there are no chunky bits remaining. Add the puree to the pot and bring the mixture to a boil, stirring well. Reduce the heat and simmer for 15 minutes. Taste and correct for spiciness, adding some of the reserved jalapeño seeds if you want to increase the heat, then continue cooking at a slow simmer for 30 more minutes to combine the flavors.

2 tablespoons finely chopped fresh cilantro or flat-leaf parsley

2 teaspoons celery seeds

• About 1½ teaspoons citric acid or ¾ cup (180 ml) fresh lemon juice

• Kosher or pickling salt

3. Set a food mill fitted with the smallest disk over a 5-quart non-reactive pot. Pass the tomatoes through the mill to remove the skin and seeds. Add the cilantro and celery seeds, then place the pot over medium-high heat and bring to a boil.

4. Ladle the hot juice into the warm jars. Add ¼ teaspoon citric acid (or 2 tablespoons lemon juice) and ½ teaspoon salt to each jar. (You can omit the salt, but I think it adds perkiness to the final product.) Clean the rims of the jars with a damp paper towel. Place the lids and rings on the jars and finger-tighten the rings.

5. Process in a boiling-water bath for 35 minutes.

The juice is shelf stable for 1 year.

VARIATION

• For simple tomato juice, omit the other vegetables. The yield will be reduced to 4½ pints. The processing time remains the same.

Tomato Nectarine Salsa

MAKES: 5 half-pint jars
ACTIVE TIME: 90 minutes

Every year in late summer, count on a food writer to remind us the tomato is a fruit, not a vegetable. And because tomatoes are a fruit, their sweet tones blend with peaches, plums, and nectarines beautifully. This salsa keeps those sunny flavors going all year. Piquant and vegetal, chunky and textural, it's perfect on poultry, pork, or fish and exceptional when paired with guacamole.

Tomato salsa is a tricky product. Adding peppers to tomatoes raises the pH (lowers the acidity) and so the salsa requires significant added acid to be safe. This can also change the flavor significantly: expect vinegar to be the first discernible flavor. To truly be safe, most tomato salsas should be pressure-canned. In this recipe, however, the fruit increases the acidity, and the end result is safe salsa processed in a water-bath canner.

2 pounds (900 g) ripe tomatoes (see Peeling Tomatoes, page 158), cored and cut into ½-inch dice

2 pounds (900 g) slightly unripe nectarines, pitted and cut into ½-inch dice (3 cups)

¼ cup (2 oz., 60 g) finely chopped red onion

1 to 2 serrano peppers, seeds and ribs removed or left intact, according to your taste for heat, finely chopped

1 cup (4 oz., 110 g) finely chopped sweet red pepper

¼ cup (0.5 oz., 16 g) chopped fresh cilantro

1¼ cups (10 oz., 285 ml) cider vinegar

1 cup (7 oz., 200 g) granulated sugar

2 tablespoons honey

2 teaspoons coriander seeds

1. Combine the tomatoes, nectarines,, onion, serrano peppers, red pepper, cilantro, vinegar, sugar, honey, and coriander into a 5-quart nonreactive pot and stir well. (The vinegar will keep the fruit from discoloring.) Bring to a boil, then reduce the heat and simmer for 25 minutes, stirring occasionally, gently, so the fruit does not break apart.

2. Ladle the hot salsa into the warm jars, leaving ½-inch headspace. Wipe the rims of the jars clean with a damp paper towel. Place the lids and rings on the jars and finger-tighten the rings.

3. Process in a boiling-water bath for 15 minutes.

The salsa is shelf stable for 1 year.

OTHER FRUIT AND TOMATO COMBINATIONS I LOVE
- Dress tomatoes, fennel, and peaches with a simple syrup. Sprinkle with torn fresh mint and basil, salt, and freshly ground pepper.
- Spread a 10-inch round of puff pastry with crème fraîche, then top with spirals of sliced yellow plums and red tomatoes. Bake at 400°F for 20 to 25 minutes.

Tomato Chutney

MAKES: 3 or 4 half-pint jars or seven 4-ounce jars

ACTIVE TIME: 90 minutes

It's green tomatoes that frequently receive top billing in chutneys, but in this recipe, ripe tomatoes are intensified with sugars and balanced with a lot of lime juice. It's totally delicious with scrambled eggs, paired with a turkey burger, or stirred into pinto beans and tucked into a burrito. It makes a beautiful glistening, sweet, spicy, and unexpected treat.

I often put this chutney into small, 4-ounce jars, as it's a perfect hostess gift. It's also picnic fare, with a bit of cured meat, a chunk of assertive cheese, and a baguette. Add salad, and call it dinner on a hot summer night.

3½ pounds (1.6 kg) ripe red tomatoes

1½ cups (9 oz., 250 g) firmly packed light brown sugar

½ cup (3.5 oz., 100 g) granulated sugar

¾ cup (6 oz., 180 ml) fresh lime juice

¼ cup (2 oz., 60 ml) cider vinegar

1 medium green or red Serrano chile, seeded and minced

2 tablespoons grated fresh ginger

1 teaspoon ground cinnamon

½ teaspoon ground allspice

½ teaspoon coarsely ground black pepper

2 teaspoons kosher salt

¼ teaspoon citric acid or juice of 1 lemon

1. Blanch and peel the tomatoes (see page 158). Halve them, scoop out the gel and seeds, and discard. Cut the tomatoes into 1-inch dice. After you have about half the tomatoes chopped, put them in a nonreactive 5-quart pot and crush with a potato masher or wooden spoon. Turn the heat to medium, add both sugars, stir well, and increase the heat to medium.

2. Chop the remaining tomatoes, add them to the pot, along with the rest of the ingredients. If you like very spicy chutney, toast the chile pepper seeds and add them to the mix for even more heat. Bring to a good rolling boil, stirring often. Reduce the heat and simmer until the texture is thick and silky, about 30 minutes.

3. Ladle into the warm jars, leaving ½-inch headspace. Clean the rims of the jars with a damp paper towel. Place the lids and rings on the jars and finger-tighten the rings.

4. Process in a boiling-water bath for 15 minutes.

The chutney is shelf stable for 1 year.

Homemade Ketchup

MAKES: three 12-ounce jars or 4 or 5 half-pint jars
ACTIVE TIME: 4 hours (with plenty of resting time while the ketchup reduces)

Growing up in Pittsburgh, I looked forward to the annual school trip to the Heinz factory. It was quite a scene: our noses assaulted by the aromas of cut onions and brining cucumbers, vats of cooking ketchup and barbeque sauce, and the assembly line, with the workers in hairnets. When the tour was over, every child received a small green plastic pickle pin and we all proudly wore our pickle pins on the collars of our jackets; I still have about eight of them in an old jewelry box.

This personal relationship with Heinz haunts me as I now admit to you that I've eschewed the familiar bottle with the white label. My childhood friend no longer joins me when I'm eating French fries or slathering a hamburger bun, because I turn to this spicy tomato spread instead. Don't tell, or I may have to renounce my Pittsburgh roots.

I know it seems like a boatload of ingredients, but most of them are already in your pantry or spice cupboard. Add everything to one big pot and let the wonderful smell of homemade ketchup fill your kitchen.

1	plump head garlic
½	teaspoon coriander seeds
½	teaspoon cumin seeds
½	teaspoon yellow mustard seeds
1	bay leaf, broken into pieces
1	teaspoon piment d'Espelette or smoked paprika
1	teaspoon ground cinnamon
¼	teaspoon freshly ground black pepper
1	tablespoon vegetable oil
2	large shallots (8 oz., 225 g) diced (about ½ cup)
3	pint jars Tomato Puree (page 161) or 6 cups (1.4 l) store-bought tomato puree
½	cup (4 oz., 120 ml) cider vinegar
2	tablespoons firmly packed dark brown sugar

1. Preheat the oven to 375°F.

2. Slice the top off the head of garlic. Sprinkle it with a tablespoon of water and wrap tightly in a double layer of foil. Steam-roast in the oven for 45 minutes, or until tender. Cool slightly, then squeeze out the soft garlic from the papery skins. Set aside. (You can make this ahead—the roasted garlic will hold for several days, well wrapped and refrigerated.)

3. Toast the coriander, cumin, and mustard seeds in a small dry skillet until fragrant, about a minute. Grind to a fine powder using a mortar and pestle, a spice grinder, or a clean coffee grinder. Empty the ground spices into a small bowl and add the bay, piment d'Espelette, cinnamon, and black pepper.

4. Heat the vegetable oil in a heavy 5-quart nonreactive pot over medium heat. Sauté the shallots until translucent, 4 to 5 minutes. Add the garlic, spice mixture, tomato puree, vinegar, brown sugar, and jam and bring to a simmer. Add the pickles, fish sauce, hot sauce, if using, and tamari and simmer gently for 1 hour and 15 minutes, or until thickened to the consistency of applesauce. Remove from the heat and cool slightly.

1 half-pint jar plum jam (page 48) or Grape Jelly (page 143)

¼ cup (2 oz., 60 g) chopped Garlic Dill Pickles (page 197)

2 tablespoons fish sauce

1 tablespoon Hot Sauce (page 175), Sriracha, or Tabasco (optional)

1 tablespoon low-sodium tamari or soy sauce

5. Puree the ketchup in a blender, in batches, until smooth. (An immersion blender will work, but be sure to blend long enough to achieve a velvety texture, without any lumps.)

6. Rinse out the pot and return the ketchup to it. Cook over medium heat, stirring regularly, until the ketchup is thick and a spoon dragged across the bottom of the pot leaves a trail, 45 minutes to 1 hour. Monitor the heat, reducing it to low as the mixture thickens: The ketchup bubbles up in an evil way, slowly building force that can send it everywhere in the kitchen; stand back when stirring.

7. Ladle the hot ketchup into the warm jars. Clean the rims of the jars with a damp paper towel. Place the lids and rings on the jars and finger-tighten the ring.

8. Process in a boiling-water bath for 15 minutes. Let the jars rest in the water for a few minutes after the processing, until the boiling stops.

The ketchup is shelf stable for 1 year.

Bonus Recipe: Avocado "Louis"

SERVES: 2

ACTIVE TIME: 15 minutes

Having company over for lunch is a treat. I suppose because I work from home, it's the equivalent of going out to lunch versus eating at one's desk. So when someone is going to be stopping by, I like to suggest lunch. There are a few stand-by dishes, especially in summer, when I don't want to eat anything but fresh garden salads. Little lettuces and warm-from-the sun tomatoes drizzled with the very best olive oil. Big olive-oil-fried croutons. Maybe a poached egg. On rainy days, soup from the pantry with grilled pimento cheese and bacon sandwiches. Sometimes I dress up last night's leftover stew. Whatever I serve, I use my pantry to make it easy. This recipe, one of my favorites for winter lunches that feel like summer, is a lunch my mother would make when she wanted to feel fancy.

"Louis" dressing is named not for my little dog but for the classic San Francisco Dungeness crab salad. It's rich and satisfying and a pretty lunch that's luxurious enough for company.

- 3 tablespoons ketchup, homemade (page 168) or store-bought
- 3 tablespoons mayonnaise, yogurt, homemade (page 376) or store-bought, or sour cream, homemade (page 384) or store-bought
- 4 Sweet Pickle Chips (page 201), minced, plus 1 teaspoon of the brine
- ¼ teaspoon Colman's dry mustard
- 2 teaspoons finely minced scallion
- 2 hard-boiled eggs, peeled and chopped
- • Kosher salt and freshly ground black pepper
- 2 perfectly ripe avocados
- 1 lemon, halved
- • Candied Chiles (page 214) for garnish

1. In a small bowl, stir together the ketchup, mayonnaise, pickles, brine, mustard, and scallion. Fold in the eggs. Season with salt and pepper.

2. Halve and pit the avocados. Run a soupspoon between the peel and the flesh to remove each avocado half in one piece. Place 2 avocado halves on each luncheon plate and squeeze lemon juice over them.

3. Divide the egg mixture among the avocado halves, letting it overflow onto the plate. This is about abundance.

VARIATION

- • If you like salty more than sweet, or if there are no sweet pickles in your refrigerator, add minced dill pickles instead. Be bold with interpretation—this sauce does it all. In fact, swap in crab or shrimp for the egg if you're feeling ritzy.

Marinated Roasted Red Peppers

MAKES: 6 pint jars
ACTIVE TIME: 90 minutes

This recipe evokes one of my favorite food memories: a trattoria in Rome, with a basket of warm crusty bread and a pile of oil-and-vinegar-laced peppers layered with plump anchovies, salty capers, and paper-thin slivers of garlic. And wine. Plenty of wine. It was quite an afternoon.

Endlessly useful, topping pizzas or focaccia, sliced into strips and added to eggs, or layered in burritos or sandwiches—there are plenty of reasons to keep jars of these peppers on the shelf. But let's be honest, I cannot think of a single person who likes roasting and peeling a big batch of peppers. It's a messy and frustrating task. To make it tolerable, wait until lovely, shiny peppers appear in the late-summer market, get some friends to share the work and the bounty, and hunker down.

While bell peppers are a reliable choice, there are heirloom varieties of sweet peppers I prefer. Look for the deliciously named Corno di Toro, Jimmy Nardello, Cubanelle, Bananarama, and The Godfather. Select bright, colorful red peppers with firm flesh and no bruises. While you may be tempted to add yellow, orange, purple, and/or green to the mix, their color doesn't hold up as well, turning gray or beige in the jar.

The salt is optional; I like it for the sprightliness it adds to the marinade, but feel free to omit it and salt to taste when serving.

8	pounds (3.6 kg) sweet red peppers (see headnote; about 15 large)
2	cups (16 oz., 475 ml) white vinegar
½	cup (4 oz., 125 ml) fresh lemon juice
½	cup (4 oz., 125 ml) white wine vinegar, plus extra for cleaning the jars
½	cup (4 oz., 125 ml) olive oil
1	tablespoon fresh oregano
1½	teaspoons red pepper flakes
6	garlic cloves, peeled
Six	1-inch-wide strips lemon zest, removed with a vegetable peeler
2	tablespoons kosher salt (optional)

1. The peppers must be peeled before processing or the skins will slip off in the heat and float around in the marinade—not pretty, and bitter to boot. Blister the peppers until deeply and thoroughly blackened (see page 172). Cool, then remove the stem, seeds, and skin and set aside.

2. Peppers are a low-acid vegetable and need plenty of added acid to be safe for water-bath canning. *Do not alter the ratios in the marinade.* Combine the vinegars, lemon juice, garlic, and oil in a 3-quart nonreactive saucepan and bring to a simmer, then remove from the heat and set aside, covered.

3. Add ½ teaspoon oregano, ¼ teaspoon red pepper flakes, 1 garlic clove, and 1 strip of lemon zest to each sanitized jar. If using salt, add 1 teaspoon to each jar. Divide the peppers evenly among the jars, fitting them in snugly and keeping the 1-inch headspace in mind.

Recipe continues

4. Whisk the oil and vinegar mixture well, then funnel into the jars, leaving 1-inch headspace. Slide a bubbler or a plastic knife or chopstick around the perimeters of the jars and in between all the peppers to remove any air bubbles. Wipe the rims of the jars well with white vinegar, to cut the oil. Place the lids and rings on the jars and finger-tighten the rings.

5. Process in a boiling-water bath for 15 minutes. Let the jars stand, undisturbed, for 12 hours.

6. Clean the jars with white vinegar to remove any oil and make them sparkle.

The peppers are shelf stable for 1 year.

VARIATION

- Artichoke hearts can be canned in a marinade too. Start with about 24 small artichokes or 12 large. To prepare the artichokes, trim off the outer leaves down to the pale soft leaves near the heart. If working with baby artichokes, these heart leaves are edible. Using a vegetable peeler, trim off the outer layer of the stem, leaving 1 to 2 inches of stem attached. Cut the hearts in half and place the trimmed halves in acidulated water (fancy term for adding the juice of 1 lemon to a bowl of water). If you are working with more mature artichokes, trim away all the leaves right down to the heart and use a melon baller to scrape away the fuzzy choke. Cut off the stems close to the heart, using a vegetable peeler to trim away any remaining tough outer layers. Hearts trimmed in this manner can be preserved whole, halved, or quartered.

  Bring a large pot of salted water acidulated with the juice of 3 or 4 lemons to a simmer. Add the hearts and simmer until tender, about 10 minutes. Drain well, then pack snugly into pint jars and cover with the marinade as above. Process for 15 minutes.

THREE WAYS TO BLISTER AND PEEL A PEPPER

For one pepper, I'll just use a gas burner, but when I have a big batch, I opt for the broiler or grill.

On the stovetop: Turn the heat to high and place each pepper directly on a gas burner. Use long tongs to turn the peppers so that all sides, as well as the top and bottom, are blackened. (If your stove is electric or the peppers are too small to set over the burner, use a very hot dry cast-iron pan or griddle.)

Under the broiler: Set an oven rack on the first or second slot, high enough to be close to the broiler element but not so high that the peppers will touch it. Preheat the broiler. Line a baking sheet with foil. Cut the peppers lengthwise in half and scoop out the seeds and cores. Set the peppers cut side down on the baking sheet and broil for 4 to 8 minutes, until the skin is blackened all over.

On the grill: Fire up the grill and get it very hot. Put the peppers on the grill rack. Monitor them carefully, turning regularly to blacken evenly. The peppers should be ready in 10 to 12 minutes.

The peppers will collapse as they blacken. After blistering, place the hot peppers in a paper bag, close it, and allow the peppers to steam. (Or place them in a large bowl and cover with plastic wrap or a tea towel.) Leave the peppers on the counter for about 10 minutes, after which the skins will slip off. Sort of.

This next step is the messy part: I set out piles of newspaper or just tear open paper bags and work over them. Slit each pepper open with a paring knife and pull out the core and seeds. Peel away the skin, scraping it with the dull side of the knife if needed. All done? Have a glass of wine. You've earned it. (Store the peppers overnight in the refrigerator before canning if this was all too much. The peppers may weep some liquid; add that to the jars too. Bring them to room temperature before proceeding with the recipe.)

OPPOSITE: Blistered and peeled peppers

Three Ways to Hot Sauce from Any Fresh Chile

MAKES: eight 4-ounce jars
ACTIVE TIME: 45 minutes
OPTIONAL CHARRING TIME: 1 hour
OPTIONAL SMOKING TIME: 30 minutes
BRINING TIME: 8 to 24 hours

Read the labels of most grocery store hot sauces, and all the multisyllabic ingredients included in the mix might surprise you. While this hot sauce will alleviate any such concerns, make it primarily because it tastes amazing. It's sweet, salty, briny. Depending on the chile, it may make tears spring to your eyes or the top of your head feel as if it is on fire—in a good way. Use a mixture for a sauce that dances on the tongue. I like a healthy blend of sweet-hot cherry bombs, gasping-hot cayennes, stinging-hot Thai bird chiles, salsa-hot Fresnos, and/or forget-about-it-hot Scotch Bonnets. And then a few brightly colored nameless-but-dangerous-looking chiles just for fun. Red chiles make the prettiest hot sauce and green the least attractive, but all chiles make a sauce that is a fantastic addition to scrambled eggs, tacos, hummus, fried rice, chili, and more.

Fresh chiles make a bright hot sauce. Charred chiles carry a deeper, richer flavor, often with more heat, but taste smoother around the edges. If you smoke the chiles with cherry wood, the fruity tones enliven the pineapple for a heady topnote.

Please remember to wear gloves when handling chiles. And when cooking and blending the sauce, the fumes can be intense, making your throat burn and your eyes water. I wear glasses, which help (or swim goggles!), and tie a bandana around my face, bandit-style, to ease the pain. (No, sorry, there will be no photographs of this outfit.)

Store in a bottle with a dispenser top and keep it close at hand. It's addictive.

1 **pound (450 g) hot chiles (see headnote)**

1. Prepare the chiles in one of three ways:

   Fresh: Wearing gloves, stem and roughly chop the chiles.

   Char: Heat a heavy cast-iron skillet or griddle over high heat. Char the chiles, turning often, until blistered on all sides, 6 to 8 minutes. Place the charred chiles in a bowl, cover with a tea towel, and let steam for 1 hour. Wearing gloves, stem and roughly chop.

   Smoke: Smoke the chiles in a covered grill over hickory or cherry wood for 30 minutes (see Smoking, page 309). Wearing gloves, stem and then roughly chop the chiles.

OPPOSITE (clockwise from top): Fresh jalapeño, serrano, and pepperoncini chiles

Recipe continues

2 cups (16 oz., 475 ml) white or
   cider vinegar
6 large garlic cloves
1 tablespoon kosher salt
¼ cup (3 oz., 85 g) honey, or to
   taste
3 tablespoons minced dried
   pineapple (3 slices)
1 tablespoon minced dried
   mango
½ teaspoon Colman's mustard
¼ teaspoon ground ginger

2. Combine the vinegar, garlic, and salt in a large jar. Shake or swirl to dissolve the salt. Add the chiles, cover, and leave overnight on the counter to brine.

3. Transfer the chile-brine mixture into a 3-quart heavy nonreactive pot. Add the honey, dried fruits, mustard, and ginger. Cover and bring to a strong boil, then boil for 3 minutes to combine the flavors; beware of the fumes.

4. Puree the chile mixture in a blender, in batches, being careful not to overfill the beaker. Run the blender for several minutes or so (depending on the strength of the motor), until the mixture is thoroughly smooth.

5. Press the mixture through a fine-mesh strainer into a bowl. If you find there are any large pieces of chile or garlic remaining in the strainer, put them back in the blender and puree until smooth, then press through the strainer.

6. Return the hot sauce to the pot, bring back to a boil, and boil for 5 minutes. Do not lean over the pot and smell this concoction: you will regret it. Instead, dip the tip of a spoon in and then taste just a drop. It's mighty powerful, or should be. If you want it to be a little sweeter, add honey by the teaspoon, stir, and taste again.

7. Ladle the sauce into the warm jars, leaving ½-inch headspace. Clean the rims of the jars with a damp paper towel. Place the lids and rings on the jars and finger-tighten the rings.

8. Process in a boiling-water bath for 10 minutes.

The sauce is shelf stable for 1 year, but it may separate in the jars. Shake before using.

OPPOSITE: Hot peppers in vinegar

QUICKLES, REFRIGERATOR PICKLES, AND SHELF-STABLE PICKLES

OPPOSITE: Seven-Day Sweet
Pickle Chips (page 201)

First-time canners are drawn to making either jam or pickles, and I imagine that has more to do with a preference for sweet or salty foods than anything else. Personally, I'm picky about pickles. I've never liked bread-and-butter pickles, so you will not find that recipe here. But I do like sweet and salty together, and you'll find evidence of that in the candied chiles and the pickled cherries. I have a fondness for dill and heat, and those flavors appear frequently. If you prefer pickles that are not too zesty, reduce or omit the red pepper flakes or the dried or fresh chiles; the pickles will still be briny, flavorful, and crisp.

I divide pickles into four types: "quickles," refrigerator pickles, vinegar-cured, and fresh-pack or lacto-fermented (sauerkraut, deli sour pickles, and kimchi). This section focuses on quickles, refrigerator pickles, and cured pickles.

As with fruits in jams, the goal of pickling is to recall summer's farm-fresh foods at winter's dinner. These sweet, spicy, dill, vinegary, candied, and/or pickled products are crisp and bright, never dull and limp, and they are welcome with everything from deviled eggs to turkey sandwiches to grain salads to pulled pork.

Before you make pickles, taste every pickle you can find and study the labels on your favorite pickles. To replicate them in your own kitchen, begin by learning about pickling spice. Buy a commercial spice mix or make my version (page 185), and spend a little time inhaling the scent. Understanding all the flavors that contribute to the whole, and deconstructing the mix to form an individual flavor will help determine your own personal blend.

Begin your pickle exploration with quickles. The batches are small and they are a satisfying addition to any simple meal. Once you see how easy they are to make, you will be pickling everything in sight. Learn about brining: how salt,

water, and time change the structure of vegetables. Then go on to make the larger batches of shelf-stable pickles.

Equipment

There is no need for a crock, a barrel, a root cellar, or a Lower East Side storefront in Manhattan to start making pickles. You can quick-pickle in any jars or containers you have. It's lovely to store quickles in attractive jars, shapes that fit the vegetables well and show them to their best advantage. Indeed, here is the best use for all those **pretty jars** you have been unable to throw away.

When working with larger batches, it is useful to have a **3- or 5-quart clamp-top glass jar or food-safe bucket** in which to ferment large batches of pickles, but a gigantic bowl (6- to 8-quart) will work fine. Be creative, look around the house, and repurpose any glass or food-safe container as a modern-day pickle crock.

All cooking equipment used for vinegar based-brines and pickling must be nonreactive, never aluminum, as that metal turns pickles odd colors and gives them a decidedly metallic taste. Instead, use **enameled cast-iron, stainless steel, or glass kitchenware and cookware.**

My favorite toy is the **crinkle cutter.** See the photograph on page 203 and Resources, page 401. And, of course, use a **scale** (see page 24).

Water, salt, and vinegar

Pickles are surprisingly simple to make, requiring only water, salt, and vinegar. This is the triumvirate to pickle, ferment, and alter the food; any other ingredients are only flavorings.

WATER

Nothing is more important to successful pickling than the quality of the water you use. Nothing. In most of the United States, tap water is filled with minerals. That's okay, as long as you can't taste those minerals. Water that smells like sulfur will make sulfurous pickles. Chlorine, which reacts with the salts and vinegars, is absolutely ruinous to a pickle. If your water smells of chlorine, leave a pitcher of water, uncovered, on the counter overnight and the chlorine, which is a gas, will dissipate. If you are unsure of the quality of your drinking water, if it has an "off" smell or high fluoride content, or worries you at all, purchase bottled water (not carbonated!) for pickling.

SALT

There are many types of salt and many sizes of salt crystals. All the recipes in this book that specify kosher salt use Diamond Crystal salt, and the recipes will work best if you use that. You can use other brands, but weigh the salt for the best results. You can also use pickling salt. Both salts have fairly small grains and dissolve quickly. Never use iodized salt in pickling; iodine can turn your pickles a dark color or make the brine cloudy. Sea salt is another good choice for pickles or for brining (see page 303), having no iodine or anticaking additives, but large crystals will not dissolve easily, so always select fine sea salt, and weigh it for the best results.

VINEGAR

The vinegar provides the underlying flavor in the pickle. Vinegar comes in all sorts of flavors, but most are not appropriate for canning. Look for a vinegar with at least 5-percent acidity (it will be marked on the label). Even if you have a favorite vinegar that is certain to make a lovely tasting pickle, if the bottle does not list the acidity percentage, there is no way to assess that without using a pH strip. So do not use that vinegar for shelf-stable pickling; reserve it for salad dressing or other cooking. Any vinegar can be used for quick-pickling, but some vinegars are better for pickles than others. Raspberry vinegar has no business showing up in garlicky pickle brine. White and cider vinegars, as well as some white wine, red wine, sherry, and rice vinegars meet the 5-percent rule, and those are my go-to vinegars for shelf-stable pickling.

Selecting and preparing ingredients

Crisp, flavorful, snappy pickles start with the freshest produce possible. Just as with making jams and jellies, of course it's ideal to process and pickle as quickly as possible after the produce is harvested, with only hours between farm and jar.

But this is real life, so loosen up and don't worry. Buy the very best organic or best-practices farm-fresh produce and make the pickles as soon as you can. Planning helps, but I've heard the call of the pickled jalapeño and have pushed aside everything else in my life to get those chiles in a brine, so I'm in no position to judge.

Early summer brings gorgeous pickling cucumbers. They may come back at the end of the summer with a successive planting, but they may not. So I pickle cucumbers in June, before cherries arrive. Beans are late-summer foods; carrots come in early spring and again in late summer; and the same is true for radishes. Onions are sweet and small in spring, while chile peppers are best in late summer, especially if it's been hot and dry. The recipes in this section follow the available produce through the seasons. Start with some quickles in springtime, then move on to water-bath processing to put up sweet or salty treasures for next winter.

Cucumbers come in many varieties, but please make me one promise: don't ever try to pickle those plastic-wrapped "seedless" horrors in the grocery store. And while the familiar smooth-skinned salad cucumber may work for relish, the Kirby cucumber—a bumpy, shorter cuke—is the best choice for slices, chips, or whole pickles. Kirbys have fewer seeds, a thinner peel, and firm flesh. Some people pickle Persian cucumbers and other small, dense varieties with good success. For me, Kirbys make the pickle I know and love. When choosing cucumbers for shelf-stable pickles, pay close attention to freshness. Old cucumbers make limp, unsatisfying pickles. The stem end should not be dried out, and the cucumber should feel full and firm. Cover cucumbers with ice water for an hour before pickling. This will dislodge any dirt and plump them up.

While it's true that any food can be pickled, that doesn't mean it should be. Tossed into a dressed salad (a form of pickling, if you think about it) tender leaves like spinach, chard, and arugula turn to slime after a couple of hours. However, it's fine to pickle the stems of chard and kale, as well as pea shoots or garlic scapes, to add a little crunch to dinner, just as you might with quick-pickled onions; they have some body. Cauliflower, broccoli, and Brussels sprouts have a lot of body. They're dense and should be blanched first—boiled for 3 minutes, then plunged into cold water to cool. Carrots and fennel, as well as turnips, kohlrabi, and beets, often need to be blanched too; they will pickle differently depending on what size they are when picked and whether or not they are sliced. I blanch older vegetables but don't bother with tender younger ones.

Pickling takes less time and fewer pots and pans than jam making, so for some people it is a more accessible entry into preserving. For me, it captures summer, delights me at most meals, and provides another addition to the practical pantry. Pickles may adorn the plate, but pickle juice is a very useful ingredient too (see Brining, page 303).

TROUBLESHOOTING PICKLES

While pickling is straightforward, there are a few disappointments that every pickler may encounter along the way.

Mushy, limp pickles. Pickles should never be limp. Use only the freshest produce. Remove the blossom end from cucumbers (or, in a pinch, slice off a small piece from both ends, without fretting about which is the blossom end). And do not use chlorinated water.

Turquoise garlic. Yes, really. Some garlic contains anthocyanin, a pigment that is activated in acid solutions like brines. Other garlic has sulfur compounds and when brined in water with a high sulfur content, will turn blue or green. The color change freaks everyone out but the good news is that the pickles are fine to eat—there's nothing wrong with them or the garlic. It's a little startling, but no big deal.

Exploding or foaming jars. The first time I made Garlic Dill Pickles (page 197), I put the jars in the garage to cure for a month. Whether I'd failed to remove the blossom end of the cucumber or used tap water, I'm not certain, but whatever I did caused the jars to explode. I walked into the garage one morning to a sea of cucumbers, glass, and funky smells. Avoid my mistakes. Always cut off the blossom end; use fresh water; and take the rings off the jars before storing them. If I had removed the rings, the buildup of gases in the jars would have only lifted the lids, not broken the glass. Remove. The. Rings.

Way too salty. I know what you did. You read the recipe and noted the yield of three jars and the salt called for—hmmm, 3 tablespoons. You put a tablespoon in each jar, didn't you? Make the brine separately and then pour it into the jars. Often there will be leftover brine, and if the salt is in the jars, not the brine, the ratios will be wrong.

Shriveled or slippery pickles. Here is another reason to invest in a scale for preserving projects. Using too strong a brine, or too weak a brine, will alter the science. Pickling is science. Salt should be weighed for pickling projects.

Soft pickles. Make sure the pickles are entirely submerged in the brine. This is challenging, fitting the pickles into the right-size jar. Jars with shoulders (not wide-mouth) tend to hold the pickles below the surface of the brine.

Bitter pickles. Using ground spices instead of whole spices is a mistake. The spices will not distribute easily and will make a murky pickle. Boiling spices for too long in the brine will make pickles bitter and tannic. Follow the recipes exactly.

Beware of cucumber pickling in dry summers. Cucumbers do not grow well under the stress of drought conditions—they have a very high water content and need the rain. I can promise you, the pickles will be disappointing. In those years, forego pickling cucumbers and explore other vegetables.

Most pickle recipes can be scaled up or down. Make half a recipe, or make a double recipe—just keep to the brining ratios indicated in the recipes and everything will work out fine.

Pickling Spice

MAKES: about ⅓ cup

ACTIVE TIME: 5 minutes

While pickling spice is available in every grocery store spice aisle, I encourage you to make your own. There are very strong flavors at work here. For every pickle maker out there, one loves allspice and hates cinnamon. Another wants a pickle without red pepper heat, and another prefers to swap black mustard seeds for yellow. There really are no rules, as the spice does not contribute to the pickling action, it only flavors it. So, alter these ingredients to suit yourself. (This is an exception to the "no changing the ratios" rule.)

3 tablespoons yellow mustard seeds

1 tablespoon coriander seeds

1 tablespoon allspice berries

1½ teaspoons red pepper flakes (optional)

1 teaspoon powdered ginger

• A 3-inch cinnamon stick

2 bay leaves

4 whole cloves

1. Crush the seeds and berries with a mortar and pestle or with the side of a knife or the bottom of a heavy drinking glass. Transfer to a small bowl and add the red pepper, if using, and ginger. Crush the cinnamon stick with a heavy pan or mallet. Crumble the bay leaf. Add both to the bowl.

2. Funnel the spice mix into a jar, cover, and shake well. It will be fragrant for 1 year.

OPPOSITE: Pickling spices

Piercing a chile

Quickles: Quick-Pickled Almost Anything (But Especially Chiles)

MAKES: 1 quart jar
ACTIVE TIME: 15 minutes
STANDING TIME: 20 minutes to 1 week

Pickles are sexy and spicy and hot and cool, with tantalizing flavors and textures: crunchy, tart, and salty. Quickles turn vegetables into something entirely different. Even odd bits: two carrots, half a fennel bulb. Cauliflower. Sweet peppers. Each one reimagined and emerging from the brine as a new and different food. Or mix and match vegetables based on color or texture or just what you have in the crisper. When I make quickles, it's all about the presentation. I want very pretty produce and I want the perfect size jar for the job.

To quick-pickle any vegetable, think in terms of ratios—equal parts water and vinegar, salty and sweet additions, herbs, spices, and chiles. There are no hard-and-fast rules. Serve quickles as a condiment, side dish, or topping for any salad.

I always have a jar of pickled serrano and jalapeño rings in the refrigerator. Pickle an onion tangle with shallots, red onion, and sweet onion, then use it to top tacos or fried rice.

8 ounces (225 g) vegetables or chile peppers
1 cup (8 oz., 240 ml) nonchlorinated water
1 cup (8 oz., 240 ml) white or cider vinegar
2 garlic cloves, slivered
1 tablespoon (0.3 oz., 8 g) kosher salt
1 tablespoon granulated sugar
1 teaspoon pickling spice, homemade (page 185) or store-bought (optional)

1. Prep the vegetables or chiles. Peel and remove any mushy parts and cut into equal-sized chunks if necessary. If you want to leave jalapeños, serranos, and other hot peppers whole, pierce each one with the tip of a knife three or four times. Fill a quart jar with the vegetables or chiles.

2. In a medium saucepan, combine the water, vinegar, garlic, salt, sugar, and pickling spice, if using, and bring to a simmer, stirring until the salt and sugar are dissolved. Pour the warm brine into the jar. Because you are not processing these pickles, the headspace is not critical, but do make sure all the vegetables are submerged. If they are floating above the brine, insert a smaller jar into the large jar to push the vegetables down into the brine. Let cool, then cap the jar.

3. Some foods, like thin-sliced onions, will be ready in 20 minutes. Others, like chile peppers, may take 3 or 4 days. Taste to judge the progress: a good pickle will be salty, acidic, and crisp. Most vegetable quickles will get sharper, tangier, and more pickled (and less crisp) every day, but the texture will suffer after 2 weeks. They should be discarded after a month.

Bonus Recipe: Salmon and Grain Salad with Red Onion Quickles

SERVES: 4

ACTIVE TIME: 30 minutes

When lunch rolls around, particularly when the garden is coming back to life in spring, I want nothing more than crunchy food. Lots of crunch. And plenty of tang. This salad gives me everything I want, with the extra boost of protein-rich grains and the luxury of my home-canned fish. More than anything, this healthy salad has a delightful counterpoint of texture and flavor.

- ½ red onion, sliced into slim half-moons
- ½ cup (4 oz., 110 g) white wine vinegar
- ½ cup (4 oz., 110 g) nonchlorinated water
- ½ teaspoon kosher salt, or to taste
- 1 teaspoon pickling spice, homemade (page 185) or store-bought
- ¼ teaspoon red pepper flakes
- 8 ounces (225 g) green beans
- 3 cups cooked grains (rice, quinoa, farro, couscous, or any combination of whole grains), warm or at room temperature
- 6 radishes, thinly sliced
- 1 half-pint jar pressure-canned salmon or tuna (see page 279), drained
- ½ cup (4 oz., 235 ml) olive oil
- 3 tablespoons mayonnaise (optional)
- Freshly ground black pepper

1. Place the onion slices in a small glass or ceramic bowl. In a small saucepan, bring the vinegar, water, salt, pickling spice, and red pepper to a simmer. Pour the brine over the onion slices and set aside for 20 minutes.

2. Trim the beans, leaving the little tails but removing the stem ends. Bring a pot of salted water to a boil Add the green beans and blanch for 3 minutes. Drain.

3. Fluff up the cooked grains on a beautiful platter. Scatter the green beans over the grains. Drain the pickled onions, reserving the brine. Sprinkle half the pickled onions over the salad. (Save the other half for tacos, sandwiches, omelets—oh, just about anything.) Top the salad with the radishes and fish.

4. Whisk together ¼ cup of the reserved pickling brine and the olive oil (or shake in a covered jar) until emulsified. Taste and season with salt, if necessary, and pepper.

5. Drizzle the salad with the dressing, add the mayonnaise, if using, and serve.

VARIATION
- Substitute other seasonal vegetables for the green beans. Try asparagus, zucchini, or diced butternut squash.

OPPOSITE: Salmon and Grain Salad with Red Onion Quickles

Fennel, Orange, and Olive Refrigerator Pickles

MAKES: one 24-ounce jar
ACTIVE TIME: 20 minutes
STANDING TIME: 2 days

This piquant pickle was inspired by a plate of olives, caper berries, and bitter oranges served with sherry at an outdoor cafe in Seville.

A wide-mouth jar will make this job a little easier. So will long tweezers or a chopstick, if you want to get fancy.

Serve with salty Marcona almonds.

2   medium fennel bulbs (24 oz., 680 g)
1   navel orange
1½ cups (12 oz., 340 g) Cerignola olives, rinsed
1   cup (8 oz., 235 ml) champagne vinegar
1   tablespoon (0.125 oz., 8 g) kosher or pickling salt
2   tablespoons granulated sugar
1   tablespoon chopped fresh tarragon
1   cup ice cubes

1. Trim the stalks from the fennel and peel away the tough outer sections of the bulb. (Put these parts in a bag in the freezer to make vegetable broth or add to a batch of chicken stock.) Remove about ½ inch of the root end of each fennel bulb, then slice vertically down the center. Set the fennel cut side down on the cutting board and slice wedges from the bulbs.

2. Wash the orange well. Slice into slim ¼-inch rounds, rind and all. Remove any seeds. Cut the slices into half-moons. Press the oranges against the inside of the jar, then fit the fennel wedges into the center of the jar, adding a few olives here and there as you go.

3. In a small saucepan, warm the vinegar, salt, sugar, and tarragon, stirring just until the salt and sugar have dissolved. Add the ice cubes and stir until cool.

4. Pour the cooled brine into the jar. Cover and place in a cool, dark spot for 2 days.

5. Chill the pickles before serving. They will keep for up to a month in the refrigerator.

OPPOSITE: Fennel, Orange, and Olive Refrigerator Pickles

Sugar Snap, Carrot, and Radish Refrigerator Pickles

MAKES: 2 tall 24-ounce or 12-ounce jars, depending on the length of the carrots

ACTIVE TIME: 30 minutes

BRINING TIME: 24 hours

If you don't have sugar snaps, the carrots and radishes are great partners *à deux*, but the peas add a nice texture and make a Palm Beach (Lily Pulitzer) color combination. Choose bright radishes; the vinegar will pull their color and make everything in the jar blush.

The carrots are vital to this recipe. Find tiny slim carrots the size of a little finger, newly pulled from the ground; their flavor is sweet and intense. They need only a good scrubbing and they are ready for anything. At my farmers' market, vendors sell "thinnings" from their planted rows: small bunches precisely the right size for this recipe. The orange, pale yellow, and deep rusty red tones are so pretty—at the first glimpse of them, I had to stop time, capture the moment, and pickle them. Be certain about one thing: these carrots are in no way the same thing as the sad carved "baby" carrots at the grocery store, which are not babies at all, but carved from mature carrots.

8	to 12 bright red radishes
12	to 16 slim young carrots
24	very fresh sugar snap peas, trimmed
1	cup (8 oz., 235 g) white wine vinegar
1	cup (8 oz., 235 g) nonchlorinated water
¼	cup (1.25 oz., 34 g) kosher or pickling salt
¼	cup (3 oz., 85 g) honey
2	garlic cloves, thinly sliced
4	teaspoons dill seeds
2	teaspoons celery seeds
¼	teaspoon red pepper flakes

1. Scrub the radishes and, depending on size, keep whole, quarter, halve, or slice thin.

2. Scrub the carrots and peel if necessary. Blanch in boiling water for 2 minutes, then cool in a bowl of ice water. Stand the carrots in the jars. If they are too tall, julienne or slice them decoratively and return to the jars. Add the peas and radishes. Make 'em pretty.

3. Bring the vinegar, water, salt, honey, and garlic to a boil in a saucepan. Divide the dill and celery seeds and red pepper flakes between the two jars and pour the hot brine into the jars. Let cool, then cap and leave on the counter overnight to brine.

4. Refrigerate the pickles and eat within a week.

OPPOSITE: Fitting carrots into a jar for Sugar Snap, Carrot, and Radish Refrigerator Pickles

TOP TO BOTTOM:
Pickled new spring onions;
pickled shallots and pearl onions

Juniper-Pickled Cocktail Onions

MAKES: two 12-ounce jars onions with stalks or 1 pint jar pearl or silverskin onions

ACTIVE TIME: 2 hours, over 2 days

CURING TIME: 2 to 3 weeks

These onions have the perfect herbal tones to complement a great gin martini or a Bloody Mary. They're also an essential ingredient in that classic London pub meal, the ploughman's lunch, or at a French bistro alongside a slice of a *pâté grandmère*. The only question here is how obsessive you feel—i.e., how much fancy knife work you're up for. I will admit to a love of carving little onions from the early stalks that appear in June. There is also an elusive perfectly shaped and sized onion called a silverskin. They are hard to find, but they are my favorite. Truly, any small onion is delicious here: cipollini, little early red or white onions, even shallots.

I can spend an inordinate amount of time carefully trimming the root ends of all of the members of the alium family, keeping the onion intact, then carefully peeling away any papery outside skin. Use sharp scissors to trim the root and top right above the bulb. Or trim the root and leave a 2- or 3-inch stalk. The former is best in a cocktail, the latter on a luncheon plate.

24 to 30 (about 32 oz., 900 g) very small red or white new onions

3 tablespoons (0.9 oz., 25 g) kosher salt

1 cup (8 oz., 235 ml) white wine vinegar

1 cup (8 oz., 235 ml) nonchlorinated water

2 tablespoons granulated sugar

1 tablespoon maple sugar or maple syrup

3 juniper berries, crushed

1 allspice berry, crushed

1 green cardamom pod, cracked open, seeds scraped out and crushed

6 black peppercorns, crushed

1 cup (8 oz., 225 g) ice cubes

2 large strips lemon peel, removed with a vegetable peeler

2 bay leaves

1. Trim the root ends and peel away any dry papery skin from the onions. Trim the stalks to 2 to 3 inches, or slice away the entire stalks, leaving only the bulbs. Pack the onions tightly into the jar(s). Add 1 tablespoon of the salt to each jar (or add 2 tablespoons salt to the pint jar), fill with cool water, and cover. Shake or agitate to distribute the salt. Leave the jars on the counter overnight.

2. The next day, drain the onions and rinse well under cool water. In a small saucepan, bring the vinegar, water, the remaining 1 tablespoon salt, the sugar, maple syrup, and spices to a simmer, stirring until the sugar and salt are dissolved. Remove from the heat, add the ice cubes, and stir until the brine is cool.

3. Place the onions back in the jar(s). Divide the lemon peel and bay leaves between the jars (or put them all in the pint jar). Pour the brine over the onions, place the lid on the jar(s), and brine the onions on the counter overnight.

4. The next day, refrigerate the onions. They will be ready to eat in 2 to 3 weeks and will keep for at least 3 months in the refrigerator.

Pickled Cherries with Star Anise

MAKES: 6 half-pint jars
ACTIVE TIME: 90 minutes
CURING TIME: 1 month

Any fruit is easily pickled with this basic recipe, but cherries are especially amenable to the heady mix of star anise and ginger liqueur. With blueberries, try juniper and gin. With peaches, cinnamon sticks and bourbon. Pickled fruit is a surprising star of the pickle plate—eye-opening and entirely complementary with meat and cheese. These little gems will also tart up a pan sauce (see page 278) or barbeque sauce (page 263). And for a tangy take on the Negroni, drop a pickled cherry into the glass. I love the way it brings out the bitter charm of Campari.

2 cups (8 oz., 235 ml) nonchlorinated water

1 cup (8 oz., 235 ml) cider vinegar

½ cup (4 oz., 100 g) firmly packed dark brown sugar

2 tablespoons (0.6 oz., 16 g) kosher or pickling salt

1 garlic clove, peeled

1 whole star anise

One 1-inch piece fresh ginger, peeled and sliced into slim coins

3 pounds (1.4 kg) sweet cherries, stemmed and pitted

¼ cup (2 oz., 60 ml) Domaine de Canton ginger liqueur (optional)

1. Bring the water, vinegar, sugar, salt, garlic, star anise, and ginger to a boil in a nonreactive pot. Remove from the heat and set aside to steep for 1 hour.

2. Remove and discard the garlic. Add the cherries to the brine and bring to a boil. Remove from the heat and stir in the Domaine de Canton. With a skimmer or slotted spoon, funnel the cherries into the jars, leaving ½-inch headspace. Pour the hot brine over the cherries. Remove the air bubbles using a bubbler or plastic knife, running it around the sides of the jars and through the fruit. Add more liquid if needed to maintain the ½-inch headspace.

3. Clean the rims of the jars well with a damp paper towel. Place the lids and rings on the jars and finger-tighten the rings. Process in a boiling-water bath for 10 minutes.

4. Let the pickles cure in a cool, dark spot for 1 month.

The pickles are shelf stable for 1 year.

Garlic Dill Pickles

MAKES: 4 quart jars
ACTIVE TIME: 90 minutes
BRINING TIME: 12 hours
CURING TIME: 1 month

People have all sorts of expectations from a dill pickle. There are the crisp and sour pickles, the pickles that sidle up to a corned beef on rye at the deli. For so many of you, that is the one and only true dill: the sour, or half-sour, dill. This is not a sour dill. It is a vinegar dill: the pickle that belongs on a hamburger, in spears next to a tuna melt, or fried, on a stick, at a county fair. These are lip-puckering, eye-scrunching pickles, and they should be served ice cold.

Because these pickles want to float in the brine, opt for regular, not wide-mouth, jars; the shoulders help hold the pickles down in the brine. To make the most of the jar space, purchase small Kirby cucumbers; if there are only larger pickles at the market, consider cutting them into spears, chunks, or chips.

¾ cup (3.6 oz., 100 g) kosher or pickling salt

14 cups (64 oz., 3.3 l) unchlorinated water

8 cups (1.9 kg) ice cubes

4 pounds (1.8 kg) small (Kirby) cucumbers, well washed

4 cups (3.2 oz., 1 l) white vinegar

4 garlic cloves, peeled and root end trimmed

4 ounces (110 g) fresh dill with seed heads or ¼ cup (7 g) dill seeds

4 teaspoons yellow mustard seeds

1. Combine half the salt and 8 cups of the water in a 5-quart non-reactive pot and bring to a boil. Add the ice. When the brine is completely cool, add the cucumbers and place a plate on top to keep them submerged. Brine in a cool spot for 12 hours.

2. Drain and rinse the cucumbers. Cut a small slice from each cucumber end; or cut into 1-inch chunks or quarter lengthwise. Pack the cucumbers into the jars, fitting them in like a three-dimensional jigsaw puzzle, as tightly as possible. Tuck one-quarter of the fresh dill (or dill seeds) and mustard seeds into each jar.

3. In a 5-quart nonreactive pot bring the remaining salt, the white vinegar, the remaining 6 cups water, and the garlic cloves to a boil. Cover the cucumbers with the hot brine, adding 1 garlic clove to each jar, and leaving ½-inch headspace. Clean the rims of the jars with a damp paper towel. Place the lids and rings on the jars and finger-tighten the rings. Process in a boiling-water bath for 15 minutes.

4. Let the pickles cure for 1 month, then chill thoroughly before serving.

The pickles are shelf stable for 1 year.

Le Peek-el: The Cornichon Imposter

MAKES: 2 wide-mouth pint jars
ACTIVE TIME: 30 minutes
BRINING TIME: 2 hours
CURING TIME: 1 month

Serve this tangy, savory little pickle next to a slice of pâté in France, and it's a corni-chon. In London, a gherkin transforms pork pie into a ploughman's lunch. These small, almost seedless cucumbers are nearly impossible to find in the United States unless you grow your own. Even then, it's difficult to get enough tiny pickles to fill several jars.

After two unsatisfactory gardening experiences, I devised this recipe for the smallest pickling cucumbers I could locate. I stand in front of the baskets of pickling cucumbers at the market and search for the very smallest. They're never going to look exactly right, but the taste is unmistakable. Someday I'll try growing the right cucumber again (the heirloom variety is Parisienne Cornichon de Bourbonne), but until then, I'll make a couple of jars of Le Peek-el every chance I get.

1 pound (450 g) tiny pickling cucumbers—the smallest, firmest, and straightest available

¼ cup (1.2 oz., 34 g) kosher salt

1 cup (240 ml) nonchlorinated water

½ cup (4 oz., 120 ml) white wine vinegar

½ cup (4 oz., 120 ml) white vinegar

4 teaspoons minced shallot

2 small garlic cloves, sliced

1 teaspoon fresh thyme leaves

½ teaspoon black peppercorns

½ teaspoon white peppercorns

2 whole cloves

2 dried bay leaves

1. Soak the cucumbers in ice water for 30 minutes to remove any dirt.

2. Drain the cucumbers, rinse well, and pat dry. Trim off the blossom ends (or, if baffled by which end is which, just trim off a little bit from both ends). Arrange the cucumbers in a single layer on a baking sheet lined with a cotton tea towel. Sprinkle 2 table-spoons of the salt over the cucumbers and roll them around until they are all well salted. (This is called a dry brine.) Spread them out in a single layer and set aside, uncovered, for 2 hours.

3. Rinse the cucumbers very well, until no salt is visible (do not soak). In a medium saucepan, bring the water, vinegars, and the remaining 2 tablespoons salt to a boil. Remove from the heat.

4. Pack the cucumbers snugly into the jars. Divide the shallot, garlic, thyme, peppercorns, cloves, and bay leaves between the jars. Funnel in the brine, leaving ¼-inch headspace. Carefully remove the air bubbles from the jars, using a bubbler or a plastic knife. Place the lids and rings on the jars and finger-tighten the rings.

5. Process in a boiling-water bath for 10 minutes.

6. Let the pickles cure in a cool, dark spot for 1 month.

OPPOSITE: Cornichons in salt

The pickles are shelf stable for 1 year.

Seven-Day Sweet Pickle Chips

MAKES: 12 pint jars

ACTIVE TIME: less than an hour a day nearly every day for a week

CURING TIME: 1 week

This traditional sweet pickle is a recipe that's been around forever in the Mennonite community. This version has been my go-to sweet pickle for many years and friends love them so much, they steal them from the pantry. Most of the recipes in this book call for three pounds of produce, but here I'm encouraging you to make ten pounds of pickles. Yes, ten pounds. If you don't believe me, go ahead and make half a recipe. Mark my words, you'll make this pickle again before the summer is over.

Alum, a crisping agent, is available in many grocery store spice aisles. It is a perfectly natural mineral, but if it worries you, opt for black tea, such as Lipton's, to ensure a crispy pickle chip. Use only nonchlorinated water. Chill the pickles thoroughly before serving.

10 pounds (4.5 kg) very fresh Kirby cucumbers

¼ cup (1.2 oz., 35 g) kosher or pickling salt

3 tablespoons alum or 5 tablespoons loose black tea from 8 tea bags

4 quarts (128 oz., 3.8 l) cider vinegar

10 cups (70 oz., 2 kg) granulated sugar, plus 1 cup (7 oz., 198 g) if needed

¼ cup (2 oz., 75 g) pickling spice, homemade (page 185) or store-bought

1. Day One: In a very large bowl or a clean cooler, soak the cucumbers in ice water for 30 minutes. Drain.

2. Trim off the ends of the cucumbers, then slice into 3/4-inch chunks; a waffle or ripple cutter produces good-looking pickles. Pack them into a 5-gallon or larger jar or food-safe container with a lid. Cover the cucumber chunks with boiling water. Let cool, then cover the container and let sit overnight.

3. Day Two: There may be some fluffy white foam on the top of the cucumbers. Don't worry, that's normal. It's called lactobacillus and it's a healthy, naturally occurring bacteria. Drain the pickles, rinse the jar, and put the pickles back in the jar. (Do not rinse the pickles.)

4. In a 5-quart nonreactive pot, bring the salt and 4 quarts of brine to a boil. Pour the brine over the cucumber slices; you may have more than you need; dispose of the extra. Cool, then cover and let sit overnight.

5. Day Three: Again, do not be dismayed by the sight of any foam or white fluff on the top of the pickles. Drain the cucumbers. Do not rinse them, but do rinse the jar, and pack the soon-to-be-pickles back into the jar.

OPPOSITE: Seven-Day Sweet
Pickle Chips

Recipe continues

6. In a 5-quart nonreactive pot, bring the alum (or tea bags) and 4 quarts water to a boil. Pour the boiling water over the cucumber slices; discard any excess. Cool, then cover and let it sit overnight.

7. Day Four: Drain the pickles and rinse the jar. The texture will have changed with the addition of the alum (or tea) and they will be crisp. The pickles are also very delicate at this stage, so place them back in the jar gently.

8. In a 5-quart nonreactive pot, bring the cider vinegar and 5 cups of the sugar to a boil, stirring to dissolve the sugar. Put the pickling spice into a cheesecloth bundle (or a tea ball) and add to the jar of pickles. Pour the vinegar mixture over the cucumber slices. Cool, then cover and let sit for 3 days.

9. Days Five and Six: Dream of what you will do with these pickles.

10. Day Seven: Drain the pickles, reserving 2 cups of the syrup; dispose of the pickling spices. Put the pickles into a giant bowl and scatter 4 cups sugar over them. Stir well and let sit for about an hour.

11. Pack the pickles tightly into the warm jars. The sugar will have drawn liquid out of the pickles. Scrape/pour this liquidy syrup over the pickles, dividing it evenly.

12. Heat 1 cup of the reserved spiced vinegar and the remaining cup of sugar in a nonreactive saucepan, stirring, until the sugar is dissolved. Fill the jars, leaving ½-inch headspace. If the jars require additional liquid, it is possible you haven't packed the jars tightly enough. Remove air bubbles and repack. If they are well packed and still short of liquid, make another batch of syrup by boiling the remaining cup of reserved vinegar with another cup of sugar and pour it over the pickles, leaving ½-inch headspace. Remove air bubbles with a bubbler, chopstick, or flat plastic knife. Carefully clean the jar rims and the threads; this is a sticky business. Place the lids and rings on the jars and finger-tighten the rings.

13. Process in a boiling-water bath for 5 minutes.

14. Let the pickles cure for a week or so, turning the jars over for the first few days to disperse and dissolve any sugar on the bottoms of the jars. Chill well before enjoying.

The pickles are shelf stable for 1 year.

OPPOSITE: Crinkle-cutting pickle chips

Dill Pickle Relish

MAKES: 3 half-pint jars
ACTIVE TIME: 40 minutes
BRINING TIME: 2 hours

While sweet relish is my choice for stirring into a tartar sauce and slathering on smoked pork sausage, there are times I want a sour, tangy relish. On a hot dog, with sauerkraut, for instance. This dill relish fits the bill. Removing the seeds from the cucumbers is a pain, but it's important. The seeds often bring bitterness and the gel that surrounds them will make for a watery relish.

3 large salad (slicing) cucumbers (24 oz., 680 g)
1 medium onion (8 oz., 225 g) roughly chopped
2 tablespoons (0.6 oz., 17 g) kosher salt
4 cups (32 oz., 950 ml) nonchlorinated ice water
1¼ cups (8.75 oz., 250 g) granulated sugar
1½ cups (12 oz., 355 ml) white vinegar
2 garlic cloves
1 teaspoon dill seeds
1 teaspoon yellow mustard seeds
¼ teaspoon turmeric (for color; optional)

1. Peel the cucumbers, cut lengthwise in half, and scoop out the seeds. Cut the cucumbers into large chunks. Put the cucumbers and onion in a food processor and process until finely chopped, nearly pureed. There should be a lot of slush but very few or no chunks.

2. Pour the cucumbers and onions into a large glass or stainless steel bowl. Scatter the salt over the vegetables, then pour the ice water over everything. It will look very watery, but go with it. The salt will plump everything. Stir well, cover, and set aside for 2 hours.

3. Pour the brined cucumber mixture into a large fine-mesh strainer and rinse very well under cold water, then shake and shake the strainer to remove as much water as possible. Press on the vegetable mixture with a spatula or wooden spoon to remove more water, then set the strainer over a bowl and let the vegetables continue draining while you start the syrup.

4. In a 5-quart nonreactive pot, bring the sugar, vinegar, garlic, and spices to a fast boil that will not stir down. Add the vegetables, bring back to a strong boil, and continue to cook at a big boil until the foam disperses and the mixture thickens, about 12 minutes.

5. Fill the hot jars with the hot relish, leaving ½-inch headspace. Clean the jar rims well with a damp paper towel. Place the lids and rings on the jars and finger-tighten the rings.

6. Process in a boiling-water bath for 10 minutes.

The relish is shelf stable for 1 year.

Sweet Pickle Relish

MAKES: 4 to 5 half-pint jars
ACTIVE TIME: 40 minutes
BRINING TIME: 2 hours

Pickle relish is a summer flavor that lives on all year long. It's sweet, tangy, and makes a sandwich extra special. Blend pickle relish with mustard and slather on a cheese sandwich. Stir it into tuna salad or egg salad. There is a world of uses for this sweet treat. If you don't have a food processor, it is a little less fun to make. Use a box grater instead.

3   large salad or slicing cucumbers (35 oz., 1 kg)

2   large sweet peppers (16 oz., 450 g; red and orange make the prettiest relish, green are fine, purple peppers are a bad idea), cored, seeded, and cut into large pieces

1   medium yellow onion (8 oz., 225 g), quartered

2   tablespoons (0.6 oz., 17 g) kosher or pickling salt

4   cups (32 oz., 950 ml) nonchlorinated ice water

3   cups (21 oz., 600 g) granulated sugar

½   cup (3.5 oz., 100 g) firmly packed light brown sugar

2   cups (16 oz., 475 ml) cider vinegar

1   tablespoon celery seeds

1   tablespoon yellow mustard seeds

1. Peel the cucumbers, cut lengthwise in half, and scoop out the seeds. Cut the cucumbers into large chunks. Put the cucumbers, peppers, and onion in a food processor and whir all the vegetables together until they are almost, but not quite, pureed. There should be no visible chunks of vegetables in the mix.

2. Transfer to a large glass or stainless steel bowl. Scatter the salt over the vegetable mix, then pour the ice water over and stir well. Cover and set aside for 2 hours. Although it will seem quite mushy, after the relish rests in this salty brine, the texture will be different.

3. Pour the relish mixture into a large fine-mesh strainer and rinse very well under cold water, then shake and shake and shake the strainer to remove as much water as possible. Use a spatula or wooden spoon to press more water out of the mixture. Set the strainer over a bowl and let drain while you start the syrup.

4. In a 5-quart nonreactive pot, bring the sugars, vinegar, and spices to a boil that will not stir down. Add the vegetables and return the mixture to a hard boil, then boil for about 12 minutes, until the foam disperses. The mixture should be thick and saucy.

5. Fill the hot jars with the relish, leaving ½-inch headspace. Clean the rims of the jars with a damp paper towel. Place the lids and rings on the jars and finger-tighten the rings.

6. Process in a boiling-water bath for 10 minutes.

The relish is shelf stable for 1 year.

Fish Sticks with Tartar Sauce

Bonus Recipe: Fish Sticks with Tartar Sauce

SERVES: 4

ACTIVE TIME: 40 minutes

Crispy, crunchy fried food tastes good—admit it. In order to get a crackling outer shell, recipes call for either a batter or a dredge. I have developed a three step do-si-do, an essential skill that does not create a huge mess. Once you have this technique in your arsenal, turn your sights on fish sticks, and mix sweet pickle relish into a creamy tartar sauce.

These plump, moist fish sticks are covered with a light, crunchy cloak that shatters at the first bite in the most satisfying way. I like to use mild-flavored firm fish fillets so the pieces are consistently sized and cook evenly. These are easy to eat, even for youngsters who aren't at all sure about fish.

Add potato flakes for crunch? That bit of brilliance came straight from Jacques Pepin. Look for potato flakes at the grocery store in the same aisle as bread crumbs.

- Juice of ½ lemon
- 3 tablespoons mayonnaise
- 3 tablespoons Sweet Pickle Relish (page 205)
- 2 pounds (900 g) fillets of cod or other firm fish
- 2 tablespoons water
- 2 cups (12 oz., 340 g) instant potato flakes
- 2 tablespoons finely minced fresh flat-leaf parsley, mint, basil, or a combination
- ½ teaspoon grated lemon zest
- Kosher salt and freshly ground black pepper
- 2 cups (8.5 oz., 250 g) all-purpose flour
- 2 large eggs
- Grapeseed, canola, or other flavorless oil for deep-frying

1. To make the tartar sauce, combine the lemon juice, mayonnaise, and sweet relish in a small bowl. Stir well, cover, and refrigerate.

2. Rinse the fish and pat dry. Slice into ½-inch-thick slabs. Make the pieces as uniform as possible so they will cook at the same rate.

3. Pile half the flour on the left side of a baking sheet and the other half on the right. Mix the potato flakes, herbs, and lemon zest into the pile on the right. Generously salt and pepper both mounds. In a medium bowl, beat the eggs with the water. Set the bowl in the center of the baking sheet.

4. With your left hand, put a piece of fish into the flour on the left side, turning it to coat well, then drop it into the egg wash. With your right hand, turn the fish over and over in the egg wash, then drop into the potato flake mixture. Use your left hand to lift the dry mixture and pat it onto the fish. Keep one hand dry, one wet. Just keep saying that under your breath. Set the coated fish at the edge of the baking sheet and repeat with the remaining fish. When all the pieces have been dredged, put the baking sheet stove-side.

5. In a cast-iron or other heavy straight-sided sauté pan, heat 1 inch of oil to 325°F. Crisp the fish, in batches, until well browned on both sides, turning only once, about 4 minutes per side. Drain the fish on paper towels set on a rack and sprinkle with salt.

6. Serve piping hot with the tartar sauce and lemon wedges.

Dilly Beans

MAKES: four 24-ounce or pint jars or five 12-ounce jars
ACTIVE TIME: 1 hour
CURING TIME: 1 week

If you have ever grown beans in a garden plot, you know the first person to make a dilly bean should be granted sainthood. Beans don't grow at a leisurely rate—they arrive like a flock of starlings in the fall, by the gazillions, far more than anyone can consume in a reasonable amount of time.

These pickled beans are so straightforward and quick, I take the time to make the jars pretty. Fit the jar to the bean—longer ones will look best in a tall 24-ounce jar, while short, stout beans fit best in a pint or 12-ounce jar. Dilly beans are made to rest on the edge of a martini glass or to be layered in a sandwich. When you are staring into the refrigerator hoping for divine inspiration, they will call out to you.

2 pounds (900 g) freshly picked green beans

¼ cup (1.25 oz., 35 g) kosher or pickling salt

1½ cups (12 oz., 355 ml) cider vinegar

1½ cups (12 oz., 355 ml) white vinegar

3 cups (24 oz., 710 ml) nonchlorinated water

4 garlic cloves, trimmed and halved

4 teaspoons crushed red pepper

¼ cup (0.75 oz., 21 g) dill seeds

4 wide strips lemon zest, removed with a vegetable peeler

1. Fit the beans to the jars by testing one, standing it upright and keeping in mind the ½-inch headspace needed. Remove the stem end but retain the elegant tail. Trim all the remaining beans to the same size.

2. In a medium saucepan, bring the salt, both vinegars, the water, and garlic to a boil. Remove from the heat.

3. Divide the red pepper, garlic, and dill seeds among the warm jars. Place the beans in the jars, leaving as little space as possible—really stuff the jars full, tucking in small pieces to fill any spaces. You may need to remove all the beans and trim them again if they pop up above the ½-inch headspace. This happens.

4. Pour the hot brine over the beans, leaving ½-inch headspace. Run a bubbler or plastic knife around the sides and through the center of the jars, removing air bubbles. Check the headspace again and add or remove brine as needed. (You may have brine left over.)

5. Process in a boiling-water bath for 5 minutes.

6. Let the dilly beans cure for at least a week before eating. They are even better after a month.

OPPOSITE: Fresh green beans

The beans are shelf stable for 1 year.

Bonus Recipe: New-Fangled Three-Bean Salad

SERVES: 4

ACTIVE TIME: Less than 30 minutes

There is nothing like a salad that is ready in an instant, taking advantage of both pantry and garden. I believe the origins of the three bean salad, that picnic staple, must have been a similar appreciation for the pantry. What that salad misses, for me, is the pickle. With dilly beans on the shelf and cannellini beans too, this is the contemporary version of that old standby. It's a good salad without the anchovies, but they really do take it over the top. I am well aware this recipe breaks many a three-bean salad rule. I suppose I am going rogue.

- 8 ounces (225 g) Romano (flat Italian) beans, trimmed and cut into 2-inch pieces
- 1 pint jar Dilly Beans (page 209)
- 1 pint jar cannellini beans (page 248)
- ½ cup (4 oz., 120 ml) olive oil
- 2 ounces (57 g) feta cheese
- 2 to 4 anchovies, chopped (optional, but not really)
- 1 cup cherry tomatoes, halved
- ⅔ cup (5 oz., 130 g) Smoked Spiced Almonds (page 312), roughly chopped
- Kosher salt and freshly ground black pepper

1. In a medium saucepan, bring 3 cups of salted water to a boil over high heat. Add the Romano beans and cook until the beans are tender but still crunchy, about 7 minutes. Drain and cool in ice water. When thoroughly cooled, drain again.

2. Drain the dilly beans, reserving the brine. Cut them in halves or thirds, about the same length as the Romanos. Stir the two beans together in a large bowl.

3. Drain and rinse the cannellini beans and stir into the other beans.

4. Put ¼ cup of the reserved dilly bean brine in a jar, add the olive oil, cover, and shake well. Dress the salad with about half the dressing—start light and then add more only if needed, and in small quantities; do not drown the beans. Crumble the feta over the salad and garnish with the anchovies, if using, and halved tomatoes. Sprinkle the smoked almonds over the top. Taste and add salt and pepper as needed.

OPPOSITE: New-Fangled Three-Bean Salad

Spicy Pickled Okra

MAKES: three 24-ounce jars or 5 wide-mouth pint jars

ACTIVE TIME: 1 hour

CURING TIME: 1 month

Pickled okra will surprise you. I know what you're thinking, but it's not slimy. It's anything but. These are crispy, briny pickles, full of fresh chile heat. The okra pods are a welcome addition to a pickle plate, the snazziest cocktail garnish, and a perfect side to salty ham or charcuterie. But here's my secret trick: stuff okra pickles with Sweet-and-Spicy Pimento Cheese (page 217) for a crazy, salty, sweet, spicy treat. Southern-snackified insanity.

3 pints (32 oz., 900 g) very fresh, firm small okra

3 to 5 jalapeño, serrano, or Fresno chiles, stemmed and seeded

3 to 5 slim lemon slices, seeds removed

3 tablespoons pickling spice, homemade (page 185) or store-bought

2 cups (16 oz., 475 ml) cider vinegar

2 cups (16 oz., 475 ml) nonchlorinated water

¼ cup (1.25 oz., 35 g) kosher or pickling salt

3 to 5 garlic cloves (optional)

1. Wash the okra well. Trim by paring away all but about ¼ inch of the stems and removing the skinny leaves that surround the crowns. With a sharp paring knife, poke 2 or 3 holes in each okra pod to help the brine soak in.

2. Divide the chiles, lemon slices, and spices among the warm jars.

3. Keeping the 1-inch headspace in mind, pack the okra into the jars, alternating tail end up and down, until they fill each jar snugly. The okra should not poke up over the headspace.

4. In a 3-quart saucepan, bring the vinegar, water, salt, and garlic, if using, to a boil. Pour this hot brine over the okra, adding 1 garlic clove to each jar and leaving 1-inch headspace. Give it a minute or two to settle, then use a bubbler or plastic knife to settle the okra back into the jars. Add more brine as necessary, debubble, and allow to settle a couple more times before reviewing the headspace. During processing and as the pickles brine, they will absorb the liquid. Adding as much liquid as possible is your goal, but maintaining the headspace is also important. This takes practice. Clean the rims of the jars with a damp paper towel. Place the lids and rings on the jars and finger-tighten the rings.

5. Process in a boiling-water bath for 15 minutes. Let the jars sit in the canner for 5 minutes to prevent siphoning.

6. Let the okra pickles cure for 1 month before eating. It seems like a lifetime, I know.

OPPOSITE: Fresh okra

The pickles are shelf stable for 1 year.

Candied Chiles

MAKES: about 4 pint jars
ACTIVE TIME: 90 minutes

These snacking chiles are incendiary. There's no getting around how searingly hot they are and, at the same time, positively addictive. Scatter a few rings over a sandwich. Chop and add to chicken salad or deviled eggs. Stuff inside tacos or burritos. Garnish a Tequila-based cocktail. Mix into Sweet-and-Spicy Pimento Cheese (page 217).

Bright red Fresno chiles are beautiful, and worth slicing and candying in long swaths. I add them to a sweet potato or winter squash gratin to serve up a sassy side dish at Thanksgiving. I must have jalapeños too, but when the garden is abundant and more and more chiles are ripening, I'll use any chile, within reason. Whole candied Shishitos are delicious and surprising. Scotch Bonnets and other Scoville-index-busting chiles should not be mixed with the milder jalapeños and serranos, but they can be candied on their own and used sparingly. If you want to temper the heat, remove the seeds before starting the candying process.

Please wear gloves to handle the chiles. Open the kitchen windows, start the fan, and, if you are sensitive, wear glasses and cover your mouth with a bandana or breathing mask. The fumes are very strong.

6 cups (42 oz., 1200 g) granulated sugar

Four 3-inch cinnamon sticks

1 vanilla bean, slit open and seeds scraped out, seeds and bean reserved

8 allspice berries

• Seeds from 12 green cardamom pods (about ½ teaspoon)

2 cups (16 oz., 75 g) cider vinegar

3 pounds (1350 g) crisp jalapeños or serranos (green or red), sliced into ¼-inch rings

1. In a 5-quart or larger heavy nonreactive pan, combine the sugar, cinnamon, vanilla seeds and bean, cardamom, and cider vinegar, stir well, and bring to a boil. Clip on a candy thermometer and boil hard until the syrup reaches 215°F, about 10 minutes.

2. Add the sliced chiles, return the syrup to a boil and boil hard for 4 minutes. Remove the chiles with a slotted spoon and pack them tightly into the warm jars.

3. Boil the syrup for 5 minutes more, then ladle over the chiles, leaving ½-inch headspace. Remove air bubbles using a bubbler or plastic knife, running it around the perimeter of the jars and through the chiles, and adjust the liquid, maintaining the headspace.

4. Wipe the rims of the jars clean with a damp paper towel. Place the lids and rings on the jars and finger-tighten the rings.

5. Process in a boiling-water bath for 15 minutes.

The chiles are shelf stable for 1 year.

WASTE NOT, WANT NOT

Save any extra chile syrup in a jar in the refrigerator. It's wonderful brushed on grilled fish or chicken or shaken over ice with lime juice and a slug of tequila for a fiery cocktail.

Bonus Recipe: Sweet-and-Spicy Pimento Cheese

MAKES: 3 half-pint jars
ACTIVE TIME: 30 minutes
CHILLING TIME: at least 2 hours

I am not from the South, but I've lived below the Mason-Dixon Line long enough to grow fond, very fond, of many classic Southern foods. Biscuits, shrimp and grits, and panfried chicken rank high on my list, as well as this riff on the classic: spicy pimento cheese. If you are not familiar with this elixir of the gods, allow me to introduce you.

Use this for truly delightful grilled cheese sandwiches, or to make cheese "coin" crackers, or pipe it into celery sticks for a snappy teatime snack. I will admit to a crazy concoction that puckers my whistle: pickled okra stuffed with spicy pimento cheese. I've even fried that stuffed pickled okra. Call me crazy, but I know you're thinking about it.

2 cups (8 oz., 225 g) grated cheddar cheese, preferably orange

1 cup (4 oz., 110 g) grated extra-sharp cheddar cheese

2 cups (8 oz., 225 g) grated Monterey Jack cheese

4 ounces (110 g) cream cheese at room temperature

½ cup (4 oz., 110 g) minced jarred pimentos, homemade (page 264) or store-bought

½ teaspoon Hot Sauce (page 175), Tabasco, or Sriracha

12 to 24 Candied Chiles (page 214), depending on your preference for heat

1. Put all the cheeses, the pimentos, and hot sauce into the bowl of an electric mixer fitted with the paddle attachment and beat until smooth, with pieces of pimento throughout. Fold in the candied jalapeños.

2. Pack the cheese into wide-mouth half-pint jars and chill for 2 hours before serving, to let the flavors come together. Stored covered, in the refrigerator, the cheese will keep for about 2 weeks.

A MIDCENTURY CHEESE LOG

- To make a classic cheese log, put a big piece of plastic wrap on the counter. Arrange 1 cup finely chopped toasted pecans in a rectangle about 12 inches long and 3 inches wide down the center of the plastic wrap. Scrape the pimento cheese from the mixer bowl onto the pecan bed.

  Use the plastic wrap to form a log of cheese evenly coated with pecan. Lift the edges of the wrap and roll the cheese around in the pecans. Lightly roll the cylinder back and forth.

  Twist the ends of the wrap closed and refrigerate for at least 8 hours. Carefully turn the cylinder every couple of hours to keep it from flattening on one side.

OPPOSITE: Celery sticks filled with Sweet-and-Spicy Pimento Cheese

Pressure gauge

Chapter Two

CANNING UNDER PRESSURE: GROCERIES YOU'LL NEVER HAVE TO CARRY HOME AGAIN

STOCK, SOUP, BEANS, VEGETABLES, CHILES, PANTRY-READY MEAT AND FISH

OPPOSITE: Canned Dried Beans (clockwise from top left): Appaloosa, black, lima, and pinto (page 248)

f the water-bath method is the general education curriculum in the school of preserving, pressure-canning is graduate school. It's more demanding, it benefits from previous experience with water-bath-canning, and it is more science based. Pressure-canning sounds scary, and the equipment has dials and gauges, so it looks as if a lab coat and an advanced engineering degree is necessary. This is an overreaction. Like every other preserving activity, it requires precision, focus, and practice. And, like no other preserving practice, pressure-canning places homemade versions of grocery store staples like chicken stock, black beans, and chile-spiked tomatoes on your pantry shelves.

For years, I reveled in the meditative nature of jam making and pickling. This was a summer activity, and I took the canning kettle and other tools out in May and put them away in September. Then, with my growing interest in eating locally and living sustainably, came a desire to preserve foods that would be unsafe to can using the basic water-bath method. It wasn't long before I was dipping my toe into the world of pressure-canning. Eager to further reduce my dependency on commercially processed foods, I looked at those items I was still purchasing: stock, soups, and beans. I realized that with the power of the pressure canner behind me, I could increase the potential of my pantry and further the notion of self-sufficiency.

In only a matter of time, I was pulling jars of chicken stock from the canner and gazing at the golden liquid, shelf stable and so much better than store-bought cans of overly salty chicken broth. With this one basic grocery store commodity, I was sold.

I began to make soups. Instead of cans of commercial soups stocked in my pantry for those nights I just don't want to cook, I have jars of my own soup recipes, and I feel better for knowing exactly what went into the jars. Pressure-canning puts all sorts of beans on the shelf too: ready-to-eat cannellini, borlotti, kidney beans, and more.

Pressure-canning opens up the possibility of canning low-acid foods like corn and beets, and salsa made with less vinegar and more chiles. The luxury of shelf-stable, home canned tuna and elegant salmon, and the jewel in the pantry, duck confit, means fancy, beautiful, delicious meals in a snap.

As in other chapters, the recipes are arranged in order of increasing complexity. Start with canning stock, then move along to soups and beans. Soon you will be preserving oil-cured fish and duck, to the amazement of everyone around you.

Pressure-canning safety

I want to allay your fears, but I also want you to be a responsible pressure canner. It is a science and that means it's serious. Low-acid foods must be pressure-canned to be safe from the botulinum toxin that causes botulism, an odorless, tasteless, deadly poison.

Botulism is the most terrifying part of any canning. Botulism is a risk when dealing with fats, meats, thick purees, and low-acid foods like beans, corn, chiles, peppers, onions, and garlic, but pressure-canning kills botulinum spores. As long as the foods are safely processed and recipes are followed to the letter, including all the processing instructions and times (adjusting for altitude), you should not have an issue.

To safely can low-acid foods, the contents of the jars must be heated to 241°F. Water-bath-canning heats the foods to 212°F, but with the power of the pressure canner, using steam under pressure, the contents of the jars can be heated to the temperature at which botulinum spores are killed. This is science.

OPPOSITE: Weighted-gauge pressure canner

Steady pressure

The temperature and pressure in a pressure canner must be maintained for the entire time the food is being canned. If the pressure slips below the recommended weight, you must begin the timing again from the start—even if only a minute or two remain of the processing time. Restarting the clock is a very sad moment. I hope it won't happen to you, but I also know it will. Because of this inevitability, try not to initiate a canning project when you have time restrictions. Things always go awry when you can least afford it.

Monitoring a pressure canner is like watching paint dry, but there is no other option. You must be careful with this piece of equipment, respect it, and not leave it unattended.

Equipment choices

There is a substantial initial equipment investment when purchasing a **pressure canner**, but it can double as a water-bath canner and, in some instances, function as a pressure cooker. Pressure canners are large and bulky, and when I had limited storage space, the pressure canner was my only canning kettle, used for all types of canning. If you are committed to preserving, it's a worthwhile financial outlay.

Pressure canners are regulated by either a dial or a weighted gauge. The dial-gauge canner is less expensive but also a little fussier; the weighted version is easier to monitor. The two types of canner function in exactly the same way, pressurizing the interior of the sealed canner so the temperature rises above that of boiling water. The processing times in the recipes have been calculated mathematically, taking into account the density of the food to be processed, the size of the jars, and how long it will take to bring the food in the very center of the jars to 241°F. This is seriously, scaldingly hot. Take care when lifting quarts of soup from the canner—the bubbling inside the jars can continue for hours.

The **dial-gauge pressure canner** is lightweight aluminum and has a rubber gasket under the lid. The **weighted-gauge pressure canner** is heavier and locks down with clamps; it doesn't have a gasket. I prefer a weighted-gauge version because of the noise it makes. The petcock (the metal piece that covers the steam vent) rattles rhythmically when the pressure is correct. My ear is trained now, and so it is easy to work on other tasks while listening. A dial-gauge canner must be monitored visually. Keeping an unerring eye on the dial is confining for those of us who are mad multitaskers.

In this chapter, you'll find recipes sized to fill a standard 20- to 23-quart canner, producing larger yields than the small-batch jam and pickle recipes in the previous chapter. This size canner holds 7 quart jars or 14 pint jars (stacked).

If these larger yields seem like too much for your household, make a half recipe. There is no need to fill the canner, but because many pressure-canned recipes require long processing times, as well as constant monitoring and scientific precision, I like to be efficient and make the largest batch possible.

Note: At the time of this printing, no pressure canner can be used safely on a ceramic cooktop. The cooktops can crack under the weight, long processing times, and heat.

The direct heat from the bottom of the canner has the potential to break the base right off a jar, so you need a rack in the bottom of the pot to set the jars on. If you don't have a rack, a folded kitchen towel will serve the same purpose.

Need to stack the jars? Place another rack between the stacks. Some canners come with an extra rack. If yours did not, measure the interior diameter of your canner and find a similar-sized round cake rack, or, again, use a folded kitchen towel.

A weighted-gauge petcock is calibrated for 5, 10, and 15 pounds and rattles to indicate the canner has reached pressure. The petcock is placed over the valve after steam has streamed vigorously for 10 minutes. Monitor the amount of pressure in the canner with the pressure gauge/dial indicator. The gauge should be calibrated once a year. My local hardware store offers this service, as do some bicycle shops, auto shops, and garden centers. If you are unable to get the gauge calibrated, contact your local Extension Service for recommendations (see Resources, page 401).

The gasket, the rubber ring inside a dial-gauge canner's lid, ensures a tight seal. Check the gasket regularly. If it is cracked, stretched, or ripped, replace it before canning again.

You will want to have jars in all sizes and shapes (see page 27), as well as the other canning tools listed in the previous chapter (see page 180).

MAINTENANCE

As with any good piece of equipment, keeping your pressure canner well maintained is vital to its long life. Clean it thoroughly, especially the bottom of the pot, where hot spots can form. If you have hard water, clean the interior of the canner with diluted white vinegar to remove mineral deposits.

Do not lock down the cover when storing the canner as it may cause gasket fatigue.

TWO CANNERS IN ONE

If you use a pressure canner as a water-bath canner, do not lock the lid down; just set it on top of the canner. This is useful during tomato season, especially, when you want to process 7 quarts or 14 pints (stacked) at a time. Some canners opt to pressure-can crushed tomatoes and tomato sauce rather than using a water bath because tomatoes are of variable acidity, even with the addition of lemon juice or citric acid. So pressure-canning's higher temperatures offer an additional layer of safety. See page 260 for instructions for pressure-canning tomatoes.

Six steps to successful pressure-canning

1. Review water-bath canning, page 28.

2. Have at the ready clean jars, with no chips or cracks. The extreme heat of the pressure canner sanitizes the jars if processing for more than 20 minutes, so you can skip the sanitizing step that precedes water-bath canning. Fill the pressure canner with 4 inches of cool water, usually 3 or 4 quarts. Measure the depth the first time you use the canner and make note of the amount necessary. The water does not need to be hot. Fill a 1-quart saucepan with water. Add the jar rings and bring the water to a boil. Turn the heat off and add the new, never-used flat lids, to soften the rubber gaskets. Set aside.

3. Fill the jars, leaving the amount of headspace specified in the recipe (the distance from the top of the jar to the surface of the food in the jar). Remove any air bubbles using a bubbler, plastic knife, or chopstick. (Metal utensils can make tiny chips in the hot glass, making the jars more vulnerable to cracking under pressure.) Wipe the rims of the jars very carefully. Use white vinegar to cut any remnant of fat or other residue that might interfere with the seal. Place the lids and rings on the jars and finger-tighten the rings.

4. Place the jars upright in the pressure canner. The water does not need to cover the jars as it does in water-bath canning, because the jars are heated by steam under pressure. Lining up the arrows on the lid and the canner, turn the lid clockwise until it locks tight. Turn the heat to high and wait for a stream of steam to escape the valve. When the steam is vigorous and loud and a solid pale gray cloud is streaming upward, set the timer for 10 minutes. During this period, the canner is expelling the air inside, preparing to pressurize. When the steam has been expressed for 10 min-

utes, place the petcock over the steam valve and watch the pressure dial or, if using a weighted gauge, listen for the rattle that indicates the correct pressure has been reached. Hold the pressure steady at the weight indicated in the recipe, adjusted for your altitude if necessary. All the recipes in this book are calculated for sea-level processing. If you are processing at a higher altitude, refer to the chart on page 227 for adjustments necessary to both the pressure and timing. If at any time the pressure falls below the required pressure, restart the timer. And sigh loudly.

5. Once processing is complete, let the pressure fall all the way to zero before removing the petcock and releasing the vacuum lock. This usually takes about 40 minutes. (I often can at night and just leave the canner overnight to cool.) Remove the jars and place them upright on a folded kitchen towel on the counter or a towel-lined baking sheet. I find a baking sheet handy when I want to move the jars. Cool the jars completely, at least 12 hours, before removing the rings. Then, grasping just the lid, lift each jar by the lid. It should hold tight, indicating a safe seal.

6. Step back and admire your handiwork. It's taken a substantial bit of effort to get to this place, and you need to gloat for a few minutes. Wash the jars well, using white vinegar. Food often siphons out of the jars during pressure-canning and leaves deposits. Pressure-canned foods are so precious. Take the time to make the glass gleam. Then label each jar with the contents and date.

Selecting ingredients

Just as selecting the most delicious, beautiful produce is essential for ethereal jams and pickles, you also want to select the very best ingredients for pressure-canning. While these are basic, essential pantry items, they should still be exquisite. Organic foods and meats that are free-range and pastured are what you want to process. It's the food that deserves to be preserved.

There are ways to manage the expense of canning, primarily by taking advantage of seasonality, even with meats, poultry, and fish. Just as you buy tomatoes or peaches at the height of the harvest for the best prices, farm animals and animal husbandry run seasonally too. When canning, look for duck in autumn, salmon in springtime, and pork in winter. Before cold weather comes, many poultry farmers slaughter chickens to control keeping costs. This is a great time to pick up backs, necks, and gizzards, my preferred triumvirate for rich chicken stock (page 230).

Again: vegetables are most affordable and abundant seasonally. There are a few other ways to trim costs: Purchase slightly bruised produce—"seconds"—from market vendors. Offer to take whatever is left at the end of the day. Most farmers don't want to take food back to the farm.

Preorder pecks, bushels, flats, and other large quantities, and you'll be remembered. Do it often enough, and you'll make friends. Bring that farmer a pint of your soup, and soon you'll be exchanging holiday cards.

Always ask questions of the farmers at the market. Most are very happy to help you learn more. The more informed you become as a consumer, the more you will expand your pantry's dependability and practicality.

If you have children or friends who are game for some hard work, take advantage of pick-your-own opportunities. When corn is abundant, drive to a farm, harvest bushels, and have a shucking party. When your grocery store displays in-season foods from local farmers, buy in quantity.

Put the best in the jar to get the best out of it. It's really that simple.

The do-not-can list

These products are too dense or absorb too much liquid to be safely preserved. This is a no-fooling-around list. Just don't do it.

- Flour products, oats, wheat, and other grains.
- Dairy products.
- Pasta and noodles.
- Mashed vegetables like potatoes, squash, parsnips, and pumpkin.
- Broccoli.
- Bananas.
- Avocados.
- Coconut milk.
- Summer and winter squashes, Brussels sprouts, cabbage, cauliflower, lettuce, and artichokes can only be safely canned when pickled (acidified).

Altitude adjustments for pressure-canning

The recipes in this book have been calibrated at sea level. Use this chart to determine the correct pressure for where you live and make the necessary adjustments.

	Pounds of Pressure	
Altitude	Dial Gauge	Weighted Gauge
0–1,000 ft	10	10
1,001–2,000 ft	11	10
2,001–4,000 ft	12	15
4,001–6,000 ft	13	15
6,001–8,000 ft	14	15
8001–10,000 ft	15	15

TROUBLESHOOTING: FOIBLES, STUMBLES, TRIALS, FRUSTRATIONS, AND SCARY STUFF

Pressure-canning is going to scare you at first, and that's all right. Because making mistakes with pressure-canning could put you and everyone you feed at risk, you should be a little worried. Rather than call it fear, though, let's call it well-earned respect.

Learning to recognize a foible from a deadly mistake helps. Sometimes liquids siphon out of the jars, so, for example, beets are exposed, without a liquid covering. They may discolor or even get wrinkly, but they are still edible. Seal failure on a jar of tuna, though, is terrible. The fish must be refrigerated and eaten within a week. Without the seal, the fish will not have the time to cure to its velvety potential. Incorrect processing, seal failure, and changing recipes in ways that alter the density can lead to the proliferation of harmful bacteria, pathogens, and microorganisms.

The biggest hiccup is **seal failure**. Many of these pressure-canned foods contain oil or fats. Oils and fats, even in the most minuscule amounts, can interfere with the seal. Wipe the rim of each jar with white vinegar. Use your clean fingertip to feel the rim of the jar for anything that shouldn't be there. It should be squeaky clean; if not, clean it carefully one more time.

More worrisome, some seals simply give up in the pantry. The jar may have gotten too warm, possibly by spending some hours in direct sunlight. Sometimes the seal releases for no apparent reason. If the button in the center of the lid can be flexed, pushed up and down, that food is NOT SAFE. Throw it away without tasting.

If there is **cheesy foam** on the surface of the food when you remove the lid, throw the food away. If there is a **sulfurous smell**, throw the food away.

Pressure-canning is a powerful process and **siphoning**, when liquids boil up out of the jar, is one outcome. If remnants of whatever is being canned are evident in the water in the canner, that's the result of siphoning. Sometimes siphoning occurs but the seals still work; other times, siphoning interferes with the seal. Avoid siphoning by double-checking headspace and debubbling the jars carefully.

And then there is the sadness known only by the sound it makes: the gut-wrenching noise of **jars exploding** in the canner. Sadly, there is no way to know when this will happen. Jars have a life span. They weaken, and then they break. Carefully examine the jars you use and repurpose any with chips or cracks.

Pressure-canning is science. And you want science on your side when facing the formidable enemy, **botulism**. There will be stumbles along the way, but being exacting and imagining your kitchen as a laboratory will help. The times and pounds of pressure under which the foods are canned have been carefully calculated, based on how long it takes for the heat to reach the center of the filled jars. This is the only way to ensure the food will be safe. Using a pressure canner does not mean you have the room to start freewheeling.

Follow directions, don't change anything other than herbs and spices, and you will preserve safely. Veer off course in any way, especially by changing the ratios of liquids to solids, and there are no guarantees.

Always use a pressure canner for any product that has meat or oil. Recipes with peppers, chiles, onions, and garlic may be unsafe unless balanced with a LOT of added acid (as in pickling), but pressure-canning allows for vegetables to be processed in water alone. Some vegetables respond well to high temperatures (beets and corn), while others do not (asparagus and peas, for instance).

Stock

Many energetic home cooks make their own stock, and certainly all good cooks rely on stock for recipes. I won't lecture you on the value of homemade stock, or the economy of using bones left from other cooking projects. Instead, I will sing the praises of stock on the shelf; of jars sized for the job, a pint or a quart, depending on whether you are making a sauce or a soup; or of a freezer free of leaky plastic bags of stock or stacks of bulky containers that leave no room for your ice cream. We have priorities, people!

Stock making is an afternoon's work, but it is not the kind of work that precludes doing other things. Get those bones in a big pot and then maintain a simmer for hours. When the stock smells wonderful, it's ready. Break the work into two days, using a long rest in the refrigerator to separate the fat. (I find it enormously satisfying to remove that cap of fat.)

If your stock boils, proteins from the bones will accumulate at the surface. These are harmless but unattractive, and they should be strained out before canning. If some remain, they can be removed when the jar is opened.

Some bones, especially those from commercially raised chicken, may throw off cloudy gray foam. Scoop it off the surface of the stock with a clean stainless steel spoon; otherwise, it will remain even after straining. Consider pastured chickens the next time.

Having shelf-stable stock was one of the primary reasons I began pressure-canning. It's exceedingly practical. Please note that these four recipes are salt-free. I never add salt to stock (or fumet), preferring to add it after opening the jar. It's far easier to add salt than take it away.

A note on equipment: The best results will come from using a 16-quart or larger pot, or two 8-quart pots or another combination that adds up to 16 (or more) quarts.

A variety of canned stocks

Chicken Stock

MAKES: 6 to 8 quart jars or 12 to 16 pint jars, depending on how fatty the chicken is (recipe may be halved)
ACTIVE TIME: 30 minutes
SIMMERING TIME: 6 hours
CHILLING TIME: 12 hours to overnight

For years, I dutifully stored wing tips, backs, and chicken carcasses in the freezer. Every few weeks, I "stocked up" and made and froze cups and quarts of it in zip-lock bags. All that is just fine until the scream-inducing moment when the bag slips from the freezer and lands on your toe. And have you ever put a zip-lock bag of stock in the sink to defrost, only to find that there was a hole in the bag and all your lovely stock escaped down the drain? Oh yes, you'll appreciate the beauty of this useful chicken stock in jars.

Any 10 pounds of chicken parts, raw or cooked, or a combination, will do. Although cooked chicken carcasses have less to offer, go ahead and throw them in. But raw backs and necks are usually inexpensive and will result in the best flavor. If there are vendors at your farmers' market selling chicken parts, they will often be willing to sell the backs and necks at a good price. Or ask at the grocery store.

5 pounds (2.25 kg) chicken backs
5 pounds (2.25 kg) chicken necks
1 pound (450 g) chicken gizzards (optional)
3 pounds (1350 g) yellow onions
2 pounds (900 g) carrots, ends trimmed
8 ounces (230 g) celery stalks, including leaves
3 bay leaves (dried or fresh)
Large bunch of parsley stems
12 black peppercorns
12 fresh thyme sprigs or 2 teaspoons dried thyme
7 quarts (224 oz., 6.6 l) cool and nonchlorinated water

1. Add the backs, necks, and gizzards, if using, to a 16-quart stockpot. Quarter the onions, leaving the skins on, as they contribute a golden color, and add them to the pot. Chop or break the carrots and celery into 3 or 4 pieces each and add to the pot. Add the remaining ingredients and cover with the cool water. Bring to a boil, then reduce the heat to low, cover, and simmer gently for 6 hours. Do not let the stock boil, or it may become cloudy.

2. Strain the stock through a colander into large bowls or big jars and let cool, then cover and refrigerate for 12 hours or overnight.

3. Skim the fat from the cold stock, then strain it through a fine-mesh sieve lined in cheesecloth into a large stockpot. Bring the stock to a strong, rolling boil and boil for 10 minutes.

4. Ladle into the clean jars, leaving 1-inch headspace. Clean the jar rims well with white vinegar. Place the lids and rings on the jars and finger-tighten the rings.

5. Process the stock at 10 pounds of pressure: 20 minutes for pints, 25 minutes for quarts. If working with mixed sizes, process for 25 minutes. Let the pressure fall naturally and the canner cool completely before opening and removing the jars and placing on a folded towel.

6. Let the jars cool for 12 hours before removing the rings and lifting each jar by the flat lid; it should hold tight, indicating a safe seal.

The stock is shelf stable for 1 year.

Beef Stock

MAKES: 6 quart jars or 12 pint jars (recipe may be halved)
ACTIVE TIME: 2 hours
SIMMERING TIME: 6 hours
CHILLING TIME: overnight

Beef stock smells so wonderful while cooking, I could be accused of making it for that reason alone. The tomato paste that roasts on the bones brings out the rich, meaty flavor and adds a deep, appetite-inducing color. This stock is hearty, especially good as the base for onion soup.

10 pounds (4.5 kg) meaty beef bones, either shanks or ribs, or a combination
5 large shallots, halved
4 garlic cloves, halved
4 cups (32 oz., 900 g) roughly chopped carrots
1 large celeriac (12 oz., 340 g), chopped into large pieces
3 tablespoons tomato paste
1 tablespoon olive oil
5 quarts (160 oz., 4.7 l) cool nonchlorinated water
12 black peppercorns
3 dried bay leaves
12 parsley stems

1. Preheat the oven to 425°F. Line a baking sheet with parchment.

2. Put the bones, shallots, garlic, carrots, and celeriac on the baking sheet. Combine the tomato paste and oil in a small bowl, then rub all over the bones and vegetables. Spread the bones and vegetables out and roast until well browned, about 40 minutes; rotate the pan halfway through.

3. Transfer the roasted bones, vegetables, and any juices to a large stockpot (see page 22). Add ¼ cup of the water to the baking sheet to loosen any tasty bits and scrape this *fond* into the stockpot. Add the peppercorns, bay leaves, and stems to the pot, add the remaining water, and bring to a boil. Reduce the heat, skim any foam, cover, and simmer gently for 6 hours.

4. Strain the stock through a colander into large bowls or jars. Refrigerate overnight.

5. Scrape the solidified fat from the stock and discard. Strain the stock through a fine sieve into the stockpot and bring to a boil.

6. Ladle into the clean jars. Wipe the jar rims clean with white vinegar. Place the lids and rings on the jars and finger-tighten the rings.

7. Process at 10 pounds of pressure: pint jars for 20 minutes, quart jars for 25 minutes. If you have a mixed batch, process for the full 25 minutes. Let the pressure fall and the canner cool before removing the jars.

8. Let the jars cool completely, then test the seal.

The stock is shelf stable for 1 year.

Brown Veal Stock

MAKES: 7 quart jars or 14 pint jars (recipe may be halved)
ACTIVE TIME: 90 minutes
SIMMERING TIME: 6 hours
CHILLING TIME: 12 hours to overnight

Veal stock is a chef's ingredient that will bump up your home cooking to restaurant quality. Veal stock has the flexibility of chicken stock with the added bonus of a velvety texture that ramps up any pan sauce (see page 123). Veal is a seasonal product, so look for bones in spring and early fall, especially.

Roasting the bones deepens the flavor and color of this stock. Do not roast the bones if you want a pale stock with the flexibility of chicken stock and the boost of collagen for a silky smoothness. It is sensational in any braise and essential for minestrone.

10	pounds (4.5 kg) veal bones
3	tablespoons tomato paste
1½	pounds (700 g) onions (about 8), peel left on and quartered
4	garlic cloves, crushed and peeled
2	pounds (900 g) carrots, roughly chopped
8	ounces (230 g) celery stalks, including tops, roughly chopped
8	quarts (7.5 l) nonchlorinated water
4	dried bay leaves
•	Large bunch of parsley stems
12	black peppercorns
12	fresh thyme sprigs or 2 teaspoons dried thyme

1. Preheat the oven to 400°F.

2. Put the veal bones on a baking sheet and rub them all over with the tomato paste. Spread the bones out on the baking sheet. Scatter the onions, garlic, carrots, and celery around the bones. Roast the bones and vegetables until well browned, about 45 minutes, rotating the baking sheet halfway through.

3. Transfer the roasted bones and vegetables to an 11- to 12-quart stockpot. Add ½ cup hot water to the baking sheet, scrape up all the browned bits (*fond*), and add to the pot. Add the remainder of the cool water, the bay leaves, parsley stems, peppercorns, and thyme, bring the stock to a boil, and skim any foam that develops. Reduce the heat, cover, and keep at a very low simmer, without boiling, for 6 hours.

4. Strain the stock through a colander into large bowls or half-gallon jars and let cool. Cover and refrigerate for 12 hours, or overnight.

5. Skim the fat from the stock and strain it through a fine-mesh sieve into an 8-quart stockpot. Heat the stock to boiling and boil for 10 minutes.

Recipe continues

6. Ladle into the clean jars. Carefully wipe the rims of the jars with a vinegar-dampened towel. Place the lids and rings on the jars and finger-tighten the rings.

7. Process the stock at 10 pounds of pressure: 20 minutes for pints, 25 minutes for quarts. If working with a batch of mixed sizes, process for 25 minutes. Let the pressure fall and the canner cool before removing the jars.

8. Let the jars cool completely, about 12 hours, then test the seals.

The stock is shelf stable for 1 year.

Fish Fumet

MAKES: 7 pint jars
ACTIVE TIME: 1 hour
SIMMERING TIME: 1 hour

F*umet*, the fancy French word for fish stock, smells of the sea, in only the very best way. It is my go-to start for seafood risotto, chowder, and cioppino. It can be a little challenging to get your hands on fish bones and heads, which is why you want to make friends with your fishmonger. Mild-flavored fish like cod, flounder, whitefish, pike, and haddock are appropriate for this broth; fish like salmon and mackerel, with their high fat content and strong flavors, are not.

1	tablespoon olive oil
2	pounds (900 g) leeks, white and pale green parts, roughly chopped (about 4 cups)
2	pounds (900 g) carrots, roughly chopped (about 4 cups)
2	tablespoons lovage leaves or 1 celery stalk, roughly chopped
5	pounds (2.25 kg) bones and heads (see headnote)
1	cup (8 oz., 235 ml) dry white wine or white vermouth
4	quarts (64 oz., 3.8 l) cool nonchlorinated water
12	black peppercorns
12	parsley stems
2	dried bay leaves
1	teaspoon dried thyme

1. Heat the oil in an 8-quart or larger stockpot over medium heat. Add the leeks, carrots, and lovage and cook until soft and translucent but not browned, about 10 minutes. Increase the heat to medium, add the fish bones, and sauté for 5 minutes, turning the bones frequently.

2. Cover the pot and steam everything for 5 minutes, then add the wine and cook until the wine simmers steadily. Add the water, peppercorns, parsley, bay, and thyme and increase the heat and bring the mixture to the edge of a boil, then turn down the heat. (Do not let the mixture boil, or the stock will become cloudy and taste bitter.) Cover and gently simmer the stock for 1 hour.

3. Strain the stock through a fine-mesh strainer lined with damp cheesecloth into another pot or a large bowl. Ladle the hot stock into the clean jars. Wipe the jar rims clean with white vinegar. Place the lids and rings on the jars and finger-tighten the rings.

4. Process at 10 pounds of pressure for 20 minutes. Let the pressure fall and the canner cool before removing the jars.

5. Let the jars cool completely, about 12 hours, then test the seals.

The fumet is shelf stable for 6 months.

VARIATION
• Substitute the fish bones with the shells from 4 dozen shrimp or from 6 lobsters for a sublime seafood stock that adds remarkable depth of flavor to fish stews and seafood risottos.

Soup

There are times when homemade soup satisfies and comforts like nothing else. Maybe you have a scratchy throat that makes you want your pajamas and a blanket. Or you've worked way too late after beginning the day way too early. Or you've just returned home from a business trip.

Sure, with all that gorgeous chicken and beef stock on the shelf, you could make a soup from start to finish fairly easily, but there are times when you don't want to do even that. That's when simply emptying a jar into a pot, then filling a favorite bowl with rib-sticking soup, is just what the doctor ordered.

Grains, flour products, cream, and other dairy products are unsafe additions to the soup before processing. But if you want to stretch the jar to accommodate more people, you can add cooked noodles or rice when heating the soup, or simply thin with a little cream or milk before serving.

I think of these recipes as a practical approach to too many leftovers. After the holidays or a big party, when the menu included turkey, ham, or beef, the leftovers readily transform into several quarts of goodness.

The roasted tomato soup? That's the result of leftovers too. It was a recipe borne of overshopping. After peeling and crushing 100 pounds of tomatoes for canning, I simply could not face the last box, so I roasted them and made soup.

For these soups, fill the jars no more than halfway with solids and then top off with the liquid, leaving 1-inch headspace. More solids will alter the density of the soup and make your soup unsafe.

Salt these soups to your own taste, or keep them salt-free, and then salt to taste after opening. Salt is not necessary for preserving.

Soups take well over an hour to process in the pressure canner, so get comfortable and settle in. It's worth it.

OPPOSITE: Roasted Tomato Soup (page 240)

Split Pea Soup, with or without Ham (Condensed)

MAKES: 7 pint jars
ACTIVE TIME: 90 minutes

Split pea soup is comforting and homey. It is a happy supper on a chilly day, served with a salad or an omelet. Split pea loves ham, and it's a great soup to make after a holiday when staring down a huge ham bone. And it's a versatile soup. You can make this vegetarian-friendly by using water instead of stock, omitting the ham, and adding a good tablespoon of smoked paprika. This soup is thick, because the peas absorb a lot of liquid during processing. So think of it as "condensed," like those soups in the red-and-white cans. To serve, add an equal measure of water (see Note).

You can use the food processor or your fierce knife skills to mince the vegetables. If using the food processor, cut the vegetables into 2-inch chunks, then pulse a few quick times. Do not puree.

¼ cup (2 oz., 60 ml) olive oil

1½ pounds (700 g) onions, minced (about 4 cups)

1 pound (450 g) carrots, minced (about 2 cups)

4 garlic cloves, minced (about 2 tablespoons)

¼ cup (0.5 oz., 14 g) fresh thyme

1 tablespoon smoked paprika (for the vegetarian option only; see headnote)

2 pounds (900 g) dried green split peas

4 quarts (3.8 l) Brown Veal Stock (page 233), or Chicken Stock (page 230), or water

2 tablespoons (0.6 oz., 17 g) kosher salt

2 teaspoons freshly ground black pepper

3 cups (24 oz., 680 g) minced ham (optional)

1. Heat the oil in a 6-quart or larger stockpot. Add the onions, garlic, and carrots and cook over low heat just until the onions turn translucent; do not let them color, or your soup may become bitter.

2. Add the thyme, paprika, if using, and split peas and stir well to coat the peas in the oil, then add the stock or water. Bring to a boil, reduce the heat, and simmer for 40 minutes. Season the soup with the salt and pepper (resist the urge to oversalt—the salty flavor may amplify with pressure canning, and there is no turning back once soup is oversalted). There is no need to blend the soup; it will liquefy in the high heat of the pressure canner.

3. For the meaty version, add 2 ounces of ham to each quart jar and 1 ounce to each pint jar.

4. Divide the soup among the jars, filling them no more than half-way with solids and leaving 1-inch headspace. Wipe the jar rims clean with white vinegar. Place the lids and rings on the jars and finger-tighten the rings.

5. Process the soup at 10 pounds of pressure: 75 minutes for pints, and 90 minutes for quarts. For a mixed batch, use the longer time. Allow the pressure to fall naturally and the canner to cool completely, about 40 minutes.

6. Remove the jars and place upright on a folded kitchen towel on the counter. Leave the jars for 12 hours to cool thoroughly, then test the seal.

The soup is shelf stable for 1 year.

Note: To serve, empty the contents of a jar into a soup pot, then fill the jar with water and pour that into the pot as well. Simmer for 10 minutes, add salt and pepper to taste, and ladle into warm bowls.

VARIATIONS

- Leave out the ham and substitute yellow or red lentils for the split peas. Replace the thyme with 1 tablespoon curry powder.
- Exchange lentils du Puy for the split peas and cooked smoked bacon for the ham.
- Swap tasso ham for the ham bone and add a big pinch of gumbo filé.
- Add a quart of chopped tomatoes, switch oregano for the thyme, and use flageolet beans. Flavor with cooked pancetta.

A Box of Tomatoes and Forty Cloves of Garlic: Roasted Tomato Soup

MAKES: 5 quart jars or 10 pint jars, or a combination
ACTIVE TIME: 2½ hours

Like the tomato soup in the familiar red-and-white can, this home-canned version is slightly condensed. With the added dimension of garlic and fennel, this soup warms the belly like no other. Serve for summer lunches or winter suppers, or in small sipping cups to greet guests on a cold day. A jar of ready-to-eat soup is a great housewarming gift and an inspired little extra to send back with a college-bound student. To serve, empty the contents of a jar into a soup pot, then fill the jar with water or milk and pour that into the pot as well. Simmer for 10 minutes, taste for salt and pepper, and ladle into warm bowls.

12 pounds (5.4 g) ripe tomatoes, cored and cut in half

1 pound (450 g) carrots, roughly chopped

1½ pounds (625 g) onions, quartered

12 ounces (340 g) fennel bulbs, trimmed, cored, and quartered

40 garlic cloves, peeled

¼ cup (2 oz., 60 ml) mild olive oil

½ cup (1.25 oz., 35 g) fresh basil leaves, stacked, rolled up like a cigar, and cut in a chiffonade (thin strips)

½ cup (1.25 oz., 35 g) coarsely chopped fresh flat-leaf parsley

3 cups (24 oz., 710 ml) Chicken Stock (page 230)

1 tablespoon kosher salt

1 teaspoon coarsely ground black pepper

1. Position the racks in the upper and lower thirds of the oven. Preheat to 425°F. Line two baking sheets with parchment.

2. Arrange the tomato halves snugly on the baking sheets, cut side up. Tuck in the carrots, onion, fennel, and garlic. Drizzle all the vegetables with olive oil. Roast the vegetables until the edges caramelize, about 1 hour. Remove from the oven and cool slightly.

3. Add the tomatoes, vegetables, basil, and parsley to the beaker of a blender. Blend in batches, pouring the smooth puree into an 8-quart heavy stockpot. (Alternatively, puree with an immersion blender right in the pot.) Add the chicken stock, salt, and pepper to the pot, stir well, and bring to a simmer. Simmer for 10 minutes.

4. Ladle into the jars, leaving 1-inch headspace. Wipe the jar rims clean with white vinegar. Place the lids and rings on the jars and finger-tighten the rings.

5. Process at 10 pounds of pressure: pints for 60 minutes, quarts for 70 minutes. If your batch includes both sizes, use the longer time. Allow the pressure to fall and the canner to cool completely.

6. Remove the jars and place on a folded towel on the counter to completely cool, about 12 hours, then test the seal.

The soup is shelf stable for 1 year.

Leftover-Turkey Soup

MAKES: 8 quart jars (recipe may be halved)
ACTIVE TIME: 2½ hours

After Thanksgiving, a sense of economy and overabundance collide. Without a doubt, it's time to make turkey soup, but who wants any more turkey? Here's your solution: pressure-can it. In the dark days of February, everyone will be grateful for jars of turkey soup. To make turkey stock, substitute turkey for chicken in the recipe on page 230.

Do not add grains or noodles to this soup before canning; grains and flour products are unsafe to process in any way (and they absorb all the liquid). Add fully cooked grains or noodles when you serve the soup instead. Clever recipe tester Christine suggested setting aside a quart of the vegetable-strewn broth for dinner. It's that good.

1 to 2 tablespoons olive oil
3 cups (16 oz., 450 g) diced yellow onion
8 quarts (246 oz., 7.5 l) Chicken Stock (page 230) or turkey stock (see headnote) or a combination
4 cups (32 oz., 900 g) diced carrots
2 cups (12 oz., 340 g) diced celery
1 cup (8 oz., 225 g) diced fennel
2 tablespoons kosher salt, or to taste
1 tablespoon coarsely ground black pepper, or to taste
1 cup (1 oz., 10 g) roughly chopped fresh flat-leaf parsley
• An herb bundle: 12 fresh parsley stems, 12 fresh thyme sprigs, 3 fresh sage sprigs, and 3 fresh rosemary sprigs, tied together with kitchen string
• Up to 4 cups (32 oz., 500 g) cooked turkey, diced, shredded, or roughly chopped

1. Heat the oil briefly in a 12-quart stock pot, then stir in the onions and cook over medium heat until they wilt but are not brown (if they brown, the soup may be bitter after canning). Just as the wilting begins, stir in 1 cup of the stock and let the onions simmer, about 10 minutes.

2. Add the carrots, celery, fennel, salt, and pepper and stir well. Allow the vegetables to soften slightly. Add another cup of stock, stir, bring to a simmer, and simmer for 5 minutes. Add the turkey, the remaining 7 ½ quarts stock, parsley, and the herb bundle and bring to a boil, then reduce to a simmer and simmer, uncovered, for 30 minutes. Fish out the herb bundle. Taste for salt and pepper.

3. Divide the turkey evenly among the clean jars. Using a perforated ladle or a skimmer, fill the jars halfway with the other soup solids. Ladle in the soup, leaving 1-inch headspace. Remove any air bubbles and adjust the liquid, adding more as necessary to retain the headspace. Clean the jar rims. Place the lids and rings on the jars and finger-tighten the rings.

4. Process at 10 pounds of pressure: 75 minutes for pints, 90 minutes for quarts. For a mixed batch, use the longer processing time. Cool the canner completely.

5. Place the jars upright on a folded towel to cool for at least 12 hours, then test the seal.

The soup is shelf stable for 1 year.

Beef and Vegetable Borscht

MAKES: 8 quart jars or 16 pint jars, or any combination (recipe may be halved)
ACTIVE TIME: 3 hours, over 2 days
BEAN SOAKING AND STOCK CHILLING TIME: overnight

This soup is an homage to my Grandmother Mary, who made a barley-studded version she called Aunt Sophie's Flanken Soup. With every mouthful, you could taste her Lithuanian homeland. The cabbage adds body and the beets contribute a rich dark color. The gigante beans fascinated me as a child. I loved their texture and chased them around the soup pot to get extras for my bowl.

This is a tummy-warming, old-fashioned bowl of goodness made rich with the addition of flanken, an Old World cut of the cow's long ribs (the opposite of short ribs). It is a rich and silky cut with brisket-like texture, reminiscent of the meat floating in excellent pho or long-cooked pulled beef barbeque. In a pinch, you can use short ribs, but try to find flanken. Your weary spirit will benefit from a bowl of this soup, full of grandmotherly love.

Serve with or without a tablespoon of sour cream floating on top.

8 ounces (225 g) dried gigante beans

3 pounds (1350 g) beef flanken

6 quarts (192 oz., 5.7 l) Beef Stock (page 232)

4 pint jars Canned Beets (page 254), drained

3 pounds (1350 g) red onions, sliced into half-moons

2 pounds (900 g) carrots, peeled and sliced into ½-inch chunks

2 pounds (900 g) white cabbage, chopped (not shredded)

2 pounds (900 g) russet potatoes, peeled and chunked

4 cups (32 oz., 950 ml) dry red wine

1. Cover the gigante beans with cool water in a large bowl, cover with a tea towel, and soak overnight on the counter.

2. Meanwhile, put the flanken in a Dutch oven or other pot wide enough to accommodate it in a single layer. Add just enough of the stock to cover. Bring to a boil, then reduce the heat, cover, and simmer until the meat shreds easily off the bone, usually about 1½ hours. Remove the meat and set aside. Strain the broth through a fine colander and refrigerate.

3. When the flanken has cooled, using your fingers, shred the meat and discard the gristle and fat. Add the meat to the broth, cover, and refrigerate.

4. The next day, drain and rinse the gigante beans. Put in a 5-quart stockpot, cover with water and bring to a boil, then reduce the heat, cover, and simmer until tender, about 40 minutes. Remove from the heat.

- **An herb bundle: 15 fresh thyme sprigs, 15 fresh flat-leaf parsley stems, and 2 bay leaves, tied together with kitchen string**
- 2 **tablespoons kosher salt**
- 1 **teaspoon freshly ground black pepper**
- 1 **cup (3 oz., 85 g) finely minced fresh dill**

5. Meanwhile, remove the fat from the (remaining) stock. In a 12-quart or larger stockpot, combine the stock, beets, onions, carrots, cabbage, potatoes, wine, herb bundle, salt, and pepper, bring to a simmer and simmer for 1 hour.

6. Drain the beans. Add them, along with the meat and broth and the dill to the stockpot and simmer for another hour.

7. Using a skimmer or perforated ladle, fill the jars no more than halfway with the soup solids. Add the broth, leaving 1-inch headspace. Wipe the jar rims clean with white vinegar. Place the lids and rings on the jars and finger-tighten the rings.

8. Process at 10 pounds of pressure: 60 minutes for pint jars, 80 minutes for quart jars. Process for 80 minutes if you have a mixed batch of jars. Cool the canner completely.

9. Place the jars upright on a folded towel to cool for at least 12 hours, then check the seals.

The soup is shelf stable for 1 year.

Fresh lima beans

Beans

Beans are an essential part of our dinner rotation, providing quick, healthy, protein-filled vegetarian meals. Just think burritos, dips, soups, salads, and cassoulet and I know you'll be ready to jump on this bandwagon.

Dried beans are widely available in the grocery store. Unfortunately, though, if the inventory doesn't turn over regularly, you may find dried beans that are old and dusty. Do your best to purchase the freshest dried beans. Sometimes in late summer, local farmers will bring fresh shell beans, in or out of the pod, to market. Until recently, these beans, sometimes called field peas, have been as rare as hen's teeth in most parts of the country other than the Southern states. They are also called truck crops, lady peas, or Southern peas. Look for pinto, white, black-eyed peas, butter beans, limas, black, cannellini, kidney, and others with fabulous names like Red Ripper and crowder and cream peas. Some farmers are now planting borlotti and other heirloom varieties. They come and go quickly, so line up your sources. Fresh beans are tender, grassy, and smooth textured and worth hunting down.

Each time I plan a bean canning session, I cook five pounds of legumes, whether dried or freshly picked. By canning different types—kidney, black, white, lima, butter, and more—I always have options right in the pantry, no cans, no trips to the store, and no waste. Sometimes, I make up a mixed batch of beans—all the different types thrown in together for that year's special blend.

Be aware that canned beans sometimes absorb the cooking liquid as they stand, so they seem to be liquid-less in the jar. They are just fine, safe, and delicious, but I always count on that deeply satisfying pot likker, the creamy elixir surrounding long-cooked beans. If you're from the South, you know what I am talking about. To use these beans, spoon them out, fill the jar with clean water, shake, and pour the water over the beans.

There is a slight possibility that certain pathogens carried by dried beans may remain beyond the canning process. To avoid any concerns, always heat canned beans for 10 minutes before using them in salads or pureeing for a dip. Beans that will be added to soups or stews and cooked again are not at issue.

Fresh field beans—
unshucked

Fresh field beans—
shucked

Canned Dried Beans

MAKES: 5 to 6 quart jars or 11 pint jars, or any combination
ACTIVE TIME: 2½ hours
SOAKING TIME: overnight

Use the very freshest dried beans you can get and process at least five pounds at a time, to make the effort worthwhile. I like to process a mix of pints and quarts; it's helpful to have just the right amount for any recipe.

I do not add salt before processing, but instead wait and salt to taste after opening the jar. By the way, those bay leaves? They help reduce the foaming, as well as the gassiness.

2 pounds (900 g) dried beans (black, pinto, lima, cannellini or kidney, or any mix)

2 dried bay leaves

• About 4 quarts (128 oz., 3.8 l) nonchlorinated water

1. Rinse the beans well and pick through them to remove any stones or debris. Cover the beans with cold water in a large bowl or pot and soak overnight.

2. Rinse and drain the beans. Add, along with the bay leaves, to an 8-quart or larger stockpot. Pour in about 4 quarts of cold water, enough to cover by 2 inches. Bring to a murmuring boil and boil gently for 30 minutes. Skim the foam from the surface.

3. Set a colander over a large bowl and pour the beans and liquid into the colander; reserve the cooking liquid. Ladle the beans into the clean jars, filling them no more than two-thirds full. Add the bean cooking liquid, leaving 1-inch headspace. Slip a bubbler or plastic knife inside each jar and remove any air bubbles. Add more liquid, or boiling water if necessary. Bubble again. Clean the rims of the jars. Place the lids and rings on the jars and finger-tighten the rings.

4. Process at 10 pounds of pressure: 75 minutes for pint jars, 90 minutes for quart jars. If processing mixed sizes, use the 90-minute processing time.

The beans are shelf stable for 1 year.

Bonus Recipe: Everyday Deep-Dish Potpie

SERVES: 8

ACTIVE TIME: 1 hour

I love a potpie, whether in ramekins sized for one or as a big deep-dish wonder. I like my potpies topped with buttermilk biscuits or tucked under flaky pie dough, crimped and decorated with fancy vents cut into the top, but sometimes I lather the pie from stem to stern with a thick coating of buttery mashed potatoes. What follows is a recipe for a deep-dish pie with a crust, but feel free to substitute mashed potatoes or biscuits. This is refrigerator-friendly, leftover-using pantry food that feeds an army and leaves everyone happily rubbing their tummies.

5 tablespoons (2.5 oz., 70 g) unsalted butter

2 cups (9 oz., 260 g) frozen pearl onions

2 tablespoons firmly packed light brown sugar

1 cup (5 oz., 132 g) diced carrots (about 3 medium)

½ cup (2 oz., 59 g) diced celery (about 1 stalk)

8 cremini mushrooms, cleaned, stemmed, and quartered

3 tablespoons all-purpose flour

½ cup (3 oz., 85 g) chopped Smoked Bacon (page 313) or country ham (optional)

1 quart jar canned butter beans or lima beans (page 248 or 251)

2 teaspoons herbes de Provence (a blend of herbs that includes lavender; substitute dried thyme or oregano if you do not care for lavender)

1. Heat 2 tablespoons of the butter in a deep wide sauté pan until it foams and then browns slightly. Add the pearl onions and cook until they begin to color. Sprinkle with the brown sugar, turn the heat to high, and shake the pan until the onions are well caramelized; keep them moving so they won't scorch. Scrape the butter and onions into a small bowl. Set aside.

2. Wipe out the pan, return to the stove, and add the remaining 3 tablespoons butter. Heat over medium-high heat until foamy. Add the carrots and celery and cook until soft, 10 minutes or so. Add the mushrooms, stir once, and then cook without stirring until they have released and reabsorbed their liquid, another 8 to 10 minutes.

3. Add the caramelized onions, then sprinkle the flour over all the vegetables. Stir to coat the vegetables in the fats and flour, then stir to create a roux and cook until the roux is lightly browned and the vegetable mixture is cloaked in the sauce. Add the bacon, if using, the butter beans, herbs, and lemon zest, then add the wine, bring to a boil, and reduce the wine by half, about 7 minutes.

4. Add the stock and bring to a boil, then reduce the heat and simmer until slightly thickened, about 10 minutes. Stir in the corn and peas. Taste and season with salt and pepper. Let cool for a few minutes. (Hot filling will make the piecrust soggy.)

5. Position the racks in the middle and lower third of the oven and preheat the oven to 425°F.

Recipe continues

½ teaspoon grated lemon zest

½ cup (4 oz., 120 ml) dry white wine or vermouth

4 cups (32 oz., 1 l) Chicken Stock (page 230), vegetable broth, or water

1 pint jar Canned Corn (page 265)

1 cup (4 oz., 125 g) frozen petite peas

• Kosher salt and freshly ground black pepper

• Mrs. Wheelbarrow's Perfect Piecrust (page 133)

6. Pour the vegetable mixture into a 9-inch deep-dish pie pan. Lightly flour the counter and roll out the dough to a 13-inch circle. Cover the filling with the crust. Decoratively crimp the edges and vent the crust with a couple of deep slashes.

7. Slide the pie onto the middle oven rack and place a baking sheet on the rack below, because it will surely bubble over. Bake for 20 minutes, then reduce the heat to 350°F and bake for 40 minutes, or until the filling is bubbling and the crust is browned. Tent with foil if the crust browns too quickly. Let the pie rest for a few minutes before serving.

VARIATIONS

• Add up to 2 cups cooked turkey, chicken, beef, pork, sausage, or any other protein, instead of beans.

• Add up to 4 cups winter squash, such as butternut or kabocha, cubed and steamed, instead of or in addition to the beans.

• Try different toppers: cornmeal crust, buttermilk biscuits, chive dumplings, or buttered mashed potatoes.

• Assemble in individual ramekins, cover with a crust, and freeze—a right-sized dinner for one. These small pies will not take as long to bake (10 minutes at 425°F and 25 minutes at 350°F, or until bubbling).

Canned Fresh Field Beans

MAKES: 5 to 6 quart jars or 11 pint jars or a combination of sizes
ACTIVE TIME: 2 hours

From mid-September until late October, a vendor at our farmers' market brings coolers filled with freshly shelled field beans: pinto, black, black-eyed peas, limas, butter beans, and even more varieties, just hours off the plant, shucked, rinsed, and sold by the pound. His arrival means hours of canning, but it's worth it. Twenty pounds of fresh field beans is a sufficient supply for an entire year for my husband and me.

Fresh field beans are very different from dried beans: spectacularly tender and flavorful. Field beans in the pod take some work to shuck, but consider it a pleasant way to spend an afternoon while storytelling with family or friends. It's a quiet, repetitive, and soothing task. Of course, if this just seems like too much work, you can always opt for canning dried beans (see page 248).

See photographs on pages 246 and 247.

2 pounds (900 g) shucked field beans (from 12 pounds, 5.4 kg beans in the pod)

2 dried bay leaves

• About 8 cups (1 l) cool nonchlorinated water

1. Rinse the beans well: rinse many times, then rinse again. Pick through to remove any stones or debris. Place the beans and bay leaves in an 8-quart or larger stockpot, add enough cool water to cover by about 2 inches and bring to a strong boil. Reduce the heat and simmer for 30 minutes; skim any foam from the surface from time to time.

2. Drain the beans, reserving the cooking liquid. Remove the bay leaves. Funnel the beans into the jars, filling them loosely about two-thirds full. Add the reserved cooking liquid, leaving 1-inch headspace. Carefully debubble the jars and continue to add liquid and remove air bubbles, maintaining the headspace.

3. Clean the rims of the jars. Add the lids and finger-tighten the rings. Process at 10 pounds of pressure: 40 minutes for pint jars, 50 minutes for quart jars to process. Use the longer time if you have mixed sizes of jars in the canner.

The beans are shelf stable for 1 year.

Canned Corn (page 265)

Vegetables and chiles

Canned low-acid vegetables harbor the danger of botulism. Tomatoes are the most frequently canned low-acid vegetable. For water-bath processing, to lower the pH, canned tomatoes must be acidified with citric acid or lemon juice (see page 38). Pressure-canning requires no added acidification, so it both preserves the flavor of the tomatoes and is a safer, quicker option. If you have a pressure canner, I urge you to move your tomato canning to this marvelous machine. Bringing tomatoes to 241°F using the pressure canner kills botulinum spores. I've included a chart with the time and pressures for pressure-canning the water-bath tomato recipes on page 260. I've included the water-bath (acidified) method so tomato canning is available to everyone, but I use the pressure canner for all tomato canning. It's dependable, fast, and safe.

Beets, green beans, corn, and potatoes, the most commonly processed low-acid vegetables, absolutely must be pressure-canned. But after a few attempts at green beans and potatoes, I gave up: I found the canned versions mealy and without flavor. Now I blanch and freeze green beans and store potatoes in our unheated garage.

Beets and corn, on the other hand, retain their freshness, flavor, and texture when pressure-canned. These two vegetables are very practical. (And let's be real here, the whole process of peeling beets is so time-consuming, why not do it all at once and enjoy the sweet, deep, rich flavor later, without all the tedium?) I open a jar of beets and add a few slices to a salad or dice up a small beet and stir into hummus for a rosy glow. Or even make a quick borscht for one.

And corn? It's ubiquitous and yet I think it's underappreciated. We love it all summer, why not enjoy it all year long? Buy at least a dozen extra ears of corn each time you are at the market. Scrape and freeze the kernels until you've gathered at least 8 cups, enough to can. Corn livens up chili, corn bread, and bean salads. It adds texture to grits and polenta and morning muffins and pancakes.

The chile-spiked tomatoes on page 259 are heaven-sent additions to just about any stew or soup. And, in much the same way, the barbeque sauce (page 263) cheers up a chicken dinner.

These foods make a self-styled grocery store in my pantry. They are modern, utterly sustainable convenience foods.

Canned Beets

MAKES: 4 wide-mouth pint jars
ACTIVE TIME: 90 minutes

Beets are a divisive vegetable. So many people love them, so many don't. In our household, I stand alone in the "love them" camp. Every summer I put up a few jars of beets to be readily transformed into any one of a dozen different salads. My favorite may be beet, orange, and pecans over leafy greens (see page 257), but I'm equally enamored of beet, grapefruit, and fennel on arugula. Or cut rounds of goat cheese and stack with slices of carmine beets and pickled shallots. While tiny new beets are marvelous canned whole, you should quarter larger beets, or slice, cube, or julienne, to fit more in the jar. These are the beets for Beef and Vegetable Borscht (page 242).

The Chioggia beet, pinkish on the outside and delightfully striped on the inside, is, unfortunately, a dreadful candidate for preserving. While it retains its stripes, it turns muddy yellow in the canner. Go figure. The same is true of the golden beet, processing turns this sweet beet murky and decidedly unappealing.

Replace the beets in this recipe with sweet young carrots and process in precisely the same manner and for the same amount of time. Scrape the carrots with a vegetable peeler instead of steam roasting. Jars of carrots are very useful for making quick work of stews and soups.

3 pounds (1350 g) beets (see headnote)
6 cups (1.5 l) nonchlorinated water
2 teaspoons kosher salt (optional)

1. Preheat the oven to 400°F.

2. Remove all but 1 inch of the stems and scrub the beets well. Leaving some of the stem means the beets will bleed less, but still, to avoid staining, wear gloves. And if your beets come with greens, don't discard them! They are sharp and tangy. Chop and sauté in a little oil with garlic, as you might cook chard.

3. Spread the beets out in a single layer on a double thickness of foil. Sprinkle with about a tablespoon of water and pinch the foil packet closed. Set the packet on a baking sheet to avoid mess and roast for about 30 minutes for small beets (up to 2 inches in diameter), or 55 minutes (larger than 3 inches in diameter) for large beets, until a knife meets only a little resistance. Remove from the oven and cool briefly.

4. Slip the skins off the beets (use a peeler if they are uncooperative) and trim the tops and bottoms to tidy them.

5. Bring the water to a boil in a medium saucepan. Small beets can be left whole, but larger ones should be sliced, cubed, julienned, or quartered.

6. Snugly pack the beets into the clean jars, leaving 1-inch headspace. If using, add ½ teaspoon salt to each jar. Cover the beets with the boiling water. Remove the air bubbles very well; they hide among the beets, I swear. Clean the rims of the jars. Place the lids and rings on the jars and finger-tighten the rings.

7. Process at 10 pounds of pressure for 30 minutes. After the jars have thoroughly cooled, test the seals, wash the jars, and label with the contents and date.

The beets are shelf stable for 1 year.

Fresh beets

Bonus Recipe: Beet Salad with Orange and Candied Pecans

SERVES: 4

ACTIVE TIME: 30 minutes

Beets pair happily with citrus, and here the deep magenta and bright orange are particularly pretty on the plate. This salad is also a good lunch or light supper, paired with simply prepared chicken or fish.

12	pecan halves
¼	cup (1.75 oz., 50 g) granulated sugar
•	Kosher salt
2	navel oranges
¼	cup (2 oz., 60 ml) olive oil
½	teaspoon Dijon mustard
•	Freshly ground black pepper
2	bunches (about 6 oz., 170 g) baby arugula
1	pint jar Canned Beets (page 254)
1	tablespoon minced, fresh chives

1. Preheat the oven to 325°F.

2. To candy the pecans, put the pecans on a small baking sheet lined with parchment and toast for 10 minutes.

3. Remove from the oven (leave the oven on). In a small deep saucepan, melt the sugar, swirling the pan until it has dissolved completely, then cook, swirling the pan occasionally, until the caramel has turned medium amber. Add the pecans and toss to coat well. Spread out on the parchment and pop in the oven to toast for an additional 5 minutes. Sprinkle with salt and let cool.

4. Cut the top and bottom off 1 of the navel oranges. Cut away the peel and pith in wide strips from top to bottom. Slice into ¼-inch slices.

5. Juice the other orange to get ½ cup juice. Add the juice to a small jar, add the olive oil, mustard, a pinch of salt, and a few grindings of fresh pepper and shake until creamy and emulsified.

6. Lightly dress the arugula. Taste and correct for salt and pepper.

7. Drain the beets and slice into ½-inch rounds if they are whole.

8. Place a good handful of the dressed arugula on each plate. Alternate the beets and oranges on top of the arugula. Garnish with 3 pecans per plate and scatter with the chives.

OPPOSITE: Beet Salad with Orange and Candied Pecans

Sliced fresh plum tomatoes

Mrs. W's Chile-Spiked Tomatoes

MAKES: 3 to 4 quart jars or 7 to 8 pint jars
ACTIVE TIME: 3 hours
COOLING TIME: 12 hours

I met my first Texan when I was a college freshman. Ann introduced me to tacos, dancing the two-step, and chili con queso made in a Crock Pot. She would unwrap a block of Velveeta cheese and open a can of RoTel tomatoes, and soon the dorm was filled with the inviting scent of warm, spicy cheese.

My reluctance to use processed foods can't keep me from this treat. A bowl of tortilla chips and warm melted cheese spiked with these tomatoes and chiles comforts like nothing else. Back in the day, it was all about the RoTels, but now my pantry has a more complex jar waiting. Adding the sear of jalapeños, the more subtle sweet heat of serranos, and the smoky flavor of roasted poblanos jazzes up that jar of tomatoes for snappy snacks, layered Tex-Mex casseroles, and spicy chilis.

½ cup (3 oz., 85 g) stemmed, seeded, and halved (lengthwise) poblano peppers

½ cup (5.5 oz., 155 g) stemmed, seeded, and slivered (lengthwise) jalapeño and/or serrano chiles

9 pounds (4 kg) ripe red tomatoes

1 tablespoon dried Mexican oregano or marjoram

• About 4 teaspoons citric acid or 1 cup (240 ml) fresh lemon juice

• Kosher salt (optional)

1. Preheat the broiler. Place the poblano halves skin side up on a baking sheet and broil until the skin is blistered and blackened, about 8 minutes. Place the chiles in a bowl, cover, and let them steam for 10 minutes.

2. Remove the blackened skin from the poblanos and slice into slivers or mince them. Add the poblanos and jalapeños to a 12-quart or larger nonreactive pot.

3. Blanch, core, and peel the tomatoes (see page 158). Add the tomatoes to the pot, crushing them as you go: I work with a 1-quart measuring cup, filling it with tomatoes and then adding them to the pot. When you add the first batch to the pot, turn the heat to medium-high and crush the tomatoes with a potato masher, then bring to a boil. Keep at a boil as you add more tomatoes and crush them. When all the tomatoes are in the pot, add the oregano, bring to a rolling boil, and boil for 10 minutes.

Recipe continues

4. Ladle the tomato sauce into the jars, leaving 1-inch headspace; leave enough room if using lemon juice to acidify. Add ½ teaspoon citric acid per pint jar or 1 teaspoon per quart jar, or add 1 tablespoon lemon juice per pint jar or 2 tablespoon per quart jar. If using, add ½ teaspoon salt to each pint jar or 1 teaspoon per quart jar. (The processing will move the salt through the jar.) Remove air bubbles and readjust to the 1-inch headspace if necessary. Clean the jar rims. Place the lids and rings on the jars and finger-tighten the rings.

5. Process at 10 pounds of pressure: 20 minutes for pint jars, 25 minutes for quart jars. Process for 25 minutes if using mixed jar sizes. Allow the pressure to fall naturally and the canner to cool completely, about 40 minutes.

6. Remove the jars and place upright on a folded kitchen towel on the counter. Cool for 12 hours before lifting each jar by the flat lid to test the seal.

The tomatoes are shelf stable for 1 year.

PRESSURE-CANNING TOMATOES

The water-bath recipes for tomato puree (page 161), crushed tomatoes (page 156), and tomato juice (page 164) can all be pressure-canned. Canners extol the virtues of the pressure canner claiming it is safer, bringing these variably acidic foods to a higher temperature. A pressure canner also holds many more jars than a traditional water-bath canner, so it can be much quicker than water-bath processing—but keep in mind, cooling the canner between batches takes up to 40 minutes. I much prefer using the pressure canner. You can decide for yourself.

Preparation	Jar Size	Dial Gauge	Weighted Gauge	Time (0–1000 Ft Altitude)
Tomatoes, crushed	Pint	6	5	20
	Quart	11	10	15
Tomato sauce	Pint	6	5	20
	Quart	11	10	15
Tomato juice	Pint	6	5	20
	Quart	11	10	15

Bonus Recipe: Layered Tortilla Lasagne with Poblanos

SERVES: 8

ACTIVE TIME: 1 hour

It was in Mexico, one of my favorite places for inspirational food experiences, that I first saw this clever use for last night's tortillas. With just a few vegetables, handy pantry items, and cheese, it's quick to get on the table. Hearty, satisfying, vegetable-filled, it is gluten free and readily vegetarian, so I call it a useful weapon in the arsenal. I often make this for big parties, and guests with eating restrictions lap it up.

I keep a dozen gratin dishes large enough for one hearty serving. This, and similar foods like mac and cheese, pot pie, and manicotti, all tuck into these dishes easily, so I make two or more "extra" servings for the freezer. Wrap in parchment, then foil, and write the cooking instructions on the foil with a permanent marker. These homemade frozen entrées are life saving after travel or a long work day, even if your family claims they don't know their way around the kitchen.

18 corn tortillas (if a little stale, even better)

5   tablespoons (2.5 oz., 75 ml) neutral oil, like grapeseed or canola

2   cups (9 oz., 260 g) diced onions

2   garlic cloves, minced

1   quart jar Mrs. W's Chile-Spiked Tomatoes (page 259)

½   cup (1.25 oz., 35 g) chopped fresh cilantro

•   Kosher salt and freshly ground black pepper

2   cups (16 oz., 450 g) diced zucchini or yellow summer squash

8   ounces (230 g) spinach, chard, or kale chiffonade (slivers)

1   pint jar Canned Corn (page 265)

8   ounces (230 g) *Cotija* cheese (substitute feta if necessary), crumbled

1. Leave the tortillas on the counter, uncovered, for about 30 minutes to dry out. The edges will begin to curl up, a good indicator they are ready to be fried.

2. Add ¼ cup of the oil to a large heavy skillet—a cast-iron pan is ideal—and heat over high heat. When the oil is smoking, slide in the tortillas one at a time and cook for 30 seconds per side. Remove to paper towels to drain.

3. Reduce the heat to medium-high, add the onions to the pan and cook until translucent, about 7 minutes. Add the garlic and cook until it releases its fragrance, another 1 or 2 minutes; do not allow the garlic to color. Stir in the tomatoes and cook over medium heat, stirring occasionally, until the sauce is slightly thickened, about 15 minutes.

4. Remove from the heat and cool slightly, then add the sauce in batches to the blender and whir until smooth (set the pan aside). Alternatively, use an immersion blender or potato masher for a more rustic, chunky sauce. Stir in the cilantro, and taste for salt and pepper. Transfer the sauce to a bowl and set aside.

5. Preheat the oven to 350°F.

Recipe continues

2   cups chopped or shredded cooked dark or light chicken; 1 pint jar canned black beans (page 248) or 3 large portobella mushrooms, sautéed; or 1 block extra-firm tofu, diced, or 8 ounces (227 g) ground beef mixed with 8 ounces (227 g) Mexican chorizo, cooked until no longer raw

1   half-pint jar canned poblano peppers (page 264); strips or dice

1   cup (4 oz., 113 g) grated Monterey Jack cheese

6. Wipe out the pan. Add the remaining tablespoon of oil and heat over medium heat until hot. Add the zucchini, sprinkle with salt and pepper, and cook until softened, about 5 minutes. Add the spinach and cook for 2 minutes. Salt and pepper to taste and set aside.

7. To assemble the casserole, slick the bottom of a 9-by-13-inch baking pan with ¼ cup of the tomato sauce. Layer 6 tortillas over the sauce. Add a cup of the vegetables, then sprinkle on half the corn, half the *Cotija*, and half the chicken. Add half the poblanos. Pour 2 cups of tomato sauce over this layer and repeat the layering, ending with a final layer of tortillas. Pour the remaining sauce over the top and sprinkle with the Monterey Jack cheese.

8. Bake for 40 minutes, or until bubbling. Let the casserole rest for 10 minutes after removing it from the oven.

Chipotle Barbeque Sauce

MAKES: 4 pint jars
ACTIVE TIME: 1 hour

This is a complex, spicy, "what is that secret ingredient?" barbeque sauce. It's also a satisfying canning project, especially at the end of canning season. Dump everything in the pot. Simmer for a while. Can it.

This sauce improves after about a month in the jar. The flavors blend and mellow, but the heat will remain. You can use only the adobo sauce or include the chiles (minced) if you like very spicy food. If you want it less spicy, omit the hot sauce. It pairs happily with chicken, tofu, pork shoulder, hamburgers, turkey, and smoked brisket (see page 327).

Sweet, smoky, spicy, and surprising, this sauce works just as well with any berry, plum, or cherry jam instead of the strawberry-rhubarb sauce.

1   **pint jar Tomato Puree (page 161)**

1½   **cups (12 oz., 355 ml) ketchup, homemade (page 168) or store-bought**

2   **half-pint jars Strawberry Rhubarb Sauce (page 64)**

2   **cups (16 oz., 475 ml) strong black coffee**

½   **cup (4 oz., 120 ml) water**

⅓   **cup (4 oz., 110 g) molasses**

¼   **cup (2 oz., 60 ml) cider vinegar**

¼   **cup (2 oz., 60 ml) bourbon or rye (optional)**

1   **tablespoon Asian fish sauce or Worcestershire sauce**

1   **teaspoon Hot Sauce (page 175), Tabasco, or Sriracha**

½   **cup (4.5 oz., 120 g) minced onion**

¼   **cup (2 oz., 57 g) chipotle chiles in adobo sauce (see headnote)**

1   **tablespoon minced garlic**

1. In a 5-quart, heavy nonreactive pot, stir together the tomato puree, ketchup, strawberry rhubarb sauce, coffee, water, molasses, vinegar, bourbon, if using, fish sauce, hot sauce, onion, chiles, and garlic and bring to a boil, then reduce the heat and simmer the sauce, uncovered, until thick and delicious, about 1 hour.

2. Ladle the barbeque sauce into the clean jars, leaving 1-inch headspace. Wipe the rims of the jars well. Place the lids and rings on the jars and finger-tighten the rings.

3. Process the sauce for 30 minutes at 10 pounds pressure.

4. Cool the jars and test the seal.

The sauce is shelf stable for 1 year.

Canned Pimentos, Poblanos, and Other Peppers

MAKES: 6 half-pint jars or 3 pint jars
ACTIVE TIME: 1 hour

If you get a hankering for pimento cheese (page 217) or poblano-laced *huevos*, having a jar of these peppers is a whole world of handy. While it seems to result in a small amount, one rarely needs a lot of pimentos or poblanos.

Select meaty peppers and pack them in strips or diced. I love Jimmy Nardellos, Turkish Sweets, and Corno di Toro red peppers for their sweet flavor, without that bell pepper funk. Anaheims have mild heat and are a good option for a broad range of tastes. Poblanos cut into strips are called *rajas* (rags) in Mexico and are often heated, doused with cream, and mixed with small boiled potatoes. Add some to chili or any one-pot dinner that wants a whisper of heat. Some of our local farmers are now growing true pimento peppers and they make a wonderful canned product.

3   pounds (1350 g) ripe peppers (see headnote)
2   cups (16 oz., 475 ml) nonchlorinated water

1. Preheat the broiler. Slice the peppers lengthwise in half and remove the stems and seeds. Place skin side up on a baking sheet and slip under the broiler until the skin has blistered and blackened, anywhere from 3 to 8 minutes, depending on the size of the peppers. Slip the peppers into a bowl, cover loosely with a tea towel, and steam them for 10 minutes.

2. Slip the skin off the peppers and dice them or cut into strips, as you wish.

3. Bring the water to a boil. Pack the peppers snugly into the clean jars, leaving ½-inch headspace. Slowly pour in the boiling water, letting it fill in the spaces between the peppers. Remove the air bubbles and recheck the headspace. Make adjustments as needed. Wipe the jar rims clean, then place the lids and rings on the jars and finger-tighten the rings.

4. Process at 10 pounds of pressure for 35 minutes. Let the canner cool completely, then remove the jars and place upright on a folded kitchen towel on the counter.

5. Leave the jars for 12 hours before removing the rings and lifting each jar by the flat lid; it should hold tight, indicating a safe seal.

The peppers are shelf stable for 1 year.

Canned Corn

MAKES: 8 to 9 pint jars

ACTIVE TIME: 2 hours

I have fond memories of summer dinners that were nothing but corn and plenty of butter, salt, and pepper, along with thick slices of tomatoes still warm from the vine.

When I began to preserve, I froze corn every summer. It was easy to buy extra corn all through the season. Then followed the ritual of stripping the ears, cutting off the kernels, and scraping the milk. I would eventually lose the corn in the back recesses of the freezer. Now I put corn in jars. Jars don't get lost, and the flavor is as crisp and sunny as the day is long.

Add these fresh tasting, plump, satisfying corn kernels to soups, salads, frittatas, and corn bread. But my favorite treat is corn, well drained and fried in butter until blackened on the edges and sticky with caramelized natural sugars. Salt and pepper well.

See photograph on page 252.

2 **dozen freshly picked ears of sweet corn**
• **Nonchlorinated water**
• **Kosher salt (optional)**

1. Fill an 8-quart or larger pot with water and bring to a brisk boil. Meanwhile, husk the corn, remove the silk, and wash the corn. Blanch the corn in 2 or 3 batches, boiling the ears for 3 minutes before removing to a large bowl filled with ice water. Drain when cool.

2. Slice the kernels off the cobs, cutting in one direction with a very sharp chef's knife. Measure the corn kernels into a 5-quart or larger stockpot. For each 2 cups corn (450 g), add 1 cup (235 ml) cool water. Bring the mixture to a full rolling boil, and boil for 5 minutes. Skim any foam from the surface.

3. Ladle the corn into the jars, dividing the corn and cooking liquid evenly and leaving 1-inch headspace. Add ½ teaspoon salt to each jar, if using.

4. Clean the jar rims. Place the lids and rings on the jars and finger-tighten the rings. Process at 10 pounds of pressure for 55 minutes.

5. Cool the jars completely, then test the seals.

The corn is shelf stable for 1 year.

Creamed Corn

MAKES: 10 to 11 pint jars

ACTIVE TIME: 2 hours

Creamed corn is naturally sweet and textural. Add a jar to your favorite skillet cornbread for an incredibly moist crumb. Substitute a jar of creamed corn for the milk in blueberry muffins. This is nursery food that is easy to love at any age.

Corn cobs make rich, rewarding, sweet vegetarian stock, and you're halfway there when you've finished prepping the corn for the jars. Put all the cobs back in the 8-quart pot, cover with water, and simmer for 4 to 5 hours. Although some people pressure-can corn-cob stock, in my experience it does not hold well, losing both flavor and color quickly. But freshly made, it is endlessly useful. Make a light corn chowder with stock, milk, plenty of salt and freshly ground pepper, corn kernels, potatoes, and a fresh green herb like parsley or basil. Or make corn-cob ice cream by making custard with the stock, cream, and eggs and freezing it in an ice cream maker.

2 **dozen ears of freshly picked sweet corn**
- **Nonchlorinated water**
- **Kosher salt (optional)**

1. Fill an 8-quart or larger pot with water and bring to a brisk boil. Husk the corn, remove the silk, and wash the corn. Blanch in batches, boiling the ears for 3 minutes before removing to a large bowl filled with ice water. Drain when cool.

2. Working over a large bowl or baking sheet, slice the kernels off the cobs, cutting in one direction with a very sharp knife. Now, run the knife in the other direction to capture the sweet corn milk. Measure the corn kernels and milk into a 5-quart stockpot. For each 2 cups (450 g) of corn and corn milk, add one cup (235 ml) cool water. Bring the mixture to a full rolling boil, and boil for 5 minutes. Skim any foam from the surface.

3. Ladle the corn into the jars, dividing the corn and cooking liquid evenly, and leaving 1-inch headspace. Add ½ teaspoon salt to each jar, if using.

OPPOSITE: Fresh corn on the cob

Spiced-Corn Chili Starter

MAKES: 7 pint jars
ACTIVE TIME: 2 hours

As long as I'm processing corn, I make a few jars of this chili starter, because I count on it all winter. Add it to soup, a lamb shank braise, or a porky stew. Serve it as a condiment with sausages or sandwiches. For a quick weeknight dinner, sauté 1 diced onion in oil over medium heat until translucent. Add 1 pound of ground turkey or beef and stir well until cooked through. Pour in 1 quart of Mrs. W's Chile Spiked Tomatoes (page 259), one 12-ounce bottle of lager, and 1 pint of Chili Starter. Heat through. Dinner is on the table in under an hour, full of heat and spice and tasting as if you'd cooked all day.

To temper the spiciness, replace some or all of the poblanos with an equal amount of pimento or roasted, peeled, seeded, sweet red peppers. If you prefer big, bold heat, use all poblanos and think about adding a piece of habanero or ghost chile.

1   head garlic
1   dozen ears of freshly picked sweet corn
1   half-pint jar canned pimentos (page 264; diced), drained
1   half-pint jar roasted poblano peppers (page 264), drained
2   cups (9 oz., 260 g) diced onions
1   tablespoon mustard seeds
1   tablespoon coriander seeds
2   teaspoons black pepper
•   Kosher salt (optional)

1. Preheat the oven to 425°F.

2. Cut off the top of the head of garlic, exposing the cloves. Drizzle 1 tablespoon water over the cloves, wrap tightly in foil, and steam-roast for 1 hour. Remove from the oven.

3. Meanwhile, fill an 8-quart or larger pot with water and bring to a brisk boil. Husk the corn, remove the silk, and wash the corn. Blanch in batches, boiling for 3 minutes before removing to a large bowl filled with ice water to cool.

4. Drain the corn and slice the kernels off the cobs, cutting in one direction only with a very sharp chef's knife. Add the corn to a 5 quart pot.

5. Squeeze out the sweet softened garlic and add to the corn. Stir in the peppers, onions, mustard seeds, coriander seeds, and pepper, bring to a brisk boil, and boil for 5 minutes.

6. Ladle the corn into the jars, dividing the solids and cooking liquid evenly and leaving 1-inch headspace. Add ½ teaspoon salt to each jar, if using. Remove air bubbles. Clean the rims. Place the lids and rings on the jars and finger-tighten the rings.

7. Process at 10 pounds of pressure for 55 minutes. Cool the jars completely, then test the seals.

The chili starter is shelf stable for 1 year.

Pantry-ready meat and fish

There are few reasons for most of us to take up canning meat and fish, except for the luxury of having these treats in the pantry and the knowledge of provenance. We are not, most of us, raising geese or ducks and facing the end of the season. Or hauling in hundreds of pounds of fish.

If you are, you are my hero.

For the rest of us, putting fish or meats into jars is just flexing those preserving muscles. It might even be showing off. For me, it is some of the most remarkable food I make because of what it becomes.

You will never look at canned tuna in the same way again. Tuna salad. Vitello tonnato. Salad Niçoise. Even plain old tuna noodle casserole, reimagined. Canned salmon becomes salmon cakes in a flash. Or salmon spread. Or pasta with salmon and peas.

Duck confit on the shelf means cassoulet at the drop of a hat. Or a scrumptious first course for a special occasion: roasted duck breast, confit duck, and duck liver terrine served with a sharp frisée salad and brioche toast.

These canned goods need to cure for months. It will require great patience, but let them sit on a shelf in a cool, dark place, then share with people you love.

Salmon and Grain Salad with Red Onion Quickles (page 189)

Duck confit under cold fat

Duck Confit

MAKES: 4 wide-mouth pint or quart jars, depending on the size of the duck legs
ACTIVE TIME: 4 hours
SALTING TIME: 6 to 24 hours
CURING TIME: 3 months

Confit is a slow-simmering cooking technique—sort of a poach, just short of a fry. It was originally a preservation technique, although now people consider confit simply another way to cook. While onions, garlic, oranges, and more are confited, duck confit is the most well known, perhaps the original, and certainly the most widely admired. Making duck confit results in rich, velvety meat; it's a tender and deeply flavored way to enjoy duck.

I learned to make confit, and to preserve it, in the kitchen at Camont, Kate Hill's gastronomic wonderland in the southwest of France, the heart of Gascony. She, like generations of French country people, preserves and cures duck with this method. Some claim there are risks associated with preserving on the bone. If you are worried, debone the duck leg quarters entirely, keeping the skin as intact as possible, pack the boneless confit into the jars, and process. As with any canning project, I weigh the risks and rewards, and here I opt to trust the French, who have yet to lead me astray.

Because confit was developed as a preserving technique, the curing is as critical to the final product as the cooking and processing. Over time, after three, or even six, months, the meat acquires an entirely different, succulent texture. To cure the confit safely, it must be pressure-canned. Yes, you could opt to freeze the confit, but it will not cure that way, and will not achieve the same texture of pressure-canned cured duck confit. In commercial applications, high-temperature pasteurization, vacuum-sealing, and sous vide are used for curing, but these are not applicable for the home kitchen.

Consider breaking up the work over three days, salt-curing the first day, confiting the second, and canning the final day.

8 duck leg quarters with thighs (Muscovy or Moulard are traditional; about 8 pounds, 3.6 kg)
- Kosher salt calculated at 3% of the weight of the trimmed duck (weight × 0.03 = salt)
- About 2 cups (16 oz., 475 ml) additional duck fat (see Rendered Duck Fat)

RENDERED DUCK FAT
Rendered duck fat is available at specialty grocery stores and from many butchers. Considerable quantities will be rendered as the duck legs are confited, so you may not need additional fat to submerge the legs. Any leftover duck fat can be reused to confit another batch of duck legs. Always taste a bit of the fat before reusing it; after a few batches, the fat will become too salty to reuse and should be thrown away.

Recipe continues

1. Trim the excess fat and skin away from the duck legs, leaving a close covering of skin on the meat, with nothing flapping around. It's easiest to see your way with the skin side down. Trace around the meat with a sharp knife.

    You'll need a very sharp knife to make quick work of dicing the fat and skin into ½-inch to 1-inch pieces. The more even the pieces, the more evenly they will render. Set aside.

2. Weigh the trimmed duck pieces and the salt. Using the heel of your hand, vigorously rub the salt into the flesh and skin side of the duck. Place the legs skin side up on a rack set over a baking sheet and refrigerate for at least 6 hours or overnight.

    In a small saucepan, render the fat from the skin, over low heat, until clear and golden. This could take up to 2 hours, resulting in about 2 cups of fat; do not let it burn or brown. The pieces of skin will rise to the surface; these are cracklin's. Strain them out, salt well, and have a snack. Strain the fat into a jar and refrigerate until ready to make the confit.

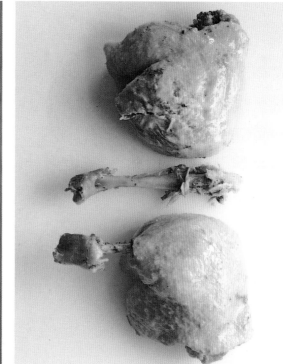

3. Remove the duck from the refrigerator and brush away any residual salt. Select a wide heavy cooking vessel. Add the reserved, strained duck fat and heat until melted. Submerge the duck leg quarters, skin side down. Add up to 2 additional cups of duck fat to ensure the legs are entirely submerged for the confit. Bring the fat to an excruciatingly slow simmer and keep it just slightly bubbling (and uncovered). Turn the duck from time to time, being careful not to tear the skin. Keeping the temperature of the oil slightly below boiling is challenging; add up to one cup water to the simmering confit to keep the duck from frying. The water will boil off and the oil will stay at the lowest possible simmer. The confit is ready when the meat has pulled away from the end of the leg bones and the fat runs clear and golden, about 4 hours. Remove from the heat and transfer the duck to a cutting board.

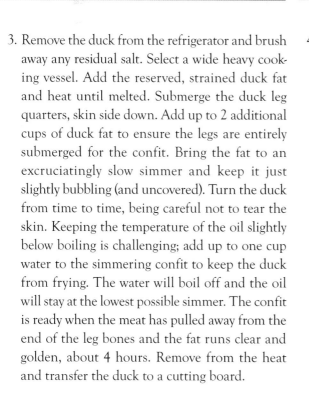

4. With a sharp knife, slice just the skin around the "ankle" of each leg bone, leaving the tendons attached. Gently disjoint the leg bone from the thigh bone and tease out the leg bone, bringing with it the tendons and small bones, but leaving the skin and meat intact. Discard the leg bone.

Tuck the duck into the jars in a snug tidy packet. Two partially deboned average-size leg quarters usually fill a wide-mouth pint jar, allowing for 1-inch headspace; if you cannot achieve 1-inch headspace, use wide-mouth quart jars.

Recipe continues

5. Carefully strain the hot duck fat remaining in the pot into a large Pyrex cup measure. Slowly pour the fat into the jars, covering the duck with the fat and leaving 1-inch headspace. Use a bubbler or plastic knife to remove any air bubbles and double-check the headspace. Clean the rims of the jars with white vinegar to cut any fats. Place the lids and rings on the jars and finger-tighten the rings. Store any extra duck fat in the refrigerator or freezer; it makes a sturdy pastry crust (see Kale and Potato Galette with a Duck Fat Crust, page 387) and stellar roasted potatoes.

6. Process at 10 pounds of pressure: 90 minutes for pints, 115 minutes for quarts. If your batch includes both sizes, process for 115 minutes. Cool the jars entirely before testing the seal. Wash the jars well, using vinegar to cut any oily residue.

7. Let the duck confit cure for 3 months in a cool, dark space before using.

8. To serve: Bring the confit to room temperature, then carefully extract a duck leg from the jar, leaving most of the fat behind.

   Set a large skillet over low heat and add the leg quarter, skin side down. Cook until the fat surrounding the leg quarter has melted. Then increase the heat to medium-high and crisp the skin side well. Turn the leg over and briefly crisp the other side. (Total cooking time is 12 to 15 minutes.) Remove from the pan and serve hot.

The confit is shelf stable for 2 years.

Note: If your stovetop runs hot, keep the confit temperature below boiling (212°F) by simmering it in the oven. Preheat the oven to 210°F. Start the confit on the stovetop and, once it's simmering, move the uncovered pot to the oven. Check from time to time, turning the legs over and making sure they remain submerged.

WHAT TO DO WITH DUCK CONFIT

Traditionally the French serve duck confit as part of a cassoulet or atop a bitter green salad. For these preparations, the leg quarter is kept whole and plated crispy skin side up. Alternatively, you can chop the crispy skin and shred the meat like pulled barbeque. Why not make a duck confit burrito? Or a duck confit salad with arugula and dried cherries? Ravioli or wontons filled with confit? Use duck confit as you might use shredded chicken, although, really, there is no comparison.

OPPOSITE: Duck Confit (page 271)

Sopes with Duck Confit, Black Beans, and
Plum-Cranberry Guajillo Sauce

Bonus Recipe: Sopes with Duck Confit, Black Beans, and Plum-Cranberry Guajillo Sauce

MAKES: 12 sopes; serves 4 for lunch or 6 as an appetizer
ACTIVE TIME: 1¼ hours

*S*opes are griddled small hand-formed corn tortillas. This two-bite finger food with little sides holds in all manner of savory fillings. Think of a *sope* as a well-crafted appetizer vehicle, perfect for the gluten-free and gluten-intolerant. I first ate these in Mexico, and I've since made dozens of combinations, ranging from fresh mango, tomato, and chile powder to roasted poblano peppers with *queso fresco*. Layered textures, layered flavors.

Make these delicious stacked-up treats for a high impact start to a dinner party or a main dish at lunch. The chocolate and smoke characteristic of the *guajillo* are echoed in the beans, and the rich duck meat is highlighted by the elegant, fruity sauce. They require some work ahead of time, but only a few minutes assembly at the last minute.

1 cup (4.25 oz., 120 g) *masa harina* (most often sold under the name Maseca)

1 cup (8 oz., 240 ml) warm water

¼ teaspoon kosher salt

1 dried *guajillo* chile

2 confit duck leg quarters, homemade (page 271) or store-bought

¼ cup (2 oz., 60 ml) duck fat (see Note), or as needed

1 pint jar canned black beans (page 248) or 2 cups (480 g) drained store-bought canned beans

• Plum-Cranberry *Guajillo* Sauce (recipe follows)

• About ¼ cup (2 oz., 60 ml) sour cream, homemade (page 384) or store-bought

• Pickled jalapeños, homemade (page 187) or store-bought

1. To make the *sopes*, in a medium bowl, mix together the *masa*, water, and salt until it forms a dough. Knead well for about 5 minutes, until smooth and pliable. Wrap the dough in plastic wrap and let rest on the counter (not in the refrigerator) for 20 to 30 minutes to allow the masa to absorb the moisture.

2. Heat a *comal* or griddle over medium heat and dry-toast the chile until it softens and becomes pliable. Flip it over and toast until it softens completely, without burning. The whole process will take only a moment or two, so don't leave your post. Set the chile aside to cool.

3. When the chile is cool, break it up and whir in a spice grinder. You'll have more than you need, but that's okay—save some for the plum sauce.

4. Divide the dough into 12 even mounds and roll each into a smooth ball. Shape one portion at a time, keeping the remaining dough covered to prevent drying it out.

5. Heat the *comal* or griddle over medium high heat. Flatten and spin a dough ball between your palms to form a pancake about 3 inches across. Try to keep the edges smooth—this takes practice and is not critical to the final product, except that they are prettier. Place the *sope* on the *comal* or griddle and form another. Flip the *sope* over after 2 or 3 minutes; it should not brown, but it will dry out some and freckle. When the *sope* has freckled on both sides, trans-

Recipe continues

fer to a wooden board. As each *sope* is removed from the *comal*, with your asbestos fingers, pinch a tiny ¼-inch rim around the outside of it. When it's warm, this is a very pliable dough, so don't let them cool. (Are you feeling like a one-man band? It gets easier after you do this a few times.)

6. Now, for the extra-special step, pinch a little round well in the center of each *sope*. This makes the *sopes* sturdier when fillings are added. (At this point, the *sopes* can be set aside for an hour. Cover well with plastic wrap or a very slightly damp towel.)

7. To fill the *sopes*, heat a cast-iron or other heavy skillet over low heat. Add the duck legs, skin side down, and cook slowly until deeply crispy and brown. Total cooking time: 12 to 15 minutes. Flip and slightly brown the other side. Set aside on a cutting board.

8. Meanwhile, reheat ¼ cup of the delicious duck fat from the confit in the same skillet. Add the black beans and 1 teaspoon of the chile powder and cook for about 10 minutes at a slow simmer, adding more fat if necessary to moisten. Mash with a potato masher for a rough or smooth puree, your choice.

9. Meanwhile, when the duck legs have cooled enough to handle, debone them if they are still on the bone. Chop the duck and skin into 1-inch chunks.

10. Warm the plum-cranberry sauce.

11. Heat the *comal* or griddle. Working in batches, schmear some black bean puree across each *sope*, add a few pieces of duck, and top with some crispy skin and a little spoonful of plum-cranberry sauce. Slide the *sopes* onto the *comal* to heat through and then get slightly toasty brown on the bottom so they are firm enough to be enjoyed as finger food.

12. Add a spoonful of sour cream to each *sope* and top with a pickled jalapeño slice. Fancy!

Note: If you pressure-canned the duck confit, the fat remaining in the jar will be more than enough. If you purchased the duck confit, you may need additional duck fat or supplement it with clean rendered lard, butter, or olive oil (about ¼ cup).

Bonus Recipe: Plum-Cranberry Guajillo Sauce

MAKES: about 1 cup
ACTIVE TIME: 15 minutes

Make this sauce up to three days ahead. Enjoy with cheese, chicken, pork, turkey, and tofu too.

½ cup (4 oz., 113 g) Whole-Cranberry Raspberry Sauce (page 103)

½ cup (4 oz., 113 g) plum jam (page 48)

2 teaspoons guajillo chile powder (reserved from *sopes*, above)

In a small saucepan, stir together the cranberry sauce, plum jam, and chile powder over medium heat. then increase the heat and boil for 1 minute. That's it!

Leftovers will hold for up to 3 weeks in the refrigerator.

Pressure-Canned Tuna

MAKES: 7 to 8 half-pint jars

ACTIVE TIME: 1 hour

CURING TIME: 3 months

Home-canned tuna or salmon is solid gold in a jar. It's expensive to produce, at about $9 per half pint, but similar high-quality imported products are $12 to $18 at gourmet grocers. Choose the very best fish, not previously frozen, preferably not farmed.

I have a wonderful fishmonger who knows my habit of putting fish in jars. He's also aware of my insistence on sustainably caught fish. He is kind enough to alert me when the fish he is selling has been line-caught, and that is when I buy and can tuna. By the same token, wild-caught salmon is the only fish I will process.

Salt is optional, but I prefer the flavor of the salted fish. You decide.

Work carefully, and clean the jars well. If your seals fail, the fish cannot be preserved and must be eaten within 2 days. Waiting for the fish to cure has to be the longest wait ever.

- **3 pounds (1350 g) fresh tuna, preferably in one piece (1-inch-thick steaks are acceptable)**
- **About 1 cup (8 oz., 240 ml) high-quality mild olive oil**
- **Kosher salt (optional)**

1. With the clean half-pint jars in front of you, cut long cubed rectangles (batons) of fish about 2 ½ inches long and ½ inch thick. Test the size in a jar, remembering you will need to maintain 1-inch headspace—cut them shorter than you think necessary. Trust me on this. Make the pieces as uniform as possible. Then turn each jar on its side and snugly but gently tuck in the fish. Cut up any leftover bits and pieces and press them between the batons to fill the jars completely. If the fish peeks out above the 1-inch headspace, remove the fish, cut it into shorter batons and start again.

2. Warm the olive oil in a small saucepan. Remove from the heat. Slowly and carefully add about a tablespoon of oil to each jar. Gently run a bubbler or plastic knife around the inside of the jar, doing your best not to break up the fish, helping the oil make its way around the pieces. Work deliberately, adding oil, removing air bubbles, and adding more oil. Let the oil fill all the nooks and crannies in the jars, leaving 1-inch headspace; it's really important not to overfill these jars.

Recipe continues

3. If using salt, add ½ teaspoon to each jar. (The processing will move the salt through the jar, so no need to stir it in.) Clean the rims of the jars with a towel moistened with white vinegar to cut any oil that might be lingering on the rims and ensure a good seal. Place the lids and rings on the jars and finger-tighten the rings.

4. Process at 10 pounds of pressure for 100 minutes. After processing, allow the pressure to fall naturally and the canner to cool completely.

5. Leave the jars on the counter for 12 hours before removing the rings and lifting each jar by the flat lid; it should hold tight, indicating a safe seal. Then store the jars in a dark closet for 3 months to fully cure the fish. (Wash the jars with a vinegar-dampened towel to make them shine.)

6. The fish is shelf stable for 2 years.

VARIATIONS

- Pressure-Canned Salmon. Follow the same procedure, using a center-cut fillet and slicing the fish into chunks instead of batons.
- Either tuna or salmon can be processed in water instead of oil. Heat nonchlorinated water until just warm, and then carefully add the water to the jars just as you would the oil.

OPPOSITE: Preparing tuna for the canner

LEFT TO RIGHT:
Air-cured pancetta (page 347),
bresaola (page 350), and pork
tenderloin (page 345)

Chapter Three

SALT, WATER, SMOKE, AND AIR: ALCHEMY IN THE KITCHEN

PRESERVED MEAT AND FISH

OPPOSITE: Barbeque-Smoked Brisket (page 327)

The recipes in the preceding chapters cover foods that tuck neatly into jars; foods that add texture, color, and layers of flavor to the plate. Almost every meal I serve has a little something on the side, whether conserve or condiment, pickle or sauce. To move preserving from the side of the plate to the center, consider how fish and meat have been preserved over the centuries. From the first mastodon hunted, man recognized the obvious: he couldn't eat all of that beast in one sitting. Human beings devised ways to save some for the off-season, using elemental methods: smoke and salt and time.

Many of the meals I make are plant-based, but a little bit of meat—an ounce or two of umami, fat, and salt—converts my husband's vegetarian dinner into a meal fit for me, an unabashed carnivore. Pasta with greens for him, and the same for me, with crisp pancetta added. Grilled stuffed portabello mushrooms are vegetarian friendly; I add crumbled bacon. Taco Night menu: black beans for him, smoked chicken for me.

It began slowly. My DIY sensibilities were tested each time I purchased bacon. With each order of bresaola at the deli counter. And with my seemingly endless need for smoked salmon. So I began to make a handful of the meat and fish items I craved, the most practical items to add to the pantry.

The transformative nature of the process lured me in. The chance to design a flavor profile, control saltiness, and dictate the provenance of the meat and fish sealed the deal.

Curing is delicious alchemy where, rather than turn straw into gold, we transform meat and fish with nothing more than base ingredients (salt, water, smoke) and time. The following recipes are organized in order of difficulty. Work your way through from bacon to bresaola to inform your skills and hone your techniques. Soon you will be sporting a white apron, wielding a cleaver, and assuming the snappy attitude of a *charcutiere*.

Selecting and eating meat conscientiously

Before I married a man who ate a mostly vegetarian diet, I consumed meats without a thought about the animals. Then came Temple Grandin, Michael Pollan, Barbara Kingsolver, Mark Bittman, and the other voices speaking about sustainability, echoing all the things Dennis had referred to for years. Worries mounted about antibiotics, hormones, feedlots, pink slime, and other scary news stories. I wondered if I, too, should change to a plant-based diet.

But the fact remained that I like the taste of meat, poultry, and fish, not to mention a more than passing fondness for dairy products. I was reluctant to give them up. Rather, I decided to become more thoughtful about my choices.

At first, I began introducing myself to vendors at the farmers' markets and then, soon after, I visited some of their farms. I learned about animal husbandry, feed choices, pasture rotation, and the seasonal nature of farming animals for meat.

I will never forget a man who raises pigs and sells at our market laughing ruefully as he said he wished pigs came with more chops, three bellies, and not as many shoulders, just one example of how challenging it is to raise and sell the whole animal. Even more memorable was watching how a poultry farmer slaughtered Thanksgiving turkeys and how carefully he maintained a calm environment for this essential yet brutal act.

Fear is an issue. It was Temple Grandin who taught us that when animals die fearfully, adrenaline courses through their bloodstream, changing the texture and taste of meat from supple and sweet to tough and gamy. The appearance of meat suffused with adrenaline is wet and sticky, with an off color. I choose to eat meat solely from animals who have lived a happy, pastured life; are fed good-quality food; and have a quick, kind death.

After being schooled by the farmers, I met a Washington, DC, butcher who taught me even more. "Pam the Butcher" Ginsberg cuts and trims meats to order at Wagshal's, a local grocer. I never refuse the opportunity to step behind the counter to watch her remove the skin from a pork belly or trim a brisket into first and second cuts. Pam introduced me to pork from Iberia, lamb from southern Virginia, and the perfectly marbled porterhouse steaks she prepares every week. Each conversation with this talented butcher gives me the chance to learn more about the whole animal, and how I might become a more thoughtful consumer. I hope you are able to find such a butcher where you live and that you become very good friends.

A two-day charcuterie class held at L'Academie de Cuisine in Bethesda, MD—curing bacon and salmon and making pâté—increased my curiosity. I wanted to learn more about butchery and preserving. Soon, through reading, experimenting,

Brisket: (From top) first and second cuts

and watching videos on YouTube, I knew what to do with those parts of the animal relatively few people were buying. Perhaps the most transformational choice was my decision to purchase only whole chickens. I learned to butcher these birds into the parts I needed for dinner, retaining the carcasses for stock (page 230), an essential ingredient in any cook's kitchen. Deboning a lamb shoulder was challenging, and the first two or three times, it wasn't pretty, but none of these activities scare me anymore. These knife—and life—skills became part of my everyday experience.

In time, I took a trip to France for the chance to work with Kate Hill, an American who makes her home in Gascony, in the southwest, a pastoral agricultural region. Kate is the Duchess of Charcuterie. She has immersed herself in the study of cured meats, from a home cook's perspective. She knows all her local producers well and takes visitors on tours to meet Jehanne Rignault, a remarkable woman who raises foie gras ducks and geese, and the Chapolards, a family of Gascon farmers and butchers who work from "seed to sausage"—growing the feed, raising, butchering, and curing the meat. Watching the informed, thoughtful circle of life on offer at the Nerac market permanently altered my carnivorous life. Together with Kate, Dominique Chapolard, and his lovely wife, Christiane, I made *noix de jambon* (a small cured ham) and *friccandeau* (a local pâté). I learned about using leaf lard for pastry and caul fat for wrapping ground meats. We skewered duck hearts and grilled them for a heady dinner alongside the famed *prunes d'Agen*. Nothing went to waste, and every mouthful was extraordinary. These animals were raised without feedlots or additives. The tastes were new and nuanced and sensual. My Gascon education made me instantly and forever a proponent of sustainability.

I urge you to purchase from people you know; eat broadly, from all parts of the beast; and cure and preserve only the finest meats or fish.

Salt-curing

Salt-curing is a way to dip your toe into the world of meat and fish preservation. Salt-curing requires no special equipment, demanding only exceptional ingredients. Bacon is a week in the making but takes no more than a few minutes of work. Gravlax is two days to delicious.

Salt draws moisture out, tightening the cellular structure of the meat or fish. Make note of the changes in texture. The pork belly will be stiffer. The salmon firmer. This is one of the most ancient of all preservation techniques, needing nothing more than salt and time.

Once again, as with the simplest fruit preserves, the water activity is a critical factor (see page 37). Control the water, and you are well on the way to safe curing. Consider that it was a matter of survival at one point to have access to meat and fish out of season; it's an elemental act. The salt draws the moisture out, reducing the water content of the meat or fish. The microorganisms living in that water are then no longer at issue, making these proteins hold far longer than fresh food could. At the same time, the salt bonds to the proteins in the meat and reduces, or slows, the actual "activity" in the water.

As with other projects in this book, I strongly recommend using a scale for precision. It is possible that the meat you buy will not weigh precisely what is called for in the recipe. Use the scale and a calculator to ensure the ratio of salt to meat is consistent. Slightly over, and the meat may be salty and unpleasant. Slightly under, and the food may not have the same shelf stability. Keep in mind this rule of thumb: a salt cure calls for **3 percent of the total weight of the meat or fish in salt.** I use grams for these calculations, as a gram scale is more precise with small quantities.

1,000 grams (1 kg) meat × 0.03 (3%) = 30 grams of salt

Basic salt-curing results in foods that satisfy, that elevate other dishes, and that tantalize the taste buds. But the more intriguing cures imbue the salty and sweet with the flavors of herbs, spices, and/or liquors. Every flavor in a cure is absorbed and amplified, so get creative with your combinations.

While I opt for kosher, pickling, or canning salt for the majority of the salt, adding a few grams of smoked salt, or substituting half the salt with miso paste or soy sauce, layers in an entirely new flavor. And don't stop there. Granulated sugar is the standard way to add sweetness, but try swapping it out for the same weight of brown sugar, agave, maple syrup, molasses, sorghum, mirin, palm sugar, or boiled cider syrup. Again, using weights instead of volume measures makes this experimentation possible. Volume measures will throw off the ratios and the results will be unfortunate. Take note: successfully expressing your creativity is impossible without a scale, a calculator, and math.

OPPOSITE: Curing equipment

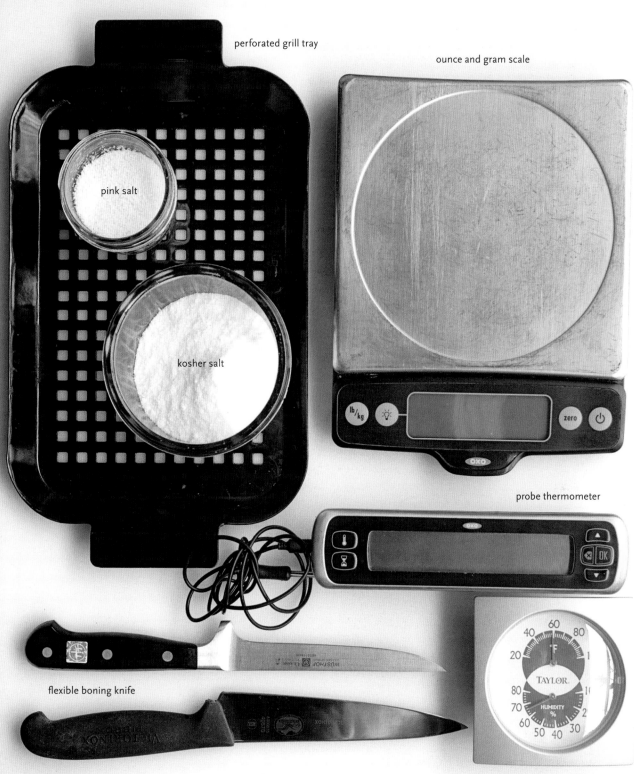

perforated grill tray

ounce and gram scale

pink salt

kosher salt

probe thermometer

flexible boning knife

general-purpose knife

hygrometer

Equipment

While there are many fancy pieces of equipment available for all sorts of home food preservation, the two essential tools for salt-curing are a scale and a thermometer.

Perhaps you have managed to cook without a **scale** until this moment, but now is the time to get one. You will never regret it, and you might learn a few things. Curing meats and fish with salt is a simple process, but using too much salt happens too easily without a scale to guide your hand. As you continue to try your hand at preserving meat, there will be more reasons to own a scale. The precision of working with weights is critical for consistent results, and for safety. Once you have a scale, try using weights instead of volume measurements in every recipe, especially baking. Many cookbooks now include both volume and weight measures. (I keep a chart of commonly used foods and their weights handy.) Notice how much better your results are. I love my scale, and once you get in the habit, I'll bet you will love yours too.

A **thermometer** ensures success when cooking meats and fish. The difference between an internal temperature of 150°F and one of 160°F may seem slight, but the former is just right for bacon, the latter is ruinous. I use an inexpensive instant-read thermometer, and that's all you need. But once I started working with a smoker, I invested in a digital **probe thermometer**. The temperature display is read from the outside of the smoker (or oven) via a wired—or wireless—probe inserted in the food in the smoker or oven. No one likes a face full of hot smoke or a blast of oven heat. (See Resources, page 401)

A **wide, shallow, food-safe container with a lid**, often called a salt box, is handy but not essential. A salt box holds the meat or fish and the dry cure in the refrigerator, can be reused, and replaces the zip-lock bags I call for in many recipes. But the bags work perfectly well.

Nitrites (pink salt)

Pink salt is a nitrite, a word that strikes fear in many hearts. Don't be scared. In these recipes, the use of nitrites is a choice. Pink salt is a curing agent. It is made up of sodium chloride (table salt) and sodium nitrite and red dye. I use it to improve both appearance and flavor of cured meats—in this book, bacon. Pink salt really is pink, not that pale peachy pink of Himalayan salt, but pink like the barrette in a five-year-old's hair. In large quantities, pink salt can cause terrible headaches and make you very sick. Keep it out of the reach of children, and always wear gloves when handling it.

In very small quantities, as in my recipes, pink salt gives some cured meats their characteristic flavor—bacony, ham-ish. It is a deeply familiar taste that has no specific name. Without nitrites, bacon will taste more like pork roast. I have made bacon with and without pink salt and like it far better with a little pink salt. The flavor is what I expect from bacon. If it worries you, skip it.

Nitrites are suspended in salt and, widely distributed through actively massaging it into the meat, work as antioxidants in the curing process—keeping meat from oxidizing, or browning. Nitrites give bacon, corned beef, salami, and many other cured meats their appealing rosy color.

Nitrites occur naturally in the world, most particularly in celery juice, spinach, radishes, and lettuces. Bacon and lunch meats advertised as "no-nitrite" use these vegetable-based curing agents.

MODIFIED CELERY JUICE POWDER ("ALL-NATURAL" NITRITE)

Newly available, modified celery juice powder works in the same way as pink salt, keeping cured meat safe. Substitute modified celery juice powder (see Resources, page 401) for pink salt equally, gram for gram. It does not provide a strong hammy flavor, but it does have anti-oxidizing property to keep your cured meats pinkish. Do not try to make modified celery juice powder at home—it is more complex than dehydrated celery.

Dip your toe in the salt: make bacon.

Nearly every home cook who becomes curious about the process of curing meat and fish begins with bacon, so that's where this chapter starts too. Bacon begins with pork belly and often requires a chat with the butcher. Although pork belly is more widely available than it used to be, I still recommend ordering it ahead of time. As with most preserving projects, this is a plan-ahead endeavor.

PROCURING PORK BELLY

Order a trimmed pork belly, skin removed, for these recipes. Ask the butcher for a piece that is squared off, like a block. If the belly you purchase has both thick and thin spots, the thinner areas will cure more quickly and may be saltier. If you purchase a whole belly, trim it into evenly thick blocks, setting aside the thin pieces for braising or red-cooking (the classic Chinese braise with soy sauce, rice wine, and sugar).

Pork belly is a commodity item and much of it comes from pigs raised on feedlots. After plenty of experimenting, I can assure you there is a vast difference in taste between the meat from farm-raised pastured pigs and the bellies sourced from large commercial producers. As we are going to be eating everything the animals did, in a sense, don't you want to know they were not fed chemicals, drugs, and hormones? Please, for so many reasons, use only the best fed, lovingly raised, carefully processed animals.

SPECIAL HANDLING: TRIMMING, SKINNING, AND OTHERWISE PATTING THE BELLY

Removing the skin from pork belly is challenging and frustrating, and it takes great skill. (And there are nipples.) So get your butcher to do it if you can. But if your pork belly comes with the skin on, here are a couple of ways to deal with it.

You can proceed with the recipe as written, curing, cooking, or smoking the pork belly, then slice off the skin (rind) afterward. It will come right off with a sharp knife inserted between the skin and the layer of subcutaneous fat below. Leave the fat attached to the bacon, not the rind! Cut the rind into chunks and store in the freezer to flavor soups or beans.

Or, if you are up for it, go ahead and remove the skin before beginning the cure. This is the best way to make *chicharrones* (page 297), the addictive pork rind snacks. Your knife must be very sharp. With the pork belly skin side up, place the tip of your knife between the skin and fat at one corner. You want to remove only the skin and leave everything else behind. Begin to remove the skin with a few small cuts at the very corner, then lift up the loosened skin and make another small cut under the skin, leaving the fat and meat intact. Continue in this fashion until there is a flap the width of your hand.

This is tedious work and is best done slowly and with great "Zenfulness." Be methodical, and leave as much fat and meat attached to the block of belly as possible. Once you have a flap, form a handhold with it by making a 3-inch slit in the skin. Grab it with your non-knife fingers and then continue to tease your knife tip slowly along the skin while simultaneously pulling it up and away. If the skin breaks or becomes unwieldy, restart again at a fresh corner.

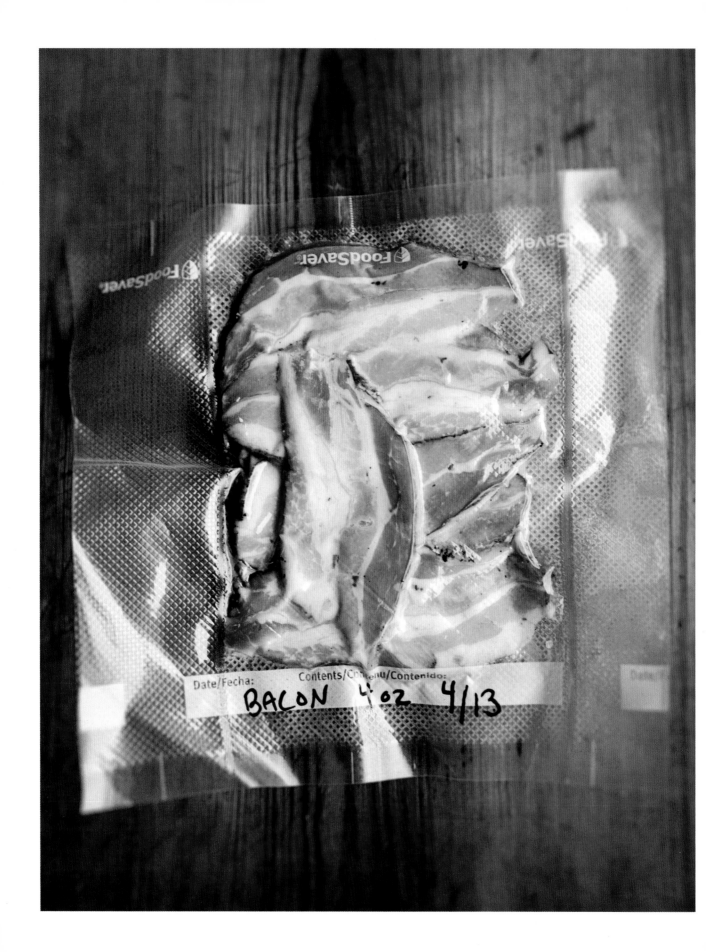

Date/Fecha: Contents/Contenu/Contenido:

BACON   4 oz   4/13

Maple-Bourbon Bacon

MAKES: 1½ pounds
ACTIVE TIME: 30 minutes
CURING TIME: 7 days plus 2 hours
COOKING TIME: 1 hour

Home-cured bacon is a revelation. You do not need a smokehouse, backyard shed, or special room. In fact, you can cure bacon in a plastic bag in your refrigerator.

When I first made bacon, the taste of good pork was the first flavor I encountered—not salt. And there were no nagging concerns about how the pork was raised, because I had purchased the pork belly from a farmer I knew. There are a million reasons to make bacon at home but you need to know only one: it will be better than any bacon you have ever eaten.

I regularly make two styles of bacon. This one, cured with maple syrup, bourbon, and coffee, has a dash of the sweet and smoky booze as an undertone. I think the bourbon makes it sing Hallelujah, but omit it if you are not a fan. The other version is cured with plenty of black pepper, rosemary, and garlic and then smoked; see page 313. I store both in the freezer in vacuum-sealed 4-ounce packets, sliced the way I like it, thick and ready to line up on top of the sliced tomato in a BLT or to serve with sunny-side up eggs for breakfast. I cut up any pieces that can't slice into pretty rashers and store them in 2-ounce packets, to be crisped and scattered on top of soup or salad.

And that's just the beginning of why bacon should always be part of your practical pantry. Use it to garnish deviled eggs, pan-roasted fish, or chicken. Candy it (see page 296). Add it to baked goods like muffins or scones. Be weekend- or brunch-ready.

2 tablespoons (0.75 oz., 20 g) kosher or sea salt

¼ teaspoon pink salt

2 pounds (1 kg) trimmed pork belly, with plenty of streaky fat and meat, skin removed

½ cup (4 oz., 120 ml) strong coffee or espresso, cooled

¼ cup (2 oz., 60 ml) maple syrup

2 tablespoons (1 oz.) bourbon or applejack

1. Wearing gloves, mix the salts in a small bowl. Rub the salt cure all over the pork belly and place it in a 1-gallon zip-lock bag in a single layer (cut the meat into 2 large pieces if necessary). Stir together the coffee, maple syrup, and liquor in a small bowl and add to the bag. Seal the bag and smoosh the liquid around. Open the bag slightly and press out the excess air, then zip it closed and lay it flat on a middle shelf in the refrigerator.

2. Let the bacon cure for 7 days. Every day, turn the bag over to redistribute the cure, and rub the belly through the bag, introducing all those nice flavors. Over the course of the week, the meat will exude juice and the cure will move through the cells of the meat; turning the bag ensures an even cure. Count the days and imagine the bacon.

OPPOSITE: Maple-Bourbon Bacon

Recipe continues

3. After 7 days, remove the pork belly from the bag. It will be firmer than it was a week ago, a sign the cure has worked. Rinse the meat thoroughly and dry with paper towels. (Discard the cure.) Place the soon-to-be bacon on a rack set over a baking sheet and place it, uncovered, in the refrigerator for 2 hours. This resting period helps move the cure through the meat and equalize the salt and flavors.

4. Preheat the oven to the lowest setting, usually around 200°F.

5. Place the bacon, still on the rack on the baking sheet, in the center of the oven and cook for about 1 hour, until the internal temperature measures 150°F on an instant-read thermometer. Remove the bacon from the oven and let cool, then wrap well in butcher's paper or plastic wrap and refrigerate until chilled.

6. Once the bacon has chilled, slice it thick or thin, as you like it. Stack the slices on butcher's paper or parchment, then vacuum-seal or place in zip-lock bags in portion sizes to suit your household. Bacon is always cooked before eating.

The bacon will keep for up to 10 days in the refrigerator or up to 6 months in the freezer.

VARIATION

- Both lamb and goat belly make terrific, deeply flavored bacon. Sometimes this cut is called breast—the current fondness for pork belly has some people renaming parts. The cut is thinner, with less fat, so it requires only 4 days in the salt and spices before cooking or smoking.

TIP: SALTY LIKE THE (DEAD) SEA

Oops? Did you cure your meat or fish longer than you should have? Put it in a bowl, cover with cool water, soak it for about 8 hours, changing the water two or three times. Drain and dry well, then roast or smoke as directed. That should fix it.

Bonus Recipe: Bacon-Onion Jam

MAKES: six 4-ounce jars
ACTIVE TIME: 1 hour
COOKING TIME: 2 hours

The moment I heard about bacon jam, I knew I had to make it. This recipe combines the tantalizing flavor of bacon with onion jam. Spread this remarkable confection on a tomato sandwich. Fill acorn squash with bacon jam and chunks of tart apple. Or make, quite simply, the naughtiest creation ever: bacon rugelach with salted peanuts.

1   pound (450 g) Maple-Bourbon Bacon (page 293), cut into small dice

1   pound (450 g) yellow onions (about 3), halved lengthwise and thinly sliced into half-moons

½   cup (4 oz., 110 g) firmly packed brown sugar

½   cup (6 oz., 170 g) pomegranate molasses

1   cup (8 oz., 240 ml) strong coffee

½   cup (4 oz., 120 ml) balsamic vinegar

¼   cup (2 oz., 60 ml) bourbon

1   teaspoon freshly ground black pepper

•   Kosher salt if needed

1. Cook the bacon in a large heavy pot over medium-low heat, stirring from time to time, until well browned. Remove and drain on paper towels. Pour off all but about ½ cup of the bacon fat from the pot.

2. Reheat the fat, add the onions, and cook over low heat until translucent and very soft, about 15 to 20 minutes. Stir in the brown sugar and caramelize the onions until very deeply brown, about 15 minutes; be careful with the heat, as this wants to burn.

3. Add the bacon, molasses, coffee, vinegar, bourbon, and pepper, stir well, and bring to a boil. Reduce the heat and simmer very slowly until the mixture is as thick and glossy as apple butter and a deep rich brown, without much liquid, about 2 hours. Taste and correct for seasoning—salt and/or pepper—but be judicious, as the flavors will develop further as the mixture cools. Remove from the heat and let cool.

4. Transfer every bit of the mixture to a food processor. It's up to you how chunky you want this spread—I like it smooth and spreadable but you can leave it chunkier.

5. Pack into jars (just a little hint, 4-ounce jars might protect you from overindulgence). Refrigerate for up to 3 months or freeze for up to a year; if you will be freezing the jam, leave 1-inch headspace in the jars to allow for expansion.

Bonus Recipe: Candied Bacon

SERVES: 4 as a snack
ACTIVE TIME: 40 minutes

I'm sure that I don't really need to offer recipes for using bacon, but this ridiculously easy, unbelievably tasty, pleasing little tidbit has to be shared. Serve it as a nibble—it's best served soon after coming from the oven, but room temperature is also fine. Toss on a salad. Mix with salty popcorn and candied nuts. If you have any left over, chop it very fine, stir into cream cheese, and add some thinly sliced scallions: instant schmear. Bacon candy fits right into bread pudding or ice cream. Don't say I didn't warn you.

4 ounces (113 g) Maple-Bourbon Bacon (page 293) in one piece

½ cup (4 oz., 110 g) firmly packed light brown sugar

1 tablespoon finely chopped fresh rosemary

½ teaspoon cayenne pepper

1. Preheat the oven to 325°F.

2. Cut the bacon into ½-inch slices, then cut crosswise into ½-inch cubes.

3. Combine the brown sugar, rosemary, and cayenne in a small bowl. Press the cubed bacon into the sugar mixture, coating it on all sides. Place the cubes on an oiled mesh rack set over a baking sheet lined with parchment (to make cleanup easier). Bake until crisp and brown, 25 to 30 minutes; watch carefully so it doesn't burn. Serve warm or at room temperature.

Bonus Recipe: Chicharrones (Spiced Fried Pork Rinds)

SERVES: 4 for a snack
ACTIVE TIME: 1 hour
RENDERING TIME: 3 hours
DRYING TIME: 1 to 2 hours
FRYING TIME: 15 to 20 minutes

I like chicharrones too much to make them often. Make these for people who eat salty, fried snacks without guilt. Remember to ask the butcher to skin the pork belly because it's really hard to do yourself. And tell the butcher you want the skin. After making the chicharrones, strain the fat into a jar and store it in the refrigerator to use again in a sauté or pinched into flour for biscuits.

½ **pound (225 g) uncured pork skin**

1 **tablespoon kosher salt**

½ **teaspoon chipotle chile powder**

½ **teaspoon ancho chile powder**

½ **teaspoon paprika**

1. Dice the rind into pieces 2 inches by 2 inches. Place in a heavy-bottomed 5-quart pot and add 2 cups of water. Bring the water to a boil, turn the heat to the lowest setting, and begin the process of rendering the fat from the skin. This will take anywhere from 1 to 3 hours, but does not need babysitting. Rendering is complete when the fat is clear. Remove from the heat and set aside.

2. Preheat the oven to 200°F. Line a baking sheet with a paper towel.

3. Remove the rinds with a slotted spoon and place on the paper-towel–lined baking sheet to drain. Then place the rinds on a rack set over another baking sheet and slide it into the oven. Dry the rinds out in the oven for 1 to 2 hours.

4. In a small bowl, stir together the salt, chile powders, and paprika.

5. Line a clean baking sheet with paper towels. Reheat the fat to 325°F. Fry the rinds in batches, using a spider or slotted spoon to remove them from the pan when they puff up and turn golden brown. Drain on the baking sheet, sprinkling with the salt mixture while still hot.

Gravlax

MAKES: 1½ pounds

ACTIVE TIME: 30 minutes

CURING TIME: 2 days

In our house, most celebratory meals and holiday gatherings start with a gravlax appetizer, served with cocktail rye, along with an herbed mustard sauce (page 301). Or drape it over a beet salad, wrap around steamed asparagus, or add a generous amount to your breakfast toast. There are people who don't care for smoked salmon, but their attitude changes when they are introduced to gravlax. It's silky and sweet and the velvety texture melts in your mouth.

What I love most about gravlax is the flexibility of the recipe. Dill or no dill, your choice. I prefer lemon verbena, fresh and fragrant; sometimes I use Thai basil or mint mixed with chervil. Try white sugar, maple syrup, or honey instead of brown sugar. Liberally sprinkle with tequila or Cognac instead of gin. In a pinch, fennel fronds can be substituted. Add ½ teaspoon dill seeds and toast the seeds with the peppercorns. If the gin lacks herbal tones, add 3 crushed juniper berries to the rub. This basic ancient Scandinavian curing technique begs to be adapted.

1½ tablespoons white peppercorns

1 tablespoon anise seeds

¼ cup (3 oz., 10 g) coarsely chopped fresh lemon verbena or dill, plus 2 tablespoons finely chopped verbena or dill (see headnote)

1 cup (8 oz., 220g) firmly packed light brown sugar

3 tablespoons (3 oz., 84 g) kosher or fine sea salt

3 tablespoon (1.5 oz.) gin, the more herbal the better (see headnote)

2 pounds (1 kg) center-cut salmon fillet (skin-on)

OPPOSITE: Gravlax with Herbed Mustard Sauce (page 301)

1. In a small dry skillet, toast the white peppercorns and anise seeds until they release their fragrance, about 3 minutes. Remove from the heat.

2. Pulse the coarsely chopped lemon verbena a few times in the bowl of a food processor, then add the sugar, salt, and toasted spices. Whir until all the herbs and spices are ground very fine. Add the gin and pulse to make a loose paste.

3. Rinse and dry the salmon. Check for pin bones and remove any you find with strong tweezers. Set a large piece of foil on the work surface and cover with a piece of plastic wrap. Place the salmon flesh side up on the plastic wrap. Dump the herb paste on top of the salmon and pat it over the surface. Wrap tightly in the plastic and then the foil.

Recipe continues

4. Place the package in a 1-gallon zip-lock bag, set it on a baking sheet or tray, and put another pan on top of the fish. Weight down the pan with heavy cans or a brick. Cure in the refrigerator for 2 days, turning the bag over a few times.

5. Remove the pan and weights, remove the fish from the bag and unwrap it. Scrape off and discard most of the green paste. (Do not rinse—you would just be adding back the moisture the salt pulled from the salmon.) Dry the fish with paper towels, then press the remaining finely chopped verbena all over the flesh side of the salmon. Well wrapped in plastic wrap, the gravlax can be stored in the refrigerator for up to 2 weeks or in the freezer for up to 3 months.

6. To serve, slice paper-thin, on a slight angle, cutting it away from the skin. A bit of verbena should adhere to each slice, forming a ruffled decorative edge for an elegant presentation.

Bonus Recipe: Herbed Mustard Sauce

MAKES: about ¾ cup
ACTIVE TIME: 15 minutes

In Sweden, sliced gravlax is served on locally made dark brown bread with a dab of mustard sauce. Sometimes I add a bit of crème fraîche or yogurt to this sauce and spread it on an open-faced sandwich of Ryvita crackers and layers of thin slices of gravlax.

¼ cup (2 oz., 60 g) Dijon mustard

1 teaspoon Colman's dry mustard

3 tablespoons clover or wildflower honey

2 tablespoons Champagne vinegar

⅓ cup (scant 3 oz., 80 ml) grapeseed oil

¼ cup (1 oz., 10 g) finely chopped fresh lemon verbena or dill

Put the mustards, honey, vinegar, and oil in a small bowl and whisk well until the sauce is emulsified and smooth. Stir in the dill. Cover and refrigerate overnight before serving.

The sauce will hold in the refrigerator for up to 2 weeks.

Brining

Wet-curing, or brining, is kissing cousin to salt-curing. A salt cure is actually a dry brine. A wet brine plumps the meat, adding moisture, while the salt cure draws out moisture and firms the meat.

If you have never brined a chicken, pork chops, or brisket, now is the time to start. For most whole birds overnight or 24-hour brining is ideal, but even 2 hours in a brine is beneficial.

A basic formula for a wet brine is 1 gallon (3760 g) of water (not chlorinated) and 1 cup (188 g) of kosher or sea salt. (Calculate safe meat and fish brines at a minimum of 5% salinity.)

I prefer a brine that balances the salty with something sweet. Other optional additions—garlic, lemons, herbs, spices, peppercorns—all contribute to the final flavor. You can substitute apple cider for some of the water; wine, beer, or any liquor will also work. The sky is the limit with added flavorings, but, really, the alchemy is in the balance of sweet and salty.

You don't even need to bother mixing a brine if you have pickles floating in brine somewhere in the refrigerator. Pour the pickle brine right over a chicken breast and let it stand for 30 minutes, then rinse, pat dry, and sauté, broil, or grill. It's a quick way to delicious.

Brining is a terrific start to roasting or grilling, and is a requirement for smoking. Smoking's arid environment removes moisture; brining plumps and moistens the meat before you start. This presents a challenge, though, as smoky flavorings adhere only to a dry surface. So you must rest the brined meat uncovered for several hours before smoking to develop a *pellicle*, a dry, slightly tacky surface.

Always rinse the meat thoroughly after brining to remove excess salt. The resting time to develop the pellicle also allows the salt to equalize throughout the meat. Never skip this step.

If ever you are unable to cook or smoke when you hoped and your food is still in the brine after 24 hours, remove it from the brine, rinse well, and refrigerate until you can cook it. If you brine the meat past the 24-hour mark, remove the meat from the brine, rinse, and then soak the meat in fresh water for an hour or so, then proceed with your recipe.

OPPOSITE: Chicken in the Basic Brine (page 304)

Basic Brine

MAKES: 2 quarts

ACTIVE TIME: 20 minutes

BRINING TIME: 2 to 24 hours

This recipe makes enough brine for about 4 pounds of meat—e.g., a small roasting chicken or two pork chops. You will need to double the recipe for larger cuts, like turkey breast, pork shoulder, or brisket. Feel free to riff with everything except the ratio of liquids to salt and sugar.

It took me years to figure out that I could dissolve the salt and sugar in some of the hot water, then cool the brine down with ice cubes. Head-slapping moment of brilliance . . . no waiting for the brine to cool down! (If you already knew this, no need to point it out, but if you didn't, thank me later.)

2 cups (16 oz., 480 ml) nonchlorinated water (substitute some or all with buttermilk, wine, bourbon, whey, or cider)

½ cup (3 oz., 80 g) kosher, pickling, or sea salt (substitute some or all by weight with smoked salt, tamari, miso paste, or pickle brine)

½ cup (3.5 oz., 100 g) granulated sugar (substitute some or all by weight with brown sugar, maple syrup, cider syrup, golden syrup, molasses, palm sugar, agave, or honey)

6 cups (48 oz., 1.425 kg) ice cubes

1. Select a deep container large enough to hold the brine and the meat or fish you will be brining or use a supersized zip-lock bag, but be sure to put the bag in a bowl to catch any possible leaks.

2. Heat the water, salt, and sugar to a simmer in a medium saucepan, stirring to thoroughly dissolve the sugar and salt. Remove from the heat and stir in any optional flavorings. Cool the brine completely by adding the ice cubes.

3. To use the brine, once it is thoroughly cool, submerge the meat or fish. If necessary, place a plate on top of it to keep it under the water. Brine for the time specified in the recipe. Then drain the meat or fish, rinse under running water, and dry well. Set on a rack on a baking sheet and refrigerate, uncovered, for at least an hour (or up to a day, if you have the luxury) to equalize the salts and flavors.

- A few fresh thyme sprigs
- A big handful of fresh flat-leaf parsley, chervil, lovage, or celery leaves, including stems
- A couple of big stalks of rosemary, lavender, or other woody herb
- 1 tablespoon Pickling Spice, homemade (page 185) or store-bought
- 12 black peppercorns
- 1 lemon, orange, or lime—halve and squeeze the juice into the brine, then add the fruit to the brine
- 1 onion, quartered
- 2 garlic cloves, crushed and peeled
- Chiles, fresh or dried

Pickling spices

Bonus Recipe: Spiced Pork Chops with Garlicky Bok Choy

SERVES: 4

ACTIVE TIME: 1 hour

BRINING TIME: 2 to 8 hours

SALT EQUALIZATION AND PELLICLE TIME: 1 hour to 1 day

Pork is amenable to many different flavor profiles, but this combination of aromatic spices may be my favorite treatment for thick-cut chops. Here some of the saltiness is from white miso, a mild form of the soy-based paste; the cinnamon and star anise are sweet and sultry—all of which begin to flavor the pork long before cooking. With all that flavor in the pork, and the spicy plum sauce, this is an everyday dinner that's great for guests too.

Brine for at least 2 hours, longer if possible, to be sure to have plump, moist chops on the plate. Then let the meat rest to equalize the salts and dry out the surface so the meat will have a tantalizing crisp crust after cooking.

The chops can also be cooked on an outdoor grill.

FOR THE BRINE

- 2 cups (16 oz., 475 ml) cold water
- ¼ cup (1.5 oz., 40 g) kosher or sea salt
- ½ cup (4 oz., 110 g) firmly packed light brown sugar
- ¼ cup (2 oz., 60 g) white miso
- 1 cinnamon stick, crushed
- 2 star anise
- 1 allspice berry
- 1 bay leaf
- 12 black peppercorns
- 2 garlic cloves, crushed and peeled
- 1 small fresh or dried Thai bird chile or other incendiary chile (optional)
- 6 cups (48 oz., 1.425 kg) ice cubes

1. To make the brine, heat the water in a 3-quart or larger nonreactive pot until simmering. Add the salt and brown sugar and stir well until dissolved.

2. Remove from the heat and add the miso, cinnamon, star anise, allspice, bay leaf, peppercorns, garlic, and chile, if using. Add the ice and stir well to combine the ingredients and cool the brine.

3. When the brine is thoroughly cool, add the pork chops. Cover and refrigerate for 2 to 8 hours.

4. Remove the chops from the brine and rinse well, then dry. Place the chops in a single layer on a rack set over a baking sheet. Refrigerate, uncovered, for 1 hour to 1 day to develop a pellicle and to equally distribute the salts.

5. Quarter the bok choy. If it is small and tender, leave in quarters but trim off the tough stem. For larger bok choy, core and chop into 2-inch pieces. Set aside.

Recipe continues

OPPOSITE: Spiced Pork Chops with Garlicky Bok Choy

4 thick-cut (1½-inch) bone-in pork loin chops

1½ pounds (700 g) bok choy, trimmed

1 teaspoon, or less, olive oil

• Kosher salt and freshly ground black pepper

1 tablespoon vegetable, canola, or grapeseed oil

One 2-inch knob of ginger, grated

2 garlic cloves, minced or grated

¼ cup (2 oz., 60 ml) tamari or soy sauce

¼ cup (2 oz., 60 ml) water

1 half-pint jar Asian-Style Plum Sauce (page 93)

6. Heat a grill pan or a large cast-iron pan over high heat until hot enough that water droplets scattered on the surface jump and sizzle. Slick with the slightest amount of olive oil, then reduce the heat to medium-high. Salt and pepper the chops, place in the pan, and sear until the pork lifts easily from the surface without pulling, tearing, or sticking, about 9 minutes. Don't fuss or move it; leave it alone, simply test to see if it will lift up. Turn and cook on the second side until the meat releases easily and the interior temperature measures 145°F on an instant-read thermometer, about 9 more minutes. Wrap the pork loosely in a double thickness of foil and place on a wooden board or a pile of towels (not the cold surface of your countertop) to rest for 10 minutes.

7. Meanwhile, cook the bok choy. Warm the vegetable oil in a 10-inch straight-sided skillet over medium heat. Add the ginger and garlic and cook until aromatic, 1 to 2 minutes. Add the bok choy, tamari, and water, cover, and cook over high heat until the bok choy is tender, about 3 minutes. Remove the lid and simmer to reduce the liquid to a glaze, 5 minutes or so. Taste for salt and pepper.

8. While the bok choy cooks, heat the plum sauce in a small saucepan until simmering.

9. Serve the chops whole (set the table with sharp knives), or cut the meat from the bone and slice. Arrange the bok choy on warmed plates. Place the pork on the choy, then drizzle plum sauce over each serving. Place a bowl of the remaining warm plum sauce on the table, a new kind of gravy.

Smoking

Adding the flavor of wood smoke to foods was originally part of a preservation technique; smoke made meat less attractive to insects and opportunistic animals. Now smoke makes meats and fish more attractive to humans. We add smoke because it tastes good. Really good. A whisper of fruitwood smoke on trout is transformative. Maple wood, maple syrup, and a chicken? Best friends. And a smoked oyster is a mouthful of happiness.

A smoker is cookware and appliance in one. Some are electric. Others sit on the stovetop. And some are jerry-rigged half barrels behind dusty gas stations across the southern United States. All require some form of wood, whether chunks, chips, or pucks. A wide variety of wood can be used for smoking, from cherry and maple (great for poultry) to alder (traditional for fish) to hickory and mesquite (for pork, beef, and venison.) Experiment with different types, using logic and whimsy to identify potential pairings—if duck goes with cherry sauce, for example, then cherry wood should work. If you like to slather salmon with maple syrup before grilling, try maple for the smoke. As with any type of home preserving, experimentation over time will inform your results.

In the case of ingredients such as nuts, chiles, or cheese, and particularly shellfish, err on the side of undersmoking. Let me assure you, oversmoking can result in a horrible, ashtray-reminiscent flavor and an acrid smell that permeates everything.

These recipes are written for a stand-alone electric smoker. It would be cumbersome, at best, to offer instructions for every smoker out there, so my hard-won advice is to read and follow the manufacturer's instructions to start, and remember that expertise takes practice. Soon you will be adding smoking to your expanding arsenal of kitchen skills.

Barbeque-Smoked Brisket (page 327)

Smoking Equipment

kitchen scale

kitchen twine

wood chips

Equipment

There are ways to add smoky flavor to food regardless of your living situation. Apartment dwellers embrace **stovetop smokers**, about the size of a lasagna pan. With these smaller stovetop models, it is possible to smoke everything in this chapter except the ham hocks and brisket. Substitute jowl for the ham hocks, and short ribs for the brisket. Keep that exhaust fan running. And when you've finished smoking, open the smoker near an open window.

A **stand-alone electric outdoor smoker**, about the size of a two-drawer filing cabinet, requires a moderate investment, but it is very sturdy and easy to use. Admittedly, this type of smoker has a seemingly insatiable hunger for fuel—pressed hockey pucks of wood chips available at the hardware store or online. (Each time I purchase a box of "brisquettes," I am reminded of college marketing classes and the adage "The razor is free, charge for the blades.") The recipes in this book were tested on a Bradley smoker. If you are using another type, your mileage may vary.

Many people rig their **gas or charcoal grill** as a smoker. Perforated foil packets of well-soaked wood chips form the smoke, placed on one side of a covered grill, while the item to be smoked is placed on the opposite cold(er) side. **Grill smokers** mimic this method with a cook surface set over a wood-filled "box" that sits on top of the grill surface, like a bunk bed.

Other home "smokemeisters" swear by the **Big Green Egg,** a bullet-shaped ceramic grill/smoker combination. Soaked wood chips provide the fuel for these smokers. The BGE is an envy-producing piece of equipment with a hefty price tag.

Before smoking, soak the **wood chips** or **chunks**. Water is fine, but consider fruit juice, malt or other vinegars, beer, wine, or bourbon to add another layer of flavor.

An accurate **thermometer** is essential. I am partial to the digital probe type, with a long cable so I can avoid opening the door to the smoker when checking the temperature. My butcher friends swear by laser or infrared thermometers.

A **perforated grill tray** is a must when smoking smaller items like scallops, nuts, vegetables, and cheese.

Kitchen twine is necessary for trussing and for suspending foods in the smoker.

Oversmoking: tastes like an ashtray

Sadly, there is nothing to do with oversmoked food but throw it away. That scent, reminiscent of Sunday morning in a frat house basement, is the odor of regret, plain and simple.

Testing, testing

Before investing in a big expensive piece of meat or fish for smoking and devoting hours to tending the fire, learn to use your smoker by practicing with the recipe that follows for a batch of satisfyingly smoky, sweet, salty almonds.

Smoked Spiced Almonds

MAKES: 1½ pounds

ACTIVE TIME: 45 minutes

Make the most of an already hot and smoky situation and pop these almonds in when making the salmon (page 321) or brisket (page 327) or any other recipe. Sometimes, while the smoker cools off, I'll make the most of the remaining heat and smoke to layer this healthy food with some smoky flavor.

4 tablespoons (2 oz., 60 g) unsalted butter or bacon fat

1 to 2 tablespoons (0.3 to 0.75 oz., 10 to 20 g) kosher salt (if using bacon fat, be careful with the salt here)

2 tablespoons firmly packed, dark brown sugar

2 tablespoons wildflower or chestnut honey (the darker the honey, the better)

2 tablespoons maple syrup

1 teaspoon smoked paprika

1 teaspoon Hot Sauce (page 175), Sriracha, or Tabasco (optional)

1½ pounds (680g) raw almonds

1 teaspoon large-crystal sea salt, such as Maldon or other flaky salt

1. Heat the smoker to 175°F, using maple, hickory, or apple wood for the smoke.

2. Melt the butter in a small saucepan. Add the salt, brown sugar, honey, maple syrup, paprika, and hot sauce, if using.

3. Place the almonds in a large bowl, pour the butter mixture over them, and stir to coat. Let the almonds hang out on the counter, covered, while the smoker heats.

4. Spread the almonds out in a single layer on a perforated grill pan. (Smoke in batches if necessary.) If there is any honey and salt mixture remaining, just dispose of it; do not try to add it to the nuts. Smoke for 25 minutes, stirring halfway through.

5. Preheat the oven to 325°F. Line a baking sheet with parchment.

6. Remove the almonds from the smoker and spread out on the baking sheet in a single layer. Sprinkle with the sea salt. Bake for about 6 minutes, rotating the pan and stirring after 3 minutes; do not let them burn. Remove the pan from the oven and slide out the parchment, letting the nuts fall back onto the warm pan. The nuts will be soft when they first emerge. Be patient—they will crisp as they cool.

7. Store in a tightly sealed jar. The nuts will keep for 2 weeks.

Smoked Bacon

MAKES: 1½ pounds

ACTIVE TIME: 30 minutes

CURING AND PELLICLE TIME: 8 days

Until I began making bacon at home, it didn't occur to me that different types of bacon could serve different purposes. Smoked, sweet, spicy, peppered—pork belly is a blank canvas wanting nothing more than your creative flavoring interpretation. This smoky version is my choice for starting braises, soups, or a pot of beans. Or add a crisp rasher to your grilled burger. Crumble over a grain salad. Add to corn bread. You get the idea.

Adding crumbled chiles to the rub makes this a very spiced bacon. If you prefer a milder flavor, omit the arbol and substitute ancho or pasilla chiles for a subtle fruity flavor without the heat.

1 or 2 dried *chiles de arbol*

2 tablespoons (1 oz., 20 g) kosher or sea salt

¼ teaspoon pink salt (see box, page 314)

¼ cup (2 oz., 60 g) firmly packed, light brown sugar

1 teaspoon dried thyme

1 tablespoon coarsely ground black pepper

2 pounds (1 kg) trimmed pork belly, skin removed

1. Toast the chiles in a small dry skillet over medium-high heat turning them over and over until flexible, about 2 minutes.

2. Wearing gloves, remove the stems from the chiles; removing the seeds is optional, but leaving them in ensures the bacon will be very spicy. Crumble the chiles into a small bowl and stir in the salt, pink salt, brown sugar, thyme, and black pepper.

3. Rub the mixture all over the pork belly and place it in a gallon-size zip-lock bag. Remove the air from the bag and seal it. Put the bag, lying flat, on the middle refrigerator shelf.

4. Let the bacon cure for 7 days. Every day, turn the bag over to redistribute the cure and rub the belly through the bag, introducing all those nice flavors.

5. After 7 days, remove the pork belly from the bag. It will be firmer than it was a week ago, a sign the cure has worked. Rinse the meat thoroughly and dry with paper towels. Place the soon-to-be bacon on a rack set over a baking sheet and place it, uncovered, in the refrigerator for another day. This will allow the salts to equalize through the meat and a pellicle to develop.

Recipe continues

6. Heat the smoker to 175°F, fruitwoods like apple and cherry are sweet and add delicious flavor to bacon, but hickory and maple work equally well. Place the cured pork belly on a rack in the smoker, fat side up, and hot-smoke for about 2 hours, until the internal temperature registers 150°F on an instant-read thermometer. Remove from the smoker, cool, and then wrap well in butcher paper, plastic wrap, or foil.

7. Chill the bacon thoroughly, at least 4 hours. The meat will firm up and slicing will be much easier.

8. Slice the bacon thin or thick, according to your preference. To store, place the slices on parchment or butcher paper, stacked in portion sizes (whatever is most convenient for your family.) Vacuum-seal or wrap snugly in plastic wrap and place in a zip-lock bag.

The bacon keeps for up to 10 days in the refrigerator or up to 6 months in the freezer. Smoked bacon is always cooked before serving.

PINK SALT AND THE SMOKER

Pink salt, a nitrite, prevents the growth of the botulinum toxin in an airless environments, like those inside a smoker, and the occasional gaps that occur inside the meat. While pink salt is optional for the salt-cured bacon on page 293, it is required for safely smoking bacon because the meat is held at a low temperature (175°F).

Smoked Whole Chicken

SERVES: 4

ACTIVE TIME: 30 minutes

BRINING TIME: 4 to 12 hours

SALT EQUALIZING AND PELLICLE TIME: 2 to 12 hours

SMOKING TIME: 2 to 2½ hours

I never make one smoked chicken. I always make two. Sometimes three. The smoked meat, carved off the bone, holds for a week in the refrigerator and up to 6 months in the freezer. And please, make stock from the carcasses for a rich soup or sauce base that adds a smoky flavor in only the very best way. Follow the recipe on page 230, substituting the smoked chicken carcasses.

Smoked chicken is as satisfying as roasted chicken and a great way to change things up in the regular dinner rotation. And the leftovers are sublime. Try this tender smoked meat in sandwiches or calzones, in pasta dishes or stir-fries, as a burrito filling, or in quiche, potpie, and enchiladas.

If serving the chicken for company, take the extra time to glaze and brown the skin for a much prettier presentation. Otherwise, remove and dispose of it before serving.

One	3½- to 4-pound (2-kg) pastured, farm-raised chicken
2	cups (16 oz., 475 ml) nonchlorinated water
6	cups (48 oz., 1425 g) ice cubes
½	cup (2.5 oz., 70 g) kosher or sea salt
½	cup (3.5 oz., 100 g) granulated sugar
1	lemon
1	orange
1	dried bay leaf
6	fresh thyme sprigs
10	parsley stems
10	black peppercorns
¼	cup (2 oz., 60 ml) maple syrup or orange juice (optional)
¼	cup (2 oz., 60 ml) olive oil (optional)

1. Rinse the chicken well inside and out. Trim off the wing tips (and freeze for making stock), or tuck them behind the back of the chicken. Trim away any loose flaps and little clumps of fat.

2. To make the brine, combine the water, salt, and sugar in a 5-quart or larger stockpot and heat over medium heat, stirring until the salt and sugar are dissolved. Add the ice to cool off the brine.

3. Halve the lemon and orange and squeeze the juices into the brine. Drop the citrus halves in for good measure. Add the bay, thyme, parsley, and peppercorns and stir well.

4. Submerge the chicken in the cold brine and refrigerate for 4 to 12 hours.

5. Remove the chicken from the brine. Rinse well inside and out and dry thoroughly. Place the chicken on a rack set over a baking sheet and refrigerate, uncovered, for 2 to 12 hours, until the skin feels dry and slightly tacky to the touch—that's the pellicle.

Recipe continues

6. Heat the smoker to 225°F, using maple, cherry, apple, or pecan wood for the smoke. Brush the breasts, legs, and wings of the chicken with the maple syrup. Place the chicken breast side down on the smoker's middle rack and smoke for 2 to 2½ hours, until the internal temperature reaches 160°F (insert the thermometer into the thickest part of the thigh, almost on the underside of the bird, without touching bone); baste the chicken two or three times during smoking.

7. At this point, you have two choices: Chickens do not emerge from the smoker with the crisp, shiny, appealing, snack-worthy skin of a roast chicken. Instead, the skin is pale, rubbery, and not very appetizing.

   If serving the whole smoked chicken: Once it emerges from the smoker, paint the skin with the remaining maple syrup mixed with the olive oil, then put the bird under a hot broiler until the skin is blistered and more appealing, 3 or 4 minutes. You want to avoid drying out the flesh while still crisping the skin, so be quick. The skin will still have a slightly rubbery texture, but the presentation is much more attractive. Let the chicken rest for at least 10 minutes before serving.

   Or if the meat from the smoked chicken will be added to another dish (or sandwiches, or served as part of a barbequed meat platter): Remove the bird from the smoker and let it rest for a few minutes; the internal temperature will rise to 165°F. Remove and discard the skin and slice the meat from the bone.

VARIATION: SMOKED TURKEY BREAST

• Smoking a turkey breast is just the ticket for any holiday, but especially Thanksgiving, whether you are a gathering too small for an entire turkey or too large for just one turkey. Follow the same procedure as above, but a 6-pound bone-in turkey breast needs twice the amount of brine, at least 6 hours brining, 4 to 8 hours to develop the pellicle, and 3 to 4 hours to smoke to 160°F.

OPPOSITE: Smoked Chicken, Porcini, and Peas (page 318)

Bonus Recipe: Smoked Chicken, Porcini, and Peas

SERVES: 4

ACTIVE TIME: 45 minutes

There are times when nothing but familiar, comforting foods will do. The weather or the end of a demanding work week might bring on this ache, or perhaps just the yearn for a simple dinner made from practical but sensational pantry goods. In another era, this might have been called chicken à la king. It's creamy and aromatic and deeply satisfying.

This recipe relies on an essential ingredient in my pantry—dried mushrooms. Whether it's porcini or morels or the musical sounding chanterelles, a whisper of any one of these treasures pumps up the umami volume in any dish. The chicken and peas make it comforting, the mushrooms make it all the more special.

See photograph on page 317.

- 1 cup (8 oz., 226 g) basmati, jasmine, or long-grain white rice, rinsed
- 3 tablespoons unsalted butter
- ½ cup (2 oz., 60 g) minced shallots
- 3 cups (8 oz., 194 g) quartered cremini mushrooms
- • Kosher salt and freshly ground black pepper
- ¼ cup (2 oz., 60 ml) dry white wine
- ¼ cup (2 oz., 55 g) dried porcini, rehydrated in ½ cup (4 oz., 125 ml) boiling water until plump, 15 to 20 minutes
- 3 tablespoons all-purpose flour
- 2 cups (16 oz., 475 ml) chicken stock, homemade (page 230) or store-bought, or water

1. Pour 2 cups water into a 3-quart saucepan with a lid, add a big pinch of salt, and bring to a boil. Add the rice and return the water to a boil, then cover, reduce the heat to barely there, and simmer for 13 minutes. Fluff with a fork and cover. It will be tender and perfectly cooked when the chicken is done.

2. Meanwhile, in a large skillet, heat the butter over medium heat until bubbling. Add the shallots and sauté until translucent, about 3 minutes. Increase the heat to medium-high, add the mushroom quarters, and salt and pepper well. Without stirring, cook the mushrooms until browned, about 5 minutes; they will release liquid. Shake the pan and continue to cook for another few minutes, until they reabsorb the liquids and are well browned. Add the wine, bring to a boil over high heat, and cook until reduced by half, 3 minutes or so.

3. Drain the porcini in a cheesecloth-lined strainer set over a bowl; reserve the mushroom stock. Roughly chop the porcini and set aside.

4. Sprinkle the flour over the mushrooms and shallots, stir to coat, and cook over medium heat, stirring, until the raw flour smell is gone, 3 or 4 minutes. Add the mushroom and chicken stocks, stirring to prevent lumps, then increase the heat to a hearty simmer and cook, until the sauce thickens, 12 minutes or so. The velvety sauce will be smooth like gravy, but not thick like porridge. Salt and pepper again to taste.

2 cups (12 oz., 230 g) shredded or cut-up (bite-sized pieces) smoked chicken or turkey (see page 315)

½ cup (2 oz., 62 g) frozen tiny peas

¼ cups (2 oz., 60 ml) heavy cream, sour cream, or crème fraîche (page 385)

¼ cup (1 oz., 11 g) chopped fresh flat-leaf parsley, plus more for garnish

5. Add the porcini, along with the smoked chicken and peas, and stir well to coat. Heat thoroughly, then remove from the heat, stir in the cream and parsley, and add salt and pepper if necessary.

6. I like to serve this dish on a big shallow platter: Pile up the fluffy rice, make a well in the center, and spoon in the chicken mixture. Garnish with more parsley. It's also pretty plated individually: Pack a ramekin with rice and invert it onto a serving plate, making a tidy little form, then spoon some of the chicken mixture over the top. Repeat on three more plates.

Hot-Smoked Salmon

MAKES: about 1½ pounds

ACTIVE TIME: 20 minutes

CURING AND PELLICLE TIME: 3 days

SMOKING TIME: 2 hours

Smoked salmon is a staple in my household. It's great for breakfast, lunch, or dinner. It's healthy and satisfying, and it keeps well. If I have the option, I ask for a center-cut fillet, from the thickest part of the side of the salmon, but a salmon steak, the tail end, or whatever piece of salmon you have all smoke beautifully.

This is hot-smoked salmon, moist, flaky, and lightly scented with alder wood. Cherry and maple woods also suit, but heavier mesquite and hickory will overwhelm the taste of the fish. This is not cold-smoked salmon or lox, which is cured and lapped with smoke—this method thoroughly cooks the fish in the smoker.

Smoked salmon starts out like gravlax (page 299), salt-curing in the refrigerator for 2 days before the smoke flavor is layered on. Once you have this technique under your belt, start to branch out: Add herbs. Change the sugar and use maple syrup. Experiment with spices like cinnamon or fennel seeds and chiles like ancho or dried chipotle.

Flake some smoked salmon with mascarpone (page 379) and stir in minced cornichons (page 199) and a squeeze of lemon juice to make a salmon spread that's great with bagels and fancy enough to top baguette toasts at cocktail hour. Mix smoked salmon and canned salmon (page 279) with fresh breadcrumbs and an egg, form, and fry up a salmon cake. Top with an egg and call it brunch. You're going to be happy to have smoked salmon in the house.

One 2-pound (1 kg) center-cut organic or wild-caught salmon fillet (skin on)

5 tablespoons (1.75 oz., 50 g) kosher or sea salt

1 cup (8 oz., 220 g) firmly packed light brown sugar

½ teaspoon grated orange zest

1 tablespoon (½ oz.) Cognac

1. Inspect the salmon for any pin bones and remove with tweezers. Combine the salt, brown sugar, and zest in a small bowl and rub it all over the flesh side of the salmon. Sprinkle the same side with the Cognac.

2. Wrap the fish tightly in plastic wrap. Place in a gallon-size zip-lock bag and put in a shallow baking dish to catch any leaks. Place a small baking pan on top of the wrapped fish, then weight with cans or a brick. Refrigerate for 2 days. The fish will exude liquid. Turn it once after 24 hours and put the weight back on top of the wrapped fish.

Recipe continues

OPPOSITE: Hot-Smoked Salmon

3. Remove the fish from the wrapping, scrape off any excess cure, and dry with paper towels. It will be firmer and a deeper color. Place the fish skin side down on a rack set over a baking sheet and refrigerate for 12 hours to develop a tacky, dry pellicle.

4. Heat the smoker to 175°F, using alder or another mild wood. Place the salmon skin side down on a center rack, or suspend it from an upper rack (see Note), and smoke to an internal temperature of 150°F, about 2 hours (see Tip, page 323).

Note: To suspend the fish, make a small hole in an outside corner of the fillet with a sharp knife. Push kitchen twine through the hole and use it to tie the fish to one of the racks in the smoker.

Hot-Smoked Trout

MAKES: 2 whole smoked trout

ACTIVE TIME: 10 minutes

CURING AND PELLICLE TIME: 2½ hours

SMOKING TIME: 1½ hours.

Serve the whole fish, warm, with corn bread and fried eggs. Or flake the flesh into yogurt or sour cream and add a big spoonful of horseradish and lots of lemon juice. Serve on pita chips, brioche toasts, or cucumber rounds.

Opt for head-on or head-off trout. Your choice.

2 **exceptionally fresh whole trout**

• **Kosher salt**

1. Rinse the trout well, inside and out. To calculate the correct amount of salt, weigh the fish and multiply the weight by 3%. (Example: 340 g × 0.03 = 10 grams of salt.) Rub the flesh of the fish with the salt. Place the fish on a rack set over a baking sheet and refrigerate for 2 hours.

2. Thoroughly wipe away the cure. Air-dry for 30 minutes, then smoke at 175°F to an internal temperature of 150°F, about 90 minutes.

> ## TIP
>
> If you overcook trout or salmon and the fish is dry, don't despair. Call it jerky. Shred or chop it, and add chopped scallions, soy sauce, and hot sauce, and serve over a hearty grain. Or stir minced chives and shredded jerky into grits and top with sour cream. Make fried rice with it. It's still delicious.

Pappardelle with Smoked Salmon
and Spinach

Bonus Recipe: Pappardelle with Smoked Salmon and Spinach

SERVES: 4

ACTIVE TIME: 40 minutes

This is a comforting meal, ready in just a few minutes. If you don't have cream, substitute sour cream or cream cheese. If you don't have smoked salmon, substitute smoked trout or a jar of your own home-canned salmon or tuna from the pantry. No spinach? Use kale. No kale? Use peas. Or even steamed carrots, if that's all you have. Add toasted chopped nuts to the bread crumbs if you want more crunch. Once you've made this a few times, it will become a go-to solution for a satisfying dinner. It is a perfect example of the practical pantry at work, and it is the dinner I crave on many cold, rainy Sundays.

3	to 4 cups (275 g) baby spinach or one 10-ounce (28.3 g) package frozen chopped spinach
½	cup (2 oz., 60 g) fresh bread crumbs
2	tablespoons (1 oz., 28 g) unsalted butter
2	medium shallots, minced
½	cup (4 oz., 120 ml) heavy cream
½	cup (4 oz. 125 ml) chicken stock, homemade (page 230) or store-brought, or light broth such as Brown Veal Stock (page 233)
12	ounces (340 g) Hot-Smoked Salmon (page 321), flaked
•	Kosher salt and freshly ground black pepper
8	ounces (500 g) fresh or dried pappardelle
¼	teaspoon freshly ground white pepper
½	teaspoon freshly grated nutmeg
1	tablespoon finely minced fresh chives
1	tablespoon finely minced fresh flat-leaf parsley

1. Fill a large deep, pot with water, salt well, and bring to a boil.

2. Meanwhile, if using fresh spinach, fill a 3-quart saucepan with an inch or two of water and bring to a boil. Insert a steamer basket (or use a colander or sieve), add the spinach, cover, and steam until tender, about 4 minutes. Remove from the heat and cool, then squeeze the excess moisture out, pressing the spinach against the steamer or colander walls. Chop well and set aside.

3. In a large dry skillet, toast the bread crumbs until dry and golden brown. Remove and set aside.

4. Heat the butter in the same skillet until foaming, then add the shallots and cook until translucent. Add the cream, stock, spinach, white pepper, and nutmeg and simmer, stirring gently, until the sauce thickens slightly. Add the salmon, stir well, and taste for seasoning, adding salt and pepper as needed.

5. Meanwhile, drop the pasta into the boiling water and cook according to the package directions. Drain the pasta, reserving ½ cup of the cooking water.

6. Add the pasta to the sauce and toss gently to coat. Add the cooking water if the mixture seems dry.

7. Serve piping hot, with a scattering of the toasted bread crumbs and chopped chives and parsley.

Barbeque-Smoked Brisket

SERVES: 8, with leftovers
ACTIVE TIME: about 3 hours over 2 days
DRY-BRINING TIME: 12 hours to 1 day
SMOKING TIME: 4 to 6 hours
OVEN COOKING TIME: 4 to 6 hours
RESTING TIME: 1 hour

Making brisket is a commitment. Without a lot of love and attention, this is a cut of beef with the potential to be tough, stringy, and dry. Say good-bye to bad brisket and tenderize and moisturize it in a long, slow braise. Adding a smoky flavor before that braise will make a memorable meal, not to mention memorable sandwiches the next day.

Brisket is cut from the long breastplate of the cow. It's a big piece of beef, and a muscle that doesn't get much use, so there isn't a lot of fat marbling the meat. First-cut brisket is leaner and suited for the person who orders lean pastrami or corned beef. I prefer the deckle, or second cut, with its gleaming fat cap that seeps slowly into the meat while it cooks. For smoking and long cooking, that fat cap ensures a tender, moist result. A smoked whole brisket is wonderful. Scale up the recipe to suit the weight.

Smoked brisket is first rubbed with a dry brine to start the cure. The brine tightens the meat's structure by drawing out some of the moisture. Then you put some moisture back with the peppery mop, basting the meat as it is slowly smoking. These two elements, a dry rub and a mop, are quintessential elements in the world of barbeque.

½ recipe Sizzling BBQ Rub (recipe follows)

One 3-to 4-pound (1.35 to 1.8 kg) deckle-cut (second cut) brisket (first cut is acceptable), trimmed

2 to 3 cups (475 to 600 ml) Peppery Mop (recipe follows)

2 to 3 medium onions, sliced ½-inch thick

One 12-ounce (375 ml) bottle dark beer

2 pint jars Chipotle Barbeque Sauce (page 263)

OPPOSITE: Massaging the Sizzling BBQ Rub (page 329) into the brisket

1. Massage the rub all over the brisket. Put it on a rack set over a baking sheet and place it in the refrigerator, uncovered, for 12 hours to 1 day.

2. Early the next day (about 12 hours before dinner), heat the smoker to 175°F, using hickory wood. Brush away excess rub, then generously brush the brisket with the mop. Place it fat side up on a center rack. Smoke for 1 hour, then mop the meat again, and continue to mop every hour for another 4 to 6 hours, until the internal temperature reaches 180°F.

3. Preheat the oven to 225°F. Line a baking sheet with a double layer of heavy-duty aluminum foil twice the length of the pan, so it extends over the short ends. Add the onions in a thick layer in the center of the lined baking sheets. Remove the brisket from the smoker and place it on top of the onions.

Recipe continues

Barbeque Brisket Sandwiches (page 329)

4. Pour the beer and ½ cup of the barbeque sauce over the meat and form a tight packet with the foil. Place the happy packet in the oven on the baking sheet and cook for 4 to 6 hours, until the meat is fork-tender. Remove the packet from the oven and allow it to rest for at least 15 minutes, or up to an hour.

5. Open the packet and inhale the wonder. Slice the meat against the grain and serve with remaining warmed barbeque sauce on the side.

VARIATIONS

If you are a small family and wondering what you would do with all of that meat, consider substituting short ribs for the brisket. If you don't have a smoker, the brisket or short ribs can be oven-braised. Oven-braising takes about half the time as smoking, so it may fit into your lifestyle a little more readily. But if you can, that whisper of woodsmoke is what makes this barbeque authentic.

- **To Oven-Braise the brisket (or short ribs) without smoking:** Skip the mop, skip the smoking. Put the rub-coated brisket, after a 12-hour rest, on top of the onions on the foil. Before sealing the packet, lay three or four ½-inch-thick slices of smoked bacon on top of the brisket. Then add the beer and ½- cup barbeque sauce, as in Step 4, seal the packet, and oven-braise for at least 8 or up to 12 hours.
- **Barbeque-Smoked Short Ribs:** Substitute 4 pounds of bone-in short ribs for the brisket. Use half the dry rub, or the meat will be too spicy, and mop the meat only once or twice. Smoke for 4 to 6 hours and oven-braise for at least 6 hours. Just because they're smaller doesn't mean a shorter cooking time to tenderize ribs, but you will need about half the mop, barbeque sauce, and beer.
- **Barbeque Brisket Sandwiches (about 8):** Shred the brisket and mix with a cup or two of the barbeque sauce. Serve in soft sandwich buns.

Sizzling BBQ Rub

MAKES: a little less than a cup

A ramped-up salt cure, this spicy rub imbues the meat with plenty of flavor while drawing out the moisture and tightening the texture, all of which contribute to the sublime barbeque experience.

3 tablespoons coarsely ground black pepper
2 tablespoons kosher salt
2 tablespoons granulated sugar
1 tablespoon smoked paprika
2 teaspoons chipotle chile powder
2 teaspoons ancho chile powder
- Pink salt calculated at 0.25% weight of the meat (optional; see Note)

Mix all the ingredients together.

Note: Because the meat is smoked at such a low temperature, pink salt is recommended to keep the meat safe to eat.

Peppery Mop

MAKES: about 1 quart
ACTIVE TIME: 30 minutes

A mop keeps meat moist while it's being smoked. This one works wonderfully with fish, chicken, or pork, as well as beef. Or try it with tofu, tempeh, or eggplant.

The mop will keep for up to a month in the refrigerator, but if you dip a brush into the jar and touch the raw meat, then put the brush into the jar again, the mop can't be reused safely. Instead, if you won't be using the entire recipe, pour the amount of mop you need into a bowl and reserve the rest for the next time.

1 tablespoon canola or grapeseed oil

1 cup (4.25 oz., 120 g) minced onion

1 tablespoon minced garlic

One 12-ounce (375-ml) bottle dark beer, such as Dos Equis

¼ cup (2 oz., 60 ml) cider vinegar

2 tablespoons tomato paste

2 tablespoons Worcestershire sauce

2 tablespoons Asian fish sauce

3 tablespoons firmly packed dark brown sugar

1 tablespoon smoked paprika

1 tablespoon black pepper

1 tablespoon sauce from chipotles in Adobo

1 teaspoon ground cumin

1 cup (8 oz., 240 ml) water

1. In a large saucepan, heat the oil over medium-high heat until shimmering. Add the onion and garlic and cook for 2 minutes, or until translucent. Add the remaining ingredients and bring to a boil, then reduce the heat and simmer for 15 minutes. Remove from the heat and let cool.

2. Pour the sauce into a quart jar.

Smoked Ham Hocks

MAKES: 4 smoked
ACTIVE TIME: 20 minutes
BRINING TIME: 5 days
PELLICLE TIME: 6 hours to 1 day
SMOKING TIME: 4 to 6 hours

Just as Italians start a recipe with pancetta and the French with ventrèche, many great recipes from the American South start with smoked ham hocks—an example of making good use of every bit of a well-raised animal. Ham hocks are cheap and easy to smoke, and they emerge mahogany-toned and smelling exquisite, worth their weight in gold.

Ham hocks are gnarly things, with thick skin and pads of fat, but, once brined, smoked, and simmered in a pot of beans for hours, they can be picked apart into luscious meat, fat, and skin, all of which, chopped well, impart glorious velvety texture and tasty little hammy bits.

4 cups (1 l) nonchlorinated water

2 tablespoons (0.75 oz., 20 g) kosher salt

• Pink salt calculated at 0.0025 of the weight of the hocks

2 tablespoons maple sugar, maple syrup, molasses, or sorghum

1 teaspoon coarsely ground black pepper

1 tablespoon fresh thyme or winter savory, chopped

4 cups (950 g) ice cubes

4 fresh ham hocks (about 3 pounds, 1.3 kg)

¼ cup (3 oz., 75 ml) maple syrup or sorghum

1. In a 3-quart saucepan, combine the water, salts, maple sugar, pepper, and thyme and heat, stirring just until the salt dissolves. Remove from the heat and add the ice cubes to cool the brine.

2. Rinse the ham hocks. Place in 2 gallon-sized zip-lock bags. Add the brine, force out the excess air, and seal the bags. Refrigerate for 5 days; turn the bags from time to time.

3. Remove the hocks, rinse, and place on a rack set over a baking sheet. Place in the refrigerator for 6 hours, or up to 1 day, to equalize the salts; the surface should feel dry and tacky.

4. Heat the smoker to 175°F, using hickory or pecan wood. Set the hocks on a middle rack and smoke for 1 hour. Brush them with maple syrup, then smoke for about 2 hours longer, until they are bronzed, and the internal temperature reaches 140°F.

5. Wrap the smoked hocks well and refrigerate or freeze until ready to use. I vacuum-seal these and other smoked meats to keep the smoky smell from permeating the freezer. The hocks will hold in the refrigerator for a month or more and for up to a year in the freezer.

Bonus Recipe: Field Beans with Ham Hock

SERVES: 4 good eaters

ACTIVE TIME: 30 minutes

COOKING TIME: 1 to 2 hours

Autumn arrives, and slowly the cold starts creeping in. Cassoulet or pasta fagioli or *borrachos* or all-American pork and beans—it's all peasant food offered up with the same intention: warm tummies.

To riff on this recipe, make cassoulet, with tarbais beans and smoked bacon (page 313). Or guanciale (page 349) and cannelloni beans for pasta fagioli. Try smoked hog jowl (page 334) with pinto beans and a dark beer for a southwestern spin.

4 tablespoons (2 oz., 55 g) butter or bacon fat

2 cups (8.5 oz., 240 g) diced onions

1 cup (4.5 oz., 130 g) sliced (½-inch-thick) carrots

1 celery stalk, cut into ½-inch dice

1 Smoked Ham Hock (page 331)

1 quart jar canned lima or butter beans (page 248 or 251)

1 dried bay leaf

5 fresh thyme sprigs or 1 teaspoon dried thyme

12 black peppercorns, crushed

1. Preheat the oven to 300°F.

2. In a 5-quart or larger ovenproof pot, heat the butter over medium-high heat until bubbling. Add the onions and cook until translucent, then add the carrots and celery and cook until softened, a total of about 12 minutes.

3. Add the ham hock and stir and turn over medium-low heat to melt some of the ham fat. This will take about 15 minutes.

4. Add the beans and gently stir to coat with all the good juices in the pot. Add the bay leaf, thyme, and peppercorns, barely cover with cold water, and bring to a boil. Reduce to a slow simmer, cover, and place the covered pot in the oven. Cook for at least 1 hour—it's even better after 2 hours. Remove from the oven and remove the ham hock; let it cool slightly.

5. Pull the meat from the ham hock and dispose of gristle and fat. Chop the meat well, and stir it back into the beans. Taste for salt. Heat the ham and beans.

6. Serve piping hot in soup bowls, with corn bread or crusty, chewy peasant bread.

OPPOSITE: Field Beans with Ham Hock

Smoked Hog Jowl

MAKES: 1 jowl
ACTIVE TIME: 1 hour
CURING TIME: 7 days
PELLICLE TIME: 1 day
SMOKING TIME: 2 hours

If you happen upon pork jowl, consider smoking it. The jowl can be served in slices, as you might serve bacon, or in chunks, as a garnish for beans, rice, or grits. The jowl has a sweeter flavor and a more soft, silky fat. It's wonderful in the bottom of a pot of long-cooked collard greens. And it lights up fried rice.

1 hog jowl
• Kosher salt calculated at 0.03 of the weight of the jowl
• Pink salt calculated at 0.0025 of the weight of the jowl
1 tablespoon coarsely ground black pepper
1 teaspoon dried rosemary
¼ cup sorghum or maple syrup

1. To trim the jowl, feel around it so you get to know the difference between the firm "good" fat and meat and the glands, small pearls clustered here and there through the surface fat. The glands have a dreadful texture and an off-putting taste. Use a sharp, flexible blade to cut them away, as well as any jiggly fat. The good fat, which is firm and white, should be retained to moisturize the meat during smoking. And because it's delicious.

2. To calculate the amount of kosher salt, weigh the trimmed jowl and multiply by 3% (Example: 900 g x 0.03 = 27 g salt). Weigh the salt and add to a small bowl. Calculate the amount of pink salt and add. Mix in the pepper and rosemary. Wearing gloves, rub this mixture into the flesh and skin side of the jowl using the heel of your hand. Place in a zip-lock bag or covered container and refrigerate for 1 week, turning the jowl over every day.

3. Remove from the refrigerator and knock off any residual salt and rub. Place on a rack set over a baking sheet and refrigerate for 6 to 24 hours, until the surface is tacky.

4. Heat the smoker to 175°F using hickory or pecan wood. Set the jowl on a middle rack, skin side up, and smoke to an internal temperature of 150°F, 1 to 2 hours, depending on the size. Baste with the sorghum after one hour and again every 30 minutes until done.

5. Remove the rind after smoking and slice the jowl into rashers, as with bacon. Cut any that won't slice easily into chunks, to flavor soups and beans or long-cooked greens. Store in the freezer for up to a year.

Smoked Oysters (page 336) with sea salt on butter crackers

Smoked Oysters

MAKES: 48 smoked oysters
ACTIVE TIME: 30 minutes
CURING TIME: 24 to 48 hours
SMOKING TIME: 20 to 40 minutes

Smoked oysters always make me think of my mother, who adored these sweet, salty, tender delights. Each summer, cans of oysters arrived with my Bostonian grandmother, visiting what surely (to her) seemed a backwater in Ohio. From time to time (predivorce), my mother would sit at the kitchen table, a cigarette burning in the ashtray, a faraway look on her face, a glass of Scotch and a can of smoked oysters in front of her, small fork at the ready. It was years before I understood how comforting smoked oysters might be in life's difficult moments.

Now that I've learned to make them, I enjoy smoked oysters without any need for a life crisis. This is a food that is more than comforting; it's luxurious and deeply satisfying and meant to be shared with someone special.

A couple of notes: Oysters range in flavor from sweet to briny. There are so many varieties of oysters it's impossible to name names here, but seek out the freshest, plumpest, sweetest oysters you can find. Small so-called "cocktail" oysters, with shells about two inches across, are best enjoyed raw. For this recipe, get large, fat oysters in shells about two and a half inches across.

See photographs on pages 335 and 338.

48 oysters in the shell (see headnote) or 2 pints shucked oysters

1. Rinse the oyster shells and scrub them well. They should be tightly closed; discard any that are not. If you are an adept oyster shucker, pop the shells and capture the oysters and their liquor in a large mixing bowl. If you are not a shucker, here's a trick: Preheat the oven to 300°F. Place the oysters rounded side down on a baking sheet and slide the pan into the oven for 5 minutes, or just until the shells pop open. If some have not yet opened, remove and shuck the ones that have and slide the pan back in the oven for a minute or two for the stragglers.

2. Drain the oysters (just-shucked or preshucked), reserving their liquor. Strain the liquor.

¼ cup (1.5oz., 90 g) kosher salt

¼ cup (2 oz., 60 ml) maple syrup

¼ cup (2 oz., 60 ml) blackstrap molasses

½ cup (4 oz., 125 ml) bourbon

¼ teaspoon cracked black pepper

¼ teaspoon hot sauce

2 cups (16 oz., 475 ml) water

4 cups (950 g) ice cubes

- Mild olive oil
- Maldon or other flaky sea salt (optional)

3. To make the brine, in a 4-quart nonreactive pot, stir together the salt, maple syrup, molasses, bourbon, pepper, hot sauce, oyster liquor, and water and bring to a simmer, stirring to dissolve the sugar. Remove from the heat and add the ice to cool the brine completely.

4. Meanwhile, gingerly rinse each oyster under cold running water to remove any bits of shell or sand. Drop the oysters gently into the cooled brine. Cover and refrigerate for 24 and up to 48 hours.

5. Heat the smoker to 225°F, using alder or mild fruit wood. Remove the oysters from the brine, gently pat dry with paper towels, and place on a perforated grill pan. Slide the oysters into the smoker and smoke until they are cooked and the edges start to ruffle and curl, 20 to 40 minutes, depending on the size and plumpness of the oysters. Check them every 5 minutes after the first 20, poking the flesh with your finger until it meets a slight resistance.

6. To serve, douse in a bit of mild olive oil and sprinkle with crunchy salt. Or submerge in olive oil in a jar and store in the refrigerator for up to a week.

Bonus Recipe: Smoked Oyster Chowder

SERVES: 4

ACTIVE TIME: 30 minutes

When I was a small child, my grandparents took me to Cape Cod to visit my great-grandmother, a tiny woman with an enormous personality. No one questioned Esther. About anything. While clam chowder wasn't part of her upbringing, she embraced it wholeheartedly when she moved to the United States from Russia. This soup reminds me of her, although it's much better. You see, she had the very best intentions, but her choice of skim milk for chowder was a mistake. Use the real deal, cream or whole milk, or half-and-half. You're worth it.

4 ounces (113 g) Smoked Bacon (page 313) or store-bought bacon, diced

2 leeks, white and pale green parts, sliced into thin disks

2 Yukon Gold potatoes, cut into 1-inch dice

2 tablespoons all-purpose flour

2 quarts (64 oz., 2 l) Fish Fumet (page 235) or Chicken Stock (page 230)

1 pint jar Canned Corn (page 265)

12 Smoked Oysters (page 336), at room temperature

½ cup (4 oz., 120 ml) heavy cream or whole milk

4 thick slices sourdough bread

1. In a 4-quart pot, cook the bacon over medium heat until crisp. Using a slotted spoon, remove to paper towels to drain. Add the leeks to the pot and wilt them in the lovely bacon fat over medium heat. Add the potatoes, toss to coat in the fat, and cook until slightly browned on the edges, about 8 to 10 minutes.

2. Sprinkle the leeks and onions with the flour and cook, stirring, until the raw flour smell is gone and the flour has taken on a slight golden tone, about 3 minutes. Stir well, add the fish fumet, and bring to a boil. Add the corn and lower the heat to a simmer, then add the smoked oysters, stir, and cook for 2 minutes. Add the cream and bacon and bring to a simmer.

3. Meanwhile, toast or grill the bread until well browned and crisp. Set aside.

4. Divide the chowder among four warmed bowls. Float the toasted bread on the top and serve piping hot.

OPPOSITE: Smoked Oysters (page 336) in olive oil

Air-curing

You probably haven't given much thought to what makes pancetta or country ham or *saucisson sec* or beef jerky so very delicious. The common thread? The modern descriptive is *umami*, the fifth sense of taste, after sweet, sour, bitter, and salty. Meaty, savory, tangy—that is *umami*.

In air-cured meats, umami is brought to life with a stew of "good" microbes and bacteria that live in your home, backyard, and neighborhood. It's a flavor created from an alchemy of time, trust, and a soupçon of obsessive. These long-lasting preserved treats provide most of my meaty satisfaction. The explosion of flavor from even a very modest quantity is the reason curing meat is considered an art form.

It takes a certain amount of gutsy "kitcheneering" to hang meat in a curing cabinet and hope for a conversion to charcuterie through the influence of "good" bacteria. That is the first big leap of faith I'm asking from you. (There's another coming in the next chapter.) Curing meat means leaving meat out of the refrigerator to ferment. The meat is not *going off*—it's transforming.

Perfect curing conditions mean good airflow, ambient temperatures between 55° and 65°F, and humidity between 55 and 65 percent. There is some wiggle room: For instance, if the temperature is below 55°F but above freezing (32°F), curing will still occur, though it will take longer and some tang and funk may be missing. Too-high humidity leads to bad molds, but too low will lead to dry, hard, dessicated meat, less unctuous but still safely edible. (Use a Microplane and grate the salty bits on absolutely everything.)

A good rule of thumb: cured meats are ready to eat when they have lost 30 percent of their original weight. (Yet another reason to have a kitchen scale.) Be hyperaware, and use touch, smell, and sight to evaluate the curing process.

While this preservation technique is completely straightforward, I urge you to take great care with every step. Above all, be safe. Err on the side of obsessive.

I selected the air-cured recipes for this book judiciously: this is Curing 101. A slab of pork belly. An eye of round. A tenderloin. These whole-muscle cuts are inherently less likely to go bad than ground or pieced meats like salami or coppacola and are the safest gateway to the world of fermented meats.

OPPOSITE (left to right):
Air-cured pancetta (page 347), bresaola (page 350), and pork tenderloin (page 345)

The curing space

Locate the best space for curing air-dried meats using a combination thermometer/hygrometer. This inexpensive device, available at a hardware store or online, measures both temperature and humidity. Depending on the weather in your part of the world, you might find the right spot in a corner of your attic, in an unheated basement, or even the back of the linen closet. One intrepid meat curer I know hung an entire ham a few inches from the ceiling of his foyer for nearly a year. Unless you looked up, you would never see it.

From October until April, I suspend curing meats from the ceiling in a corner of an unheated, partially underground garage. The conditions are perfect, and there are no opportunistic bugs or critters (though when the dog walks into the garage, he does gaze up hopefully). If there is no suitable area in or around your home, repurpose a wine or other refrigerator into a curing cabinet. It should have temperature controls that will modulate the temperature at between 55°F and 65°F and keep the humidity at between 55 and 65 percent.

The cabinet's humidity will likely vary, starting off high when a fresh, moist piece of meat is hung. To reduce the humidity if it is above 65 percent, place a small bowl filled with raw rice in the cabinet to absorb moisture. As the meat dries, the humidity may fall below 55 percent. If that happens, place a small bowl of nonchlorinated water in the bottom of the cabinet. Place one end of a clean cotton kitchen towel in the bowl and drape it over an upper rack of the cabinet leaving the towel in the water. The water will wick up the towel and increase the overall humidity in the cabinet. If the reading remains too low, thoroughly dampen the towel and replace it in the same setup, still with one end dipped in the water. It may take an hour or more to adjust the cabinet's humidity; be patient and continue to check in.

The last, and equally important, requirement for a suitable curing space? Airflow. The best foods are evenly cured, a result that is helped along by moving the air in and around the hanging meat. Even a battery-operated fan will do the trick in the curing cabinet.

TROUBLESHOOTING: BAD BACTERIA, MOLDS, AND DESICCATION

Air-curing is a serious kitchen craft, practiced for centuries. There is a very real possibility that things will go awry, but most problems will be very obvious. Good practices are the best defense.

When curing meat, it's necessary to be obsessive. Check in on your preservation project at least once a day, more often if possible. Keep notes. If you pay close attention, follow the recipe instructions to the letter, and use common sense, you will create a flavorful, safe product.

Here's what you need to know. Botulinum bacteria can grow in any damp, airless pockets and will take advantage of intramuscular cuts. When trimming, use a very sharp knife and take care not to pierce the meat. Don't do any fancy knife work that cuts into or otherwise challenges the integrity of the muscle. Err on the safe side. Yes, trim away excess fat to avoid rancid meat, but intramuscular marbling is good, safe to leave, and contributes to the silky texture and deep flavors of air-cured meat.

Trim and square off the meat to help it cure evenly. Truss snugly to close any possible entryways for pathogens. There are two ways to truss. The safest way is to bring the string around the meat and tie a knot every inch or so. Make the string very snug so it doesn't slip when the meat cures and shrinks. The second trussing method is to use a running loop. With this method, one piece of string runs the entire length of the meat. This is not for beginners, but it's nice looking, stays firmly in place, and is aspirational.

To prevent mold from growing on the meat while it hangs, some home meat curers use sodium erythorbate (see Resources, page 401). This all-natural product, derived from beets, keeps mold at bay. Mix 25 g in 1000 ml warm water, then brush all over the meat until thoroughly drenched.

In the best conditions, cured meats develop a chalky-white bloomy mold on the outside. This is expected and indicates a healthy curing environment. But be wary. If the meat smells at all rotten, or if that bloom of mold is deep black or oddly green, or if long, and hairy mold develops, dispose of the entire experiment right away. These conditions tell you something has gone wrong and you must throw the meat away. All of it. DO NOT TASTE IT. Throw it out.

After any creepy molds or experiments gone wrong, clean the curing cabinet well with a 10% chlorine bleach to water solution. Air it out for a few days. Try again. We learn from failure.

Dry, tough, desiccated meat happens when the humidity is too low. Or when airflow becomes a brisk Nor'easter. Airflow is a soft breeze, not a weather system.

Cured Pork Tenderloin

MAKES: 6 ounces cured meat

ACTIVE TIME: 30 minutes

SALT EQUALIZATION TIME: 12 to 24 hours

CURING TIME: 10 days to 2 weeks

Because I am the only person in my household who eats cured meats, and someone who perhaps loves them a little too much, curing a pork tenderloin is just right. I use Aleppo pepper, a chile common to Middle Eastern cuisines. I like the mild heat and the way the fruity flavor accents the pork. Whatever you call it, however you spice it, it is a delightful addition to the *apéro* hour.

Wrapped loosely in parchment paper, the cured meat will keep for a month in the refrigerator but will continue to dry out. If it becomes so dry it cannot be sliced, use a microplane and grate the last bits over pasta or scrambled eggs.

1 **pork tenderloin (about 1 pound, 454 g; about 12 oz., 340 g after trimming)**
- **Kosher or sea salt**
1 **tablespoon Aleppo pepper**

1. Trim any obvious fat away from the exterior of the tenderloin. Cut off the tapering ends, forming a uniform thickness.

2. To calculate the correct amount of salt, weigh the trimmed tenderloin and multiply the weight by 3% (Example: 340 g × .003 = 10 grams salt). Using volume (tablespoon) measurements can lead to oversalted meat; use a scale. Rub the salt into the meat well, using the heel of your hand. Place the meat on a rack set over a baking sheet and refrigerate, uncovered, for 12 to 24 hours.

3. Knock off any apparent salt. Do not rinse. Truss the tenderloin, tying it off every inch, keeping the string snug, and ending with a long piece of twine to suspend the meat as it cures. Weigh the tenderloin in grams and make a note of the starting weight and the goal weight, which is 30 percent less. (Starting weight × 0.7 = ending weight).

4. Spread the pepper out on a board and roll the trussed meat in the pepper until it is entirely coated, including the ends.

5. Hang the tenderloin in your curing space for 10 days to 2 weeks, checking in on it every day. Check the weight after 10 days. When the tenderloin feels firm, with a slight give, and is near or at the ending weight, it is ready to enjoy.

OPPOSITE: Cured Pork Tenderloin

6. Slice the tenderloin into thin coins and serve.

Pancetta Tesa

MAKES: 1½ pounds

ACTIVE TIME: less than 1 hour

CURING TIME: 7 days

AGING TIME: 3 days to 3 weeks

The Italians have their own way of curing all sorts of meats, but their spin on pork belly is especially earthy, with a slight funk. This peppery, herbal meat is delicious in pasta and, especially, crisped and served with fruits or vegetables. *Pancetta*, Italian unsmoked bacon, and guanciale (recipe follows), are cured for anywhere from a few days to 3 weeks. More time equals more funk in the flavor—expect gamy, acidic, and slightly tangy after a long cure.

This recipe details the preparation for pancetta cured as a plank, flat and unencumbered, not rolled as it often is into a tight spiral. As pretty as a spiral of pancetta is, the stress surrounding forming a perfectly trussed pork belly with no air pockets that could attract "bad" bacteria convinced me to embrace this supersafe method.

- **Kosher or sea salt**
- One **2-pound (900-g) slab pork belly (see Procuring Pork Belly, page 291), rind removed and squared off**
- **Pink salt calculated at 0.25% of the weight of the meat (optional)**
- ¼ **cup (1 oz., 28 g) coarsely ground black pepper**
- 1 **teaspoon dried rosemary**
- 3 **dried bay leaves, crushed**
- ½ **teaspoon ground nutmeg**
- 3 **whole cloves, crushed**
- 10 **juniper berries, crushed**

1. To calculate the correct amount of kosher salt, weigh the trimmed belly and multiply by 3% (Example: 900 g × 0.03 = 27g salt). Weigh the salt and add to a small bowl. Calculate the amount of pink salt, if using, and add to the bowl. Mix in the pepper, rosemary, bay, nutmeg, cloves, and juniper. Wearing gloves, rub the cure all over the meat. Place in a zip-lock bag, or vacuum-seal it, and refrigerate for 7 days. Turn the bag over every day and massage the cure into the meat through the bag.

2. After 7 days, take the meat out of the bag and carefully knock all the cure and herbs and spices off the meat. Do not rinse, just brush off as much as possible. Pierce a corner of the belly with a knife to make a hole for hanging it. (A hole pierced all the way through the muscle gets sufficient airflow to be safe.) Thread a long piece of kitchen twine through the incision. Some people opt to wrap the pancetta in a double thickness of cheesecloth before curing it, but it is not necessary; wrapping does keep the meat consistently moist, but it is harder to review the progress of the curing, so I don't recommend it when you're new to curing.

OPPOSITE: Pancetta Tesa

Recipe continues

3. Hang the meat in your aging space for at least 3 days, and up to 3 weeks. Even after just 3 days, it will have developed a remarkable zestiness.

4. Store the pancetta well wrapped in butcher's paper or wax paper. My preference is to slice and vacuum-seal it in 4-ounce packages. Once the bag is opened, the pancetta will keep in the refrigerator for up to a month. Unopened and well wrapped, it will keep for a year in the freezer.

5. Slice the pancetta thinly or cut it as you need it. It must be thoroughly cooked before it is eaten.

Guanciale

MAKES: 1 jowl
ACTIVE TIME: 1 hour
CURING TIME: 7 days
AGING TIME: 7 days

Guanciale is cured pork jowl, fatty and meaty and much sweeter than the belly. Get to know the pig farmers at your farmer's market or ask your butcher, because this cut is difficult to source.

- 1 hog jowl
- • Kosher salt
- • Pink salt calculated at 0.0025 x the weight of the jowl
- ¼ cup (1 oz., 28 g) coarsely ground black pepper
- 1 teaspoon dried rosemary
- 3 dried bay leaves, crushed
- ½ teaspoon ground nutmeg
- 3 whole cloves, crushed
- 10 juniper berries, crushed

1. To trim the jowl, feel around it so you get to know the difference between the firm, "good" fat and meat and the glands, small pearls clustered here and there through the surface fat. The glands have a dreadful texture and an off-putting taste. Use a sharp, flexible blade to cut them away, as well as any jiggly fat. The good fat, which is firm and white, should be left on. A 3-pound jowl might weigh under 2 pounds trimmed. Trimming is critical to a pleasing end product, so take your time.

2. To calculate the amount of kosher salt, weigh the trimmed jowl and multiply by 3% (Example: 900 g x 0.03 = 27 g salt). Weigh the salt and add to a small bowl. Calculate the amount of pink salt and add. Mix in the pepper, rosemary, bay, nutmeg, cloves, and juniper. Wearing gloves, rub the cure all over the meat. Place in a zip-lock bag and refrigerate for 7 days. Turn the bag over every day and massage the cure into the meat through the bag.

3. After 7 days, take the meat out of the bag and brush off the cure, herbs, and spices. Do not rinse. Pierce a corner of the jowl with a knife to make a hole for hanging with kitchen twine. (A hole pierced all the way through the muscle gets sufficient airflow to be safe.) Hang the meat in your aging space for at least 7 days, and up to 3 weeks.

4. Store the guanciale well wrapped in butcher's or wax paper. I prefer to slice and vacuum-seal it in 4-ounce packages. Once opened, the guanciale will keep in the refrigerator for up to a month. Unopened and well wrapped, it will keep for a year in the freezer.

5. Slice the guanciale thinly or cut it as you need it. It must be thoroughly cooked before it is eaten.

Bresaola

MAKES: about 1½ pounds
ACTIVE TIME: 30 minutes
CURING TIME: 2 weeks
SALT EQUALIZATION TIME: 8 to 12 hours
AGING TIME: 3 weeks

Centuries ago, Italians, fond as they are of beef, identified the eye of round as a difficult cut to cook. So they cured it. Simple and straightforward, *bresaola* is rubbed with salt and spices, cured for 2 weeks, and hung for another 3 weeks. Patience is the most difficult ingredient to source.

Once the bresaola is ready, with a pretty white bloomy mold on the outside it's meltingly tender, herbal, and unique in the world of air-cured meats. Slice it paper-thin and serve with a generous drizzle of the very best olive oil, cracked black pepper, and shaved curls of Parmigiano-Reggiano cheese.

If your bresaola dries out during aging, vacuum-seal it and refrigerate for 1 week, then slice and serve. It will keep for months if stored in a vacuum-sealed package.

One **2-pound (900-g) eye-of-round roast, trimmed meticulously of any evident fat**
 • **Kosher or fine sea salt**
 2 **tablespoons coarsely ground black pepper**
 ¼ **cup (2 oz., 60 g) firmly packed light brown sugar**
 1 **teaspoon juniper berries, crushed**
 1 **teaspoon dried oregano**
 1 **teaspoon dried rosemary**
 1 **teaspoon fennel seeds, crushed**

1. Trim the ends of the eye of round to create an evenly shaped cylinder so the meat will cure evenly (reserve trimmings and grind into sublime hamburgers). Because it is a lean cut of beef, butchers often wrap the eye of round in thin pieces of fat. Remove that, and trim away any fat remaining on the outside of the roast. Do not dig into the meat or stab at it; deep cuts are places for bacteria to grow.

2. To calculate the correct amount of salt, weigh the trimmed meat and multiply by 3% (Example: 900 g × 0.03 = 27 grams of salt). Weigh the salt and place in a shallow dish. Add the pepper, brown sugar, juniper, oregano, rosemary, and fennel seeds. Put the meat in the dish and rub the spice mix into the meat, pressing firmly.

3. Put the meat and any extra seasoning into a gallon-sized zip-lock bag for 2 weeks in the refrigerator. Turn the meat over every day or so and continue to rub the spice mixture into the meat, through the bag.

4. Remove the meat from the bag and wipe away the cure. Dry very well, first knocking away any herbs that are adhering, then wiping it thoroughly with paper towels. Put the meat on a rack set over a baking sheet and refrigerate uncovered, for 8 to 12 hours. This allows the salt to equalize throughout the meat.

5. Truss the meat tightly (see photograph below). Weigh the meat and make a note of the starting weight. I use grams for precision. Make a note of the goal weight (start weight × 0.7 = end weight). Hang the meat vertically in your curing space and cure for 3 weeks, or until it reaches the end weight. If white mold appears, this is not a worry, but if you find it unsightly, or it gets too enthusiastic, wipe the outside of the bresaola with a cloth dampened with red wine or red wine vinegar.

6. To store, wrap the bresaola in parchment or cheese paper. Thinly slice to serve. The bresaola will last for a month or more in the refrigerator.

Trussing the bresaola

Bonus Recipe: Arugula and Bresaola Salad with Parmigiano-Reggiano and Hazelnuts

SERVES: 2

ACTIVE TIME: 15 minutes

My first trip to Italy was one eye-opening food experience after another. Some tastes stand out, even decades later, especially this bitter, crunchy, chewy, salty salad served at a tiny trattoria in Verona. At the time, I had never tasted any cured meat beyond salami and corned beef from the deli. The silky texture and juniper tones in the bresaola made me gasp. While it may seem astonishing, I had never tasted arugula before that moment, either. Now it grows in my garden and this salad makes lunchtime appearances all summer long.

- 1 teaspoon minced shallot
- Juice of 1 lemon
- 1 large bunch arugula, well washed and dried
- 2 ounces (56 g) Bresaola (page 350), sliced paper-thin
- A chunk of Parmigiano-Reggiano (don't fool around—go for the very best)
- 3 to 4 tablespoons fruity green olive oil
- ⅔ cup (3 oz., 86 g) toasted, skinned hazelnuts (see page 72), roughly chopped
- Kosher salt and freshly ground black pepper

1. In a small jar, combine the shallot and lemon. Set aside while you plate the salad; the shallot will pickle a little, taking the sharp edge away.

2. Divide the arugula between two salad plates. Arrange the slices of bresaola attractively atop the arugula. Using a vegetable peeler, shower a generous amount of Parmigiano over the lettuce and meats.

3. Add the olive oil to the shallot and lemon juice, shake to emulsify, and drizzle lightly over the salads. (You may have more than you need.) Sprinkle the hazelnuts here and there. Add salt and pepper to taste.

4. Serve with a crisp Italian white wine and a Fellini film.

OPPOSITE: Arugula and Bresaola Salad with Parmigiano-Reggiano and Hazelnuts

Spicy Scrapple with fried egg

Spicy Scrapple

MAKES: 1 loaf

ACTIVE TIME: 30 minutes

CHILLING TIME: 8 hours to overnight

The Pennsylvania Dutch serve this pork loaf for breakfast, using cornmeal as a filler. It can be wonderful, spicy, rich, and aromatic—crispy on the outside and creamy on the interior, all light as a feather. The secret to the very best scrapple is the pork liver, which may be difficult to locate.

Talk to your butcher, a farmer who raises pigs, or directly to an abattoir. The liver can be portioned and frozen if you have to buy the entire (huge) thing. Or you may be lucky enough to get a gift of a small amount, which is really all you need for some scrapple.

Serve scrapple sliced and crisped in a pan. Add a fried egg with a runny yolk and a buttermilk biscuit with butter and honey. You'll want to go raise a barn.

1   pound (500 g) pork shoulder, tenderloin, or belly (any uncured trim; this is a great way to use trim from the tenderloin or from making bacon)

8   ounces (250 g) pork liver (chicken livers can be substituted, but it's not the same)

1   tablespoon dried sage

1   teaspoon dried thyme

1   teaspoon herbes de Provence

1   teaspoon crushed red pepper, or to taste

1   tablespoon (0.3 oz., 10 g) kosher salt

1   teaspoon coarsely ground black pepper

2   cups (9 oz., 255 g) fine cornmeal

1. Line a 9-by-5 inch loaf pan with plastic wrap. (Moistening the inside of the terrine can make this task less frustrating.)

2. Chop the pork and liver into 1-inch dice and add to a 3-quart saucepan. Cover with 3 cups water and bring to a simmer over medium-high heat. Simmer for 10 minutes. Remove the meat, using a slotted spoon, and reserve the cooking liquid. Pulse the meats in a food processor until almost smooth; a few tiny pieces add a textural element in scrapple.

3. Bring the cooking liquid to a boil, add the pureed meats, and stir well. Add the sage, thyme, herbes de Provence, red pepper, salt, and pepper and stir well. Stirring constantly to prevent lumps, add the cornmeal to the boiling mixture in a slow stream. Reduce the heat and simmer slowly, stirring all the while, until the mixture pulls away from the sides of the pan, about 5 minutes. Remove from the heat.

4. Pack the mixture into the prepared loaf pan. Cover with parchment, put a piece of cardboard on top of mixture, and weight with cans or jars. Chill at least 8 hours, or overnight.

5. To unmold, invert the pan over a cutting board and lift it off. Peel off the plastic wrap. The loaf can be rewrapped and refrigerated for a week. Or slice ½ inch thick and freeze for up to a year.

6. To serve, lightly oil a skillet and fry slices of scrapple over medium-high heat until crispy and heated through.

Cheese-Making Equipment (see pages 361–64)

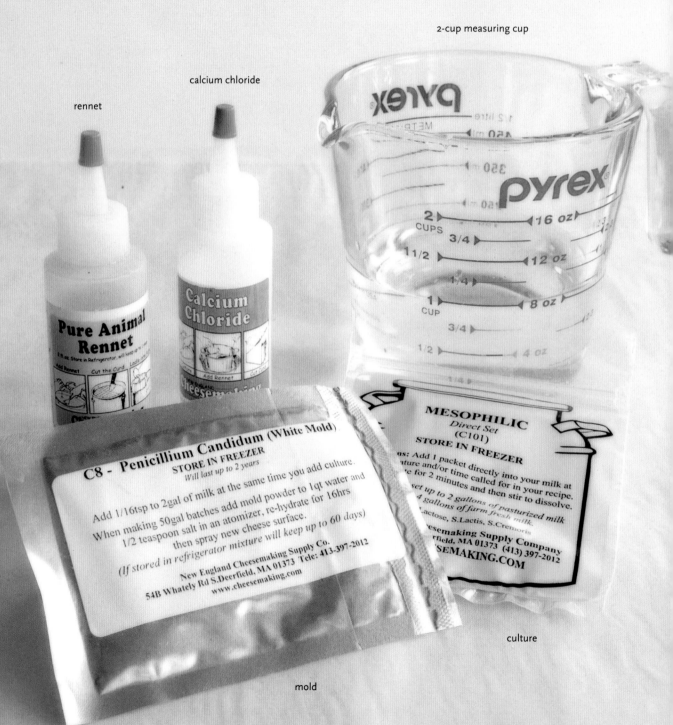

rennet

calcium chloride

2-cup measuring cup

Pure Animal Rennet

Calcium Chloride

C8 – Penicillium Candidum (White Mold)
STORE IN FREEZER
Will last up to 2 years

Add 1/16tsp to 2gal of milk at the same time you add culture.
When making 50gal batches add mold powder to 1qt water and
1/2 teaspoon salt in an atomizer, re-hydrate for 16hrs
then spray new cheese surface.
(If stored in refrigerator mixture will keep up to 60 days)
New England Cheesemaking Supply Co.
54B Whately Rd S.Deerfield, MA 01373 Tele: 413-397-2012
www.cheesemaking.com

MESOPHILIC
Direct Set
(C101)
STORE IN FREEZER
...s: Add 1 packet directly into your milk at
...ature and/or time called for in your recipe.
...te for 2 minutes and then stir to dissolve.
... set up to 2 gallons of pasturized milk
... gallons of farm fresh milk.
...Lactose, S.Lactis, S.Cremoris
...eesemaking Supply Company
...rfield, MA 01373 (413) 397-2012
...SEMAKING.COM

culture

mold

Chapter Four

CURDS AND WHEY: WHY BUY THE COW?

FRESH CHEESE MAKING

OPPOSITE: Whisking curds for Cottage Cheese (page 391)

When fresh cheese is part of your pantry (and when I say pantry here, I mean refrigerator), there is no end to inspiration for the nightly dinner quandary. A little crème fraîche turns a handful of mushrooms into a creamy mushroom ragout, to spoon over thick toast spread with fresh butter. Homemade ricotta turns pasta, home-canned tomatoes, and a few leaves of basil into a creamy, mouthwatering meal. Homemade cottage cheese for lunch, served with halved peaches from the pantry, is a far cry from diet food. And wait until you taste your home-smoked salmon draped across a bagel with a schmear of your own cream cheese.

Most of these foods are readily available in your grocery store, so why make cheese? With no stabilizers, with the very best milk, and with your loving attention, handcrafted fresh cheeses are remarkable, even spectacular, treats.

I first explored fresh cheese making when faced with an excess of heavy cream after a big dinner party. (Yes, I forgot to serve the whipped cream with dessert. It happens.) I hate waste, and I'm not a milk drinker as a rule. I do, however, adore anything and everything cheesy. That left-over cream was transformed into butter in a snap, and the taste was flavorful, rich, and sweet.

After adding just a cup of it to a Mornay sauce, I bemoaned the remains of a quart of milk. But once I learned to make ricotta from that left-over milk, those moans turned happy. Soon I was culturing and embracing homemade yogurt.

That was it. I was enthralled with the process of converting dairy to cheese. If you never move beyond those three projects, that's okay. Making your own yogurt, ricotta, and butter will change your relationship to leftover dairy forever.

But if you love to learn new skills and making everything yourself is part of your credo, you may find your way to homemade crème fraîche. Here the technique is less about using leftover milk and more about intentionally converting excellent dairy into a sensational dairy product. From there it is a slippery slope to Camembert, and after that, you'll be hooked. Homemade Camembert is too good; consider this fair warning.

Like most preserving projects, cheese making is an ancient culinary art. I imagine dairy farmers turning milk to cheese in the barn, with creamy milk fresh from the cow, goat, or sheep.

Cheese was made centuries before refrigeration or industrialization, and so cheese making requires few special tools or ingredients. It relies on nothing more than an excellent base ingredient: the very best, freshest milk available.

What follows is a small collection of approachable recipes. These are useful cheeses to have on hand and making them will allow you to explore the nuances of truly fresh cheese.

As in the previous chapters, the recipes are organized in order of increasing difficulty. Work your way through the recipes, from butter to Camembert, to gain skills, expertise, and knowledge, just as an apprentice *fromagier* might.

Equipment

I won't lie. Advanced cheese making requires special ingredients and tools, but plenty of fresh cheeses can be made without cultures and molds. Here are a few of the items I keep on hand so I can make cheese whenever I want.

Covered nonreactive deep saucepans or pots for culturing. Stainless steel and enameled cast-iron pans are nonreactive and hold the heat well. I use 1-, 3-, and 5-quart pots.

A **deep 10-quart or larger pot** for sanitizing the curd cutter, whisk, molds, cheesecloth, mats, and other tools.

A long **thermometer** that clips onto the side of the pot is essential for making cheese safely. Measure the temperature deliberately; remember, milk will heat at the bottom of the pot more quickly. Stirring and lifting the milk from the bottom of the pan up to the surface distributes the warmth and equalizes the temperature, and your readings will be more accurate.

A probe-style **instant-read thermometer** with a flat top is best for cheese making, where the temperatures most often range from 65° to 190°F. I credit Sally Canatsey for teaching me this brilliant trick: thread the thermometer through the "handle" of a medium binder clip clamped onto the side of the pot. Ta-da: a hands-free thermometer.

A **draining basket or colander** for separating curds and whey. I use a stainless steel colander for draining cheese, but a sturdy plastic colander or even a produce basket, like those used to pack berries, is reliable and completely safe.

Cheesecloth, butter muslin, or all-cotton tea towels. I have a ridiculous number of all-cotton kitchen towels, some that are old and thin and perfect for draining cheese. If your kitchen towels are thick and thirsty, they will not work. Instead, opt for cheesecloth or, even better, butter muslin,

a tightly woven type of cheesecloth that is washable and can be used over and over.

A long-handled nonreactive perforated **flat skimmer or slotted spoon** for stirring and ladling curds. The longer the handle, the easier it will be to reach the bottom of the culturing pot.

For the more complex preparations, curds are cut. A **long-handled stainless-steel whisk** will gently break the curds for cottage cheese, but for Camembert, the curds are cubed, and for that, use a **14-inch round-bottomed stainless steel palette knife**.

When you become obsessed with cheese making, you may want to invest in sturdy **cheese molds** to make perfect rounds of Camembert. In the meantime, any food-safe container will work, such as straight-sided 1-quart yogurt containers. Clean the container well inside and out. Using a sharp knife or scissors, cut off the bottom to form a cylinder. Using a clean skewer or rust-free sharp nail, and working from the inside out, poke 25 holes in the container, spacing them about 2 inches apart, from top to bottom and all around. You'll need two such molds for the Camembert recipe.

Draining mats are used for drying and aging cheeses, to keep the cheese elevated above the weeping whey. A classic sushi mat stands in here perfectly, and inexpensively. Plastic cheese draining mats, which resemble a needlepoint canvas, are slightly easier to keep clean.

Cheese paper, parchment that is waxed on one side, allows cheese, a living organism, to breathe in the refrigerator. Even if you don't make any of the more complex cheeses in this book, cheese paper is useful. If you love cheese, if you buy way too much every time you see a cheese display, if you are on a first-name basis with the raw milk cheese producer at the farmers' market, you need cheese paper. Your cheeses will keep for weeks and your refrigerator won't smell like Époisses.

butter muslin

skimmer

fine-mesh colander

long-handled whisk

cheese paper

palette knife

very small measuring spoons

bamboo draining mat

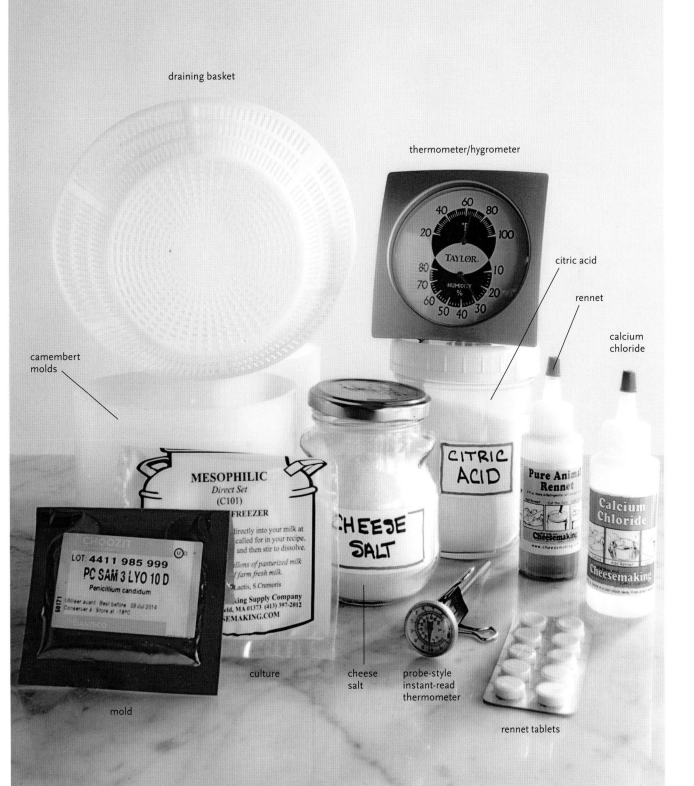

draining basket

thermometer/hygrometer

citric acid

rennet

calcium chloride

camembert molds

MESOPHILIC
Direct Set
(C101)

FREEZER

directly into your milk at
called for in your recipe.
and then stir to dissolve.

allons of pasturized milk
f farm fresh milk.

Lactis, S.Cremoris

king Supply Company
eld, MA 01373 (413) 397-2012
SEMAKING.COM

CHOOZIT

LOT: 4411 985 999
PC SAM 3 LYO 10 D
Penicillium candidum

Utiliser avant Best before 03 Jul 2014
Conserver à Store at -18ºC

CHEESE SALT

CITRIC ACID

Pure Animal Rennet

Cheesemaking

www.cheesemaking.

Calcium Chloride

Cheesemaking

culture

cheese salt

probe-style instant-read thermometer

mold

rennet tablets

Cheese salt is quick to dissolve. Kosher and fine sea salt are adequate substitutions.

Cultures like buttermilk and lemon juice are very effective agents, but **powdered cultures** like *mesophilic* (cultures at body temperature), *thermophilic* (cultures with heat), and even *penicillium candidum* (for snowy-white-molded rinds) are more precise and more reliable. This makes a difference with the more complex processes for making cream cheese, cottage cheese, and Camembert. Dry cultures are sold in small packets that tuck into a corner of the freezer and stay fresh for a year; see Resources, page 401.

In some cheeses, **rennet** is used to firm the curd. Rennet is derived from bovine (calf) stomach enzymes. Vegetarians can opt for a vegetable-based alternative, most frequently derived from artichokes and other thistles. Rennet coagulates milk and forms a firm curd. While milk would coagulate naturally if left out to lacto-ferment, it would also develop a sour flavor, as in sour cream. Rennet gives you the ability to calculate coagulation, control it, and maintain the fresh, grassy taste of good milk. Rennet is available as tablets or liquid, each equally easy to use and interchangeable in any recipe. Both forms of rennet must be kept refrigerated, or they will lose their effectiveness rapidly. (See Resources, page 401.)

When raw milk is not available, home cheese makers rely on **calcium chloride** to boost coagulation. Diluted and added before the rennet, it acts as a coagulation insurance policy with no negative effects.

Know your dairy cows

Great homemade cheese depends on excellent, fresh dairy. Finding the best source for your dairy products can be the most challenging aspect of cheese making. The grocery store milk generally sold in plastic jugs or waxed cartons is both pasteurized and homogenized and will not work for home cheese making.

Because of their source (animals and barns), dairy products carry a lot of bacteria. Not that there's anything wrong with bacteria. "Good" bacteria is essential not only for cheese making, but also for making bread, wine, beer, and pickles. We embrace many bacteria, but not all bacteria are good.

Pasteurization helps. Milk is heated to 145°F and held there for 30 minutes, so the milk retains the healthy microbes and flora and tasting notes. Pasteurized milk keeps longer and is safer for consumption. Thank you, Dr. Louis Pasteur.

Homogenizing is another thing altogether. Homogenizing is the industrialized world's answer to commodity dairy products. There was a time when milk from one dairy came from one herd of cattle, but then industrialization meant several dairies' milks were often combined, and wider strains of bacteria were present. They were also less traceable. Homogenized milk is forced through a very fine strainer that breaks down the individual cells and fats, to blend all the milks. Cheese making is frustrated by homogenized dairy products. Homogenizing removes beneficial enzymes, counteracts culturing, reduces yield, flattens the flavor, and produces very unsatisfactory cheese. Without all those good bacteria and enzymes contributing to culturing, there can be no cheese.

Heavy cream is rarely available raw. If you can locate nonhomogenized, pasteurized cream, your cheeses will have a more complex flavor. But don't worry, it is possible to make delicious cheese from many of these recipes with grocery store cream.

In some parts of the country, raw milk is sold without regulation. When I can purchase raw milk, I do. I buy from the most reputable farmers, the ones with clean, well-kept barns and happy animals. If you have access to raw milk, your cheese will be just that much more complex and nuanced.

Lack of access to raw milk does not mean homemade cheese is out of reach. I've written these recipes assuming the use of nonhomogenized pasteurized milk, often sold in glass bottles in upscale grocery stores and at many farmers' markets. Some local dairies are now producing nonhomogenized pasteurized milks, even bringing back the milkman and home delivery. Elsewhere, dairy farms sell products at their own, onsite, farm stores.

If cheese is your preserving interest, you will find the milk. And when you do, you will be happy. Nonhomogenized pasteurized milk is a far cry from the ultrapasteurized dairy products of the last few decades. You will taste the difference. There will be essences of the pasture—sweet with the scent of clover in springtime, like hay with a little funk in high summer, grassier and tangier in fall.

When you purchase raw or glass-bottle milk, open it up and take a long slow sniff. Smell the grassiness, the sweetness, the *terroir* of the milk. Taste it. Do this every week for a while, and you will train your palate. This simple act will make you a better cheese maker; you will experience how the flavor of the milk changes and how all that character is amplified in the cheese.

Three keys to successful cheese making

Cheese making is a culinary art, like charcuterie, jam making, and pickling. It's a technique, a skill, and a creative expression. Your talents will grow over time, as will your understanding of dairy. Be patient and practice for predictably stellar results.

As with any project, being organized helps. Read the recipe several times before starting. Most cheese making takes less than an hour of active time but timing errors, too-high temperatures, or adding the salt too early, for example, will interfere dramatically with culturing and yield.

SANITIZING

Before making cheese, clean everything you will be using meticulously. Surfaces and equipment should be sanitized, or as close to sterile as you can get in a home kitchen. Have a pile of clean tea towels available.

To sanitize your equipment, put the curd cutter, colander or sieve, skimmer, muslin or cheesecloth, and measuring cups and spoons—all the tools needed—in a very large pot. Cover with water and bring to a boil. Let boil hard for 10 minutes, then remove the equipment and let it air-dry on clean tea towels. Wash and return utensils to boiling water to sanitize between uses.

PASTEURIZING

Raw milk carries all the *terroir* of the farm. To make raw milk safe for cheese making, particularly when aging cheeses, you should pasteurize the milk.

Pour the milk into a nonreactive pot (the heavier the better, as it will hold the heat). Bring the milk to 145°F and hold it there for 30 minutes. If your kitchen tends to be cold, once the milk is at temperature, cover and wrap the pot in a thick towel to insulate it and keep the temperature steady. Be careful to keep the towel away from the heat source, of course.

After pasteurization, the milk is ready to be made into cheese, but it will need to cool down. In a large heavy pot, this could take an hour or two. To speed the process, put the pot in a sink holding two or three inches of ice water.

"Flash-pasteurizing" is faster but harder to control. Bring the milk to 163°F for just 30 seconds, then plunge the pot into an ice bath in the sink to reduce the temperature quickly. If it overheats, cheese making may be compromised, so don't walk away.

CULTURING

Culturing milk is the first step in making cheese. Culturing, or fermenting, uses, among other things, lactic-acid bacteria, found in the air around us. Culturing increases shelf life—cheese lasts much longer than fresh milk—and also changes the flavor. Some fresh cheeses, like crème fraîche, culture naturally via microbes and bacterias in the air; others, like Camembert, require the addition of powdered culturing agents.

Culturing agents—such as buttermilk, lemon juice, yogurt, and powdered mesophilic and penicillium cultures—transform dairy products into different cheeses. They are added to the milk at specific temperatures and allowed to set up for a specified period of time. During these rest periods, the culturing agents react with the milk and start the act of controlled aging, blooming in the same way yeast blooms in bread making. Use a perforated skimmer or slotted spoon to distribute the agent, lifting the milk from the bottom of the pot to the top. Avoid breaking the surface. The act of incorporation isn't about whipping or stirring hard; rather, it's gently moving the cultures through the milk.

The next essential ingredient in culturing is warmth. All cheese making begins by bringing milk to room temperature. In many ways, this is your first leap of faith. The milk will not spoil as it sits out; it will simply change. And hidden in that change is cheese.

Going against everything you have been taught, you leave the milk out, rather than in the refrigerator. On purpose. You must find the spot that is not too hot and not too cold, but just right. Somewhere in the 70° to 75°F range is perfect. If it's a little cooler, culturing takes longer and the end product may be tangier; even just a little warmer, and culturing happens quickly and unpredictably and has a high risk of spoilage.

There are several ways to keep your pot of culturing milk at the right temperature (depending on the technique), but the easiest is just to wrap the warm pot in a thick towel as soon as it comes off the stove. Cover the pot and lid with the towel, then place the whole thing on a wooden board or a stack of towels or anything that isn't the stone-cold surface of a countertop.

If that won't keep the milk warm, place the covered pot in a few inches of warm water in the sink—not too warm, or the milk will heat. This may seem like fussy work, but remember that cheese was made in the open air, without refrigeration and without thermometers, for centuries. Relax. You can do it.

Salting the cheese

Salt is important in cheese making. *Really important.* Salt stabilizes the culturing process, slowing it, and prevents spoilage. You can use fine sea salt, kosher salt, or cheese salt. Use it sparingly, but use it. Do not use large-crystal salt, because it won't dissolve entirely, and crystallized bits aren't appreciated in cheese.

Salt is always added by weight. Weigh the finished cheese and then calculate 1 percent of the weight in salt. For accuracy, use a gram scale for this calculation. For example, if the cheese weighs 650 grams, multiply that by 0.01 to get 6.5 grams salt and add that amount.

Do NOT add salt with the culture; add it after the culturing, just before forming, firming, or finishing the cheese. The salt dissolves and will be distributed through the cheese as it rests.

If you forget to add salt, you will know right away. Sometimes green moldy spots can appear as quickly as a day. Just cut out the green spots, add the salt, if possible, and continue to enjoy your cheese. If black mold grows, discard the cheese and try again.

TROUBLESHOOTING CURDLES, BAD MOLD, FUNK, AND WRINKLED SKIN

Cheese making is straightforward, but there are some stumbles I never expected when I started. I want to help you avoid these mistakes.

Never make a **yeast bread** the same day you are making cheese. The yeast and cheese cultures don't like to intermingle, so your cheese will fail and your bread will be leaden.

It's not just the milk that's important, it's also the water. The **chlorine** in your water can interfere with the culturing. Minerals insinuate themselves into the flavor. Boil tap water for 10 minutes or leave it out for 12 or more hours in an open container so the chlorine gases fade, or purchase filtered water.

If you are having trouble with **curd set**, try adding calcium chloride, available as a powder or liquid, using an amount equal to the rennet called for and add it to cool water to dilute.

Always use a **clean spoon** to serve yogurt. This keeps the culture clean for the next yogurt-making session.

Always loosen or remove **the lid** of a bottle of raw milk that is sitting out on the counter. The active bacteria can blow the lid off the bottle or, even worse, break the bottle, allowing all that lovely milk to run down the cabinet fronts, into the drawers, or, well, you get the idea.

If a cheese grows some green **mold**, you can cut it away and still enjoy the cheese. If the mold is black or any other weird color, don't eat it. Either the humidity or temperature in your cheese cabinet was off, the milk was bad, or something worse. Throw the cheese out and try again.

Sometimes cheese **smells funky**. I like this scent and associate it with interesting cheese flavors, but not everyone feels this way. Raw milk carries more funk, and milk from deep summer will be the funkiest. If you like a milder flavor, make cheese in the spring and fall.

If the milk gets too hot when you are heating it, a **skin** will form, like the skin on pudding. When milk (water + casein + whey + fat) is heated, the water evaporates, the proteins concentrate, and presto! skin forms. Don't worry. Just continue with the recipe and incorporate that skin right into the cheese.

If you **overheat** the milk too much, though— for example, to 200°F or higher—I'm sorry to say, the milk will not be reliable for cheese making.

WHAT TO DO WITH WHEY

Whey is the by-product of making cheese. When cultures are added to milk, curds form, and the watery remainder is whey, a combination of waters, lactose, protein, minerals, and trace amounts of milk fat. When you start to have fun with cheese making, you'll end up with a lot of whey. A lot. But whey has many uses. I have tried some, but not all, of them over the years.

- **Know any bodybuilders?** They love whey. It's essential to building muscles, and many bodybuilders depend on protein drinks made with whey powders. Here's the real deal.

- **Drink it.** Whey is full of protein and pumps up your morning smoothie. The flavor is mild but sour, with some redolent tones from the milk. Make sure it is icy cold. Some people make iced tea with whey. I haven't done that.

- **Cook with it.** Use whey in place of stock in soups or sauces. Cook pasta, rice, or noodles in whey. It adds tang, creaminess, and body.

- **Bake with it.** Substitute whey for water or other liquids in bread baking. Its sour tang transfers to the flavor of any bread or roll.

- **Ferment with it.** Accelerate the speed of lacto-fermentation (think pickles, kimchi, and sauerkraut) with some whey.

- **Whey has so much natural fizziness** that if you bottle it and keep it at room temperature, it makes a sparkling soda-like drink that's good on its own, or with fruit juice. Try making lemonade with whey.

- **Whey will make your dog's coat shiny**. Dogs and cats like a little whey. If you keep chickens, give them a bit of whey when they moult. Pigs love whey.

- **Use whey as a post-shampoo rinse**. It makes hair shiny and lustrous.

- **Feed azaleas, rhododendrons, hydrangeas, camellias:** Pour cooled whey around the root zone of these acid-loving shrubs.

- **Spray roses or other plants** affected by powdery mildew with a 1:4 mixture of whey and water. It's a miracle worker.

- **Feed tomato plants and blueberry bushes** with whey to increase yield.

- **Country people will tell you** that whey helps with sunburn, eczema, and other skin problems. A whey bath is recommended for poison ivy or skunk spray.

Cultured Butter

MAKES: 4 ounces (the equivalent of 1 stick of butter) and about 1 cup of full-fat buttermilk
ACTIVE TIME: 20 minutes
CULTURING TIME: up to 2 hours

Butter made by hand (or mixer) is spectacularly different from any other butter. I'm not saying that you'll never again buy grocery store butter, or that it rivals European butters, but homemade butter is lovely and fresh and exhilarating to make and serve.

Culturing cream for butter is gentle and only requires an hour or two on the counter. If you want a very tangy butter, though, leave the cream out for as long as 48 hours, as when making crème fraîche (page 385), then proceed with the recipe.

If your kitchen is warm, it may be challenging to work with butter. If you have a stone or marble countertop, a surefire way to keep the butter cold while you knead it is to chill the counter first: just place a bag of ice on the stone or marble surface for 10 minutes.

1 **pint (16 oz., 475 ml) heavy cream (nonhomogenized pasteurized cream is best)**
¼ **teaspoon kosher or sea salt (optional)**

1. Leave cream out on the counter, uncovered, for an hour or two to culture.

2. Whip the cream using the whisk attachment, in the bowl of a stand mixer, or use a hand mixer and a large bowl. The cream will go through several stages, foamy, then frothy, then soft peaks, stiff peaks, and, eventually, butter. Start at medium speed, then increase quickly to the top speed. It will take anywhere from 6 to 15 minutes until the butter separates from the buttermilk and starts to spatter. Early spring cream makes butter in a snap, later-season cream takes longer. If you have children who might benefit from some distraction, they can shake the cream in a wide-mouth quart jar with a tight-fitting lid until the butter separates from the buttermilk, 15 to 25 minutes.

3. Pour the buttermilk into a container. This makes exquisite biscuits, and it can be used in place of dry mesophilic cultures to make many fresh cheeses. The buttermilk will keep for 2 weeks in the refrigerator, but its culturing strength fades quickly. If you will not use it immediately, freeze it in ice cube trays (most ice cube trays freeze 2 tablespoons, or 1 ounce, of liquid per mold).

Recipe continues

4. Gather up the butter with impeccably clean hands. Working over a colander in the sink, make a ball of the butter and wash it under cold running water. (Is the butter too soft? Float it in a bowl of ice water for 20 minutes, then continue.) Squeeze and form the ball of butter again and again to remove all the buttermilk. (If there is buttermilk remaining in the butter, it will turn rancid in a day or two.)

5. Once the water runs clear from the butter in your hands, knead it firmly to remove all the moisture. You can use butter paddles to press and form the mass into a block or a disk, but two bench scrapers work just as well. Lift, fold, and press it into shape again and again. If the butter (or kitchen) is warm, use a flexible spatula to spread the butter against the side of a bowl to press out the water.

6. If you want to salt the butter (this increases shelf life), or add any optional flavorings (see box), now is the time. Knead the salt and/or flavorings into the butter, then wrap in wax or cheese paper or pack into ramekins. Unsalted fresh butter will keep for 4 days in the refrigerator and up to 3 months in the freezer. Salted butter keeps for 2 or more weeks in the refrigerator and up to 3 months in the freezer.

COMPOUND BUTTERS

Top a grilled steak with a bit of compound butter; place a pat on a pile of steamed asparagus; tuck a knob into the hollow of a halved acorn squash; finish a pan sauce (see page 123).

To make compound butter, while the butter is soft, knead in:

1 tablespoon minced fresh herbs, such as chives, parsley, thyme, chervil, or rosemary

1 teaspoon minced garlic, scallions, or pickled shallots

2 tablespoons toasted sesame seeds

1 tablespoon grated lemon zest and ½ teaspoon crushed black pepper

¼ cup blue cheese and ¼ cup chopped toasted walnuts

OPPOSITE: Separating butter from buttermilk

ABOVE: Pressing out the water

Whole-Milk Ricotta

MAKES: 1 cup
ACTIVE TIME: 30 minutes
DRAINING TIME: 15 minutes

Many countries have a version of a soft spoonable cheese, whether it's *fromage blanc,* *queso blanco, paneer,* farmer's cheese, or ricotta. Whole milk makes a creamy ricotta that fills pasta or substitutes for milk or cream in scones, cakes, and muffins. And a small bowl of ricotta with fruit preserves is a first-rate breakfast.

Traditionally ricotta is made from the whey left after making mozzarella and many other cheeses but this is made from whole milk—more fats, more flavor, more texture. It's spoonable and creamy, and it melts magnificently.

⅓ cup (scant 3 oz., 90 ml) fresh lemon juice or white vinegar or 1 teaspoon citric acid

3 quarts (96 oz., 2.8 l) raw or nonhomogenized pasteurized whole milk

1. Line a colander with a dampened clean, threadbare tea towel, butter muslin, or a triple thickness of cheesecloth and set it over a bowl if you wish to save the whey.

2. In a 3-quart stainless steel pot, heat the milk and lemon juice (or vinegar or citric acid) over medium heat until small bubbles appear around the edges of the pan, just under a boil; the milk will measure 190°F. Watch for the moment the curds separate from the whey and the whey becomes more clear than opaque, about 10 minutes. Remove the pot from the stove, cover, and set aside for 10 minutes. The separation of the curds and whey will be even more evident.

3. Lift the curds from the pot using a slotted spoon or skimmer and snuggle into the tea-towel-lined colander. Drain for 15 minutes for a soft, spoonable cheese, or for up to an hour for a drier version, better suited to stuffing pasta.

4. Invert the cheese onto a plate or into a bowl, cover, and refrigerate. Ricotta will keep for about 3 days, but it is best when freshly made.

OPPOSITE: Nestle egg yolks into ricotta for Ricotta-and-Egg Pasta Pillows (page 374)

Bonus Recipe: Ricotta-and-Egg Pasta Pillows

SERVES: 4 as an appetizer
ACTIVE TIME: 1 hour

There are times when I like to get downright fancy. These plump ricotta pillows are a show stopping appetizer for a dinner party. In fact, they are also a favorite pantry-friendly dinner.

When I want to ramp up the clever, I'll make small pillows and use quail eggs. When I want to boost the rich flavor, I make them even larger and use duck eggs. It takes some patience and skill, but it's nothing you can't manage.

1 cup (4 oz., 110 g) sliced almonds

1 pound (450 g) fresh pasta sheets

• Fine cornmeal for dusting

• Whole-Milk Ricotta (page 372)

½ cup (2.5 oz., 70 g) freshly grated Parmigiano-Reggiano cheese

⅛ teaspoon freshly grated nutmeg

8 large extremely fresh egg yolks

• Kosher salt and freshly ground black pepper

8 tablespoons (4 oz., 110 g) unsalted butter

3 tablespoons chopped fresh flat-leaf parsley

3 tablespoons chopped fresh chives

1. Toast the almonds in a dry wide skillet until fragrant, about 5 minutes. Spread the nuts out on a baking sheet to cool.

2. With a sharp knife, cut sixteen 4-inch squares from the pasta sheets. Line up 8 squares on a baking sheet dusted with cornmeal. Cover with a slightly damp towel and set aside.

3. In a medium mixing bowl, stir together the ricotta, Parmigiano, nutmeg, a big pinch of salt, and a few grinds of black pepper.

4. Lay out the remaining 8 pasta squares on a work surface. Drop 2 tablespoons of the ricotta mixture into the center of each square. Form a well in the cheese on each square and slip an egg yolk into each well. Moisten the edges of each square of pasta, then top with one of the remaining squares of pasta and press the edges together to seal.

5. Fill the largest straight-sided sauté pan in your arsenal with enough water to cover your pasta packets. Salt the water well and bring to a brisk boil. Reduce the heat to a strong simmer and, using a wide spatula, gently lift up the large lovely pasta squares and settle into the simmering water. Cook until floating, about 5 minutes.

6. Meanwhile, as the pasta cooks, brown the butter in a sauté pan, cooking it until the milk solids turn toasty and drop to the bottom of the pan.

7. Gently lift each pasta packet and place two on each warm plate. Drizzle the butter over the pasta, sprinkle with the parsley, chives, and almonds, and serve.

OPPOSITE: Ricotta-and-Egg Pasta Pillows

Whole-Milk Yogurt

MAKES: 1 quart
ACTIVE TIME: 45 minutes
CULTURING TIME: 4 to 8 hours

It's so satisfying to make yogurt at home that it's been years since I purchased any. If I want Greek-style yogurt, I drain it for a couple of hours in a fine-mesh strainer lined with cheesecloth. This thick yogurt is creamy and tangy and appropriate for tikka masala, raita, and so many dishes well beyond breakfast. If I want a fruit-filled yogurt, I add jam, fruit sauce, or fresh or canned fruits.

In the mood for *labneh*, the Middle Eastern yogurt cheese? Just let it drain a little longer; overnight is perfect. It's traditional to serve *labneh* drizzled with fruity olive oil and sprinkled with salt and pepper and *za'atar*, a Middle Eastern mixture of dried herbs, sumac, and sesame seeds. Dig into this bowl of goodness with warm pita.

Use yogurt instead of milk in quick breads and muffins. Add to waffles. Brine chicken in yogurt, then wipe away and grill. Add flour to make a loose batter for onion rings. Spoon into smoothies. Add herbs and a little vinegar for a ranch-style dressing.

Yogurt, like most cheeses, requires a culturing agent—a starter—and the best is exceptional yogurt. Once you've started making yogurt at home, you will have the ½ cup needed to culture more. Your fresh yogurt becomes the next culture and so on. But yogurt has to start somewhere. Purchase a small container of the very best plain yogurt you can get. Check the ingredient list—it should have only milk and active cultures. Anything else is unnecessary and can affect your culturing.

½ cup (4 oz., 110 g) plain full-fat yogurt

1 quart (32 oz., 1 l) raw or nonhomogenized pasteurized whole or 2 percent milk

1. Spoon the yogurt into a sanitized glass jar or divide it between 2 pint jars or four 1-cup jars.

2. Clip an instant-read thermometer to the side of a medium saucepan, add the milk, and heat until small bubbles appear around the edges of the pan; the milk will be about 185° to 190°F. Turn off the heat, leave the thermometer in the pan, and let cool until the temperature has reached 110°F, about 30 minutes.

3. Pour the milk into the jar(s). With a clean stainless steel spoon, give the milk three lazy stirs. Cap the jars and place in a warm culturing spot (see box). My culturing spot is right next to the stovetop, near a wall, where the temperature is reliably 75°F or higher. I place the jar on a wooden board, to keep the chill of the counter away.

4. Check the yogurt after 4 hours. If it has set to your preference, put it in the refrigerator. If you would like it to be firmer, leave it to culture for as long as 8 hours. Keep in mind that the yogurt will thicken further when chilled. Chill completely before draining for Greek yogurt or *labneh*.

FINDING THE PERFECT CULTURING SPOT

I've been known to put yogurt jars near the furnace, where it's toasty warm in February. You'll find the sweet spot in your kitchen if you purchase and then poke around with a thermometer. Test the back of the top shelf of a closet, the laundry room, or maybe near your old computer monitor that runs hot. Keep the jars away from drafts; proximity to cold takes the heat right out of the jars and halts culturing. Set the warm filled jars on a wooden board or a stack of newspapers, or anything that will not draw cold from stone counters (a single folded towel is not enough shelter from the cold). Often the inside of a (turned-off) oven is perfect for this project, especially if there is a pilot light. Even the oven lightbulb is warm. In cool weather, wrap a towel around the jars to keep them warm. If your kitchen is in Maine or Montana, was built in the eighteenth century, and just never warms up, you might want to set the jars on a heating pad set on Low. Aim for 78°F ambient room temperature or warmer.

A slow cooker is another option for yogurt culturing. Place a folded kitchen towel in the bottom of the cooker and set the jar(s) on the towel. Set the cooker to run at the lowest possible temperature for 6 hours.

Mascarpone

MAKES: 1 cup

ACTIVE TIME: 20 minutes

DRAINING TIME: 8 hours to overnight

How many recipes have you made requiring three tablespoons of cream? Or half a cup? Then the remaining bit of cream either goes sour in the refrigerator or is added recklessly to coffee. Instead, when that cream languishes but before it goes off, add a bit of lemon juice and make mascarpone, the smooth, creamy Italian fresh cheese. Slather it on a peach half, sprinkle with light brown sugar, and broil until bubbly. Stuff dates with it, roast for 5 minutes in a 425°F oven, and sprinkle with crunchy salt and olive oil. Fill a meringue with key lime curd and mascarpone folded into whipped cream. There are many uses for this Italian treat.

2 cups (16 oz., 475 ml) heavy cream (nonhomogenized pasteurized cream is best)

1 tablespoon fresh lemon juice

• Fine sea salt

1. In a small saucepan, heat the cream to boiling. Reduce the heat, add the lemon juice and salt, and simmer the cream for 5 minutes; it should be at a temperature of 185°F. Remove from the heat, cover, and set aside for 30 minutes.

2. Set a fine-mesh sieve lined with a double thickness of damp cheesecloth over a bowl. Without stirring, gently tip the cream into the lined sieve, letting the whey run into the bowl below. Sprinkle a small pinch of salt over the cream. Cover and refrigerate the bowl and sieve for at least 8 hours, or overnight.

3. Remove the mascarpone from the sieve by lifting the cheesecloth by the corners and twisting it into a packet; discard the whey. Mascarpone will keep, wrapped in the cheesecloth in a covered glass or ceramic bowl for up to 2 weeks. Wipe away any collected whey in the bottom of the dish daily to keep the cheese fresh.

OPPOSITE: Mascarpone draining

Cajeta

MAKES: 3 cups

ACTIVE TIME: 2 hours

SIMMERING TIME: 4 hours, with occasional stirring

I am crazy for caramel: I love it in every form. A favorite caramel has always been *dulce de leche*, the sweet Mexican caramel tinged with cinnamon and vanilla. *Cajeta* is *dulce de leche* made with goat's milk, so it has a goaty tang that balances the sweet exquisitely. It's sensational, buttery and complex, and it holds in the refrigerator for months.

Make this recipe in a much larger, wider pot than you think you will need. More surface area will help reduce the *cajeta* quickly without scorching, and a large pot keeps it from boiling over, which happens fast and is, without a doubt, the worst mess in the world of kitchen messes.

2 **quarts (64 oz., 1.9 l) goat's milk (even ultrapasteurized homogenized will work for this recipe)**

2 **cups (14 oz., 400 g) granulated sugar**

Two **3-inch cinnamon sticks**

1 **vanilla bean, split**

½ **teaspoon salt**

½ **teaspoon baking soda, dissolved in 1 tablespoon cool water**

1. In a 5-quart or larger heavy stainless-steel or enameled cast-iron pot (such as Le Creuset), warm the milk and sugar over low heat, stirring until the sugar is dissolved. Add the cinnamon, vanilla bean, and salt and slowly increase the heat to bring the milk to a boil; this should take about 45 minutes.

2. Stir in the baking soda mixture. Be careful—be prepared to remove the pot from the heat when it starts to bubble up. And it will. Do not turn your back for even an instant. Once the *cajeta* settles back down to a simmer, reduce the heat to the lowest possible setting and cook the caramel, uncovered, for about 4 hours. You do not need to babysit the *cajeta* until the last 60 minutes or so; just stir it from time to time. Don't worry about the foam; it will all be resolved as the mixture thickens.

3. During the last hour, be very attentive: Stir often and thoroughly. Avoid sticking and burning at all costs. If you sense it is burning, transfer the *cajeta* to a clean pot without scraping the bottom, and continue cooking (the burnt taste can permeate the *cajeta*).

4. When the *cajeta* is deeply colored and as thick as maple syrup, remove the cinnamon sticks and vanilla bean. Funnel into a sanitized jar or two, cover, and refrigerate for up to 3 months. The caramel will thicken more as it cools. To clean the pot, fill with water and bring to a boil. The caramel will melt away with no scrubbing.

5. When ready to serve, warm the jar of *cajeta* in a saucepan of simmering water, not the microwave.

WHAT TO DO WITH CAJETA

- **Pour** the warm *cajeta* over ice cream or pound cake.

- **Fill** sandwich cookies.

- **Dip** apples, pears, bananas, or pineapple wedges into the warm caramel.

- **Sneak** a spoonful. No one's watching.

Bonus Recipe: Tropical Tart

MAKES: one 9-inch tart

Imagine a banana split married Bananas Foster. And ready in an hour. I go back and forth on whether this needs salted peanuts or toasted coconut on top. It's all good.

4 tablespoons (2 oz., 57 g) unsalted butter, melted

3 tablespoons granulated sugar

1 large egg yolk

1 cup (4.25 oz., 125 g) all-purpose flour

¼ cup (1 oz., 28 g) almond meal (see Note)

½ teaspoon ground cinnamon

½ cup *Cajeta* (page 380) plus extra for garnish

1 half-pint jar Drunken Pineapple Sauce (page 108)

½ cup (4.5 oz., 125 g) Whole-Milk Ricotta (page 372), or substitute Mascarpone (page 379) or Crème Fraîche (page 385)

2 bananas, sliced into ¼-inch coins

1. Preheat the oven to 350°F.

2. In a medium bowl, combine the melted butter, sugar, and egg yolk with a fork. Add the flour, almond meal, and cinnamon and mix with the fork until combined.

3. Using your fingertips or a flat-bottomed drinking glass or measuring cup, press the dough over the bottom of a 9-inch tart pan and push it partway up the sides. If you don't have a tart pan, press or roll out the dough to a rustic circle about 10-inches across, ½-inch thick. Transfer to a baking sheet lined with parchment. Bake the tart crust until golden brown, 18 to 20 minutes.

4. Remove the baking sheet from the oven, place on a cooling rack, and spread the *cajeta* over the crust while it is still warm.

5. When the crust is cool, carefully lift it and place it on a serving dish or cake stand. Using an offset spatula, spread the pineapple sauce over the *cajeta*. Whisk the ricotta to lighten it, then spread it over the pineapple sauce. Make a pretty spiral with the banana coins atop the ricotta. Decorate the banana slices with more *cajeta*. Brush it on, spoon it on, or dip a fork in the caramel and hold it high above the tart to form a squiggle. You should chill the tart for 1 hour, but I rarely manage to wait that long.

Note: Almond meal is available in the baking aisle of many grocery stores. Or make your own by blitzing blanched almonds in a food processor or Vitamix until finely ground.

OPPOSITE: Tropical Tart

Sour Cream

MAKES: 1 pint

ACTIVE TIME: 5 minutes

CULTURING TIME: 24 to 36 hours

Sour cream is a delightful, gentle float in a bowl of soup; a tangy, creamy addition to peaches or bananas; or the cooling agent served with incendiary chili. Homemade sour cream has a different texture. It's creamier. There are no stabilizers to coat your mouth, no added preservatives. It's the taste of pure cream and tang.

Feeling blue? Try lathering a sour cream layer on butterscotch pudding. Sprinkle with turbinado sugar and broil. Lift your spirits with every spoonful.

2 cups (16 oz., 475 ml) heavy cream (nonhomogenized pasteurized cream is best)

¼ teaspoon mesophilic culture (see Resources, page 401) or 2 tablespoons freshly cultured buttermilk (see page 369), at room temperature

1. Gently heat the cream to 70°F. (As this is close to room temperature, you may be able to leave the cream out for a bit and it will reach 70°F without heating it on the stove at all.) Pour the cream into a sanitized pint jar or a glass bowl, sprinkle the culture over the cream, and let it sit for 5 minutes to bloom. (If using buttermilk, just add it to the cream. Be aware that buttermilk may require a longer culturing time.)

2. Stir the cream very gently with a clean stainless steel spoon. Cover the jar with a square of cheesecloth and secure it with a rubber band. Place the jar in a warm culturing spot where the temperature is reliably 75°F or higher and culture for 24 hours.

3. Check the set. If the sour cream is not firm enough, check again in 4 or 5 hours; it may need to be cultured for as long as 36 hours. (Much longer, and it's crème fraîche. Too long, and it spoils.) It should be thick and creamy, smell faintly sour, and taste tangy.

4. Cover and refrigerate. The sour cream will firm up further as it chills. It will keep for 10 days to 2 weeks in the refrigerator. Pour off the accumulating whey (the liquid that floats to the top) to extend its freshness.

Crème Fraîche

MAKES: 1 pint
ACTIVE TIME: 5 minutes
INACTIVE TIME: 36 to 42 hours

Crème fraîche is sour cream Frenchified. It's made in the same way but cultured a little longer, so it's tangier and stiffer and more subtle. I love crème fraîche. And making it at home is much more cost effective than buying the precious containers in the grocery store. I'll add a whisper to soup for a touch of smooth and tart in the finish or blend it with yogurt or mayonnaise to make a base for a dip or spread. Whip it into an ice cream base. Cold-smoke it (see page 309). A dollop served over roasted beets is as delightful as one alongside roasted figs. It's a shape-shifter.

2 cups (16 oz., 475 ml) heavy cream (nonhomogenized pasteurized cream is best)

¼ teaspoon mesophilic culture (see Resources, page 401) or 2 tablespoons freshly cultured buttermilk (see page 369), at room temperature

1. Gently heat the cream to 70°F. (As this is close to room temperature, you may be able to leave the cream out for a bit and it will reach 70°F without heating it on the stove at all.) Pour the cream into a sanitized pint jar or a glass bowl, sprinkle the culture over the cream, and let it sit for 5 minutes to bloom. (If using buttermilk, just add it to the cream. Be aware that buttermilk may result in a longer culturing time.)

2. Stir the cream very gently with a clean stainless steel spoon. Cover the jar with a square of cheesecloth and secure it with a rubber band. Place the jar in a warm culturing spot where the temperature is reliably 75°F or higher and culture for 36 hours.

3. Check the set. If necessary, leave the cream for up to another 6 hours. It should be stiff and taste tangy, with a velvety texture.

4. Cover and refrigerate. The crème fraîche will firm up further as it chills. It will keep for 10 days in the refrigerator.

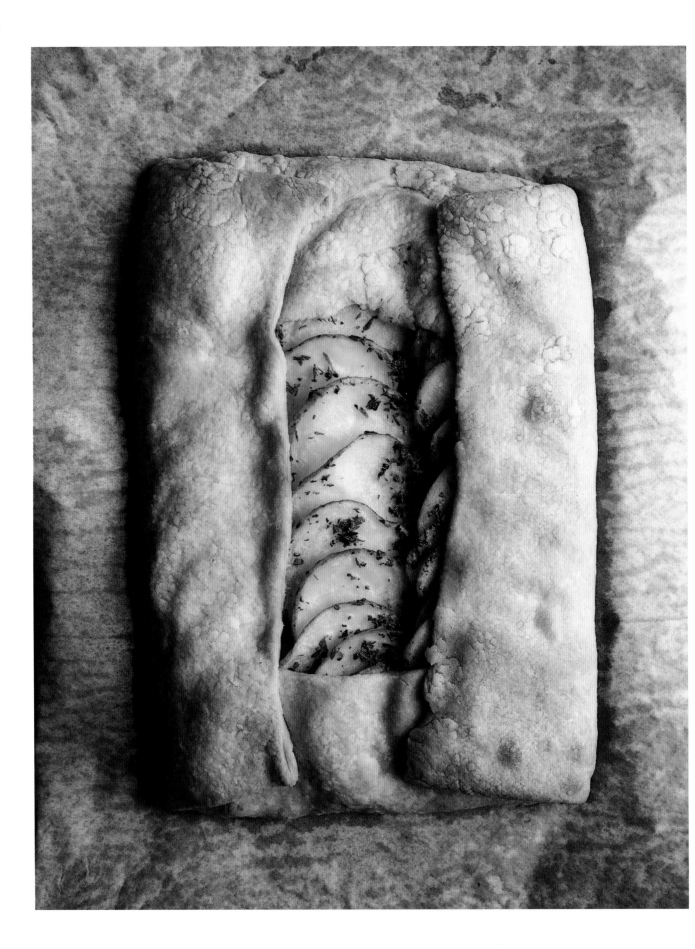

Bonus Recipe: Kale and Potato Galette with a Duck-Fat Crust

MAKES: one 10-by-12-inch or 12-inch round galette; serves 6–8

ACTIVE TIME: 1 hour

CHILLING TIME: 4 hours

BAKING TIME: 80 minutes

Without a doubt, my favorite use for crème fraîche is as a tart base. Cooking crème fraîche does something remarkable to the fresh tangy cheese. I learned this technique from my dear friend and teacher Kate Hill. It was in the beautiful small town of Kate's adopted home in Gascony that I was exposed to modern interpretations of Old World ways with animal husbandry, butchery, and charcuterie.

FOR THE DOUGH

- 10 **tablespoons (5 oz., 150 g) unsalted butter**
- 6 **tablespoons (3 oz., 85 g) duck fat (see Duck Confit, page 271)**
- 3 **cups (12.75 oz., 375 g) all-purpose flour**
- • **Kosher salt**
- ⅓ **cup (scant 3 oz., 80 ml) ice water**

- 8 **ounces (225 g) lacinato kale**
- 2 **tablespoons olive oil**
- 2 **pounds (900 g) Yukon Gold potatoes, thinly sliced**

1. To make the dough, cube the butter and duck fat and place in a single layer on a small baking sheet or plate. Freeze for 1 hour.

2. Combine the flour, ½ teaspoon salt, and frozen butter and duck fat in the bowl of a food processor and pulse exactly fifteen times, until the mixture resembles small pebbles. Add the ice water and pulse until the dough forms a ball. Turn it out, form into a 6-inch disk, wrap, and refrigerate for at least 4 hours.

3. Set a rack in the center of the oven and preheat the oven to 425°F.

4. Wash the kale and remove the ribs, then cut the leaves into a very slim chiffonade (thin ribbons). Heat a large skillet over medium-high heat. Add the oil and sauté the kale until wilted but not cooked through. Remove from the pan and set aside to cool.

5. Fill a 3-quart saucepan with water and bring the water to a boil. Add 1 teaspoon salt and the potato slices and allow the water to return to a boil, then drain the potatoes and shock (cool) them in ice water. Be gentle, as they break easily and you want them intact.

6. On a board or counter well dusted with flour, roll the dough into a 12-by-14-inch rectangle or a 12-inch circle, about 1/4 inch thick. If the dough is very tender and sticky, roll it out between two sheets of parchment. Transfer to a baking sheet (and peel away the top sheet of parchment).

Recipe continues

OPPOSITE: Kale and Potato Galette with a Duck-Fat Crust

- 2 tablespoons chopped fresh flat-leaf parsley
- 1 tablespoon chopped fresh mint
- 1 teaspoon chopped fresh thyme
- Freshly ground black pepper
- 1 cup (8 oz., 230 g) crème fraîche (page 385)
- ¼ cup (2 oz., 57 g) fresh goat cheese
- 4 ounces duck confit, homemade (page 271) or store-bought, shredded, or bacon, cooked until crisp and crumbled (optional)

7. Stir the parsley, thyme, mint, a good pinch of salt, and a few grindings of pepper into the crème fraîche. Spoon 1/4 cup of the crème fraîche over the crust, leaving a 2 inch border. Scatter the kale over the crème fraîche, then pinch off pieces of goat cheese and scatter them over the kale. If using, dot the tart galette with the duck confit or crisp bacon. Arrange the potatoes over the top, in rows for the rectangular tart or in a spiral for the circular tart. Fold the edges of the dough over by 2 inches or so. Embrace the rustic nature of the galette and don't fret too much about perfection. If making a rectangular galette, pinch the corners together. Pour the remaining crème fraîche over the exposed potatoes, gingerly filling the crust.

8. Pop the galette into the oven and bake for 20 minutes, then reduce the temperature to 350°F and bake for another hour or so. It should be a bubbly golden beauty. Cool the galette for at least 20 minutes before serving.

Cream Cheese

MAKES: 11 to 12 ounces
ACTIVE TIME: 30 minutes
CULTURING TIME: 24 to 36 hours
DRAINING TIME: 8 to 12 hours
CHILLING TIME: 8 hours

We're not in Philadelphia any more. One taste of this cream cheese, and you'll see what all the fuss is about. Without stabalizers and gums, cream cheese is a whole new schmear. Making cream cheese is a little tricky—it takes a nice warm spot to culture and plenty of patience. Why make your own? The tang and the texture are so much more refined. It will be better than any other cream cheese.

2 cups (16 oz., 475 ml) whole milk

2 cups (16 oz., 475 ml) heavy cream

¼ teaspoon mesophilic culture (see Resources, page 401) or ½ cup (4 oz., 120 ml) freshly cultured buttermilk (see page 369)

¼ teaspoon kosher salt, cheese salt (see Resources), or fine sea salt

1. In a 3-quart saucepan, bring the milk and cream to 75°F. Sprinkle on the mesophilic culture and allow to bloom for 5 minutes, then stir gently a few times. (If using buttermilk, just pour it in and stir.)

2. Cover the pan and culture the mixture in a warm, draft-free spot until the whey has separated and the curd has become thick, like Greek yogurt, 24 to 30 hours. There will be some, but not a lot, of whey. If there seems to be mostly liquid below a thick cap of thickened cream, culturing is not complete. Allow to culture for another 2 or 3 hours, checking for set until you are satisfied with the curd consistency. The firmer the curd at this stage, the more quickly it will drain in the next stage.

3. Line a colander with a dampened threadbare tea towel and set the colander over a bowl. Gently pour the cultured cheese into the colander. Drain for 30 minutes. There will be nearly a cup of whey.

4. Gather the towel up by all four corners, turn one corner around the others, and tie up into a hobo pouch. Tie a length of kitchen twine around the knot. With the twine, tie the pouch securely to a cabinet handle, faucet handle, or any place it can be suspended over a catch bowl, to allow gravity to drain off the whey and dry out the cheese. Get creative, but realize that wherever

Recipe continues

you hang it, it will be in the way. (In my dream kitchen there is a special place to suspend bags of curds and whey.) The room temperature should be around 78°F. Cooler temperatures will mean the cheese takes longer to form, which is fine but nerve-wracking. If the temperature rises above 85°F, the cheese will sour and may spoil. Drain the cheese for 8 hours.

5. Untie and unwrap the towel and scrape the cheese out onto a board. It should be smooth, thick, and hold together (it will firm up further in the refrigerator); if it is still liquid in the center, put the cheese back in the pouch, tie it up again, and hang for as many as 6 more hours, then scrape out onto the board.

6. Add the salt to the cheese and incorporate it by using a bench scraper to lift and fold the cheese over. The cheese may be somewhat soft and a little hard to control, but it will firm up in the refrigerator. Fear not, the salt will dissolve and work through the cheese as it rests, so a fold or two is all that is needed. (As with other cheeses, salting is necessary for shelf stability.)

7. Form the cheese into a log or brick and wrap well in plastic wrap. Chill for at least 8 hours, during which time the cheese will firm up further. Cream cheese will keep in the refrigerator for up to 2 weeks. Store in wax paper or cheese paper to extend the shelf life.

TRY ADDING . . .
- Smoked salmon or trout (page 321 or 323)
- Chopped chives, lovage, borage, or parsley
- Diced apples and celery, walnuts, and a pinch of cinnamon
- Minced pickled serranos
- Minced candied jalapeños (page 214)
- Diced Marinated Roasted Red Peppers (page 171)
- Chopped capers and sun-dried tomatoes
- Caramelized shallots

USE HOMEMADE CREAM CHEESE IN . . .
- Rugelach (page 51)
- Cheesecake
- Cream cheese frosting
- A cookie recipe or pie dough—substitute for one-third to one-half the butter

OTHER IDEAS . . .
- Serve cream cheese with chutney or jelly—try Heat-and-Sweet Habanero Jelly (page 142).
- Spread cream cheese on a cracker and top with a candied jalapeno (page 214).
- Spread cream cheese and jam on brioche, trim the crusts, and quarter. Serve with milky tea.
- Grill cream-cheese-and-conserve sandwiches on pumpernickel.

Cottage Cheese

MAKES: 2 cups (16 oz.)

ACTIVE TIME: 2½ hours

CULTURING TIME: 5 hours

Forget those thoughts of cottage cheese as a diet food. Or lady food. This is textural, moist, tender, creamy food. Mixed with avocado, hot sauce, and soft scrambled eggs, or with tuna, or with fruit preserves, or pickled peppers, or plum sauce, it's just the most wonderful addition to the refrigerator, creating breakfast or lunch in a snap.

Calcium chloride will help with curd set if you do not have access to raw milk. If you are lucky enough to get raw milk, omit the calcium chloride. Skim milk makes the best squeaky curds, the sign of perfect cottage cheese; your yield will also be lower with a higher-fat milk.

See photographs on pages 358 and 393.

4 quarts (128 oz., 3.8 l) nonfat (skim) raw or nonhomogenized pasteurized milk

¼ teaspoon calcium chloride (see Resources, page 401) if not using raw milk

¼ to ¾ cup (60 to 180 ml) filtered water

¼ teaspoon rennet (see Resources)

¼ teaspoon mesophilic culture (see Resources) or ¼ cup (2 oz., 60 ml) buttermilk or white vinegar

• About ½ teaspoon fine sea salt

• About ¼ cup (2 oz., 60 ml) heavy cream

SANITIZED EQUIPMENT

• Threadbare all-cotton tea towel

• Skimmer or whisk

• Long-handled curd knife

• Colander or sieve

1. If using raw milk, pasteurize it by heating to 145°F and holding it at that temperature for 30 minutes; let cool. If using pasteurized milk, remove the caps or lids and leave the milk on the counter for a couple of hours to bring it to room temperature.

2. If using, dissolve the calcium chloride in ½ cup of the filtered water. Dissolve the rennet in ¼ cup filtered water.

3. Set the colander or sieve over a catch bowl and line it with a threadbare, dampened tea towel.

4. Add the milk to a 5-quart pot with a cover. Check the temperature and, if necessary, heat the milk to 70°F. If you accidentally overheat the milk, let cool to 70°F before proceeding. Sprinkle the mesophillic culture over the milk and allow it to bloom for 5 minutes, then stir gently with the skimmer. You're not beating or whisking, just combining. (If using buttermilk or vinegar to culture, just stir it in.) Allow the mixture to stand for 5 minutes.

5. Add the diluted calcium chloride, if using, and disperse it gently through the milk with the skimmer. Add the diluted rennet and combine in the same way. Cover the pot, wrap in a warm towel to keep the milk at 70°F, and let the cheese develop for 2 hours.

Recipe continues

6. Look for a clean break in the curds: Make a 2-inch-deep slice into the surface with the curd cutter and press the curd apart—you want a texture like firm custard, not scrambled eggs. If it still seems loose, cover the pot for another 10 minutes and then test again. (With vinegar or buttermilk, the curd will be less firm than curd made with a mesophilic culture.) Then cut the curds with the curd knife, drawing it through from front to back, side to side, and top to bottom to create 1-inch cubes, or a close approximation. With the skimmer or whisk, stir lazily for 5 minutes, raising the curds from the bottom of the pot to the surface and breaking them into pieces the size of a kidney bean.

7. Put the pot on the stove and turn the heat on very low. Stir lazily once or twice, then walk away for 5 minutes.

8. Stir the mixture with the skimmer or whisk to break apart the curds. The curds may clump, but don't worry; just keep it moving. Slowly bring the temperature up to 102°F (the slower the increase in heat, the more creamy and pleasing the curds). Aim for about 45 minutes to complete this climb. I use a diffuser on my gas stove to keep the heat very low.

9. Taste a curd at 102°F. Is it just a little squeaky and then creamy in the center? That's what you're looking for. It shouldn't collapse. Keep tasting as the heat goes up to find a texture you find pleasing, but do not heat to above 110°F, or the curds may become rubbery.

10. Using the skimmer, spoon the curds into the lined colander. Using your fingers, break apart bigger clumps into curds the size of a kidney bean. Rinse the curds well under warm water to get rid of all the whey. (Whey will make your cottage cheese spoil more quickly.)

11. Weigh the curds. Add salt measured as 1% of the weight of the cheese and enough heavy cream to moisten the curds. Try the cheese now, while still a little warm. It's so good. Stir well and chill.

The cottage cheese will keep for a week in the refrigerator.

OPPOSITE: Cottage Cheese (page 391) with a canned peach

Camembert

MAKES: 2 classic rounds, 5 inches in diameter
ACTIVE TIME: 3 hours
DEVELOPING THE RIND: 12 to 14 days
AGING TIME: 4 weeks

Raw milk, especially in early spring when the grass is new, will make the most complex cheese. In lieu of that, try to find a cream-top milk, the kind sold with a layer of thick cream. This recipe also works with raw or nonhomogenized pasteurized goat milk.

It's wonderful to bring out your very own homemade soft, gooey, runny cheese with a bloomy rind to serve friends. You'll be proud.

4 quarts (128 oz., 3.8 l) raw or nonhomogenized pasteurized whole or cream-top milk
⅛ teaspoon calcium chloride (see Resources, page 401) if not using raw milk
⅛ teaspoon liquid rennet (see Resources)
½ cup (120 ml) filtered water
⅛ teaspoon mesophilic culture (see Resources)
1/16 teaspoon penicillium candidum mold (see Resources)
2 teaspoons kosher salt

1. Take the milk out of the refrigerator about 2 hours before starting the recipe and uncap, letting it come to room temperature and culture slightly. If using raw milk, pasteurize it by heating to 145°F and holding it at that temperature for 30 minutes.

2. Set up the draining tub with the board and one mat and stand the molds on the mat (see photograph, page 396).

3. Dilute the calcium chloride, if using, in ¼ cup of the filtered water. Dilute or dissolve the rennet in the remaining ¼ cup water. Empty the milk into a large pot, clip on a thermometer, and heat slowly to 85°F. Stir, especially before reading the temperature. If it goes above 85°F, cool to 85°F before culturing.

4. Sprinkle the mesophilic culture and penicillium mold across the surface of the milk. Let the cultures bloom for 5 minutes, then incorporate gently for 30 seconds, using an up-and-down stirring motion. Add the calcium chloride, if not using raw milk, and the rennet. Stir in the same way for a minute, then cover. Wrap the pot in a towel to keep it at 80° to 85°F. Culture in a warm spot for 90 minutes. (Raw milk may set in an hour.)

Recipe continues

TOP LEFT: Cutting the curds with a long palette knife. TOP RIGHT: Drawing the palette knife through the curds. BOTTOM LEFT: Stirring the curds with a skimmer. BOTTOM RIGHT: Spooning the curds into the prepared molds.

- Stainless steel skimmer or slotted spoon
- 10-inch stainless-steel palette knife
- Two Camembert molds, 5 inches in diameter and at least 5 inches deep (see Resources, page 401)
- Rimmed baking sheet
- Two boards or flat platters that will hold both molds side by side and fit on the baking sheet
- Two bamboo sushi-rolling mats large enough to hold both cheeses
- Lidded plastic or glass draining tub (13 by 9 inches and at least 4 inches deep)

5. Look for a clean break in the curds: Make a 2-inch-deep slice into the surface of the firm curd and press it apart—you want a texture of firm custard, not scrambled eggs. If it seems loose, cover the pot for another 10 minutes and test again. Cut the curds with the palette knife, drawing it from front to back, side to side, and top to bottom to create 1-inch cubes of curd, or a close approximation. Using a skimmer or long-handled whisk, move the curds with a slow stir here and there for 10 minutes to further separate the curds and whey. They will be about the size of a lima bean.

6. Using the skimmer, ladle the curds into the two molds; move back and forth between the molds, allowing the whey to drain out and waiting a couple of minutes between each ladle. Expect the process of filling the molds to take about 30 minutes. The two molds will be completely full at the end. Put the entire draining contraption aside for 2 hours.

7. When you go back to the tub, you'll see gravity at work: The whey will have been expressed through the holes in the molds, the cheeses will be tightening up, and they will have dropped down. This next step is scary but surprisingly easy once you do it. Put the second bamboo mat on top of the molds, and then the other board, and flip the whole thing over. Okay, you can breathe again.

8. Let the cheese drain for another 2 hours, then flip the molds again. Do this four more times over the course of the next 24 hours. Don't get hung up with how often, do it when you have a moment.

9. After 24 hours, you're ready to salt the cheese. Spread out 1 teaspoon of salt on a plate. Remove the cheese from one mold and gently tap the sides of the cheese into the salt, then rub the salt over the top and bottom of the round. Place the cheese in the draining tub on a clean bamboo mat. Salt the other round of cheese and put in the tub.

Recipe continues

10. Cover and place the draining tub in your curing space. Flip the cheese over every day, placing a clean mat on top of the cheeses, then turning the cheese over. Wipe away any moisture that gathers in the bottom of the draining tub. In a few days, the cheese will be covered with a pretty white, snowy mold. Sometimes the mold will stick to the mat, but that's all right—more mold will form. If the mold is green, pink, black, or hairy, something isn't right. It could be the humidity in your cheese cave, or the temperature. It could be bacteria and pathogens that got into your cheese. It could be so many things, but it's not edible, that's certain. Sorry, toss out the cheese and try again.

11. Once there is white fuzz thoroughly covering the rounds, usually within 12 to 14 days, wrap the cheeses in cheese paper or parchment. Age the wrapped cheese rounds in a single layer in your cheese cave (see Creating a Cheese Cave) for 1 month. You will be able to feel the give in the center of the wrapped rounds of cheese—it will feel gloriously oozy.

12. When the cheese is ready to eat, move it from the cave to the refrigerator. It will stop developing and will hold until you are ready to enjoy it. Eat the cheese within 1 month for the best results.

13. Remove the cheese from the refrigerator 3 or 4 hours before serving. Complement the cheese with items from the pantry, such as your own chutney, or preserved fruits, or pickles paired with dried meats, and you've got the start to quite a picnic.

CREATING A CHEESE CAVE

Temperature and humidity are critical when aging cheese, so a thermometer/hygrometer combination is very handy. Use it to suss out a suitable space in a garage, basement, or pantry, or even that old refrigerator in the basement.

My cheese cave is a jerry-rigged wine refrigerator, similar to the space I use for curing meats (see page 342). I set the temperature at 56°F and keep the humidity in the 60 to 65 percent range. If the humidity runs low, I put a small bowl of water on the floor of the refrigerator. If the humidity is too high, a small bowl of uncooked rice will take the moisture out of the air. While I have successfully aged both meat and cheese in this wine refrigerator, I do not recommend curing both at the same time.

Your kitchen refrigerator is probably set at around 36°F, and that is quite a bit cooler. If you are using your kitchen fridge to age cheese, plan on additional time to develop a snowy mold and sometimes seven or eight weeks to ripen. Keep the cheese in the back on a center shelf, which is likely to be the warmest spot. It will work, just more slowly.

OPPOSITE: Well-drained ricotta (page 372)

Resources

Equipment and ingredients

Online shopping has made the acquisition of equipment and ingredients far easier than it once was, but because I always prefer to support local merchants, I do my best to find what I can in my own neighborhood.

FOR GENERAL COOKING

It's easy to collect kitchen equipment that is useful for only one task, but I try to avoid that. Nevertheless, I admit to a packed kitchen tool drawer. Listed below are the tools I reach for over and over.

Stainless steel colanders and strainers in different sizes
Meat thermometer (for foods in the oven, grill, and smoker and for cheese making, I am partial to the probe thermometer from OXO, but I use a classic instant-read thermometer most of the time)
Candy thermometer (I prefer the Taylor candy thermometer because of the way it sits flat on the bottom of the pot)
Gram and ounce scale (my favorite scale is from OXO)
Food mill with interchangeable disks
Long-handled stainless steel ladle
Long-handled stainless steel skimmer
Microplane or other grating rasp
Vegetable peeler
Citrus zester
Cherry pitter

Spice grinder and/or mortar and pestle
Stainless steel potato masher
Crinkle cutter
Long-handled silicone spoons and spatulas
Kitchen twine
Cheesecloth
An endless supply of cotton kitchen towels, including a couple of soft threadbare ones
A well-honed heavy chef's knife and a sharp little paring knife

FOR CANNING

Hardware stores have always been the place to seek out canning jars and equipment. Most carry a wide range of jar sizes and shapes and all the utensils and doo-dads necessary for filling and lifting jars.

There are several online sources for jars. I like Fillmore Container's range of canning products: www.fillmorecontainer.com.

Canning kettle
Jars of all sizes, lids, and rings
Preserving pot (I always reach for my Le Creuset)
Tools: lid lifter, jar lifter, jar funnel, and bubbler
Jelly bag and stand
Pressure canner

Many of the recipes call for various dried fruits. I purchase several of these, as well as whole and chopped nuts, from www.nuts.com.

OPPOSITE: Buttered toast and Double Strawberry Preserves (page 53)

FOR CURING AND FOR
PRESERVING MEAT AND FISH

Curing bacon calls for pink salt. For many years, I "borrowed" some from my butcher. Then I found www.butcher-packer.com and www.sausage makers.com, which sell very affordable packages that remain shelf stable for years.

Pink salt (curing salt #1)
Modified celery juice powder
Sodium erythorbate
Perforated grill pan
I use an electric Bradley smoker; it is compact, dependable, and easy to manage

FOR CHEESE MAKING

Molds and cultures are necessary for the more complex cheese recipes. If there is no cheese-making shop near you, try home-brew stores, as they use the same cultures. Alternatively, order supplies through New England Cheesemaking, www.cheesemaking.com, or amazon.com.

Keep rennet and calcium chloride in the refrigerator and cultures in the freezer.

Citric acid
Rennet
Calcium chloride
Mesophilic culture
Penicillium candidum mold
Butter muslin
Curd cutter
Cheese molds
Draining mats and tubs
Cheese paper

Bibliography

BOOKS AND WEBSITES I TURN TO OVER AND OVER

Tall filled-to-overflowing bookcases in my kitchen hold hundreds of food and writing books, and dozens that I cook from regularly, but only a handful that furthered my culinary education and honed my skill set. These are the books that taught me to cook:

Child, Julia. *Mastering the Art of French Cooking*, volumes 1 and 2. New York: Alfred A. Knopf, 1961 and 1970.

Cunningham, Marion. *The Breakfast Book*. Alfred A. Knopf, 1987.

Cunningham, Marion. *The Fannie Farmer Cookbook*. Alfred A. Knopf, 1984.

Goins, Suzanne. *Sunday Suppers at Lucques: Seasonal Recipes from Market to Table*. Alfred A. Knopf, 2005.

Hazan, Marcella. *The Classic Italian Cookbook*. MacMillan, 1980.

Heatter, Maida. *The Book of Great Desserts*. Alfred A. Knopf, 1977.

Hesser, Amanda. *The Cook and the Gardener*. W. W. Norton, 2000.

Katzen, Mollie. *The Moosewood Cookbook*. Ten Speed Press, 1977.

Keller, Thomas. *Bouchon*. Artisan, 2004.

Kennedy, Diana. *The Art of Mexican Cooking*. Clarkson Potter, 1989.

Lewis, Edna. *The Taste of Country Cooking*. Alfred A. Knopf, 1982.

Madison, Deborah. *The Greens Cookbook: Extraordinary Vegetarian Cuisine from the Celebrated Restaurant*. Bantam Books, 1987.

Rodgers, Judy. *The Zuni Cafe Cookbook*. W. W. Norton, 2002.

There are dozens of preserving books I adore, all of them packed with interesting recipes. I encourage you to explore broadly to both inform and inspire your cooking. The following four books contributed to my preserving education:

Bertolli, Paul. *Cooking by Hand*. Clarkson Potter, 2003.

Carroll, Ricki. *Home Cheese Making: Recipes for 75 Homemade Cheeses*. Storey Publishing, 2010.

Ferber, Christine. *Mes Confitures: The Jams and Jellies of Christine Ferber*. Michigan State University Press, 2002.

Ruhlman, Michael, and Polcyn, Brian. *Charcuterie: The Craft of Salting, Smoking, and Curing*. W. W. Norton, 2nd edition, 2013.

I stay up to date with preserving, particularly with regard to safety, via these websites:

The Department of Agriculture (USDA) canning guide provides the most up to date safety information for water bath and pressure canning: www.csrees.usda.gov/newsroom/news/2011news/home_canning_guide.html.

Every state and most counties have a cooperative extension service, also part of the USDA, an office offering education and support for gardeners and home food preservers. Find the office nearest you (they are always looking for new volunteers): www.csrees.usda.gov/Extension.

The National Center for Home Food Preservation at the University of Georgia, nchfp.uga.edu, covers all types of preserving with recipes and safety information.

Jarden Home Products (Ball Canning), the company that makes the jars, has a vibrant website full of information for canners, both new and experienced: www.freshpreserving.com.

Canning Across America hosts the Canvolution every summer. Check the website for this year's date and host a canning party along with thousands of other canners across the country: www.canningacrossamerica.com.

Find a farmers' market at www.farmersmarkets.com, or at www.nfmd.org, which lists locations and dates for U.S. markets.

Pick-your-own farms can keep costs down when preserving large batches (especially useful for tomatoes). Find one near you at the Pick Your Own website, listing PYO farms around the country: www.pickyourown.org.

Fresh blueberries

Acknowledgments

Five years ago, the idea of writing a cookbook had not even crossed my mind. With encouragement, though, I began to dream about writing a cookbook, and now that it is here, a look back reveals an enormous warm, encouraging community that hovered around me through the entire process.

Five years ago, I was drowning—so deeply unhappy after the economy changed and my small but satisfying landscape design business dried up. Capie Baily, Carrie Collins, Julie Goos, Holly Hassett, Francesca Kelly, and Julie Stewart, with whom I cried and laughed for a year, helped me find my way. With their encouragement, I offered cooking classes, started a blog and tiptoed into the world of food writing.

A nudge of approval came next from the community at Food52, where I discovered similarly passionate home cooks. Founders Amanda Hesser and Merrill Stubbs brought us together to compete and celebrate via weekly contests in the most cooperative way conceivable. Soon we connected on Twitter and Facebook, and became real friends. Then the Charcutepalooza participants joined the party, and I developed an even wider world of friends, where I could have a conversation about canning or making cheese. I was not the only DIY dork. Sean Timberlake deserves a shout-out for being curator of all things DIY at Punk Domestics.

For an even bigger dose of encouragement, no first-time author could have asked for a better agent, one sure to dole out straight-shooting advice along with a belt of Scotch, than Martha Kaplan. For months, she waited patiently while I played cat-and-mouse with my book proposal, corralling my enthusiasm into something workable. Did I mention she has an uncanny knowledge of fabulous but unknown restaurants in every neighborhood in New York City? For that reason alone, I think she has to be the best agent in the world.

The book process often seems endless. Winnie Abramson, Abby Dodge, Elizabeth Kadetsky, Domenica Marchetti, and Emily Nunn read drafts here and there and offered advice, solace, laughs, and long telephone conversations when that's exactly what I needed. Carol Sacks did all of that as well and tested recipes too, with help in the kitchen from her daughter, Claire Stotts.

Absolutely every writer needs an editor. Somehow I have managed to work with the best in the business. From the beginning, as I moved from dabbling with a little blog to the larger world of professional food writing, Bonnie Benwick was incredibly generous and encouraging, just as she has been through this entire book process. I treasure our friendship and think of her every time I make a sour cherry pie.

I have learned so much from Susan Edgerley, who edits with deft moves, exquisitely extracting only the best, only what is necessary, but retaining nuance, voice, and style. It surprises and delights me to see my byline in the *New York Times*, and I am so grateful to Susan for taking a chance on this unknown writer.

The legendary Maria Guarnaschelli always brings great intelligence to editing. Reading her comments was illuminating, sometimes hilarious, and generally brilliant. This is a better book because of her. I apologize now for the heartache she must have suffered over mangled Italian words. The team at W. W. Norton shepherded me through this process: Mitchell Kohles, Devon Zahn, Susan Sanfrey, Lauren Opper, and Nancy Palmquist. I owe enormous thanks to Judith Sutton for her copyedits. Designer Beth Tondreau made it beautiful.

Great big overflowing buckets of appreciation go out to the extraordinary team of Christopher Hirsheimer and Melissa Hamilton. They immediately understood my desire to create photographs of real food, locally grown, in season. The women of Canal House threw the doors open wide. They welcomed me, Dennis, and our little dog, Louie, into their light-filled studio. Far beyond the magnificent images in this book, they offered me a gentle education in food prepared for photography, cookbook production, the beauty of natural light, and a good Sidecar.

Testing recipes for the third chapter meant Friday night "Bring Your Own Vegetable" parties. Thank you, Morris and Nancy Deutsch, Nancy Dunn, Tammy Gordon, Lisa Howard, Laura Kadetsky and Jonah Kaplan, Alejandra Owens, and Gabby Rojchin for tasting and commenting. The Practical Pantry Posse did early recipe testing: Jennifer Avellino, Lu Bennett, Pam Bianco, Jill Warren Lucas, Gillian Miller, Anna Saint John, Catherine Del Spina Shereshewsky, Victoria Sostock, Carri Thurman, and Susan Wagner.

Norman's Farm Market, Bending Bridge Farm, Nob Hill Farm, and Redbud Farm grew the glorious fruits and vegetables photographed and lovingly preserved here. Meats and fish came from Wagshal's ("Pam the Butcher" Ginsberg), as well as Painted Hand Farm, Our Springfield Farm, and D'Artagnan.

The precision and clarity in the recipes is a direct result of careful testing by Christine Burns Rudalevidge. She may have 123 jars in her pantry now, but I have a book full of proper recipes.

I will always be grateful to my assistant in the kitchen, Ally Kirkpatrick, who washed a lot of dishes, weighed a lot of fruit and vegetables, and tried, valiantly, to bring home the bacon jam rugelach. I hope you continue to love the kitchen and preserve with gusto, my friend.

Even though she has yet to lower a canning jar into a pot of boiling water, Gail Dosik, the always remarkable, übertalented, imaginative pastry chef and cookie decorator, has been uncomplainingly available (my own Baking 411). Gail is the reason I understand anything about sugar.

Bob del Grosso has been endlessly patient with my questions about butchery, charcuterie, and meat curing, and he graciously agreed to review the curing recipes and instructions. Mary Reilly turned her precise and attuned chef's eye to the weights and measures.

For cleaning up my syntax, for being the first to read the entire manuscript, for the excellent notes, in the midst of moving her household across the Atlantic Ocean, Francesca Kelly, I thank you.

Jennifer Steinhauer is one of those late-in-life surprises—a new friend. I am grateful for her welcoming kitchen table, for cocktails on Saturday afternoons, for tasting and commenting on nearly every recipe, and for substantial, often life-altering advice, support, and encouragement. This book is better, and maybe even a little bit funnier, because of her.

My best and most wonderful friend, Katrin Achelis, who nearly throttled me toward the end of this process, no doubt for good reason, generously offered a room to write, a space to think. I am always inspired to write when I stay in her ancient home on Martha's Vineyard, the Captain Joseph Norton House, and every good thing that happened on the road to this book happened there. Thank you from the bottom of my heart, Kaki.

My kitchen skills and curiosity were handed down from my mother, grandmothers, and great-grandmothers. While they are no longer alive, it would be an enormous oversight not to list them here.

Bill Cohn has been there for me throughout, with unconditional support and encouragement.

How can I ever thank my darling husband sufficiently? I don't think either of us expected this process to be so upending and, yet, through it all, he has been supportive and generous and loving. What a marvelous life we have, Dennis. *Merci, mille fois.*

Sugar Snap, Carrot, and Radish Refrigerator Pickles (page 193)

Fresh black currants

Index

Page numbers in *italics* refer to illustrations and charts; recipe page numbers are in **boldface**.

Fresh strawberries

About the Author

Cathy Barrow is the author of the food blog Mrs. Wheelbarrow's Kitchen. She has written for the *New York Times, Washington Post, Garden and Gun, Southern Living,* and NPR, among others. She lives in Washington, DC, with her husband, Dennis; Louie and Morty, the two terriers; and an all-white cat.

Conversion Tables

Compiled by Molly Stevens

LIQUID MEASURES

Exact conversion: 1 fluid ounce = 29.57 milliliters

U.S. Standard	UK Imperial	Fluid Ounces	Practical Metric Equivalent	Exact Metric Equivalent
1 teaspoon	1 teaspoon	$\frac{1}{8}$ fl oz	5 ml	4.93 ml
2 teaspoons	2 teaspoons	$\frac{1}{4}$ fl oz	10 ml	7 ml
1 tablespoon	1 tablespoon	$\frac{1}{2}$ fl oz	15 ml	14.8 ml
$1\frac{1}{4}$ tablespoons	$1\frac{1}{2}$ tablespoons	$3\frac{3}{4}$ fl oz	22.5 ml	22.2 ml
2 tablespoons	2 tablespoons	1 fl oz	30 ml	29.57 ml
3 tablespoons	3 tablespoons	$1\frac{1}{2}$ fl oz	45 ml	44.4 ml
$\frac{1}{4}$ cup	4 tablespoons	2 fl oz	60 ml	59 ml
$\frac{1}{3}$ cup		$2\frac{1}{2}$ fl oz	75 ml	73.9 ml
$\frac{1}{2}$ cup		4 fl oz	125 ml	118 ml
$\frac{2}{3}$ cup	$\frac{1}{4}$ pint or 1 gill	5 fl oz	150 ml	148 ml
$\frac{3}{4}$ cup		6 fl oz	185 ml	177 ml
1 cup		8 fl oz	250 ml	237 ml
$1\frac{1}{4}$ cups	$\frac{1}{2}$ pint	10 fl oz	300 ml	296 ml
$1\frac{1}{2}$ cups		12 fl oz	375 ml	355 ml
2 cups		16 fl oz	500 ml	473 ml
$2\frac{1}{2}$ cups	1 pint	20 fl oz	600 ml	591 ml
1 quart (4 cups)	$1\frac{2}{3}$ pints	32 fl oz	1 liter	946 ml
2 quarts (8 cups)		64 fl oz	2 liters	1.9 liters
1 gallon (4 qts)		128 fl oz	4 liters	3.78 liters

WEIGHT EQUIVALENTS

Exact conversion: 1 ounce = 28.35 grams

U.S. Standard (Avoirdupois) in Ounces	U.S. Standard (Avoirdupois) in Pounds	Practical Metric Equivalent	Exact Metric Equivalent
$\frac{1}{2}$ oz		15 g	14 g
1 oz		25 g	28 g
2 oz		50 g	56 g
4 oz	$\frac{1}{4}$ lb	125 g	113 g
$5\frac{1}{4}$ oz	$\frac{1}{3}$ lb	150 g	149 g
8 oz	$\frac{1}{2}$ lb	225 g	226 g
12 oz	$\frac{3}{4}$ lb	350 g	342 g
16 oz	1 lb	450–500 g	453 g
24 oz	$1\frac{1}{2}$ lb	750 g	680 g
32 oz	2 lb	1 kg	907 g